www.wadsworth.com

wadsworth.com is the World Wide Web site for Wadsworth and is your direct source to dozens of online resources.

At *wadsworth.com* you can find out about supplements, demonstration software, and student resources. You can also send email to many of our authors and preview new publications and exciting new technologies.

wadsworth.com
Changing the way the world learns®

Introduction to Teaching

Rewards and Realities

Lynda Fielstein

University of Central Arkansas

Patricia Phelps

University of Central Arkansas

WADSWORTH

THOMSON LEARNING ™

Australia • Canada • Mexico • Singapore • Spain • United Kingdom • United States

Education Editor: *Dan Alpert*
Associate Development Editor: *Tangelique Williams*
Marketing Manager: *Becky Tollerson*
Signing Representative: *Suzanne Harris*
Project Editor: *Trudy Brown*
Print Buyer: *Mary Noel*
Permissions Editor: *Joohee Lee*
Production Service: *Graphic World Publishing Services*
Text Designer: *Lisa Mirski Devenish*

Photo Researcher: *Sue C. Howard*
Copy Editor: *Beth Hayes*
Illustrator: *Alex Raffi*
Cover Designer: *Harold Burch*
Cover Image: *Rieder & Walsh, Photonica*
Cover Printer: *Phoenix Color*
Compositor: *Graphic World, Inc.*
Printer: *World Color*

Wadsworth/Thomson Learning
10 Davis Drive
Belmont, CA 94002-3098
USA

For more information about our products, contact us:
Thomson Learning Academic Resource Center
1-800-423-0563
http://www.wadsworth.com

International Headquarters
Thomson Learning
International Division
290 Harbor Drive, 2nd Floor
Stamford, CT 06902-7477
USA

UK/Europe/Middle East/South Africa
Thomson Learning
Berkshire House
168-173 High Holborn
London WC1V 7AA
United Kingdom

Asia
Thomson Learning
60 Albert Street, #15-01
Albert Complex
Singapore 189969

Canada
Nelson Thomson Learning
1120 Birchmount Road
Toronto, Ontario M1K 5G4
Canada

Library of Congress Cataloging-in-Publication Data
Fielstein, Lynda.
    Introduction to teaching : rewards and realities /
Lynda Fielstein, Patricia Phelps.
        p. cm.
    Includes bibliographical references and index.
    ISBN 0-534-56547-6 (alk. paper)
    1. Teachers. 2. Teaching—Vocational guidance. I. Phelps,
Patricia H., 1955- II. Title.

LB1775 .F46 2001
371.1—dc21
                                00-063419

This book is dedicated to those role models who showed us that teaching is an honorable profession and a worthy calling. Our hope is that our nation's children and future generations continue to be inspired and blessed in the 21st century with equally wise, just, and caring teachers who will guide them as we were guided.

UNIT 2 — Whom Teachers Teach

UNIT **5**   Professional Issues and Political Realities

16 / Is Teaching for You? Expectations for the Future

Introduction to Teaching: Rewards and Realities offers an exciting yet realistic glimpse into what it is like to be a teacher in today's schools and classrooms. Many individuals taking an introductory education course want to know if they have the attitudes, aptitudes, skills, as well as disposition to be successful in this field. One of the primary purposes of this introductory textbook is to provide those who are considering teaching as a career with information to make an informed decision. Our aim is to be straightforward and realistic in our portrayal of what it is like to teach, without deterring capable and caring individuals from this field.

Our Approach

Today's teachers are expected to play a multitude of demanding and complex roles. In addition to the traditional role of classroom instructors, teachers are community activists, school reformers, empirical scholars, student advocates, disciplinarians, character models, and more. Successful teachers are able to establish healthy, positive relationships with students, parents, administrators, colleagues, and other community members. In this text, we attempt to delicately balance the rewards of teaching with the responsibilities in an effort to provide a fair perspective of what it means to teach. We pose problems as challenges, and show how challenges can be transformed into solutions.

We realize our readers represent a wide spectrum of diverse cultures and backgrounds with equally diverse life experiences. We also know that many of our readers have already had teaching experiences of some kind. Therefore, we have tried to present the material in a way that every reader can relate to, regardless of past experiences. Throughout the narrative, you will find questions that prompt the reader to think about how he or she would react to various situations that arise in teaching.

The *Contents* represents the subjects we think exemplify the major components of the knowledge base underlying teacher education. Many of these topics will be explored in greater depth in subsequent education courses. Respecting the uniqueness of teacher education programs, each chapter is self-contained, to give instructors more latitude in determining what content to cover and in what sequence. If specific topics are more thoroughly discussed in other chapters, we have noted this.

We have tried to write a text that is grounded in research and practice. Although there are no absolute rules in teaching, there are scientific findings that guide teacher practices. At the same time, we have tried to balance the science of teaching with coverage of the art of teaching—the personal style that each teacher brings to the classroom. We believe that exemplary teachers are both practicing "artists" as well as "scientists."

Our approach in this text is a candid one. Deciding on a career is an important decision that requires deliberate and careful thought. A major goal in this text is to help readers discern if teaching might be a good career choice for them. Many prospective teachers have misconceptions about teaching: some students are overly optimistic, while others are unduly pessimistic in their expectations. Although idealism has its advantages, naiveté for a beginning teacher could be problematic. Likewise, negativity can be detrimental.

We, the authors, have had the privilege of being teachers for more than 40 years collectively in public and private schools and in universities. Because we believe that teaching is a highly rewarding profession that continues to bring joy and substance to our lives, we are honored to convey this to our readers.

Admittedly, finding a productive and satisfying career can be difficult, yet it is a worthwhile goal to pursue thoughtfully, earnestly, and diligently. When a good match is found, it truly can be rewarding, particularly in education. Therefore it is in our best interests to identify those teachers who have the vision, ability, passion, and courage to lead our schools and children into the 21st century. The process of becoming a teacher is a compelling lifetime journey about self-awareness. We welcome our readers to join us on this journey of self-discovery.

Features

To invite frank dialogue, our writing style is conversational and friendly. To engage our readers, we periodically ask probing questions that demand personal reflection. By using a self-reflective approach, the reader will actively participate in the process of application. The ultimate goal is to help readers discern whether teaching is a good match for them personally and professionally. Some reflective questions are woven into the narrative; other questions appear in features such as *Assess Yourself, A Case Study,* and *Reflection Questions*.

A feature we added to capture the emotional side of teaching and the practicalities of teaching is called *Reflections from the Field*. In this section we interview teachers representing all grade levels who share their wisdom and "real stories" from the field. In addition, we intersperse quotes from individuals that seem to capture the essence of the material; this feature is aptly labeled *Notable Quote*. In some chapters we add biographies of distinguished educators (past and present) to supplement the knowledge base; we label this feature *Great Teachers*.

To help our readers organize their thoughts and review for exams, we start each chapter with *"At the end of this chapter, you will be able to . . ."* and *"A bird's eye view of what to expect in this chapter."* At the end of each chapter are *Key Terms*; the definitions are found in the margins and in the *Glossary*. And throughout the text we have scattered *Web Sites* to provide additional sources of online information.

To supplement readers' knowledge, *Suggested Reading* and *References* follow the key terms at the end of each chapter. And for easy access, a complete list of references (in alphabetical order) can be found in the back of the book.

Supplements

To help instructors present—and students to better understand—the rewards and realities of teaching in today's classrooms, several supplements are available to accompany this text:

- A comprehensive *Instructor's Resource Manual,* including many instructor tools and a test bank
- *Exam View®* testing software (for Macintosh and Windows), to create and customize tests and study guides
- *PowerPoint™ Presentation Tool*—for great lectures
- *Transparency Acetates—Education 2001,* to reinforce key content
- *The Wadsworth Education Video Library,* including a great selection of videos to enhance student learning
- *The Homeroom: Wadsworth's Education Resource Center,* http://education.wadsworth.com, featuring links to a variety of education-related sites, journals and publications, conference sites, and grants/funding information, as well as password-protected instructor's materials
- *InfoTrac® College Edition*—four months of free online access to hundreds of journals and periodicals

Acknowledgments

Many people's efforts made this book possible. Particularly, we would like to thank our chairpersons, David Skotko and Terry James, in our respective departments, Psychology & Counseling and Curriculum & Instruction, for supporting us in this endeavor. We also appreciate the University of Central

Arkansas Research Council, Faculty Development Committee, and Sabbatical Committee for providing Lynda with release time and other forms of assistance to support the writing of this textbook.

We would like to thank a number of individuals who made noteworthy contributions to this project. A special thanks is extended to Carolyn Kelley who contributed the chapter on school governance, Lloyd Hervey, the chapter on student diversity, Billy Smith, the chapter on technology, and Sharon Gibb Murdoch and Rulon Garfield, the chapter on schools. Further, the personal account by Carol Shestok, describing the process of becoming National Board certified, made a significant contribution to the chapter on teaching as a profession. Also, we would be remiss if we did not thank Stephanie Beasley for her invaluable contribution to the feature "Great Teachers." Her help during the final stages of text preparation did not go unnoticed. We are truly indebted to these talented and generous individuals for providing their expertise to the writing of this text.

Additionally, we are grateful to those teachers who contributed "Reflections from the Field." These teachers were from Horace Mann Magnet Middle School, Little Rock, Arkansas; Bob Courtway Middle School, Conway, Arkansas; University of Central Arkansas Summer 1999 Writing Project; and many others. Without their written reflections, the rewards and realities of teaching might not be so evident.

And it would be quite an oversight if we failed to acknowledge our colleagues for their support and encouragement over the past three years. Many colleagues, Terry James, Ann Witcher, and Terry Smith (to name a few), were willing to read sections of the manuscript at various points and offer ideas for improvement. A special thanks goes to Christina Adams who proofread for us under tight deadlines. And, of course, our kind students should be thanked for excusing our absentmindedness and tolerating our idiosyncrasies during stress points.

We would like to thank our former editor, Dianne Lindsay, who was our mainstay during the past two years. And a special thanks to Joan Gill—the editor who read our initial prospectus—and believed in our concept (and in us). In addition, Tangelique Williams, the associate development editor, has gone beyond the call of duty to assist and encourage us during the latter stages of this adventure. Last but not least, to Michael McConnell, our production editor, your willingness to respond promptly (and patiently) to our last-minute inquiries was immensely appreciated.

Further, we would like to thank our reviewers for their helpful comments and recommendations at various stages of development.

Patty Adeeb
Nova Southeastern University

Carolyn Babione
Indiana University, Southeast

Reene A. Alley
Youngstown State University

Douglas A. Beed
University of Montana

John Caruso
Western Connecticut State University

William S. Forney
Texas Wesleyan University

Mark J. Guillette
Valencia Community College

Bruce Gutknecht
University of North Florida

Dennis Herschbach
University of Maryland, College Park

Harold Jaus
University of North Carolina,
Charlotte

Deborah Bainer Jenkins
The Ohio State University,
Mansfield

William R. Martin
George Mason University

Theodore S. May
North Dakota State University

Henry M. McCarthy
Appalachian State University

Barba Patton
University of Houston, Victoria

Lucy L. Payne
University of St. Thomas

Geoff Quick
Lansing Community College

Eleanor Reimer
California State University, Stockton

Judy Reinhartz
The University of Texas, Arlington

J. Karen Reynolds
Texas Technical University

Rita Seedorf
Eastern Washington University

Betty Jo Simmons
Longwood College

David R. Stronck
California State University,
Hayward

John R. Zelazek
Central Missouri State University

A Tribute to Our Families

We would like to thank family members for tolerating our hectic lifestyle over the past three years. Even though we know you were tired of hearing us obsess over this book, you were saints for keeping it to yourself and for giving us the time and space to pursue this dream. Because of you, we were able to go forth.

And most important, we want to thank our husbands, Elliot and Hank, for their incredible patience and abiding love and support. Without them to take up the slack on the home front, this book would still be "in our minds" rather than on paper. A special thanks goes to Callie, Patty's daughter, who tolerated "Mom" on the computer many evenings. And Lynda would like to thank her new Chinese daughter, Jodie Bea, for giving her hope and inspiration, as well as a good reason to persevere.

Take a few minutes to read this orientation to this text to benefit your plan of study. To introduce ourselves, Patty and I have had the privilege of being teachers for more than 40 years (collectively, that is), and from these wonderful years of teaching in public and private schools and in universities we have accumulated knowledge and experiences upon which to draw while writing this textbook. Teaching is a highly motivating and intrinsically rewarding career, and we particularly appreciate this opportunity to tell you about it.

Introduction to Teaching: Rewards and Realities is designed to give you an idea of what it is like to be a teacher in today's classrooms. Besides providing an overview of teacher education, we include helpful information to use when deciding whether teaching would be a good career option for you. We have tried to portray teaching in contemporary schools as realistically as possible, without diminishing the rewards that come from daily interaction with students.

The book's content is mainly derived from professional literature and best teaching practices. You may want to preview the *Contents* to get an idea of the topics we will address. To enhance this knowledge base, we intersperse tidbits of wisdom gleaned from interviews with former and current school teachers to provide a practical and human side to the act of teaching. Furthermore, we share a few of our own "unforgettable" teaching experiences with you.

For those readers contemplating teaching as a career, we hope this textbook will answer many of your questions. However, it would not be wise to rely solely on this textbook for all the answers to your questions. For the record, we are not "the" authority on teacher education, nor is anyone for that matter. Although we do know a great deal, based on our academic preparation, teaching experiences, community service, and empirical research, this does not qualify us to be the definitive word. You have probably noticed that many textbook writers today refrain from using an authoritarian voice; contemporary authors are prone to admit the extent to which personal values, beliefs, and backgrounds have influenced and shaped their writing.

It is important to seek one's own answers to life's dilemmas and problems. Skills such as observation, reflection, and inquiry are valuable traits to cultivate and use. For example, if you are exploring the idea of becoming a teacher, you should start the habit of careful observation and thoughtful reflection. We examine the process of decision making in more depth in

Chapter 1. The following section discusses how you can gain the most from this textbook.

How to Gain the Most from this Textbook

Be a Reflective Decision Maker and Active Learner

This textbook will help you discern whether teaching fits your academic and career goals, as well as your preferences and personality. We have chosen a reflective decision-making model to actively engage you in the learning process. **Reflective thinking** is a processing skill whereby a person consistently questions and evaluates his or her attitudes, beliefs, values, and actions in an effort to improve. We suggest you cultivate and refine this practice. Effective teachers continually think about and evaluate their decisions so they can improve professional practice. To determine whether teaching is right for you, reflect on the questions posed in this textbook.

Some features in this text are student-centered (i.e., learner-centered), which means that they are designed to actively engage you in learning. A **student-centered approach** encourages an individual to become actively involved in and responsible for his or her learning. In the literature this is commonly referred to as **active learning.** The feature *Assess Yourself* is an example of a student-centered activity because after you have read a section, you will be asked to find personal meaning in the content.

Additionally, *Reflection Questions* will give you further opportunities to formulate your thoughts about the subject matter. You may want to use some of your responses as entries in a portfolio. A **portfolio** is an educational assessment tool used to display and evaluate an individual's achievement and growth. If your program or instructor uses portfolio assessment, these questions can be used as possible entries. These activities can help you organize and clarify thoughts as you prepare for your future teaching career.

Attend to Features

In addition to the student-centered features, there are other worthwhile features to note. In a **teacher-centered approach** the teacher is primarily responsible for dispensing the information; the teacher plays a more active role in learning as opposed to student-centered learning. *Reflections from the Field* is an example of a teacher-centered approach to learning. This feature highlights excerpts from interviews with former and current teachers. From their stories, perhaps you will gain a better understanding of what to expect if you become a teacher.

Speaking of teacher-centered, we *advise* you to attend to all the features and incorporate the information into your reading. Many teachers (and

---

reflective thinking

A processing skill whereby one consistently questions and evaluates his or her attitudes, beliefs, values, and actions in an attempt to improve practice.

student-centered approach

An approach to instruction in which the student is primarily responsible for his or her own learning.

active learning

An approach to learning in which the individual is actively involved in finding personal meaning in the material being studied.

portfolio

An assessment tool used to display and evaluate an individual's achievements and personal growth.

teacher-centered approach

A traditional approach to teaching in which the teacher is deemed responsible for dispensing knowledge and information to the student.

writers) use instructional approaches that are in between teacher-centered and student-centered or alternate between the two for variety in their lessons. We use a variety of features to demonstrate the benefits of diversity not only to effective writing, but to effective teaching as well. Just as effective teachers tend to do, we shift our pedagogical style to prevent fatigue, monotony, and loss of concentration.

To help prepare for tests, you should notice that each chapter begins with *"A bird's eye view of what to expect in this chapter"* in addition to stated objectives for that chapter: *"At the end of this chapter, you will be able to . . ."*. At the end of each chapter are the *Conclusion* and *Key Terms*. The definitions to those terms can be found in the margins of the accompanying chapter and the Glossary at the back of the book.

Lastly, there are many current educational links on the Internet that can add to your storehouse of information. We suggest you make note of the *Web Sites* presented intermittently throughout the text. You can also contact Wadsworth Education Resource Center at http://education.wadsworth.com for additional educational sites and instructor tools that may be valuable in your career search.

Adopt a Constructivist Approach to Learning

constructivism

A philosophical approach to learning that suggests individuals connect new learning with familiar experiences to gain personal insight.

Another tip for gaining optimal results from your study is to take a constructivist approach to learning. **Constructivism** is a philosophical approach describing learning that grew out of cognitive theory. Briefly, a constructivist looks for connections between new ideas and familiar experiences, and in the process constructs personal insight from the experience. Creating or "constructing" your own knowledge makes learning meaningful, which in turn makes it easier to retrieve later. Inevitably, new learning will conflict with present patterns of thinking. Being challenged to see things from a different slant or in a unique way is what makes learning exciting.

Discord in our cognitions (i.e., conflicts in our thoughts) produces genuine growth. As we acquire more knowledge our concepts inevitably change, and we start to perceive things differently. For example, you are reading this book to learn more about what it is like to be a teacher. Every piece of information contributes to a clearer image of the field. In time you will see how the pieces fit together into the big picture. However, the picture will never be complete. Your perception will continually evolve about what it is truly like to be a teacher in today's society. Consequently, the knowledge base in teacher education is fluid; it expands with every new discovery.

Construct Knowledge in a Social Context

As you read and seek personal meaning from the material, we also suggest that you seek information from others. Constructivism has basically two versions, each equally important. One variant of constructivism is that one

social constructivism

A philosophical approach to teaching that suggests learners actively construct meaning from the acquisition of new material gleaned in a social context.

makes his or her own meaning, independent of others (Airasian & Walsh, 1997). The other version—**social constructivism**—contends that learning is "constructed by an individual's interaction with a social milieu" (Airasian & Walsh, 1997, p. 445). Although slightly different, both versions of constructivism are linked to growth and, therefore, learning.

You will be encouraged throughout the pages of this text to solicit input from others as you learn more about this field. If you rely solely on this book or the professional literature to determine whether teaching is a compatible career choice, you would miss the knowledge others might offer on the subject. Therefore it is important to consult with teacher education faculty and former teachers, peers, friends, and family when gathering information about your suitability for teaching.

community of learners

The concept of teachers and students working together to learn.

In the professional literature this concept of learning from others is often referred to as **community of learners.** Effective teachers apply this principle in their classrooms (regardless of the age or grade level of the students). Recognizing that we are members of this community of learners, teachers and students can work cooperatively to achieve learning goals. The teacher facilitates a positive learning environment by respecting all students' contributions. Effective teachers understand that we learn many worthwhile and meaningful lessons in context with others. Begin now by acknowledging the contributions your peers can make to this process.

Read Critically

critical thinking

A higher-order type of thinking in which one carefully evaluates the reliability and validity of sources before making decisions.

In this information age, we are bombarded daily with oral and written communication. It is up to us to decipher the truth and determine the authenticity of our sources. To determine the reliability and validity of our sources, it is imperative to develop the skill of **critical thinking**. Critical thinking demands that we analyze what we read or hear to determine credibility. For example, information on the Internet (like all sources) must be examined closely to judge not only its worth but its authenticity as well. Although the Internet can be a valuable storehouse of information, one cannot accept at face value everything that appears in print—or on screen. As with all data, you must be selective, analytical, and evaluative.

The bottom line is that critical thinking is an important attribute, especially if you intend to become a teacher. For example, we tried to be impartial as we selected sources to quote for this textbook. Nevertheless, our life experiences and background may have influenced us. To illustrate, in an introductory book we could not possibly include every topic, nor acknowledge every researcher or author who has made a worthy contribution to the literature. Consequently, we had to select which to include. It makes sense that our decisions were probably affected by our backgrounds. A person's background shapes perceptions, and for this reason, it is a good practice to be a critical thinker and reader, and to teach your students the value of a curious and "critical" mind.

Textbook Themes

Several themes are embedded in this text that mirror our philosophies and ideologies. We believe that for too many children the teacher is the only stable and reasonable adult figure in their lives. Therefore future teachers must be aware of the influence and power they wield. *Teachers are responsible for modeling appropriate attitudes and behaviors to their students*.

Many students today bring a myriad of emotional problems to the classroom; therefore *teachers must be willing to play multifaceted roles*. Sometimes teachers are coaches, advisors, disciplinarians, parents, and counselors to their students. Of course we are not insinuating that teachers are trained counselors, but they are "front-line" helpers. On a daily basis, teachers are called to make judgments about the mental and physical health of their students and respond appropriately to those needs.

In effect, *teachers are human relations specialists*. Successful teachers must be able to establish healthy, positive relationships with students as well as parents, administrators, colleagues, and other people in the community. Forging relationships with others requires that teachers be in relatively good mental health. One cannot successfully connect with others until he or she first connects with self. We have found that intrapersonal skills of teachers are sometimes overlooked in education textbooks, and yet these qualities are as vital to success as one's interpersonal skills (if not more so). In fact, we believe the psychological health of teachers is so critical that we devoted an entire chapter to describing the cultivation of healthy attributes and coping skills. Hence, *teachers need to possess good intrapersonal skills and interpersonal skills*.

We have found that many future teachers worry about their ability to handle student misbehavior. To alleviate these concerns, we also devoted a full chapter to discussing ways to prevent behavioral problems from developing. Although it is true that *teachers need instructional and management skills to create learning environments that engage learners*, we have seen that many concerns and fears beginning teachers have about classroom management are distorted or unwarranted. Fortunately, the majority of classroom problems can be prevented by adopting positive teacher attitudes and proactive behaviors. The fear of losing control of a class should not dissuade a prospective teacher from entering this profession.

Caring teachers advocate for their students—all students— regardless of family income, ethnicity, gender, disability, sexual orientation, religion, or cultural background. Some prospective teachers are concerned that cultural differences between them and their students may be too great to overcome. We contend that student diversity is an opportunity for growth for you and your students. As class leader, you will be in a position to model acceptance and appreciation for student differences. The teacher sets the tone for class cooperation and harmony. We believe that *successful teachers respect and welcome individual differences among students in their classrooms*. The differences among your students can make teaching more interesting and rewarding.

In sum, becoming a teacher is a journey not a destination. As part of the process, *professional educators commit to lifelong learning*. Being a student of life for life is an exciting idea. Along the path, you will find many people whom you will learn from, including your students. Fortunately for all of us who teach, the students are like "on-the-job" consultants; we are partners in learning. Thus *facilitative teachers create collaborative learning environments where everyone learns from one another*. You may find it reassuring to know that you and your students (as members of a community of learners) will be learning life's lessons together. And naturally no one person will have all the answers to life's perplexities, but each individual along the path might contribute a piece or more of the puzzle.

In an introductory book we could not possibly address all your questions. At the end, you may discover you actually have more questions than you do now. If this happens, this is good; it means you learned a great deal and you are now in a position to ask more relevant and pointed questions. In the final analysis, choosing a satisfying career is such a crucial decision that it cannot be rushed into or resolved definitively. Career choice is a process, and like anything else that is worth pursuing, it is an on-going investigation that requires careful deliberation and serious reflection.

The Art and Science of Teaching

Have you ever thought about whether teaching is an art or a science? This philosophical question is often debated among professional educators. There are many esteemed educators who argue that teaching is an art, whereas other equally esteemed educators argue it is a science. By the way, does taking one position preclude the other? Could teaching be both an art and a science? To appreciate both sides of this contentious debate, we will discuss each stance separately.

The Art: The Qualitative Side of Teaching

Can you identify those who were "naturals" at teaching? They had the ability to teach you when you least expected it; learning happened like magic. You found yourself stimulated by what was transpiring in their classroom, and abracadabra, you were hooked on the subject. You were captivated by their charm; you were swept into their learning web. These dynamic teachers probably found life intriguing, learning exciting, and people fascinating. Their zest for living spilled spontaneously over into the classroom.

In reality, there are many things that teachers do that cannot be studied systematically or explained definitively. These attributes are "qualitative" not "quantitative"; thus they defy measurement. Although we cannot precisely define or validate these subjective qualities, we can experience them.

At best, the professional literature can cite "attractive" qualities for teachers to possess, such as enthusiasm, but cannot tell you exactly how to acquire those attributes. Nor can studies accurately predict which traits consistently yield what outcomes under which conditions.

A classic we suggest you read is *The Art of Teaching* by Gilbert Highet (1951). According to Highet, teaching is an art, not a science. Highet warns against applying the scientific method to human beings, because human interactions are beyond cause and effect manipulations; however, he does contend that science can be useful when making predictions about large groups of people (p. vii).

The Science: The Quantitative Side of Teaching

Those who argue that teaching is a science contend that teaching practices must be studied scientifically and applied to human behavior. Teachers should not only be schooled in principles derived from empirical studies, but they should model scientific inquiry and methodology to their students. The curriculum should emphasize quantitative knowledge and be driven by the latest research findings.

Theoretical questions that beg to be measured include: How do students learn? What do we know about learning? Which teacher behaviors produce better outcomes with what students under what circumstances? Pursuit of answers to questions such as these has produced findings that have improved teacher practices. Empirical research continues to add to the professional literature and knowledge base. As a result of scientific inquiry, teacher education training has improved over the decades.

Colleges of education encourage faculty to participate in research that enhances the existing knowledge base. Incentives for teacher education faculty to collaborate with colleagues in public schools have resulted in cooperative research projects and development grants. This partnership has proven to be productive and beneficial to all parties. Higher-education faculty and school faculty learn from each other, and teacher candidates benefit from this sharing of knowledge and expertise. Ask your instructors what grants or research projects they have been involved in with community schools and what they learned from these collaborative efforts.

Resolved: Teaching Is Both an Art and a Science

In this text, we take the position that teaching is both an art and a science. We will show throughout how art and science complement each other. Any artistic work is fraught with ambiguity. It is open to various interpretations depending on the person viewing it. A group of people can look at a painting, read a poem, or hear a song, and have varying interpretations of what the artist intended.

This same ambiguity also characterizes teaching. One of the purposes for the self-reflective questions in this textbook is to point out that many situations you will face or issues that you will deal with do not have conclusive answers. Thus, teachers must be able to deal with many problems and situations that do not have clear-cut solutions. Palmer (1998) notes that persons who think in "either/or" terms may have difficulty with paradoxes that contain "both/and," and therefore they might have trouble as teachers (p. 74). What this means is that it is imperative that teachers are comfortable with ambiguity.

However, believing in the art of teaching should not preclude one's desire to seek definitive answers to human problems. Fortunately for teacher education, many scholars have made significant contributions to the professional literature, giving us an empirical body of knowledge from which to operate. We look forward to further research that will improve the delivery of instruction and facilitate learning.

In this textbook, we demonstrate the interrelated role of the teacher as scientist and practitioner. We translate theory to practice to make the content more understandable and applicable. We make every effort to present research findings that complement rather than detract from the artistic side of teaching. We recommend that future teachers recognize the value of both the science and art in teaching practice. The goal is to become the best teacher you can be—which translates to being open to both persuasions.

REFLECTION QUESTIONS

- **What would be the unique benefits of viewing teaching as an art?**

  ....

- **What would be the unique benefits of viewing teaching as a science?**

  ....

- **If you had to choose between the art of teaching or the science of teaching, which would you choose as more compatible with your views about education? Why?**

  ....

Reflections from the Field

Even though Patty and I have commonalities, we, like all people, have our differences. In common, we are both white, European-American females, and raised in the South; yet our teaching philosophies and pedagogy (how we teach) are markedly different. Case in point: When I asked Patty what she thought that teacher preparation programs should emphasize the most—the art or the science of teaching—she answered this way:

"If forced to choose between art and science, I believe a teacher preparation program should lay a strong foundation by emphasizing the 'science' of teaching. From research we derive principles that teachers can use to direct their decisions and actions. Although there are no hard and fast rules in teaching, there are valuable contributions from the scientific perspective. For example, research has documented effective strategies teachers can implement when teaching basic skills. Prospective teachers should be exposed to this kind of knowledge in their preparation program of study. Once teachers acquire the teacher education knowledge base, they can then turn their attention toward the 'art' of teaching."

Patty's response is quite different from my opinion. Read mine (below) to see how we differ. These statements should give you a sense of who we are as people and professionals.

"If I had to choose, I believe the 'art' should be emphasized the most, especially in teacher education programs. I would assume most students are well-versed in their specialty area when they graduate. Education courses, then, should stress the affective domain. Beginning teachers should not assume that mastery of a subject or discipline automatically translates to teaching success. If students think this is all they need, they are in for an unpleasant surprise when they are confronted with a host of problems having little to do with curriculum or instructional methods. I contend it is a disservice to our students to fail to address intrapersonal and interpersonal skills.

"Patty, after reading your response to my question, I was reminded of how well you and I complement each other. Our divergent philosophical views and teaching backgrounds bring a balanced perspective to this book. I also think our differing teaching styles prevent us from being too teacher-centered or too student-centered in the narrative. Hopefully we have constructed a story that conveys a respectful appreciation of both the art and science of teaching. Indeed, this was a challenging assignment."

Teaching Demands a Unique Person

Hardly ever does one hear a teacher (novice or veteran) complain that the job is too easy or the problems that students bring to the classroom are not challenging enough. Quite the opposite, teaching is a full-time, demanding job that requires unique attitudes, skills, and talents that most people neither possess nor care to acquire. In this book we try to explain why teaching requires a unique person.

For starters, just think who your audience is: You will be teaching children and teenagers who by definition are in a state of transition. Young people develop at varying rates; hence, every child you teach will be at a slightly different level of maturity—physically, emotionally, cognitively, socially, and so forth. In addition to that, many physically and mentally challenged students (who may have been taught separately by resource room teachers), are now being placed more frequently into the regular classroom to learn alongside of peers. This is called **inclusion.** In theory, inclusion makes sense and is meritorious, but as you might suspect, it requires great flexibility on the teacher's part to efficiently and effectively accommodate for the range of motivations, abilities, interests, and learning styles existing among his or her students.

inclusion

The practice of placing physically and/or mentally challenged students in regular classrooms as much as possible.

As you read about what teachers do, you may be surprised that some people have the idea that teaching is easy. Quite the contrary, teachers face a multitude of pressures, internally and externally. And although we offer many effective strategies for handling these demands, we also ask you to consider whether you believe you have the temperament, stamina, and commitment that the job requires.

Be Part of the Solution

Before we go any further, we would like to forewarn you: There are many people out there with an opinion about what's wrong with education today. Many authorities claim to have "the" solution to school and community problems. In reality, the answers to educational and societal problems are far from simple. Even recognized giants in the field of education can (at best) offer only a new angle or fresh perspective to think about when seeking solutions to educational problems.

It's a shame that education has at times become a convenient target to blame for many of society's problems. Granted, education has the potential to make societal changes, but it cannot single-handedly conquer the ailments in contemporary society (e.g., violence, addictions, poverty, racism, and oppression). In reality, it takes a joint effort between school and community to fully address these issues. The exciting part is that as a member of a collective team, teachers can make differences in the lives of students. As individuals, teachers can also make discernible differences—one student at a time.

Conclusion

In this text you will see how teacher education has evolved, its current status, and where it is headed. By having a historical perspective on education, you will be in a better position to evaluate present issues and challenges facing schooling in America. Because teaching is part of a larger system, it should be presented in context with the home and community. By placing the act of teaching in context, therefore, you will be better able to conceptualize the role teachers play in the system.

There is an abundance of qualities, beliefs, values, and behaviors associated with effective and satisfying teaching. *Fortuna fortes iuvat* is a Latin phrase from Vergil's *Aeneid* that translates, "Fortune (or success) favors the brave." This saying truly applies for those who are considering teaching as a career. In *The Courage to Teach: Exploring the Inner Landscape of a Teacher's Life,* Palmer (1998) contends that because teaching comes from the heart, the trait of courage is essential for good teachers to possess. This text describes amazing and effective teachers. You will find that deciding to become a teacher takes courage, knowledge, and preparation.

There needs to be a commitment to the pursuit of excellence on the teacher's part (Evans & Brueckner, 1992). To pursue excellence in teaching requires that you be open to new challenges and ideas and that you continually seek ways to improve yourself. You will begin to understand as you read this textbook how important it is that a teacher commit to lifelong learning to be successful in the classroom.

Finally, learning about teaching is a process that requires a curious mind and a patient soul. The teaching profession continually looks for bright, enthusiastic, caring, creative, committed, and brave individuals who have the courage to make a difference in the lives of students. Therefore, please stay with us as we tell you more (much more) about this challenging, gratifying, and never-dull career called teaching. Who knows, you may be the ideal candidate for the position.

KEY TERMS

active learning

community of learners

constructivism

critical thinking

inclusion

portfolio

reflective thinking

social constructivism

student-centered approach

teacher-centered approach

REFERENCES

Airasian, P. W. & Walsh, M. E. (1997). Constructivist cautions. *Phi Delta Kappan, 78*(2), 444–449.

Evans, J. M. & Brueckner, M. M. (1992). *Teaching and you: Committing, preparing, and succeeding.* Boston: Allyn & Bacon.

Highet, G. (1951). *The art of teaching.* London: Methuen.

Palmer, P. J. (1998). *The courage to teach: Exploring the inner landscape of a teacher's life.* San Francisco: Jossey-Bass.

Introduction to Teaching

Rewards and Realities

WHAT IT MEANS TO TEACH

© Michael Newman/PhotoEdit

At the end of this chapter, you will be able to

- Identify factors that affect career decision making.

- Describe reasons people are attracted to teaching as a career.

- Differentiate extrinsic from intrinsic rewards.

- Discuss reasons people leave teaching.

- Identify useful sources of information for deciding whether to teach.

- Assess your own motives for becoming a teacher.

Motivation to Teach

A bird's eye view of what to expect in this chapter

In this chapter you are given the chance to think about what it's like to teach and why you might want to become a teacher. We will help you sort through many factors that can influence your career decision. Take this time to consider more seriously your desire to become a teacher and to learn more about yourself.

As you read this chapter, we suggest that you be open to self-reflection so that you understand better why you may or may not want to teach. A sample of some of the questions raised in this chapter are: What do you wish to achieve in your life? What are your strengths? Do you think your interests will be compatible with a career in teaching? Are you enthusiastic about learning? Do you like challenges? Do you like young people?

These and other pertinent questions are asked to compel you to consider whether teaching is a good match. We hope that by the end of the chapter you will have a better idea about your present motivations and possible career goals.

By the way, choosing to teach is not a "one-shot," irreversible decision. Decision making is a developmental process. You may decide, for example, that this is not the right career for now but that it could be later. In the last chapter, we revisit these issues and offer suggestions for what to do if you decide teaching is not right for you.

eachers are frontline helpers; they help students recognize their potential and develop strengths. At the end of each day, teachers know that in some small way they have helped someone. Making a child feel successful is indeed a laudable achievement. Many identify this "helping component" as key to retaining teachers. Not many jobs pay employees to make positive changes that ultimately can improve the human condition. The bottom line is that teachers are in pivotal places where they can make significant contributions to the lives of young people on a daily basis. If you become a teacher, you will be choosing a profession that allows—in fact, expects—you to serve others.

Factors in Career Decision Making

In the following section we examine relevant factors that may influence your decision to teach or not to teach. You may think of other factors we omitted; discuss those in class.

Role Models

By the time you enter college, most of you know more about teaching than any other occupation. Perhaps you have visited the dentist once or twice a year, exchanged information with a banker three times in your life, and in-

Engaging in the act of teaching can bring personal pleasure and satisfaction.

© Mary Kate Denny/PhotoEdit

Percent of public school students' interest in a career in education, by student characteristics: 1996

Item	Total	School level Grades 7 and 8	School level Grades 9 through 12
Interest in becoming a teacher			
Very interested	8	8	8
Somewhat interested	24	23	25
Not very interested	25	23	27
Not at all interested	41	45	39
Don't know	1	1	1
Ever talked to a teacher about becoming a teacher?			
Yes	12	9	14
No	87	90	85
Don't know	1	1	1
A teacher has told you they thought you would make a good teacher			
Yes	22	20	24
No	73	75	71
Don't know	5	5	5

Source: Metropolitan Life/Louis Harris Associates, Inc., The Metropolitan Life Survey of The American Teacher, 1996, Part II. "Students Voice Their Opinions on: Their Education, Teachers and Schools."

teracted with a performing artist twice in your past. In contrast, you have had a *minimum* of 12 years of daily contact with teachers. The direct contact you have had with teachers over the course of your school years has undoubtedly shaped and influenced your perceptions and understanding of what teachers do.

Who are your role models? What characteristics do they exhibit that you admire? How have these role models influenced your desire to teach? Place (1997) found that students who were influenced by a former role model were more likely to select education as a field of study than those whose major career motivation was the hope of financial reward. Although past school experiences will certainly color your present understanding of the teaching profession, it's important to realize that these perceptions may not be entirely accurate. Nonetheless, your familiarity with teaching and perhaps the influence of an individual teacher or several teachers may have precipitated your consideration of teaching as a career.

REFLECTION QUESTIONS

- Recall some of your most memorable school experiences—both positive and negative. Taking the time to write down these recollections can be a useful activity at this point.

- Describe early encounters with teachers who have positively affected your perception of teaching.

- Describe early encounters with teachers who have negatively affected your perception of teaching.

Self-Knowledge

A good starting point for deciding whether to become a teacher is assessing your knowledge of yourself. What is important to you? What are your personal strengths? What needs do you hope your career will meet? What do you care about most deeply? Although answering questions such as these may not be easy, it is, nonetheless, vital that you confront them honestly in order to make a wise choice.

values

Those things that matter the most to a person.

A significant aspect of your self-knowledge pertains to your **values,** which play an important role in determining your career choice. "A value is a personal standard that you feel to be extremely important" (Chapman, 1988, p. 21). As you contemplate your values, you should be able to identify a few that define who you are.

Take a few minutes to reflect on the work values listed below. Which ones matter most to you? (Check all that apply.)

❑ Being your own boss

❑ Being in charge of, or directing, others

❑ Doing new and different things every day

❑ Making a significant contribution to society

❑ Having job security

❑ Earning a lot of money

❑ Helping others

❑ Being recognized for your contributions

❑ Enjoying your work and having fun

❑ Using your creative skills and abilities

❑ Other: _____

Which two or three values are most important to you? Prioritizing your values will help you determine what really matters to you. Once you know that, it's much easier to decide which career would be a good match for you.

career anchor

The values that draw one to a particular occupation or job.

Closely related to the notion of career values is what Schein (1993) calls a **career anchor,** defined as "the *one* thing a person would not give up if forced to make a choice" (p. 50). A career anchor serves to pull a person back on course. From career history interviews, Schein (1993) identifies the following eight career anchor categories:

1. *Technical/functional competence:* This career anchor attracts people whose identity is derived from the content or specialization of their work.

2. *General managerial competence:* This career anchor attracts people who like to identify and solve problems and desire high levels of responsibility.

3. *Autonomy/independence:* This career anchor attracts people who like to do things their own way and dislike close supervision.

4. *Security/stability:* This career anchor attracts people who need stable, predictable work.

5. *Entrepreneurial creativity:* This career anchor attracts people who have a strong need to create. If this need is not met, these individuals become bored.

6. *Service/dedication to a cause:* This career anchor attracts people who want to improve the world.

7. *Pure challenge:* This career anchor attracts people who are drawn to the idea of challenge and the opportunity to overcome obstacles.

8. *Lifestyle:* This career anchor attracts people who perceive teaching as a way to integrate several areas of life, such as personal time, family commitments, and career goals. These people place a high value on flexibility (p. 50).

Career anchors pull a person back on course throughout the person's working life. Teaching is most closely aligned with the career anchor of service or dedication to a cause. Being drawn to this anchor means that you will not want to miss an opportunity to pursue work that allows you to achieve something of value (Schein, 1993, p. 78). It is certainly possible for people to hold the same job and be anchored by different motives. Not all teachers would say that the anchor of service or dedication to a cause draws them to the profession. Many teachers are also drawn by the anchors of security/stability, pure challenge, and lifestyle. However, the need for congruence between a person's career and his or her anchor helps explain why people do or do not make career changes.

As you contemplate your personal anchor, consider also those things about which you are most passionate. According to Fried (1995), passion is what distinguishes good teachers. Take time to ponder your passions. What do you care about deeply? What do you get so immersed in that you lose all sense of time? Do you have a passion about people (e.g., children or young people), a passion for a particular subject area, or a passion for the process of teaching and learning? Your passions reflect your values. Being aware of one's passion can result in powerful teaching.

Personality Type

In addition to your values, anchors, and passions and your past encounters with various careers, your personality influences the career path that will lead to success. Your personality will not only play a part in your degree of satisfaction with the teaching profession but will also shape your individual teaching style. Understanding your own personality can help you decide whether a "fit" exists between you and the requirements of a specific work environment.

John Holland's (1985) theory of vocational choice offers one way of looking at the congruence between different personality types and work environments. Holland stated that there are six types of personalities: conventional, enterprising, realistic, investigative, artistic, and social. Teaching is most closely aligned with the social type, yet it also contains elements of the artistic and enterprising types. The social personality type is concerned with others' welfare and derives satisfaction from interacting with people. Having a keen ability to empathize, these individuals like to solve problems through discussion of feelings and interaction with others. Corresponding to Holland's six personality types are six occupational, or work, environments. Holland describes a social work environment as one that involves caring, helping, and instructing others (Holland, 1985).

What traits and characteristics make you unique? Numerous personality tests and vocational and personal inventories are available to help you learn more about your personality type and determine what setting would be most compatible with your traits. We suggest you start by contacting your campus counseling center for information on the tests appropriate for you. Bear in mind, however, that no inventory or questionnaire can accurately predict the career in which you will be most successful.

AssessYourself

What kind of person are you? What five words best describe you? Do you prefer working with things, information, or people?

Are you flexible or rigid? Are you curious? Are you persistent?

Are you sensitive to others' thoughts and feelings? Are you an avid learner?

Are you comfortable interacting with others? Are you at ease speaking in front of a group?

Are you creative? Are you a risk taker or do you prefer to maintain the status quo?

Do you seek variety? Do you enjoy coordinating events?

NOTABLE QUOTE

In teaching, as in all human service professions, satisfaction from work is very much a function of the interaction between the requirements of role and one's temperament or personality style. *(Seymour Sarason)*

Reasons People Select Teaching

Now that you know more about yourself and what factors may influence your career decision, consider next the reasons people choose teaching as a career.

Attractive Features of Teaching

Lortie's classic study of teaching as an occupation resulted from extensive interviews of teachers. In *Schoolteacher*, Lortie (1975) shared his sociological findings. Of particular note are five "attractors" identified by Lortie as themes: interpersonal, service, continuation, material benefits, and time compatibility. The *interpersonal* theme encompasses the intense contact with young people that teaching provides. This theme emerges as a primary reason for people choosing to become teachers (Hutchinson & Johnson, 1994). Other than teaching, very few occupations are characterized by such direct and constant interaction with children or adolescents. The *service* theme relates to the altruistic nature of teaching and the importance of education in society. The *continuation* theme refers to being able to remain in a setting and in an endeavor that one has found pleasurable. Teachers often mention that school has always been an enjoyable experience and that they wish to continue their work in that environment.

Salary, status, and security are associated with the *material benefits* theme. Finally, the theme of *time compatibility* has to do with the flexibility of teachers' schedules, which allows them to pursue other interests, especially during the summer months. This theme attracts to teaching those who seek its suitability for having a career and meeting family needs and concerns. However, those who become teachers tend to consider the material benefits and time compatibility themes as secondary attractors.

Timing

In the book *On Being a Teacher*, Gehrke (1987) traces the stages of teachers' career paths and examines the "timing" of a person's decision to become a teacher. She differentiates between early deciders and late-comers by

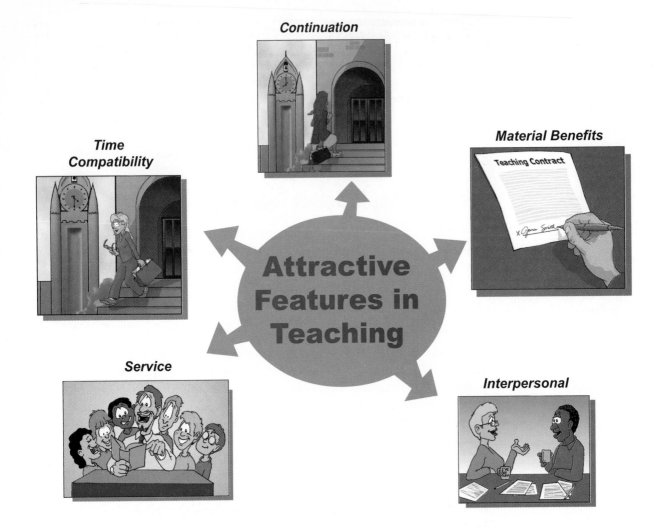

labeling different categories of teachers according to the timing and reason for their decision.

For some people, deciding to become a teacher is a decision that is made early in life. According to Gehrke (1987), there seems to be an almost intuitive **occupational fit** among these individuals who easily identify with the work of teachers and see themselves fulfilling the demands of that role. Others enter teaching as *crusaders, content specialists, converts,* or *freefloaters.*

Crusaders are drawn to teaching primarily because they believe that they can "make a difference." These individuals have a sense of mission about teaching and desire to change society. Idealistic and committed to a cause beyond self, crusaders are concerned with social issues and conditions. As teachers, they perceive their role as crucial in ameliorating such conditions as inequality, poverty, or illiteracy.

Converts have tried and been successful in careers other than teaching, yet they may have not found satisfaction. They have decided that teaching is re-

occupational fit

An intuitive calling among those who easily identify with the work of teachers and who see themselves fulfilling the demands of that role.

Knowing at the end of the day that you made a difference in the life of even just one student can be a powerful motivator to stay in the profession.

© Eric Fowke/PhotoEdit

ally what they want to do, perhaps having pushed aside that thought earlier in life.

Content specialists become teachers primarily because they love their chosen subject area. Teaching allows them an opportunity to stay involved in a discipline they enjoy studying. Sometimes, effective teaching is hindered by a strong devotion to subject matter. Teachers whose primary motive is linked to a specific area of study may overlook important aspects of teaching by placing more emphasis on "*what* is taught" and less on "*who* is being taught." Prospective teachers should be aware of the detrimental effects of such a tendency so they can avoid making the same mistake.

Freefloaters lack true commitment to teaching and have not actually decided to become teachers. They are merely seeking teacher certification until they discover what they really want to do with their lives. Admitting that you might be a freefloater requires honest self-appraisal. It's best for students if freefloaters screen themselves out of the profession early, because their hearts will never be in it. A lack of commitment certainly influences the manner in which a teacher performs the duties of the profession.

The critical consideration, then, is *why* you decide to become a teacher rather than *when* you make such a decision.

Let's now examine the rewards of teaching and explore more deeply the reasons for choosing to become a teacher.

Rewards in Teaching

extrinsic reward

A benefit that is determined by the tangible "positives" of a job, such as salary, security, and schedule.

Every career offers rewards. One way of classifying rewards is according to whether they are of extrinsic or intrinsic value to a person. **Extrinsic rewards** are visible, external, measurable and objective; they include salary, power, status, and schedule (e.g., holiday breaks and time off in the summer). Teachers achieve status when they are looked up to as knowledge experts. Being in authority over others and deciding their fate (i.e., grade) can place teachers in a powerful position—one with important ethical implications discussed later in the book.

intrinsic reward

A benefit that is derived from the feelings of satisfaction gained.

In contrast, **intrinsic rewards** are invisible, internal, immeasurable, and most often emotion based (or subjective). Intrinsic rewards include the feeling of satisfaction derived from helping others, the pleasure of engaging in

Teachers provide emotional support to students.

© Elizabeth Crews

Many people are drawn to the intense contact with youth that is inherent in teaching.

© Spencer Grant/PhotoEdit

the act of teaching and providing assistance in understanding to others, and the sense of personal fulfillment from knowing that you have made a difference in someone else's life. Interacting with one's teaching colleagues can also provide much satisfaction.

In a survey conducted by MetLife (Harris, 1995), 89% of the teachers queried cited intrinsic rewards to describe what they liked most about their jobs. In a review of the research literature, Ellis (1984) found that intrinsic rewards contribute more to teacher morale and job satisfaction than extrinsic rewards. According to Gehrke (1987), having a desire to work with and help people is the most compelling reason for choosing teaching as a career. Do you agree or disagree? Why? Toward which rewards are you drawn most strongly? When comparing the types of rewards among professions, the weight of intrinsic rewards is heavier in teaching than in some other professions. Those who remain happy in teaching recognize that these intrinsic rewards are what make it worthwhile.

Reflections from the Field

When asked about the rewards in teaching that are particularly attractive, Denise Jenkens, with 12 years' teaching experience in the

Mayflower School District, offers the following information. "There are many rewards in teaching: the sense of accomplishment when observing students learn under my tutelage, watching young men and women reach maturity, and the sharing of day-to-day life. But the biggest rewards come from the students themselves when they express their thanks in words and deeds. I am reminded of the student who said my art class had made her trip to Europe more meaningful and enjoyable. She brought me a piece of the Berlin Wall when it was being torn down. I also bask in the glow of being twice nominated by students for inclusion in *Who's Who of American Teachers,* once in 1992 and again in 1996. As you can see, the list is unending, but my biggest reward came unexpectedly at the local Wal-Mart when I ran into a former student. Three years earlier, he had been a student in my art class. Although he was frequently absent from school, when he did show up, he loved to draw. I really don't recall giving him any more attention than any other student at the time. There we stood in the main aisle of Wal-Mart, reminiscing and catching up on his life. He informed me that he had a steady job and was about to be married. I gave him some motherly advice and a few words of encouragement and started to walk off. He detained me by saying, 'I'm *really* glad I ran into you. I've been wanting to tell you all these years that when I was in high school, you were the one teacher who kept me going.' That did it! It all came together. If I teach 100 years, this student's words are all the reward I will ever need."

Dionne Bennett, a middle school teacher, shares these observations relative to the rewards found in teaching. "The greatest reward that I receive from being a teacher is knowing that every day I can affect the lives of my students in a positive way. This is only my fourth year of teaching, but as I watch my students progress from middle school to high school, it gives me such pleasure knowing that I influenced their lives. It means so much to me to see them in the community and hear their comments about what they are using from what they learned in my class. It warms my heart to know that being a member of my class enhanced their future. I also consider summer vacations a reward of teaching. Summers off allows me to go back to school and also travel. The extra knowledge that I gain during these months off helps improve my classroom instruction while also keeping me abreast of new trends in education."

Reasons People Leave Teaching

After reading the excerpts in *Reflections from the Field*, you might wonder why anyone would leave teaching. Nevertheless, some people do leave the profession early. Let's examine the reasons; an understanding of these reasons might be helpful as you examine your motives for pursuing teaching as a career choice.

From the Huberman, Grounauer, & Marti (1993) study, the top three reasons for considering leaving (not necessarily doing so) were as follows: (1) a positive motive—leaving without a crisis (e.g., raising one's family); (2) institutional reasons (e.g., employment conditions such as a long commute, difficult schedule, out of field subject matter assignment, overwhelming school system mandates); and (3) fatigue, routine, and frustration.

The occurrence of a phenomenon known as **burnout** is a common reason given by those who leave teaching. Burnout is an expression used to describe a condition that teachers experience as a result of a high level of stress on the job. Burnout is usually accompanied by a feeling of mental and/or physical exhaustion and a belief that one has nothing more to give. The significant amount of giving of self required on the job often leaves teachers with little left to give to themselves or their families, and thus they easily burn out.

Stress caused by the working conditions in schools is often a problem for teachers. Having too much paperwork, too many students, too many discipline problems, and too little administrative or parental support takes a toll on even the most physically and emotionally stable teacher.

Some teachers create undue stress by holding unrealistic expectations. New teachers are especially susceptible to this kind of stress because they often have idealistic views about teaching. For example, do you envision being a teacher as an opportunity to receive unconditional love and acceptance from a group of wonderful children? Do you picture yourself as being respected and admired by everyone in the school community? Holding mental images such as these contributes to frustration and burnout when the practice of teaching (i.e., reality) proves to be much different.

Once you are teaching and you find yourself approaching burnout, look for change and new challenges. Be willing to experiment and to take on new assignments so that you do not get stuck in a rut. If you invest all your time and energy in your teaching efforts, it's easy to lose your personal identity. It's important to maintain interests outside of school. Even as you prepare to become a teacher, find stress-relieving activities (such as exercise) that suit your lifestyle and meet your needs. Be sensitive to the signs of burnout and be willing to give yourself a break.

It's important that you consider and confront now whether you harbor any unrealistic expectations for teaching. Realize that you can work to change the working conditions in schools. By developing your leadership skills and level of commitment, you can do much to improve the atmosphere of the school where you will eventually work. Be willing to become involved and to speak up for the improvement of education.

A study conducted by the National Center for Education Statistics (NCES, 1997) revealed that 66% of teachers would "certainly or probably" become teachers again; 16% thought that the chances were "about even"; and 18% said they would "probably or certainly *not*" become teachers again. The re-

burnout

A condition caused by high levels of job stress, usually accompanied by a feeling of mental and/or physical exhaustion.

Web Site

For more information, visit http://www.ed.gov/NCES/pubs97/97460.htm

sults from this study should provide some reassurance for those who decide to teach. Statistically speaking, if you choose a career in teaching, you will most likely not regret your decision.

Reflections from the Field

A senior high English teacher in a small rural school left teaching after 10 years, citing the following reasons for her dissatisfaction. "The administration was too focused on figures and money. They did not support those of us in the trenches (or did in your presence but not in your absence). It was discouraging to see other colleagues who were there only for the paycheck (small though it was). Also, some co-workers tried to make all students fit into the same mold, leaving no room for individuality or expression. Some co-workers did not think the best of students or expect the best from them. Extracurricular activities took students from class, so that the amount of teaching time became less than activity time. Also, I had to either buy supplies from my own pocket or do without. These are a few aggravating things that come to mind, and that may have something to do with my decision to quit teaching."

In her list of reasons for leaving teaching, the English teacher quoted above did not once cite problems with students. In fact, her frustrations were rooted in her perceptions of how administration and other colleagues were doing their jobs. When asked about things she liked about teaching, she listed the following—all of which are related to her passion for learning and for students. Read on:

"I liked many things about teaching: it was fun to watch students grow as individuals, noting them succeed when they thought they could not, challenging them to be better than they thought they could be, showing them they could grasp the subject matter they had come to believe they could not, leading them to believe in themselves even though they had been convinced by others that they were failures."

Web Site
A valuable information source is Recruiting New Teachers (a national non-profit organization) at www.rnt.org. Check it out.

field experiences
School-based placements designed to help future teachers learn more about the profession.

Information Sources

Many sources of help are available to assist you in making a decision about whether to teach. This section discusses several of these valuable sources.

Field Experiences

Most of your teacher education courses will have **field experiences** as a learning component. Basically, field experiences are opportunities to learn more about what it means to teach and to determine whether you are suitable for the demands inherent in teaching. You will be placed in a classroom at first to observe the teacher; later in your teacher education program you will assist the teacher. Placements will be made in different types of settings (e.g., elementary, middle school, junior high, or high school). What you may see in one setting may intrigue you more than what you observe in another setting. By observing different levels of schooling, you may find that you particularly enjoy working with children of one age over those of another age.

Work Experiences with Youth

In addition to your required field experiences, look for opportunities to work in settings that provide contact with children and youth. You might find a job in a daycare center, at a summer camp, or at a youth center. If you cannot secure paid work, seek volunteer opportunities to apply yourself and assess your ability to interact effectively with children and youth. By tutoring a neighbor or relative you will find out what providing one-on-one instruction is like.

Mentors

mentor

A wise and trusted counselor or friend who offers advice, insight, and encouragement to another person.

Along with actual experience working with children, find yourself a trusted mentor in whom you can confide. A **mentor** is a wise and trusted counselor or friend who can give you insights and encouragement. A mentor may be a college professor, a former teacher, an employer, a family member, or a close friend. Mentors can be helpful assistants as you sort out feelings and beliefs about what is important and what you want to accomplish. We recommend interviewing teachers as a way to learn more about what they do and how they feel about their work. These interviews can help you gain greater understanding by providing a "behind the scenes" look at teaching.

Family Members and Friends

Much learning in life takes place in a social context, and therefore your communication with others serves as a valuable source of information. Solicit feedback from family members and friends (who know you well) about your skills and abilities. This input could be of great value in your career search. These people can offer you "personal" insights that you may have inadvertently overlooked (or conveniently suppressed).

Self

Although many people, including your peers in class, can be helpful consultants when deciding on whether teaching is a good match, the final decision will be made by you. In the final analysis, *you* are the one most qualified to know what is best. Thus you must continually engage in self-assessment. Find ways to learn more about yourself. Become involved in campus activities that provide leadership opportunities. Keep a journal to record your thoughts, feelings, and plans for the future. The more you know about yourself, the better prepared you will be to make wise decisions. Should you decide teaching is *not* right (which could happen, because it's not for everyone), all we ask is that you reach this decision after careful reflection and deliberation.

REFLECTION QUESTIONS

- What are your motivations for wanting to become a teacher? Share your thoughts with a close friend, mentor, family member, former teacher, or class-mate. Solicit that person's reaction and feedback.

- Answer these questions raised by Laurence Boldt (1996, p. 60): What was I born to do? What would be my greatest contribution to others? What would I really love to do? What is the best use of my time?

Reflections from the Field

When we asked the question, "What made you decide to become a teacher?" Rugenal Anderson, with 26 years' teaching experience, offered this explanation. "I was brought up in a small, rural community during a time when professional careers for aspiring black students were limited. Becoming a teacher was much like obtaining one of the most rewarding and challenging jobs on the face of the earth. The best and the brightest, as I knew them, were all teachers. The people who lived in my neighborhood were poor and lived in somewhat smaller, less equipped homes while the teachers in the community lived in nicer homes and even drove cars. At a very early age, I knew I could not work at menial jobs in the field or in someone's hotel or kitchen. Many of my early teachers modeled a work ethic and lifestyle I thought might be something I could do. After all, I had taught my nieces and nephew everything I knew when I was only in the fourth grade. Once out of high school and in college, my choices were narrowed even more and my decision became clear. Although becoming a teacher was only one of the few choices available to young, black women during my formative years, it was a choice I made freely and it continues to be my driving force."

Anita Cegers-Coleman, keyboarding and mathematics teacher with four years' teaching experience, made this observation. "I have several educators in my family, such as teachers (my mother, an uncle, and some cousins), principals (a cousin and an uncle), and even an uncle who is a former superintendent. Growing up around them, I became fascinated by the stories they would tell me. I used to "play school" when I was younger, and I would even "teach" my younger brother and some others. I worked hard to make good grades when I was in school, partly because that was expected of me, and also because I enjoyed being there (most of the time, especially in the lower grades). Like many other people might agree, the schedule is wonderful, also!"

Reflections from the Field

Patty and Lynda discuss their motives for becoming teachers.

Patty: "I made the decision to teach when I was in upper elementary school. It seemed that I had the 'occupational fit' profile. In the ninth grade I had the opportunity to try out teaching when on two occasions my Latin and algebra teachers had me take the role of substitute teacher for a week. What an exciting and satisfying experience it was to explain skills and content to my peers! I found that I truly enjoyed the act of teaching. However, I did not receive reinforcement to become a teacher from my family (becoming a doctor or engineer was strongly suggested). Thus when I graduated from college I did not have my teaching credentials. My former high school Latin teacher (who was by then retired) called and told me that she had recommended me for a teaching position at a private high school. I then got my teaching certificate. I have never regretted becoming a teacher and am grateful to Mrs. Houchin for giving me the lead on my first teaching job."

Lynda: "I remember as far back as primary school thinking how much fun it would be to teach. Unlike Patty, though, I received a great deal of support from family to be a teacher. My grandmother, aunt, and mother were all teachers—and loved it! They inspired me to want to teach. My earliest recollections were coming home from school in the afternoons and playing 'teacher' with neighborhood chums. The younger children made the best pupils because they were most compliant. After all, they were thrilled by the attention I bestowed on them, and I was grateful for the practice. Hopefully we all gained something from this. I guess you would say that teaching is an 'occupational fit' for me."

AssessYourself

As you learn more about the career of teaching, you will soon realize that it's clearly not for the weary or faint-hearted. Actually the reverse is true, teachers must have inordinate amounts of energy, endurance, patience, devotion, and courage.

Some people (including us) consider teaching a "calling," which means it calls for the rare individual who is willing to sacrifice personal needs for students' needs. Could you be that special person?

Conclusion

Choosing a career is much like the process of selecting a mate (Sarason, 1993). As you get to know a potential mate better, you can determine whether your interests and values match. Do you think the two of you will be compatible? Would you enjoy being with this person over the long haul? Making a final decision usually takes thoughtful deliberation. When deciding on a career, you go through a similar decision-making process by examining your own values and those supported by a particular career. You then weigh the chances that your own personality and needs will be fulfilled in that career choice. It's always somewhat of a gamble, but the more information you have about yourself and about your selected career, the more likely you are to make an informed and meaningful decision.

Therefore we suggest that you read and study with an open heart and mind and be willing to ask plenty of questions of those around you, such as your instructor and other faculty members. In the last chapter of this book, we will return to the question of whether or not teaching is the right career move for you. If teaching appears to be a good fit, we will provide you with additional ideas on what to do next. If it does not seem right, we will offer further suggestions and alternatives to explore.

As you study about the teaching field, keep in mind that becoming a teacher is a process rather than an outcome; it's a journey not a destination. We learn as we go. For many of you the trip has just begun; for others you are already en route. Regardless of where you start, you will learn many new things along the way. Hopefully you will begin to see things in a different light. Isn't that the purpose of travel—to open ourselves up to new possibilities? Providentially, there will be many caring and wise mentors to guide you along the way and steer you in the right direction. Fortunately, this journey does not have to be taken alone.

KEY TERMS

burnout

career anchor

extrinsic reward

field experiences

intrinsic reward

mentor

occupational fit

values

SUGGESTED READING

Boldt, L. G. (1996). *How to find the work you love.* New York: Arkana.

Fried, R. (1995). *The passionate teacher.* Boston: Beacon Press.

REFERENCES

Boldt, L. G. (1996). *How to find the work you love.* New York: Arkana.

Chapman, E. (1988). *Be true to your future.* Los Altos, CA: Crisp Publications.

Ellis, T. I. (1984). Motivating teachers for excellence. ERIC Clearinghouse on Educational Management: ERIC Digest, 6, *ERIC Document Reproduction Service,* No ED259449.

Fried, R. (1995). *The passionate teacher.* Boston: Beacon Press.

Gehrke, N. J. (1987). *On being a teacher.* West Lafayette, IN: Kappa Delta Pi.

Harris, L. (1995). *The Metropolitan life survey of the American teacher 1984–1995: Old problems, new challenges.* New York: MetLife.

Holland, J. L. (1985). *Making vocational choices* (2nd ed.). Englewood Cliffs, NJ: Prentice Hall.

Huberman, M., Grounauer, M., & Marti, J. (1993). *The lives of teachers.* New York: Teachers College Press.

Hutchinson, G., & Johnson, B. (1994). Teaching as a career: Examining high school students' perspectives. *Action in Teacher Education, 15*(4), 61–67.

Lortie, D. (1975). *Schoolteacher: A sociological study.* Chicago: The University of Chicago Press.

National Center for Education Statistics. (1997). *America's teachers: Profile of a profession 1993-94.* Washington, D.C.: U.S. Department of Education.

Place, A. W. (1997). Career choice of education: Holland type, diversity, and self-efficacy. *The Journal for a Just and Caring Education, 3*(2), 203–214.

Sarason, S. (1993). *You are thinking of teaching? Opportunities, problems, realities.* San Francisco: Jossey-Bass Publishers.

Schein, E. H. (1993). *Career anchors: Discovering your real values.* San Francisco: Pfeiffer.

© Elizabeth Crews

At the end of this chapter, you will be able to

- Explain factors that contribute to teachers' vulnerability.

- Recognize signs that suggest potential psychological problems for beginning teachers.

- Identify intrapersonal skills that are psychologically healthy and facilitative.

- Identify issues from your past that might interfere with your effectiveness as a teacher.

- Describe ways to handle intrapersonal conflicts so they do not negatively affect your relationships with students and others.

Connection to Self: Intrapersonal Skills

A bird's eye view of what to expect in this chapter

It is critical that teachers be able to make caring connections with students, families, colleagues, administrators, and other people in the community. Equally important is the ability to connect in a caring way to self. Liking oneself and treating oneself with respect is crucial to liking and respecting others. Self-esteem, the value one places on self, is essential to being an effective teacher who can relate easily to students and to others.

One of the themes embedded in this book is the importance of teachers having good mental health. In this chapter we explore the psychological health of the teacher in more detail. You are asked to reflect on areas in your life that could create problems for you as a teacher. For example, teachers must deal with student misbehavior. Would you be comfortable addressing issues such as these? You may have trouble with the role of disciplinarian if you are harboring unresolved anger from your past regarding how you were treated as a child. Reconciling one's past is essential to one's present mental health.

Some questions raised in this chapter are: What unresolved conflicts do you foresee being problematic if you become a teacher? What specifically are you doing to address these areas of your life? Will you be able to set healthy boundaries with your students? Basically, you will be asked if you can cope with the psychological demands imposed on teachers.

I n the next chapter we will discuss prospective teachers' abilities to re-late to others. You will see how important it is that teachers have good interpersonal skills. In this chapter, however, you will come to under-stand that it is equally important to have good intrapersonal skills. In fact, many believe that intrapersonal skills are more important because you can-not successfully interact with others until you first successfully connect with self (Locke & Ciechalski, 1995; Purkey & Novak, 1996). A general rule in psychology is that people tend to treat others as they treat themselves. Purkey and Novak (1996) assert that people who accept and like them-selves have a "much greater capacity to understand, accept, and like stu-dents" (p. 47). Clearly, self-acceptance is a cardinal attitude for a teacher to possess.

The Importance of Mental Health for Teachers

From our experiences, we believe the mental health of a teacher is so cru-cial that we have devoted an entire chapter to the subject.*

Note that we are not implying that teachers are problem-free or in per-fect mental health. If that were the case, there inevitably would be a severe shortage of teachers in schools and in higher education—undoubtedly few people would qualify. Corey, Corey, and Callanan (1998) maintain that it is not "*whether* you happen to be struggling with personal questions, but *how* you are struggling with them" (p. 37) that counts. This practical advice ap-plies to prospective teachers as well as counselors and therapists.

Socrates was quoted, 2,500 years ago, as saying: "An unexamined life is not worth living." We believe that future teachers should be willing to openly examine their lives and honestly acknowledge those trouble spots that may interfere with effective and abundant living. Furthermore, they should prepare themselves by actively working on those unresolved is-sues. Perhaps this chapter will reveal certain areas in your life that may need attention.

> **❝ NOTABLE QUOTE**
>
> What the teacher is, is more important than what he teaches. *(Karl Menniger)* ❞

*We would like to give credit to Corey, Corey, and Callanan (1998) for their in-sightful ideas regarding the mental health of those entering helping professions. In particular, we found Chapter 2 in their book, *Issues and Ethics in the Helping Profes-sions* (1998), very informative.

Teachers Are Not Immune to Emotional Problems

Indeed, teaching can be mentally draining. It has been found that teachers are not any more immune to emotional problems than their students (Persi, 1997). School counselors realize that the child being referred by the teacher for counseling is not the only one in distress; in many cases, the referring teacher may actually need psychological help more than the student (Persi, 1997).

Statistics suggest that teachers may be *more* susceptible to emotional disturbances than their students. To illustrate, it has been found that 28% to 30% of adults need psychological treatment compared with 17% to 22% of children and adolescents (Kessler et al., 1994). When teachers were compared with other adults, it was found that teachers had higher rates of psychological problems and substance abuse because of stressors inherent in the job (Punch & Tuettemann, 1990; Watts & Short, 1990).

Unfortunately, however, many teachers who need professional help refuse to seek treatment for fear of losing credibility and/or their jobs (Deane & Chamberlain, 1994); hence their emotional problems go undiagnosed and untreated. Because teaching could be hazardous to your "mental" health, we discuss some of the emotional demands of teaching that have the potential to put a teacher at risk for psychological problems.

REFLECTION QUESTIONS

Which areas in your life could be problematic for you as a beginning teacher? Note ways that you are working on those areas so they will not interfere with your effectiveness as a teacher.

Factors Contributing to Teachers' Vulnerability

What is it about the teaching job that makes teachers vulnerable to emotional disturbances? Why are teachers more susceptible to substance abuse, chronic depression, and other mental conditions compared with other professionals?

The following are some unique characteristics of the teaching profession that make the job emotionally demanding.

Living in a Fish Bowl

Teachers live in a fish bowl. They are scrutinized by administrators, parents, taxpayers, and students. The degree to which one's private life is considered

public record depends on several factors, such as the type of school, size of the school, and locale. With dismal reports of the status of education, the public is looking frantically for someone to blame for current problems. Unfortunately, schools have become convenient scapegoats; thus teachers may find that their actions are being watched more than they would like. Policymakers are holding teachers accountable for their actions more than ever.

Therefore in many communities, school boards and parent groups may feel they have a moral obligation to monitor and restrict teachers' professional and private lives. Some constituents believe that the way a teacher conducts his or her personal life is directly related to job performance. Consider politicians, for example—the news media capitalizes on the public's "right to know" about the professional and private lives of public officials. The rationale is that people who hold public office and who are paid by public monies should be held to certain minimum standards of personal conduct. You may also agree that school boards have the right to set standards of conduct. But this raises two interesting questions: (1) Who determines what is "appropriate"? and (2) Do these standards apply to a teacher's behavior outside of school?

To what extent does a community—that is, the taxpayers—have the right to inquire into a teacher's private life? As a judge, where would you draw the line regarding a teacher's civil rights and the public's right to know? Even when the law upholds the teacher's right to privacy (which in most cases it does), does this guarantee that a teacher's job is secure? How could administrators and school boards, for example, pressure a teacher to conform to community standards? Occasionally a teacher will have to seek employment elsewhere to avoid potential trouble with school districts. Teachers have had to resign under duress because their beliefs or lifestyle were offensive to a particular community or school. You should think about these kinds of issues before accepting a teaching job.

Reflections from the Field

Lynda recalls this story from the early 1970s: "At the end of the first semester, I was called in by my principal. He had been informed by a 'respected' member of his church that I had been a 'hippie' in college. At that point, I knew my days were numbered, because in the early '70s it was assumed that a former 'flower child' was associated with illicit drugs. I admitted that I had been politically active during my college days and had participated in a few peaceful war and civil rights demonstrations. But I shortly realized my defense of my past was falling on deaf ears. This community did not want me, or at least the administration did not. I began looking for employment elsewhere, in a larger, less provincial school district. This ordeal raised a host of questions for me: Maybe I was too liberal to teach in the South? Perhaps I was in the wrong profession? What if this becomes a pattern—always being at odds with the administration and never fitting in? This was certainly not a good way to end my first year of teaching. Fortunately, however, I was accepted and appreciated at the second school."

AssessYourself

Would you decline a job offer if you knew in advance that the community standards were too liberal, or too conservative, for your political beliefs? Or would you take the job and challenge the system to change?

Would you prefer to avoid confrontation, admit it would be a mismatch, and apply to another school district whose politics are more in line with yours? This is a dilemma. What would you do?

In addition to public scrutiny, students will also be watching you. Fortunately, most students' interest in a teacher's personal life is less threatening and judgmental. As a rule, the younger the children, the less interested they are in a teacher's private life. As children mature, however, they are more prone to be curious about adults who are significant role models to them. But not all students' motivations are pure. For example, if revenge were the motive, a student might pry to get information about a teacher to use it against that teacher. Consequently, teachers must be careful.

You may be thinking that teenagers are too self-absorbed to find teachers personally interesting. Some may be. Did you find your teachers' private lives of interest? How old were you when you started wanting to know more about your teachers on a personal level?

When I asked two eleventh grade girls from a private Catholic school whether they were interested in the personal lives of their teachers, they instantly responded affirmatively. This single question launched a spirited conversation about every scoop of information they held about every teacher. They behaved as if they had the "right" to know and that somehow they were entitled to personal details.

Which teachers were you most curious about—those who were single, divorced, young, attractive, and outgoing or those who appeared shy, withdrawn, and socially insecure? Are you less interested now in your professors' private lives? Does this fascination depend on maturity level, or is this tendency to be curious about people in positions of authority and influence a common reaction?

Although the idea of living in a fish bowl may seem innocuous and even amusing to some prospective teachers, it can be very disconcerting to others. To be constantly scrutinized can evoke undue stress for some. Others might not like the idea of having to justify their actions or lifestyle outside of class, perceiving it to be an encroachment on their civil liberties.

REFLECTION QUESTIONS

- Does the notion of being expected to live your life according to some arbitrary standard of conduct sound too intrusive and suffocating to you?

- Would you be willing to have your privacy challenged?

- To what extent would you tolerate such an intrusion?

- It takes an emotionally stable person to be at odds with the majority opinion. Do you think you could handle this?

> ❝ **NOTABLE QUOTE**
>
> Students share and risk themselves only to the degree that [teachers] are willing to share [them]selves and take similar risks. *(Joe Wittmer & Robert D. Myrick)* ❞

Working with Minors

Teaching involves working with children and adolescents who are underage (minors), and therefore teachers are always at risk of being sued. A drawback to increased awareness about child abuse matters and sexual harassment is that some students have maliciously accused teachers of sexual misconduct as a means to get revenge. A teacher must not only be on guard about his or her behavior, but also must not do anything that could be perceived as inappropriate. Even a hint of impropriety could lead to charges of misconduct.

Even with best intentions and impeccable behavior, some teachers have been unfairly accused. No one wants to be charged; even if a person is acquitted, his or her reputation as a teacher has been virtually ruined (Villaume & Foley, 1993). Suggestions for minimizing litigation will be discussed in Chapter 13, Ethical and Legal Issues.

Interacting with Students in Close Quarters

The school milieu is designed to bring teacher and student into close proximity. On the surface it makes sense: we want teachers and students to interact with one another. On second glance, though, this closeness can be stifling (for some more than others). The amount of space between two people, sometimes referred to as **social distance,** suggests the kind of relationship those two people have (Hall & Hall, 1987). It is known that people need space to thrive, yet teachers are confined with students in small, overcrowded classrooms (Gehrke, 1987).

social distance

The amount of distance between two people that defines the terms of the relationship.

Jackson (1968) alludes to this problem in the following way:

> There is a social intimacy in school that is unmatched elsewhere in our society . . . while buses and movie theaters may be more crowded than classrooms, the difference is that people do not stay in these conditions very long, nor are they expected to concentrate on work or to interact with each other . . . while they are there. Only in schools do thirty or more people spend several hours each day literally side by side. (p. 8)

Each student has a threshold for intimacy, and teachers must be respectful of that distance. How close should teachers get to students? Admittedly there is a fine line between appropriate and inappropriate behavior regarding teacher/student interactions. Regardless of the ambiguity, however, the teacher (being the adult) must know the difference between healthy and unhealthy boundaries and he or she must be the one to draw that arbitrary line. When teachers interact personally with students, they must be aware of the risks involved and be careful to maintain appropriate boundaries. As a teacher you must know how to keep the appropriate distance from students, or you will be vulnerable to potential misunderstandings and possible lawsuits (Villaume & Foley, 1993). More will be said about boundaries shortly.

Being Held Accountable for Student Achievement

Increasingly, teachers are being expected to produce results in spite of high teacher to student ratios, space problems, meager resources, and outdated materials. National concern about declining standardized test scores and "inflated" grades has made teachers convenient targets. As the public holds teachers more accountable for student achievement, vulnerability increases proportionately. In some locales, teachers' jobs have been threatened by poor test results. The incessant demands to improve student achievement and meet local and state mandates add more stress to an already stressful job.

Working in a Precarious Setting

Finally, schools today have become precarious work settings. This is not surprising when you realize that a school system is nothing more than a mi-

Teachers have to be objective in handling disputes between students inside and outside of the school.

© Elizabeth Crews

Unlike many professions, teaching is always done at the dangerous intersection of personal and public life. *(Parker Palmer)*

Liking oneself is crucial to feeling comfortable in the presence of others.

© Elizabeth Crews

crocosm of society, meaning that it reflects the problems of the larger community. Regrettably, we live in a violent society, and inevitably violence will spill over into schoolyards and classrooms. Who can forget the series of news bulletins in the spring of 1998, reporting that children and teachers had been gunned down at school? Or, in the spring of 1999, the killing spree at Columbine High School in Colorado? The most sinister part was that these murderers were not outside agitators, but fellow classmates. It was unfathomable that such a thing could happen—children killing children at school!

These tragedies did not occur in high-crime neighborhoods or inner-city schools, which should be a warning that incidences of violence can happen anywhere. Americans are forced to come to terms with the realization that schools are not as safe as once assumed. Apparently, zero-tolerance laws, security guards, and metal detectors are not enough to deter some students from bringing guns and weapons on school grounds.

Being a victim of violence or even witnessing an act of violence can be a terrifying experience. Notably it is traumatic for a teacher who has experienced past abuse. Any act of aggression or even a hint of violence could evoke painful memories for some, and this could result in erratic and inappropriate responses. For example, a teacher harboring long-suppressed memories of trauma and violence can experience flashbacks (sudden, vivid memories) by simply witnessing an act of violence on the playground (Persi, 1997). Generally, when relationships are harmonious an individual's unpleasant memories lie dormant; however, stress can reopen earlier wounds, possibly wreaking havoc on the person's mental stability. The bottom line is that as a prospective teacher you must be aware that suppressed issues could resurface.

As you can see from these examples, stressors are a serious consideration in the teaching profession. Teachers must be relatively well adjusted to handle its unrelenting demands and pressures. We think the mental health of the teacher must be addressed.

Warning Signs of Potential Problems for Teachers

What are the warning signs that indicate potential "emotional" problems for beginning teachers? From personal experiences and the education literature, we have compiled a list of possible warning signs that could indicate that a teacher is at risk. This list is hardly exhaustive; think of other signs we have omitted. The purpose of this section is to help you assess the extent to which you might be vulnerable to emotional distress.

Berates Self

Self-talk, what a person says to oneself, conveys what a person thinks about himself or herself (self-concept). If your thoughts are constantly negative and disparaging of self and others, it could be a warning sign. An example is a teacher who says "I'm so stupid" every time a colleague makes a suggestion. Conversely, when you value yourself, you will generally say encouraging things to yourself (even when you fail). A teacher with a positive self-image when confronted with a suggestion from a colleague will say to himself or herself, "Now that's good advice that will likely improve my instruction."

It is no surprise that positive self-talk has been linked to personal effectiveness (Fuqua, Newman, Anderson, & Johnson, 1986). What do you say to yourself? Are you generally nice in your remarks, or are you your own worst enemy? Monitor your thoughts; note when they turn sour, and note when they are upbeat. Are your thoughts relatively consistent, or do they vacillate depending on your moods? What situations evoke negative self-talk?

Exhibits Inappropriate Anger

Distraught people who cannot manage their anger appropriately may direct their anger toward self or others (or both). You may have heard of a defense mechanism called "kick the cat," which means taking out one's anger on an innocent person instead of the real source of the anger. Displaced aggression is not a healthy approach to venting anger. There are many "healthy" defense mechanisms for handling frustration, disappointment, and anger, but displaced aggression is *not* one of them.

You may recall a time when you were a convenient target for someone else's misery. The bottom line is that children are vulnerable and should be protected from erratic teacher behavior. Teachers who cannot control their temper and/or who cannot handle the emotional demands of the job should be dissuaded from teaching. Students should not be targets for frustrated, angry, and insecure teachers.

As a prospective teacher, it is wise to remember that regardless of your personal predicament, it is not appropriate to vent adverse feelings on others—especially in school. Parents and guardians are entrusting their children to the care of teachers, and they have every right to expect that their children will be treated with dignity and respect. You also must treat your colleagues and others respectfully.

However, some people who are angry take their frustrations and disappointments out on themselves. You may know people who are depressed and withdrawn. Sometimes depression is organic and can be treated with antidepressants and therapy. Other times, it is situational—a psychological reaction to stress, disappointment, or hurt. Regardless of its origin, proper treatment should be sought.

Directing anger and frustration inward may be a way to cope, but it is not a healthy defense mechanism. People who are chronically depressed may express self-loathing (unconsciously) by engaging in high-risk behavior such as speeding, drinking to excess, staying out late, bingeing or refusing to eat, spending extravagantly, engaging in unsafe sex, avoiding exercise, or other self-destructive behaviors. Of course being self-indulgent and engaging in high-risk behaviors signals trouble for anyone, not just teachers.

Needs to Feel Powerful

Teachers, by virtue of their position, are conferred power in order to be effectual at imparting knowledge to students. Yet power has the potential to be misused or abused by the one in authority. Naturally an enormous responsibility goes with being entrusted with power. Because students are vulnerable, teachers must not take advantage of their authority to harm students. Teachers simply must be able to manage their emotions and not take frustrations out on unsuspecting (and undeserving) students. As a prospective teacher, you must meet your power needs through outside activities, such as biking, running, hiking, or other forms of exercise.

Lacks Boundaries

Many people have trouble relating to others because they want to get close but do not know how. People with boundary problems are usually insensitive to the boundaries of others and unknowingly encroach on their space. As we have mentioned, every person has his or her own space, and those boundaries, which are both physical and psychological, vary accordingly. For example, a child who has been severely abused by an adult may cower when the teacher comes too close and invades the child's space. Most people retreat when someone invades their physical space, but students (especially younger ones) do not always have that prerogative when confronted by an imposing authority figure such as a teacher.

Emotional boundaries are slightly different. A teacher who asks a student about a personal matter—and does not notice the student wincing—has more than likely crossed the line. When confronted, people who violate emotional boundaries may use the defense, "I was just kidding," or as in the latter case, "I was only trying to help." Admittedly, we have all been guilty of teasing or asking questions of someone and later discovering that our words were perceived as hurtful or intrusive by that person. When we realize this, we usually apologize for our faux pas. However, if this is a frequent occurrence in a person's interactions with others, then that person may have a genuine "boundary problem." Sometimes professional assistance is required to help a person develop sensitivity toward others.

Seeks Undue Attention

Another red flag is a teacher who craves inordinate attention from others and seeks that attention from his or her students. Sometimes new teachers disclose information about themselves that is too personal for their students to handle. A teacher's social life is to be conducted outside of class, and students must not be included in the teacher's circle of friends. Flirting with students of either gender is not appropriate, either. The tendency for beginning teachers to want to be liked and accepted by their students should be resisted. We suggest you heed this sound advice from Banner and Cannon (1997): "Teachers should never be students' close friends or companions, never their intimates" (p. 28).

Lacks Discipline

Teachers must be self-disciplined before they can reasonably expect to teach their students self-discipline. Therefore we recommend that you start with yourself—look at *your* behavior first. How self-disciplined are you? What could you do to develop greater self-discipline?

> ## ❝ NOTABLE QUOTE
>
> I have come to a frightening conclusion that I am the decisive element in the classroom.... As a teacher, I possess tremendous power to make a child's life miserable or joyous. I can be a tool of torture or an instrument of inspiration. I can humiliate or humor, hurt or heal. *(Haim Ginott)* ❞

Reflections from the Field

"Tell future teachers that they can't bring personal problems to school and dump them on the students or anyone else who is in their range," said a psychological examiner who had just returned from an elementary school where she had been assigned to test a student for learning problems. When she had arrived at the school earlier that day, she was greeted by a hostile teacher who said, 'I don't have time for this today. I have bigger problems right now than testing students from my class.' The principal later apologized and explained that this teacher was going through a bitter divorce. Although the examiner acted in a professional manner and did not react in a negative way to the teacher's remark, she had this to say: "In spite of a teacher's personal problems, it is unacceptable to behave in this way. As teachers we have to accept that even when we are in the midst of a family crisis, we cannot take it out on our students or on other people. This is not part of the job. You can't wear your feelings on your sleeve."

Healthy Intrapersonal Traits and Attitudes

emotional intelligence

A type of intelligence that includes self-awareness, impulse control, persistence, zeal, self-motivation, empathy, and social skills.

Goleman (1995), in his book, *Emotional Intelligence,* argues that people who are "emotionally adept—who know and manage their own feelings and who read and deal effectively with other people's feelings—are at an advantage in any domain in life" (p. 36). This model of "emotional intelligence" was first advanced by Salovey and Mayer (1990).

Realizing how important it is for teachers to possess **"emotional intelligence,"** we have identified some intrapersonal characteristics and attitudes

Consultation and collaboration are necessary for creative teaching. Teachers should not be afraid to ask colleagues for help and also be willing to share ideas.

© Michael Newman/PhotoEdit

Engage in Self-Examination

Some teachers are very quick to ask students why they said or did something, but are unwilling to ask these same questions of themselves. You must be willing to ask probing questions of yourself to better understand why you behave as you do. As we have already seen, being a reflective thinker is undoubtedly a key ingredient to effective teaching. You must be sensitive to your own likes, dislikes, moods, and values and continually evaluate how these factors affect your response to situations.

Know When to Ask for Help

Do not let insecurities prevent you from asking more experienced educators for advice. Also, know when you need professional help and be willing to seek medical assistance when needed. Stay alert to your body; know when you need help from a physician. Your doctor can assess your situation and determine whether you need psychological and/or medical assistance. You can use your time in school to learn more about yourself. Fortunately, almost all colleges and universities have counseling centers where you can receive affordable therapy in a confidential setting. It may be to your advantage to avail yourself of these services.

Model Self-Discipline

In conclusion, there is one more intrapersonal skill we believe is essential to successful teaching—self-discipline. If teachers want to help students become self-disciplined, they must possess and model management skills themselves. In the literature you will find many names for self-discipline such as self-assessment, self-planning, self-direction, self-monitoring, and self-evaluation (Miller, 1998). For this discussion, we have elected to use the more traditional term "self-discipline."

One of the optimal ways to teach self-discipline to students is through example (Locke & Ciechalski, 1995). To reiterate, a teacher cannot expect students to manage their behavior, when his or her behavior is apparently out of control. "Students need good models to emulate, especially younger children [who] imitate their teachers" (Locke & Ciechalski, 1995, p. 67).

Stoops and King-Stoops (1981, p. 58) recommend that teachers discipline themselves in "manners, voice, disposition, honesty, punctuality, consistency . . ." so they can set an example for students to follow. To illustrate, if you want to teach students how to control their temper, you must keep your own in check.

"To be an effective teacher, how disciplined do I have to be?" A general rule is that a person should be "relatively" self-disciplined; at least *good enough* to be able to teach basic management skills to students and maintain sufficient order in the classroom so students can learn. To answer this question, we suggest you think in terms of a continuum. On one end of the continuum is an extremely undisciplined person and on the other end an extremely disciplined person. As a rule, extremities on a continuum are unhealthy and thus should be avoided. In light of this, a "healthy" teacher seeks moderation—a balance between extremities.

Alan Lakein (1973), a renowned time management expert, demonstrates how to work smarter not harder. Many suggestions made by Lakein in his best-selling and now classic book, *How to Get Control of Your Time and Your Life* (1973), can be directly applied to effective teaching. We highly recommend this book and suggest that you read it more than once. Lakein (1973) explains that gaining control of one's time and life is "analogous to good muscle tone; you don't want control to be too tight (i.e., compulsive, restrained, obsessive) nor too loose (i.e., apathetic, indifferent, lazy)" (p. 14). Lakein (1973) suggests ". . . balance; you want enough control to get the work done, without sacrificing flexibility and spontaneity" (p. 14).

An extremely disciplined person tends to be rigid. He or she imposes inordinate demands on self and others. Inevitably, this person will fail (as will others) to meet these unrealistic demands. Failure to meet self-imposed, arbitrary standards produces an exasperated and discouraged person. Perfectionism can be an addiction. Trying to excessively control one's behavior and the behaviors of others is neither feasible nor healthy.

One way to avoid rigidity is to think more about taking charge—not control. As a teacher you will be ineffective if you try to control every action or behavior in the classroom. This will only frustrate you, because it cannot be done. Taking charge means staying on top of those things you do have control over, and letting go of those things you do not. To illustrate, it is not necessary for a teacher to interrupt a lesson every time a student is daydreaming. Good teachers know they do not need unanimous attention from students at all times.

Defiant students are challenged by authority figures who are rigid and dictatorial. Rigidity in a teacher is like waving a red flag in front of an angry child. This is especially true of prepubescent and adolescent youths who are defiant and want to prove the teacher wrong. Rigidity seldom works; it has the potential to backfire and create greater problems and disorder in the long run. The best advice is to avoid power struggles with students. Therefore, instead of trying to control every student action, attend to those behaviors that need prompt attention. Use discretion regarding when to stop and correct and when to ignore.

An extremely undisciplined person is equally unhealthy. These people are self-indulged; they lack goals and direction. Being disorganized and delinquent in tasks is especially problematic in teaching. Classroom tempo is fast and hectic, and teachers must be able to keep pace. Unrelenting paperwork with strict deadlines is another problem area. Carelessness and disorganization has other implications that teachers should consider. An easygoing teacher, for example, can be inconsistent in enforcing class rules and may be negligent teaching students basic skills and essential knowledge. Students suffer when teachers do not set goals, fail to plan instruction, and are indifferent to time schedules or lesson plans. Remember, students bear the brunt of dilatory teachers.

In summary, teachers have influence; consequently they must be vigilant about what they say and do. We believe that a teacher should have his or her own locker in order before asking this of students. It is pointless, as well as hypocritical, to expect something from someone that you cannot or will not do yourself. "Practice what you preach" is an old cliché, but it speaks volumes.

Reflections from the Field

When asked if she thought it was necessary to discuss the mental health of teachers in an introductory textbook on teaching, Patty replied: "Early in my career as a teacher educator, I ran into a beginning teacher whom I had taught the previous year. She had been teaching for one month. She shared with me that she was enjoying teaching but that I did not prepare her for the emotional toll of the job. According to her, she was unprepared for how emotionally drained she felt. That comment was a reminder for me not to overlook the emotional side of teaching. I do not think we can be too sensitive about this aspect; I would rather err on this side than risk being too objective in our portrayal of the teaching profession. From this encounter with a former student I learned that I had been remiss in not addressing the emotional side of teaching, focusing too much on the technical dimensions instead."

Patty's response concurs with my belief that if we fail to explore the subject of psychological health we are doing a disservice to our reader. It is far better to know at the outset, rather than to find out later in the program or after the first year, that teaching is mentally challenging. If in some small way we can assist you to start thinking now about these issues, you will be better prepared. As Palmer (1998) points out in his book, *The Courage to Teach: Exploring the Inner Landscape of a Teacher's Life*, ". . . teaching is a daily exercise in vulnerability" (p. 17). Think about it.

AssessYourself

Clearly, there are aspects about teaching that can indeed be emotionally draining. Would you be willing to examine your past, especially those memories that caused you great pain, in order to deal with them?

If your past were interfering with your ability to be an effective teacher, would you be willing to go for personal counseling? Why or why not?

Conclusion

This chapter offers a glimpse of the emotional side of teaching. Connection to self is a prerequisite for connection with students and others. If you are unkind to yourself, you may have trouble getting along with others, particularly students and parents.

Individuals considering teaching as a career should be aware of the stressors inherent in the job and be willing to face their past. A person's past, however, should not prevent that person from becoming a teacher, as long as he or she is willing to admit problems and actively work on them. A reflective teacher is one who continually examines past memories to understand why he or she behaves in certain ways. One cannot afford to be driven by destructive impulses and unhealthy compulsions. If you deny your past, you could be hurting yourself and, in turn, your students. The bottom line is that you are less effective with others when you are preoccupied with your own needs.

The teaching profession desperately needs people who are enthusiastic and undaunted by challenge. Teaching, as you have seen, can be very imposing and exhausting because everyone's needs take precedence over yours. An irony of this emotionally draining profession is that many people are actually stimulated by the premise that teaching is a taxing profession. Recall the adage, "When the going gets tough, the tough get going!" Does this expression apply to you? Are you the type of person that is attracted to challenges. Now that you have read this chapter, we hope you are saying, "Sign me up!"

KEY TERMS

emotional intelligence
social distance

SUGGESTED READING

Goleman, D. (1995). *Emotional intelligence.* New York: Bantam Books.

Lakein, A. (1973). *How to get control of your time and your life.* New York: Penguin Group.

Palmer, P. J. (1998). *The courage to teach: Exploring the inner landscape of a teacher's life.* San Francisco: Jossey-Bass.

REFERENCES

Banner, J. M., & Cannon, H. C. (1997). *The elements of teaching.* New Haven: Yale University Press.

Corey, G., Corey, M. S., & Callanan, P. (1998). *Issues and ethics in the helping professions.* Pacific Grove, CA: Brooks/Cole Publishing Company.

Deane, F. P., & Chamberlain, K. (1994). Treatment fearfulness and distress as predictors of professional psychological help-seeking. *British Journal of Guidance and Counseling, 22*(2), 207–217.

Fuqua, D., Newman, J., Anderson, M., & Johnson, A. (1986). Preliminary study of internal dialogue in a training session. *Psychological Reports, 58,* 163–172.

Gehrke, N. J. (1987). *On being a teacher.* West Lafayette, Indiana: Kappa Delta Pi.

Ginott, H. G. (1976). *Teacher and child.* New York: Avon.

Goleman, D. (1995). *Emotional intelligence: Why it can matter more than IQ.* New York: Bantam Books.

Hall, E., & Hall, M. (1987). Nonverbal communication for educators. *Theory into Practice, 26,* 364–367.

Jackson, P. (1968). *Life in classrooms.* New York: Holt, Rinehart & Winton.

Kessler, R. C., McGonagle, K. A., Zhao, S., Nelson, C. B., Hughes, M., Eshelman, S., Wittchen, H. U., & Kendler, K. S. (1994). Lifetime and 12-month prevalence of DSM III-R, psychiatric disorder in the United States. *Archives of General Psychiatry, 51,* 8–19.

Lakein, A. (1973). *How to get control of your time and your life.* New York: Penguin Group

Locke, D. C., & Ciechalski, J. C. (1995). *Psychological techniques for teachers,* (2nd ed.). Washington, D.C.: Accelerated Development.

Miller, D. (1998). *Enhancing adolescent competence: Strategies for classroom management.* Belmont, CA: West/Wadsworth Publishing Company.

Palmer, P. J. (1998). *The courage to teach: Exploring the inner landscape of a teacher's life.* San Francisco: Jossey-Bass.

Persi, J. (1997). When emotionally troubled teachers refer emotionally troubled students. *The School Counselor, 44,* 344–352.

Punch, K. F., & Tuettemann, E. (1990). Correlates of psychological distress among secondary school teachers. *British Educational Research Journal, 16,* 369–382.

Purkey, W. W., & Novak, J. M. (1996). *Inviting school success: A self-concept approach to teaching, learning, and democratic practice.* Belmont, CA: Wadsworth.

Salovey, P., & Mayer, J. D. (1990). Emotional intelligence. *Imagination, Cognition, and Personality, 9,* 185–211.

Stoops, E., & King-Stoops, J. (1981). Discipline suggestions for classroom teachers. *Phi Delta Kappan, 63*(1), 58.

Villaume, P. G., & Foley, R. M. (1993). *Teachers at risk: Crisis in the classroom.* Bloomington, MN: Legal Resource Center for Educators.

Watts, W. D., & Short, A. P. (1990). Teacher drug use: A response to occupational stress. *Journal of Drug Education, 20,* 47–65.

Wittmer, J., & Myrick, R. D. (1989). *The teacher as facilitator.* Minneapolis, MN: Educational Media Corporation.

© Bill Aron/PhotoEdit

At the end of this chapter, you will be able to

- Describe humanistic practices that affect teacher-student relationships.

- Identify benefits and barriers to family involvement.

- Cite strategies to overcome barriers and thus increase parental involvement.

- Outline principles that underlie effective relationships with students, families, colleagues, and administrators.

- Appraise your ability to establish positive relationships with others.

Connection to Others: Interpersonal Skills

A bird's eye view of what to expect in this chapter

Teaching is a service profession. Whom do we serve? On first glance the answer is easy—we serve students. Although this is true, it is not the whole picture, because teachers serve many others besides students. In reality, teachers' constituents extend far beyond the four walls of the classroom. Teachers must be able to relate to many people in addition to students if they are to be successful.

Metaphors often are helpful tools in understanding complex concepts. One way to view teaching is that it is like engaging in a dance such as square dancing. As the dancers change partners, the bonds among the participants become stronger and the dance becomes more exhilarating. Likewise, effective teachers "dance" not only with their students but also with their families, colleagues, administrators, and community members. The complexity of teaching in today's society requires that teachers adapt to and interact with many different partners.

Getting along with others is therefore a prerequisite for teacher effectiveness. In the last chapter we asked you to examine your intrapersonal skills to determine whether you have the disposition for teaching. In this chapter, we ask if you think you have the interpersonal skills to connect effectively with students and others. You will be asked some penetrating questions that demand self-appraisal. Remember that the primary goal of this textbook is to help you determine whether teaching is a good match for you. Thus self-examination is critical, especially if you are considering teaching as a career.

Being able to relate to others is essential for teacher effectiveness. Teachers must be socially facile and comfortable in their interactions with other people. Earlier we talked about the "art" of teaching; clearly connecting with students is an essential aspect of this artistic expression. As artisans, teachers facilitate positive relationships as part of their craft. To some people, establishing relationships with others is second nature. For others it may take more work. However, the good news is that relating to others is a skill that can be cultivated and improved through practice.

We begin this chapter with teacher-student relationships, then move to relationships with parents, colleagues, administrators, and the community. We suggest ways that teachers can increase parental involvement. In addition, you will be introduced to basic communication principles and skills that facilitate relationship building.

Teacher-Student Relationships

In 1977 a three-year investigation by the National Consortium for Humanizing Education (NCHE) found that teachers' interpersonal skills were correlated with positive student outcomes. The study's findings were published in a book aptly titled *Kids Don't Learn from People They Don't Like* (Aspy & Roebuck, 1977). Gordon (1974), in his landmark book, *Teacher Effectiveness Training (T.E.T.)*, suggested that students learn best when a "unique relationship exists—some kind of connection, link, or bridge between the teacher and the learner" (p. 3). More recently, correlational studies verify this premise—a quality teacher-student relationship is related to student morale and learning (Birch & Ladd, 1996; Wentzel, 1997). Many authorities—which we will discuss later—such as John Dewey, Maria Montessori, Carl Rogers, and James Comer, have stated that the relationship between teacher and student is essential to student motivation and learning (Comer, 1988).

Caring Teachers

Words such as *caring, respect,* and *just* are often used in the literature to describe effective qualities for teachers to possess (Haberman,1995). Nel Noddings (1992) has written a great deal about the importance of teachers exuding caring qualities. She believes that schools today must instill an "ethic of care," and that children should observe "caring in action."

Robert Myrick is another educator who distinguishes "caring" as a fundamental quality for teachers to cultivate. He defines six conditions that must be present in the classroom to facilitate student learning: caring, understanding, acceptance, respect, friendliness, and trustworthiness. "Caring suggests to students that you are personally interested in and concerned about a person's well-being; you value the person enough to psychologically

Being able to relate to students on a personal level is key to effective teaching.

© Mark Richards/PhotoEdit

reach out and be attentive" (Myrick, 1993, p. 115). Perronne (1991) succinctly captured the essence of caring when he said, "Teachers need to be seen as real people who care" (p. 31).

Martin Haberman (1995), who has extensively studied what makes some urban teachers "star teachers" and others not, has found that "stars have a relationship with children that demonstrates a consciously premeditated caring" (p. 57). However, this kind of caring is not always "predicated on children always doing the right thing"; in fact, the sign of a caring teacher is one who demonstrates to the student that he or she is "worthy and capable—even at the lowest and worst moment of his or her offense" (p. 58). Can you recall "caring" teachers who you would consider "stars"? Could you still care for a child who misbehaved in your class? What if a student swore at you, for example; could you be there for that student in his or her lowest moment?

"Students don't care what you know until they know you care." We are not sure who first made this remark, but we like the notion. When you think about it, it makes a lot of sense. On the first day of class students scrutinize their teachers to determine whether the teachers will care about them as persons. You must find ways to show your students that you care about them as persons.

As an example of what a caring teacher might do we selected a passage from *Marva Collins' Way* (Collins & Tamarkin, 1982). Collins writes, "My approach was to teach the whole child. A teacher should help develop a child's

The Caring Teacher

Respectful

Accepting

Understanding

Trustworthy

Caring

Friendly

🍎 GREAT TEACHERS

Nel Noddings

Courtesy of Dr. Nel Noddings

Nel Noddings is a Professor of Education at Teachers College, Columbia University. She has challenged the educational system to critically examine the liberal arts curriculum, which has been the basis of public education. Noddings claims that the emphasis on verbal and mathematical performance neglects those students who excel in other areas. She argues for educational reform in curriculum and instruction so that all children will reap benefits from the educational system. Instead of pushing students to score higher on achievement tests, Noddings proposes that educators see the classrooms as large families. She believes that the main goal of education is moral development, rearing children to be competent and caring individuals.

Noddings has written several books, including *Caring: A Feminine Approach to Ethics and Moral Education; Women and Evil; Awakening the Inner Eye: Intuition and Education* (with Paul Shore); *The Challenge to Care in Schools: An Alternative Approach to Education;* and *Educating for Intelligent Belief or Unbelief.*

character, and build a positive self-image. I was concerned about everything—attitudes, manners, and grooming. I made sure my students' faces were clean, their hair combed, their shirts tucked in, and their socks pulled up. I told them to walk with their heads up and their shoulders back, to have dignity and confidence" (p. 58). Is Marva Collins a caring teacher? Do you see yourself doing this?

Limitations to Research on Teacher-Student Relationships

Studies linking quality teacher-student relationships to student learning show a correlation between variables; however, they cannot prove cause-and-effect like experimental studies do. A correlation is a descriptive statistic that indicates the degree to which variables are related. Research that

affective attributes

Traits that cannot be measured quantitatively, such as attitudes, feelings, values, and emotions.

studies **affective attributes** such as attitudes, values, emotions, and feelings do not conform to the standards of experimental research. At best, those studies that examine affective variables can show an association (or correlation).

Studies that explore the "soft" sciences (e.g., behavioral and social sciences) as opposed to "hard" sciences (e.g., mathematics and physics) have this limitation. In an experiment, a researcher demonstrates "cause and effect" by isolating (and thus controlling for) known variables that could affect outcomes. So, although the teacher-student relationship is found to be *associated* to student motivation and learning, researchers cannot fully explain how or why this happens. Naturally, it would be impossible to isolate for all the variables existing in interpersonal relationships. But who would want to? Part of the beauty of relationships is the mystery; the intrigue of human interaction is not knowing for sure what your outcomes will be. Unpredictability, aside from being an element of surprise, keeps us constantly looking for better ways to get along with other people.

Humanism

humanism

An approach to teaching developed from existential philosophy that recognizes the worth and dignity of all human beings.

Humanism emerged in the 1950s as a philosophical stance and approach to teaching. The fundamental goal was to strengthen the teacher-student relationship to advance learning. Many educators, who felt that schools were placing too much emphasis on academics at the expense of positive student interactions, were eager to embrace humanism. The growth of humanism as a movement was seen by many to be a natural reaction and alternative to behaviorism and cognitivism. Briefly, a behaviorist focuses more on what students do (behaviors), whereas a cognitivist focuses more on what students think (cognitions). (For further discussion see Chapters 6 and 8.) In contrast, humanistic education focuses more on how students feel (emotions).

A humanistic teacher emphasizes affective concepts; the curriculum used by a humanistic teacher reflects that emphasis by including affective goals with cognitive and behavioral goals. A humanist would take a **holistic approach** to student learning and motivation, which means that all aspects of a student's life are considered when planning and delivering instruction (e.g., physical, mental, social, cognitive, and spiritual). Marva Collins's approach is considered holistic because she contends that the whole child should be considered.

holistic approach

A teaching approach that takes into account all aspects of a student's life.

Humanism stems from the human potential movement in psychology. However, in education its roots can be traced to educators such as Arthur Jersild, Arthur Combs, and Donald Snygg (Ornstein, 1982).

In this chapter we examine the philosophies of Carl Rogers and Arthur Combs. Education borrowed the term "student-centered" from Carl Rogers (1902–1987), a renowned psychologist whose **client-centered**

client-centered counseling

Popularized by Carl Rogers, a nondirective therapeutic approach to counseling that focuses on the needs of the client.

Teachers encourage students by taking an interest in them as people with unique needs, skills, and talents.

unconditional positive regard

An attitude that projects total acceptance of another person's worth.

genuineness

A trait that expresses sincerity in thought and motivation.

empathy

The ability to put yourself in another person's shoes to more fully understand his or her feelings and present situation.

counseling (now referred to as person-centered psychotherapy) became popular in the 1950s. Rogers highlighted the teacher's role as counselor. Traits such as **unconditional positive regard** (accepting a student's worth without judgment or evaluation); **genuineness** (being real); and **empathy** (being able to see another's point of view) were seen as necessary qualities for teachers to possess (Rogers, 1961, 1962). Teachers who advocate student-centered teaching assume a more nondirective approach to instruction.

According to Arthur Combs (1965), a sensitive and caring teacher attempts to understand each student by putting himself or herself "in the student's shoes" (which Carl Rogers called "empathy"). An empathic teacher understands the emotional world of his or her students without having had the exact experiences. For example, although a teacher may not have associated with the "wrong crowd" when in school, he or she still can understand how some students who are rejected by peers and significant others might consider gang affiliation as their only recourse.

Practices Based on Humanistic Concepts

This is a good point at which to describe some humanistic practices that affect teacher-student relationships in a positive way.

Teachers who assume humanistic attitudes and behaviors . . .

- Are sensitive to the physical and emotional needs of students that could hinder their abilities to learn. When possible, teachers should attempt to meet their students' deficiency needs so that potential can be realized. Example: "Hannah, I noticed you are squinting when you take notes off the overhead projector. Is the print too small?"

- Demonstrate empathy by inquiring into the subjective world of the student. Example: "Shawn, this is the third time you have been late turning in your assignments. Is there anything I could do to help?"

- Show an interest in their students by giving them opportunities to choose projects that are appropriate to the subject *and* meaningful to the student. Example: "Josie, what topic from the list did you select for your oral presentation?"

- Give students choices when feasible. Example: "For class today, I am giving you two options: You can go to the library and work on your research papers or stay in class and locate sources on the Internet. It's up to you."

- Realize that students' self-concepts are related to achievement and learning. Look for self-perceptions that might sabotage a child's academic success. Provide plenty of opportunities for students to recognize personal worth. Example: "Lee, you must feel very proud of yourself for having completed your assignment on time." Have students identify characteristics they like about themselves. Example: "Lee, tell me five things you like about yourself." Or, "Name five things you do well."

- Demonstrate respect for students by encouraging them to voice their opinions and ideas without experiencing judgment or reprisal. Example: "Thank you for your suggestion. To be honest, I had not thought of it in that way before, but I will consider your suggestion." Or, "This class has been operating under my rules for the first nine weeks of school; now I want to know your opinions on these class rules. Which ones work for you and which ones should be changed?"

- Convey unconditional positive regard by accepting students as unique persons. Spending time with students and encouraging them to talk about things of interest or concern is one way of doing this. Attending events such as plays and athletic contests helps teachers get to know their students' gifts and talents. Assigning projects that allow students to express themselves also shows acceptance. Example: "Students, I want you to select a hobby or interest of yours for the oral presentation."

Critics of Humanism

Although humanism is intuitively appealing, it has limitations (and its critics). Some critics argue that humanism places too much responsibility on the student for his or her own learning. These critics point out that students are not capable of such responsibility and instead need guidance from authority figures. By giving students too many choices in their learning, teachers may end up losing their control over student learning.

Opponents of humanism believe that students' intellectual development is being neglected at the expense of "good intentions." Declining national test scores and underachievement, critics contend, is linked to an undue emphasis on students' personal and social development (i.e., student-centered activities).

Furthermore, critics argue that it is difficult (if not impossible) to measure student performance (outcomes) when carrying out affective objectives. Teachers today are being held more accountable for student achievement, and some argue that "humanistic" activities cannot be documented or defended quantitatively. In other words, how would you demonstrate that your students made significant gains in social skill development or moral reasoning? By pointing out how well they now cooperate in group work? Adversaries of humanistic education claim that outcomes such as these are beyond the realm of measurement, so why bother? What do you think?

Humanism has suffered bad press in recent years by being associated with New Age thinking and secularism. This is sometimes referred to as "secular" humanism. Spring (1998) defines *secular humanism* as "a set of ethical standards that place primary emphasis on a person's ability to interpret and guide his or her own moral actions" (p. 267). Secular humanism is perceived by some to be antithetical to God. In certain geographic regions and among specific parent groups, some humanistic practices are perceived to be anti-God.

This conception is compounded by the fact that several prominent humanists were and are self-avowed agnostics or atheists. Consequently, some religious leaders and conservative parents are suspicious of any practice labeled humanistic. As teachers we must be careful that parents do not feel diminished or usurped in their critical role as guardians and teachers of their children. Teaching self-reliance and self-acceptance should not in any way supplant or undermine the valuable role religion and parents play in the lives of children.

Consideration of the Limitations of Humanism

Admittedly, humanism does have limitations, and many have raised objections to this theory. However, we offer another perspective for consideration. Teachers should use reason and moderation when applying humanistic practices. It is impossible to give students choices every time a teacher gives an assignment. One novice eighth grade teacher complained that she had followed humanistic practices and within weeks her class was completely out of control. When questioned about her approach, she said she had given them choices about what they would learn, how she should teach, and when they wanted to learn the material. She now scoffs at the notion of giving students choices. In our opinion this is a classic case of taking humanistic principles to the extreme. No one is suggesting that teachers suspend logic and reason when implementing humanistic practices.

The term *humanism* has the potential to offend certain groups; therefore we suggest that the word be avoided. Obviously, it is not prudent for a teacher, especially a novice, to alienate parents or community groups. Therefore teachers should handle tactfully any sensitive issue that may inflame passions and refrain from using any practice perceived to be objectionable by parents or guardians. For example, if it is known that guided imagery is considered questionable by some parents, do not use it. Substitute other strategies that will help your students engage in hypothetical and abstract thinking.

Keep in mind that your intention is to help students learn—not attack or change the community and/or parental attitudes and religious beliefs. It is not our place to do this; we need the goodwill of parents, families, and communities in our effort to educate students. Do not sacrifice students' success to quibble over semantics. Nothing stops you from behaving humanistically towards others—just don't call it that.

Focusing on students' needs and interests does not necessarily preclude students' mastery of basic skills and core knowledge. Affective goals can augment academic goals; they do not replace them. Taking a humanistic approach in the classroom should not negate the teacher's responsibility of imparting knowledge to students. There is time for both, especially if you integrate personal and social development with academic growth.

Reflections from the Field

One third grade teacher, Emily Bradley, offered these ideas for promoting self-esteem in children: " I believe children require many of the same things adults do to feel good about themselves. They need you to listen, encourage, validate, and mostly acknowledge them. I make an effort to stop and make eye contact when my students are talking to me. I listen, comment, and ask questions. I even jot down notes so that I can remember to ask Shane how his birthday party went or Kandis about her grandfather's health. These gestures show your students that you value them not only as students but also as persons. Kids have a built-in radar for sensing insincerity. They instantly know when you mean it and when you are faking it."

Teachers' Relationships Beyond the Classroom

Along with relationships with students, other equally important relationships are forged by teachers. Effective teachers are receptive to the idea of extending their relationships beyond those of the four walls of their classroom. These "other" relationships are sometimes overlooked, but they too must be nurtured. The next section addresses these essential relationships and offers advice for successfully forging these vital partnerships.

A CASE STUDY

Early one November, Ann, a seventh grade social studies teacher, sat at her desk after school. She was troubled by several situations in her classroom. She was feeling frustrated and did not know what to do. Many problems weighed on her mind. First, there was Billy, whose behavior was becoming more and more disruptive. Ann had tried several approaches she had studied in her teacher education courses. Nothing seemed to be working. She had moved Billy to different locations in the classroom, she had talked with him privately, and she had kept him in at lunchtime. What could she do next? Because of Billy's behavior, Ann was beginning to dread third period every day, and teaching that class was becoming more and more impossible. Then there was Sally, whose grades continued to slide. Every day Sally just sat in class—not being disruptive, but not participating either. Sally had not completed a single assignment in the last two weeks. Ann was worried about Sally. How could she help Sally turn things around?

Actually, there was a pervading lack of interest in all her classes. Most of her seventh graders seemed to think that social studies was a drag and had no personal meaning to them. "Who needs social studies?" and "Why do we have to study this stuff?" were questions her students frequently voiced. The more Ann thought about these problems, the more overwhelmed she became. Teaching was getting her down. Was this just a November slump? Shouldn't she be able to handle these dilemmas? How could she remedy these difficulties? As she packed her bookbag that afternoon, Ann had a thought about something that had been lacking in her classroom and teaching.

> **" NOTABLE QUOTE**
>
> The nature and complexity of teaching diverse students what they will need to know for success in the next century cannot be accomplished by even the most knowledgeable individuals working alone. *(Vito Germinario & Henry Cram)* **"**

What do you think that missing ingredient for Ann might be? What solutions would you offer her at this point? One of Ann's problems is her attempt to single-handedly take on the challenges of classroom teaching. She has neglected to involve anyone outside the classroom in addressing the needs of her students. Some teachers see asking for help as a sign of weakness. However, by enlisting the aid of Billy and Sally's parents, Ann is more likely to develop workable plans for helping them to improve. Also, by making links with the community, Ann can increase her students' levels of interest and motivation and thus enrich their learning experiences. Inviting to class guest speakers who "use" social studies daily (e.g., meteorologist, government official, historian, newspaper reporter), designing projects based on authentic problems (e.g., recycling in the city or running an election campaign), and arranging local museum tours are ways to bring social studies to life for students. These activities are not possible unless Ann makes connections to the community.

Relationships with Families

Goals 2000: Educate America Act

An act passed by the U.S. Congress in 1994 outlining eight national education goals to be realized by the year 2000.

national education goals

Passed by the U.S. Congress in 1994, the Educate America Act outlined eight national education goals to be realized by the year 2000.

With the passage of the **Goals 2000: Educate America Act** (1994), partnerships with those outside the classroom moved to the forefront of American education. This federal legislation stipulated eight **national education goals**; the one pertinent to this discussion is goal 8, which states that "every school will promote partnerships that will increase parental involvement and participation in promoting the social, emotional, and academic growth of children" (National Education Goals Panel, 1995, p. 13).

Until recently most of the responsibility for school involvement fell on parents, and most contact with schools was initiated by parents. Now schools try to reach out to families. Twenty-first-century teachers must be able to form productive partnerships with students' families, as recommended in the report *New Skills for New Schools* (Harvard Family Research Project, 1997).

The need to interact with more than students is best understood by examining a model proposed by Joyce Epstein, executive director of the Center on School, Family, and Community Partnerships at Johns Hopkins University. Her overlapping spheres of influence theory views students at the center; students are affected by three overlapping spheres of influence—the school, the home (or family), and the community. To strengthen the positive influence of these three forces, Epstein (1995) suggests that schools should become more "family-like," that families should become more "school-like," and that communities should create more "school-like" opportunities for reinforcement within more "family-like" settings.

Similarly, Morrison (1997) advocates the creation of "family-centered" teaching and learning. Teachers must recognize that education is not the responsibility of schools alone. Learning should permeate all aspects of life whether in school or not.

In a partnership model, there is widespread involvement on the part of families and the community; communication is two-way. Comprehensive, rather than "hit or miss," programs are implemented. In planning these programs to involve families, school-based action teams frequently employ Epstein's (1995) model of involvement, which specifies the following six types of involvement: parenting, communicating, volunteering, learning at home, decision making, and collaborating with the community. As more schools are adopting a partnership approach to working with families, teachers will become more proactive in their encounters with parents rather than waiting for a crisis to erupt.

Benefits to Family Involvement

The U.S. Department of Education's *Strong Families, Strong Schools: Building Community Partnerships for Learning* (1994) cites sound research support for the critical role of families in education: "Thirty years of research show that greater family involvement in children's learning is a critical link to achieving a high-quality education and a safe, disciplined learning environment for every student" (p. iii).

Of course, teachers have known for years that the conditions within a student's home (e.g., frequent encouragement, the value placed on education, the provision of resources to support learning, and adult guidance and supervision) contribute to a child's success in learning. However, teachers have little control over these conditions (Mager, 1980). Students are at school approximately six hours each weekday. Thus, "The family, not the school, provides the primary educational environment for children" (Henderson, 1988, p. 153). Henderson points out that positive attitudes toward school are largely formed at home. Therefore, by connecting more closely with families, schools are more likely to influence attitudes in a positive direction and parents can fulfill the role of "lifesavers" in the learning process.

The following benefits of involving parents in education have been identified by Greenwood and Hickman (1991): (1) higher academic achievement, (2) improved school attendance, (3) positive student and parent attitudes toward school, (4) better student grades, and (5) parent satisfaction with teachers. It is important to note also the power of modeling and the positive message working together sends to students. When students see teachers working with others to achieve educational outcomes, they are more likely to engage in similar behaviors as adults (Germinario & Cram, 1998). We can best *teach* collaboration *through* collaboration.

Barriers to Parental Involvement

Before we can successfully engage in partnerships with families, it is important to be aware of the various obstacles to productive relationships. Numerous authors (Finders & Lewis, 1994; Germinario & Cram, 1998; Harvard Family Research Project, 1997) have identified barriers to involvement. The most frequently mentioned barriers are changing demographics, hands-off orientation, limited resources, lack of information, and parents' psychological blocks.

Changing demographics. Families are more diverse today than in the past and will continue to be so. No longer are students a homogeneous group, nor are the families from which they come. There is a greater range of cultural backgrounds, ethnic origins, economic differences, parental employment patterns, and family configurations (e.g., there are more single parents and grandparents as guardians). Such a wide range of differences in the population makes relating to families more challenging in today's schools. Stresses on families are greater today. Elkind (1995) indicates that the rapid changes in society during the last 30 years have transformed many families into what he calls "permeable." In a **permeable family** the boundaries between parents and children are not as distinct; consequently, adults' needs are being placed before children's needs. Teachers must understand the implications of these cultural changes occurring in modern homes.

permeable families

Elkind's term to describe families in which parental boundaries have been diffused and children's needs have been overlooked.

Hands-off orientation. Schools often project the stance of "Don't call us, we'll call you." This attitude influences daily practices and interaction patterns. Moreover, school norms have not encouraged adult-to-adult interaction and collaboration, but rather have stressed individualism and isolation. In the past, many schools tried to avoid problems by not involving parents. It is now believed that this practice was not helpful; interaction reaps benefits more than trouble. There may still be reluctance on the part of some schools and families to interact on a regular basis. Teachers may feel that parents are not interested; parents may feel intimidated. However, educators should take steps to close the gap and enlist families as allies.

Limited resources. Developing relationships takes time. Today, both teachers and families are stretched for time. Furthermore, designing programs is expensive. No school district or educator would agree that there is an abundance of money appropriated for education today. The lack of financial resources have hindered schools' efforts to reach out to families.

Lack of information. Sometimes schools do not reach out because of a lack of understanding about how to form partnerships with parents (Germinario & Cram, 1998). This reluctance suggests that schools and teachers need in-service training; the Harvard Family Research Project (1997) predicts that such training is likely to occur in the near future. The more skills and knowledge you can acquire now working with families, the better prepared you will be.

Parents' psychological blocks. Sometimes parents are reluctant to interact with school personnel because of their own negative school experiences as students. When dealing with educators, many adults are fearful and insecure. Additionally, there may be a history of negative messages received from the school about one's child, which leads to a basic feeling of mistrust between parents and teachers. Batey (1996) discusses the importance of parents feeling psychologically secure before they enter a school setting. It is the teacher's role to help parents feel comfortable; they must not convey the attitude of "I'm the teacher, and I know what's best for your child." Instead, a partnership approach that says "together we can help Jasmine" will invite parents to participate in their children's education.

It is vital that schools initiate contact with parents and provide a welcoming environment in order to increase parental involvement. Educators often project an uncaring attitude on parents who are less involved in their children's education. Batey (1996) reminds us that "sometimes what we perceive as an uncaring attitude is actually a barrier in communication or a fear of the unknown" (p. 18). In our interactions with parents, we must try to help them overcome any fears and anxieties they may have.

REFLECTION QUESTIONS

- **Which family barrier do you think will be the most difficult to overcome? Why?**

  ....

- **How could a school become more "family-like"?**

  ....

- **Ask a teacher to describe one difficult experience he or she had with parents. Write down what you would have done in the same situation.**

  ....

Now that we have looked at reasons to involve families and barriers that prevent this involvement, let's consider ways to establish positive relationships with students' families. You cannot expect family involvement to "just happen"; you have to plan for it. The following list presents several suggestions.

❏ *Survey students' families to determine their needs and interests.* Find out what goals parents have for their children each year. Use this information in planning lessons for students and in providing feedback to parents.

❏ *Invite parents into your classroom.* Do not assume that family members feel welcome at school. Extend a personal invitation for them to come and share their expertise. Everyone has something to contribute, but some individuals may not recognize the value of their contributions. Let parents (or other family members) share with students their personal interests or hobbies. They might also tell about their travels, childhood experiences, or careers.

❏ *Consider making home visits early in the school year.* The purpose of such face-to-face contact is to become better acquainted with students' families to open lines of communication. Coordinate these visits with your building principal.

❏ *Make opportunities for involvement convenient to families' schedules.* Be sensitive to the time constraints of working parents and plan activities that fit their situations. Give sufficient notification for special events so that parents can plan to attend. One or two days ahead is not enough time for busy parents to make arrangements. You can also videotape special events such as student presentations and allow each student the opportunity to take home the tape to share it with family and friends.

❏ *Create a newsletter to send home to parents.* Incorporate students' work and ideas. Older students can compose columns, interviews, stories, and poems. In this way the newsletter can be an extension of the curriculum by providing an avenue for students to apply skills.

❏ *Help families help their children.* For example, provide information on ways parents might assist students with learning tasks. Also design interactive homework assignments that consist of activities students can do with their families. These types of assignments, as suggested by Epstein, Salinas, and Jackson (1995), allow parents to assist students without knowledge of the content. The student becomes the teacher, and the parent assumes the role of student through TIPS (Teachers Involve Parents in Schoolwork). Make homework more relevant by relating assignments to current events. Items in the news can lay a common ground among students, their families, and the classroom.

❏ *Aim to be understood.* Use words with which parents are familiar. Avoid educational jargon in written and oral communication. Parents are often "turned off" when school personnel use specialized vocabulary.

❏ *Contact parents with good news.* Unfortunately, too many times parents only have contact with teachers when there is "bad news." Telephone calls or brief notes can be used to send home positive messages.

A CASE STUDY

Mr. Garcia is unhappy with the instruction his daughter Casey has been receiving in science class. It seems that every few days Casey tells him about another guest speaker that her science teacher, Mr. Block, has invited to class. Mr. Garcia is not convinced of the value of these experiences, so he writes a memo to Mr. Block expressing his displeasure. If you were Mr. Block, how would you respond?

Believing that his or her competence has been questioned, a teacher might become defensive about situations such as the one described in the case study. However, we must remember to consider the case from the parent's perspective. According to Faber and Mazlish (1995), parents want respect. Therefore teachers must be willing to listen to parents' concerns. We must also note that Casey may have given the impression that a guest speaker came to class daily, when in reality there had been only two guest speakers in the past three weeks. Thus the problem might be due to miscommunication.

Before responding to this parent, we should remember that one of our primary goals in working with parents is mutual support (Mager, 1980). Difficulties often arise when there is a conflict between the attitudes, values, and/or practices of teachers and parents. It may be tempting for Mr. Block to ignore Mr. Garcia's complaint. However, such avoidance will not result in greater understanding. As Mager (1980) suggests, more interaction leads to greater support. In relating to parents, teachers would do well to remember the words of Faber and Mazlish (1995): "Both parents and teachers need appreciation, information, and understanding from one another" (p. 241). How might teachers provide these "essentials" to parents? More specifically, what should Mr. Block do?

teacher efficacy

A teacher's belief that he or she can make a positive difference in the lives of students.

A key factor influencing a teacher's efforts to involve parents is self-perception. Research has found that **teacher efficacy** is one of the strongest predictors of whether teachers involve parents (Hoover-Dempsey, Bassler, & Brissie, 1987). Teacher efficacy consists of a teacher's belief in his or her own effectiveness and ability to make a difference. Teachers who have a high degree of efficacy do not view requesting help as an inadequacy. This willingness to collaborate is essential to your future success with parents.

Teachers can provide information and learning strategies to help parents help their children.

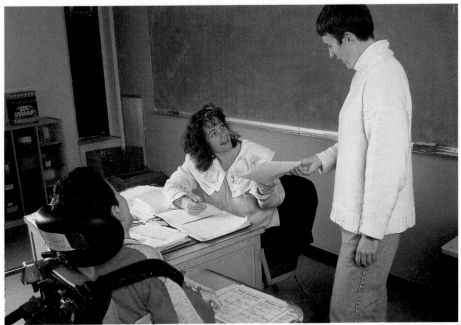

© Michael Newman/PhotoEdit

Remember that connecting with students' families requires commitment—it takes extra time, but the benefits far outweigh the inconvenience. The first step is to examine yourself and determine whether you really want parent involvement and why. The second step is to develop a proactive plan for involving parents. "Parent involvement is most effective when it is comprehensive, well-planned, and long lasting" (Henderson, 1988, p. 153).

REFLECTION QUESTIONS

In thinking about how you as a teacher will relate to your students' families, you should examine your own assumptions about teachers' relationships with parents/guardians. One way to accomplish this is by reflecting on your own family's interaction patterns with your teachers and schools. Respond in writing to the following questions:

How frequent was the contact between your home and school? Describe the type of interaction.

How did such interaction change as you progressed through school?

How might your school performance have been affected differently by the various levels or types of parental involvement?

Tips for Productive Parent-Teacher Conferences

Conferences often cause anxiety on the part of teachers. It is important to note that parents, too, become anxious about these occasions. To make parent-teacher conferences more meaningful and less stressful, we offer the tips outlined in the illustration on the following page.

When we think of communicating with students' families, we most often think about parent-teacher conferences. But there are many other informal ways to establish relationships with parents. For example, talk to parents when you see them in the grocery store, at the post office, and at various school events. Informal conversations with parents (away from the school premises) can yield valuable information that could help you foster better relationships with your students. Admittedly, face-to-face communication is probably the best form of communication, but there are other effective modes. For example, teachers can use notes, phone calls, e-mail, voice mail (i.e, answering machines), newsletters, and surveys to facilitate communication. Look for opportunities to use these methods of reaching students' families.

Web Sites
To learn more about improving relationships with families, check out these sites: www.csos.jhu.edu/p2000 (Center on School, Family, & Community Partnerships at Johns Hopkins University); http://npin.org/ (National Parent Information Network); and www.ncpie.org/ (National Coalition for Parent Involvement in Education).

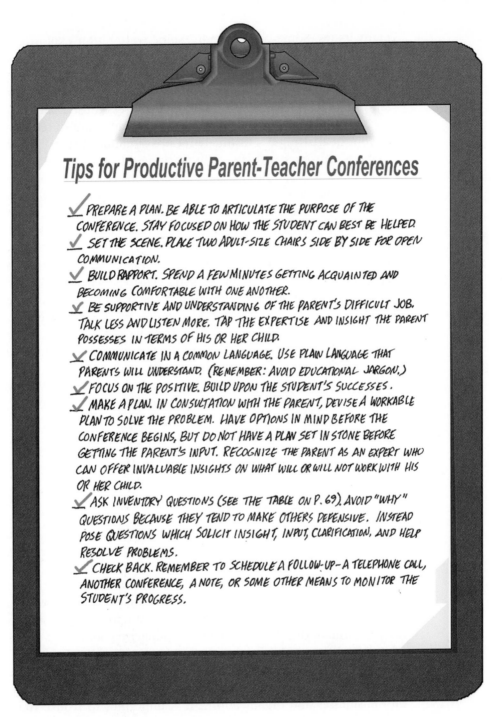

Tips for Productive Parent-Teacher Conferences

✓ PREPARE A PLAN. BE ABLE TO ARTICULATE THE PURPOSE OF THE CONFERENCE. STAY FOCUSED ON HOW THE STUDENT CAN BEST BE HELPED.

✓ SET THE SCENE. PLACE TWO ADULT-SIZE CHAIRS SIDE BY SIDE FOR OPEN COMMUNICATION.

✓ BUILD RAPPORT. SPEND A FEW MINUTES GETTING ACQUAINTED AND BECOMING COMFORTABLE WITH ONE ANOTHER.

✓ BE SUPPORTIVE AND UNDERSTANDING OF THE PARENT'S DIFFICULT JOB. TALK LESS AND LISTEN MORE. TAP THE EXPERTISE AND INSIGHT THE PARENT POSSESSES IN TERMS OF HIS OR HER CHILD.

✓ COMMUNICATE IN A COMMON LANGUAGE. USE PLAIN LANGUAGE THAT PARENTS WILL UNDERSTAND. (REMEMBER: AVOID EDUCATIONAL JARGON.)

✓ FOCUS ON THE POSITIVE. BUILD UPON THE STUDENT'S SUCCESSES.

✓ MAKE A PLAN. IN CONSULTATION WITH THE PARENT, DEVISE A WORKABLE PLAN TO SOLVE THE PROBLEM. HAVE OPTIONS IN MIND BEFORE THE CONFERENCE BEGINS, BUT DO NOT HAVE A PLAN SET IN STONE BEFORE GETTING THE PARENT'S INPUT. RECOGNIZE THE PARENT AS AN EXPERT WHO CAN OFFER INVALUABLE INSIGHTS ON WHAT WILL OR WILL NOT WORK WITH HIS OR HER CHILD.

✓ ASK INVENTORY QUESTIONS (SEE THE TABLE ON P. 69). AVOID "WHY" QUESTIONS BECAUSE THEY TEND TO MAKE OTHERS DEFENSIVE. INSTEAD POSE QUESTIONS WHICH SOLICIT INSIGHT, INPUT, CLARIFICATION, AND HELP RESOLVE PROBLEMS.

✓ CHECK BACK. REMEMBER TO SCHEDULE A FOLLOW-UP—A TELEPHONE CALL, ANOTHER CONFERENCE, A NOTE, OR SOME OTHER MEANS TO MONITOR THE STUDENT'S PROGRESS.

Reflections from the Field

When we asked Gerianne Jarolim, an elementary teacher, what her experiences have been working with students' families, she gave us this valuable insight: "Over the years I have dealt with students' families on many issues. Some were friendly; some were rather explosive. One thing I have found helpful is to try not to put the parent on the defense, because the outcome will typically be negative. I approach parents or guardians as allies. I say something such as, 'Your child has some problems or issues. How can we, as a team, address those issues?' "

This story from Corey Oliver, an eighth grade English teacher, will tug at your heartstrings: "I distinctly recall a situation that will forever live with me. During my first year of teaching, I had a student named Rod who showed great enthusiasm and earnestness in his work. During the second nine-week grading period, I sent a note home to Rod's parents, explaining to them how proud I was of his behavior and progress in class. Merely considering this an appropriate gesture, I was totally unprepared for the reward that lay ahead for me. One week later I received a letter from Rod's mother expressing her appreciation for my note. She went on to say that in all of her son's eight years in school, she had never received a positive letter from a teacher. I tucked her note safely away into the file I keep for special things. By the way, the letter from Rod's mother was accompanied by balloons and gourmet cookies. I thought the story was over. Then I discovered that Rod's mother had sent a carbon letter to my vice principals, principal, and superintendent's office. They, in turn, expressed their appreciation to me. Who would have thought such a simple gesture would have such an impact?"

Relationships with the Community

You may have never imagined that you would need public relations (PR) skills in teaching. Yet, you will find that you must be a salesperson in the field of education in order to "sell" the value of what you do to those in the community (and even in your own classroom). Members of the community, including those without school-age children, pay the local taxes that support the schools and pay your salary. To win the support of the community, keep them informed. Use the local media to publicize good things that happen at school. Too often only the "bad news" from schools makes it to the media. Teachers should function as spokespersons for their students' achievements.

An increasing number of schools are forming partnerships with community businesses and organizations. It is important to realize that there are many resources in the community that can be tapped by teachers. "Communities have much to offer teachers who are willing to seek out and build the relationships to support collaborative and cooperative ventures" (Morrison, 1997, p. 222). Guest speakers from the business community can be invited to talk with students. Mentors can be recruited to work with individual students. Building school-business partnerships can result in significant donations of time, personnel, and materials.

Community

Family/ Parents

Students

TEACHERS NEED A GOOD RELATIONSHIP WITH...

Colleagues

School Administration

Additionally, schools should be willing to "give back" time and talent to their communities. For example, students may be placed as volunteers in nursing homes to complete service projects. In return, students receive "hands-on" career guidance experiences. Interactions with community members have the potential to reinforce for students the connection between school learning and the outside world.

It is important to know the community in which you teach, even if you do not live in that community. Take a driving tour through the neighborhoods. Frequent the businesses in the area. Talk with those who live there. Read the local newspaper. Cultivate relationships with those in the community who may become powerful allies in the education of the young people you teach.

Relationships with Colleagues

As a teacher you will be part of a team with others on your school staff. No doubt you know the meaning of the acronym TEAM: Together Everyone Achieves More. This saying is quite applicable to the school environment. As Johnson (1990) so aptly states:

> A lone teacher can impart phonics, fractions, the pluperfect tense, or the periodic table, but only through teachers' collective efforts will schools produce educated graduates who can read and compute; apply scientific principles; comprehend lessons of history; value others' cultures and speak their languages; and conduct themselves responsibly as citizens. (p. 149)

As interdependent beings, teachers can offer many benefits to each other. Other teachers cannot only help meet your need for adult-to-adult contact but can also provide a rich source of ideas on resources and materials to enhance your teaching. Teaching colleagues are vital links to overcoming the isolation so readily felt by teachers (Johnson, 1990). Your attitude toward those with whom you teach should be one of cooperation. Competition has no place among teachers. Instead, all efforts should be focused on what is best for the students.

There are many people in a school to whom you can turn for assistance. The guidance counselor is an invaluable resource person. The counselor often has knowledge of family situations about which the classroom teacher may be unaware. Specially trained in interpersonal skills, a counselor can serve as a sounding board for examining problems and as a neutral third party in resolving conflicts.

Special education teachers are also extremely helpful individuals within a school. They can offer advice on meeting the unique needs of students, because they understand the learning requirements of students with special needs. Teachers should interact regularly with counselors and special education teachers to maintain current knowledge of students. They should then use this knowledge to enhance their relationships with students.

Relationships with School Administrator

Your building principal sets the tone in the school. Your relationship with this individual greatly affects your level of satisfaction. Therefore cultivating a positive relationship with your principal will be advantageous to you (as well as to your students). Keep the principal informed of special situations and any potential problems. Share with school administrators interesting things you are doing in your classroom. Extend an invitation to the principal to visit your classroom—don't wait until it's time for a formal evaluation. Discuss new ideas with your principal. Volunteer to serve on school committees and become involved in other ways. When teachers work together to support the administration's goals, the likelihood that students will succeed is strengthened.

AssessYourself

Do you have the interpersonal skills necessary to develop relationships with students?

Could you be empathic when a student is disrupting your class?

Would you have the patience to spend time getting to know and understand your students as individuals?

Would you be willing to forge relationships with the families of your students?

Would you be willing to extend yourself beyond the classroom to establish relationships with others who are involved directly or indirectly with student learning and success?

Basic Communication Skills

Think about a relationship that works for you. This can be a relationship with a group, an individual, or a business entity. Now consider what attributes make that relationship work. Create a list of descriptors. Perhaps your list includes attributes such as trust, honesty, respect, and common interests. These same attributes characterize effective relationships with your students and constituents—parents, community members, teaching colleagues, and administrators.

Underlying all effective relationships is **rapport**—a feeling of harmony and connection that leads to positive outcomes. Rapport is established by mutual respect, trust, and open communication. Underlying all relationships characterized by rapport is the notion of respect. "Respect means prizing another person simply because he [or she] is a human being" (Egan, 1975, p. 94).

rapport

A feeling of connection that develops between two people based on mutual cooperation and respect.

attending

The ability to give one's full attention, physically and psychologically, to another person.

Rapport begins with a behavior known as **attending.** To attend is to give one's full attention to someone else. Attending exists along two dimensions: the physical dimension and the psychological dimension (Egan, 1975). Physical aspects of attending include looking at the other person, turning one's body toward the person, nodding one's head in response to the other person's speech, and mirroring the person's facial expressions (e.g., returning a smiling face with a smile). Psychologically, when we exhibit attending we accept the other person and do not impose our preconceived notions on him or her.

Attending requires that we be honest with ourselves. We must be aware of our prejudices regarding a person or topic in order to be open to listening. Effective attending also involves verbal cues (Garrett, Sadker, & Sadker, 1994). Verbal cues include the effective use of silence and minimal verbal acknowledgments, such as "I see," "I understand," and "Yes."

active listening

The ability to separate the emotional content from the intellectual by focusing on the core message a person is trying to convey.

Closely related to attending is the use of **active listening,** which is a critical skill for relating to others (Garrett, Sadker, & Sadker, 1994). This skill involves being able to separate emotional content from intellectual content by focusing on the core message of what a person says (Egan, 1975). As you consider the feelings you think the speaker is communicating, you must listen without becoming defensive. To listen actively means that you summarize what you hear the other person saying and ask for clarification to determine the accuracy of your perceptions (Garrett, Sadker, & Sadker, 1994).

As an active listener you function as a mirror for the other person. The importance of both these skills is indicated by the following quote: "When you model attending and active listening behaviors, you are communicating to students, parents, and colleagues that you have put aside other business and are ready to listen and interact with them" (Garrett, Sadker, & Sadker, 1994, p. 219).

As mentioned previously, empathy is the ability to see things from another's perspective. For example, a teacher who is empathic is able to understand the fears and insecurities a parent must be feeling as a conference begins. A teacher who relates to a colleague in an empathic manner identifies the anxiety that teacher feels as she prepares to face a potentially hostile parent.

clarity

The quality of a message communicated in an intelligible manner.

An essential trait for teachers to develop is **clarity.** Send clear messages when you speak; do not hide behind educational jargon. Aim for clarity and brevity when you communicate with others. Being succinct helps to get a point across more efficiently and effectively.

The art of questioning dovetails with clarity. Questions play an important role in communication; they can either enhance or hinder further communication. Focus on problem solving, not on blame. Poorly phrased questions may cause another person to misunderstand your intentions. Garrett, Sadker, and Sadker (1994) note that questions worded inappropriately "can be threatening, interrupt thought processes, [and] generate defensiveness and hostility" (p. 220). Thus teachers must learn how to pose questions appropriately as they form productive relationships with others. Those questions that are most helpful in facilitating communication are clarification questions. Garrett, Sadker, and Sadker (1994) call these types of questions "inventory questions" and delineate four levels (see the table on p. 69).

It is important for the teacher to make parents feel at ease in the school setting.

© Robert Daemmrich/STONE

Inventory Questions

Type of Question	Explanation	Examples
Level 1	Invites the other person to talk	"Tell me what happened at the meeting."
	Increases the likelihood of thoughts and feelings being shared	"What are your goals for Billy this year?"
Level 2	Seeks additional information	"What do you mean by that?"
		"What exactly does Sally enjoy about school?"
Level 3	Helps identify outcomes and consequences	"What would happen if we did that?"
	Pinpoints discrepancies	"Is this what you want for Billy?"
Level 4	Seeks alternatives or solutions	"What else could we do to help Sally?"
		"Which solution do you think best meets Billy's needs?"

Based upon Garrett, Sadker, & Sadker from *Classroom teaching skills*, Fifth Edition, edited by James M. Cooper. Copyright © 1994 by Houghton Mifflin Company. Used with permission.

Conclusion

In this chapter we found that correlational studies have linked positive teacher-student relationships to student learning and morale. Even though relationship building is more of an art than a science (and consequently difficult to measure) it is, nonetheless, a core factor in student achievement and motivation. Humanism emerged in the 1950s among educators who wanted to emphasize the importance of the teacher-student relationship to student motivation and learning. During the 1960s and 1970s, the philosophy of humanism gained momentum and became a popular approach in the classroom among educators who believed students' affective needs were being overlooked. In effect, humanistic teachers focus on students' feelings, personal needs, and uniqueness. An underlying premise is that every child has worth and dignity and should be treated respectfully.

Further, we learned that no teacher is an island. The isolation that exists within the classroom can be overcome when teachers are willing to extend themselves to others who can, in turn, have a positive impact on students' learning. These "others" include colleagues, counselors, administrators, family members, and community associates.

Imagine the concentric ripples that result from a pebble being dropped into water. To have an impact on students' learning and success, teachers must see the importance of reaching out to those ever-widening circles of individuals who can also enhance the process. Further, we stressed that teachers, regardless of background and/or differences in life experiences, can develop effective relationships if they apply simple communication principles. The approaches and strategies presented in this chapter can facilitate positive relationships with students and others.

KEY TERMS

active listening

affective attributes

attending

clarity

client-centered counseling

empathy

genuineness

Goals 2000: Educate America Act

holistic approach

humanism

national education goals

permeable families

rapport

teacher efficacy

unconditional positive regard

SUGGESTED READING

Banner, J. M., & Cannon, H. C. (1997). *The elements of teaching.* New Haven, CT: Yale University Press.

Elkind, D. (1995). *Ties that stress.* Cambridge, MA: Harvard University Press.

Noddings, N. (1992). *The challenge to care in schools: An alternative approach to education.* New York: Teachers College Press.

REFERENCES

Aspy, D. N., & Roebuck, F. N. (1977). *Kids don't learn from people they don't like.* Amherst, MA: Human Resource Development Press.

Batey, C. S. (1996). *Parents are lifesavers: A handbook for parent involvement in schools.* Thousand Oaks, CA: Corwin Press.

Birch, S. H., & Ladd, G. W. (1996). Interpersonal relationships in the school environment and children's school adjustment: The role of teachers and peers. In J. Juvonen & K. Wentzel (Eds.), *Social motivation: Understanding children's school adjustment.* New York: Cambridge University Press.

Collins, M., & Tamarkin, C. (1982). *Marva Collins' way.* Los Angeles: J. P. Tarcher.

Combs, A. (1965). *The professional education of teachers.* Boston: Allyn & Bacon.

Comer, J. P. (1988). Is "parenting" essential to good teaching? *NEA Today, 6,* 34–40.

Egan, G. (1975). *The skilled helper: A model for systematic helping and interpersonal relating.* Monterey, CA: Brooks/Cole Publishing.

Elkind, D. (1995) *Ties that stress.* Cambridge, MA: Harvard University Press.

Epstein, J. (1995). School/family/community partnerships: Caring for the children we share. *Phi Delta Kappan, 76*(9), 701–712.

Epstein, J., Salinas, K. C., & Jackson, V. E. (1995). *TIPS manual for teachers: Language arts, science/health, and math interactive homework in the middle grades.* Baltimore: Center on School, Family, and Community Partnerships, Johns Hopkins University.

Faber, A., & Mazlish, E. (1995). *How to talk so kids can learn.* New York: Simon & Schuster.

Finders, M., & Lewis, C. (1994). Why some parents don't come to school. *Educational Leadership, 51*(8), 50–54.

Garrett, S., Sadker, M., & Sadker, D. (1994). Interpersonal classroom skills. In Cooper, J. (Ed.). *Classroom teaching skills* (pp. 189–231). Boston: Houghton Mifflin.

Germinario, V., & Cram, H. (1998). *Change for public education: Practical approaches for the 21st century.* Lancaster, PA: Technomic Publishing.

Greenwood, G., & Hickman, C. (1991). Research and practice in parental involvement: Implication for teacher education. *The Elementary School Journal, 91*(3), 279–288.

Gordon, T., & Burch, N. (1974). *Teacher effectiveness training.* New York: Peter H. Wyden.

Haberman, M. (1995). *Star teachers of children in poverty.* West Lafayette, IN: Kappa Delta Pi.

Harvard Family Research Project. (1997). *New skills for new schools: Preparing teachers in family involvement.* Cambridge, MA: Author.

Henderson, A. T. (1988). Parents are a school's best friends. *Phi Delta Kappan, 70*(2), 148–153.

Hoover-Dempsey, K., Bassler, O., & Brissie, J. (1987). Parent involvement: Contributions of teacher efficacy, school socioeconomic status, and other school characteristics. *American Educational Research Journal, 24*(3), 417–435.

Johnson, S. M. (1990). *Teachers at work: Achieving success in our schools.* New York: Basic Books.

Mager, G. (1980). Parent relationships and home and community conditions. In D. R. Cruickshank & associates, *Teaching is tough* (pp. 153–197). Englewood Cliffs, NJ: Prentice-Hall.

Myrick, R. D. (1993). *Developmental guidance and counseling: A practical approach.* Minneapolis: Educational Media Corporation.

Morrison, G. S. (1997). *Teaching in America.* Boston: Allyn & Bacon.

National Association of Secondary School Principals. (1996). *Breaking ranks: Changing an American institution.* Reston, VA: Author.

National Education Goals Panel. (1995). *The National Education Goals Report.* Washington, D. C.: Author.

Noddings, N. (1992). *The challenge to care in schools: An alternative approach to education.* New York: Teachers College Press.

Ornstein, A. C. (1982). Curriculum contrasts: A historical overview. *Phi Delta Kappan, 63*(6), 404–408.

Perrone, V. (1991). *A letter to teachers: reflections on schooling and the art of teaching.* San Francisco, CA: Jossey-Bass.

Rogers, C. R. (1961). *On becoming a person.* Boston: Houghton Mifflin.

Rogers, C. R. (1962). The interpersonal relationship: The core of guidance. *Harvard Educational Review, 32,* 416–429.

Spring, J. (1998). *American education.* Boston, MA: McGraw-Hill.

U. S. Department of Education. (1994). *Strong families, strong schools: Building community partnerships for learning.* Washington, D. C.: Author.

Wentzel, K. R. (1997). Student motivation in middle school: The role of perceived pedagogical caring. *Journal of Educational Psychology, 89*(3), 411–419.

WHOM TEACHERS TEACH

© Elena Rooraid/PhotoEdit

At the end of this chapter, you will be able to

- Describe familial and societal problems that adversely affect young people and the implications of these problems for teachers.

- Identify positive teacher attitudes and practical interventions that can lessen the impact of outside forces that negatively affect students' performance and well-being.

- Identify ways schools can address societal forces deterring students.

- Describe the vital link between school and community as a way to combat societal and familial problems.

- Cite ways you can assist students to overcome problems they face in their homes and neighborhoods.

CHAPTER 4

Challenges in Society

A bird's eye view of what to expect in this chapter

Many problems that beset society today negatively affect young people and, in turn, schools. It is naive to believe that problems children face in their homes and neighborhoods can be contained therein. In Chapter 3 we discussed how effective teachers forge partnerships with other team players such as parents, colleagues, administrators, and community leaders in an effort to help students with school-related problems. In this chapter, we examine some of those familial and societal influences that not only hinder students academically but also affect their psychological and social well-being.

In this chapter we consider ways that teachers and schools can individually and collectively lessen societal pressures that distract and discourage children. The understanding that teachers have about students' social and personal development allows them to play a valuable role in community efforts to improve students' physical and psychological health. Most teachers are happy to offer expertise and time to community efforts that have children's welfare at heart. Fortunately, there are many things teachers can do to mitigate the outside influences encumbering young people. We hope this chapter will motivate you to seek solutions to perplexing societal problems that burden our youth.

Many students and their families need the assistance of medical and psychological services. It is unrealistic to believe that either the community or schools could (or should) handle these needs single-handedly. Acting alone or separately is not the answer to the complex problems facing families and society. A concerted effort on the part of communities and schools is required to adequately address these needs. In many communities, social agencies and schools are becoming partners in an effort to improve the living conditions of children.

The first half of this chapter highlights major familial and societal problems affecting children and therefore teachers and schools. The second half offers practical suggestions based on current research and educational best practices for alleviating societal ills that are detrimental to young people. Although the interventions and programs we offer are effective, they are not panaceas. There are no easy answers for these contemporary problems. However, today's teachers must be willing and prepared to help students negotiate the difficult situations they will inevitably encounter.

Responding to At-Risk Students

Perceptive teachers realize that many of their students come to school unprepared mentally and often physically for the challenges they must face. It is disheartening to discover how many students are saddled with problems that children should not have to bear. Students whose life circumstances place them at jeopardy for failure are often referred to as **at-risk students.** These students are "at risk" for failure in life academically, vocationally, and personally. As many as one out of four children is at risk for failure in school because of social, emotional, and health problems (Dryfoos, 1994). Children who are performing poorly at school may be "victims of poverty, hopelessness, or mental illness . . . that came to the attention of schools due to disruptive and disturbing psychosocial problems" (Hendren, 1994, p.1).

at-risk students

Students who because of adverse circumstances and backgrounds are at a greater likelihood for failure in life academically, vocationally, and personally.

Some people argue that it is a waste of time to look for ways to alleviate the social problems in students' homes and neighborhoods, because such problems are too complex and school personnel have little control over what happens to students once they leave school property. As you might surmise, we believe that giving up without a fight is inexcusable. To say familial and societal problems are too complicated and beyond our purview is to surrender to defeat, which we believe socially responsible teachers should not—nor will not—do.

It is critical, then, that as teachers we do not throw up our hands in frustration at the challenges but instead realize we can do something. Specifically, teachers can control what occurs in their classrooms. They can make tangible differences in students' lives by teaching healthy attitudes and responsible behaviors. Students who acquire fundamental life skills are in a much better position to cope with life's adversities.

Many students are at risk academically because of social and emotional problems.

© Stewart Cohen/STONE

Many future teachers have in mind a particular school or locale in which they want to teach. Unfortunately, you may not get your first choice (at least initially). Thus you must be prepared to teach children regardless of their background and the location of the school. Ironically, new teachers tend to be placed in the least desirable schools (often in crime-ridden neighborhoods)—work settings that challenge the most experienced teachers. The good news, however, is that during this interval some teachers find they actually prefer working with at-risk students. They may not have known this about themselves until they were "thrown into the ring." You may have this inclination and not even know it—now that's an exciting thought.

Reflections from the Field

When we asked one of those truly gifted teachers what she does that makes her so successful at teaching disadvantaged and underachieving students, she said she had no idea. "I'm not sure what it takes to teach at-risk kids, or how I do it, but I do know—I have it." She was not being overly confident, she really does "have it," although she couldn't articulate why. Later, while glancing over the interview notes, a comment she had made earlier caught my attention: "Very shortly I realized I was teaching my students something much more important than English." Does this give you a clue to the secret of her success?

Resiliency

resilient

The ability to overcome seemingly impossible odds to become a well-adjusted and contributing member of society.

Some individuals mistakenly think that children (because of their youth) are **resilient** and therefore able to overcome adverse circumstances, allowing them to become well-adjusted, contributing members of society. Although many children are amazingly resilient, not all children are so fortunate. For some children, deprivation and other forms of neglect and maltreatment leave lasting emotional scars. When we as a society conclude that children are resilient, we often stop searching for solutions to their problems, which is detrimental to both the children and society.

As educators we are concerned about what we can do to help students negotiate life's adversities. Consequently we are curious about the traits that resilient people possess so we can try to develop those qualities in our students. If research can pinpoint traits or factors that foster resiliency, this information can be invaluable to teachers in assisting students to develop these qualities. Fortunately, over the past two decades many studies have investigated this phenomenon of resiliency.

One study we found particularly informative was conducted by the Search Institute during the 1996–1997 school year. Data were collected nationwide on a sample of nearly 100,000 students in grades 6 through 12 in 213 communities. The findings were published in *The Asset Approach: Giving Kids What They Need to Succeed* (Search Institute, 1997). The researchers identified 40 experiences and qualities that lead to positive student behavior, which they labeled as "developmental assets." These developmental assets were grouped into eight categories: support, empowerment, boundaries and expectations, use of time, commitment to learning, positive values, social competencies, and positive identity (p. 1).

As you might guess, the findings revealed that the more developmental assets students possessed, the more likely they were to become healthy, re-

Teachers console children when they are upset.

© Mary Kate Denny/STONE

sponsible, and caring individuals. As we read the results of this study, we were disturbed by how few assets our children possess. To explain, the average student's score was 18 out of a total of 40 assets. And 62% of the students had 20 or fewer assets from which to draw. Equally disturbing was the statistic that only 26% of the students reported positive family communication, and only 20% reported feeling valued by the community. Of the student sample, 37% reported they lacked the strength to resist negative peer pressure and dangerous situations (Search Institute, 1997, p. 2).

These findings demonstrate the magnitude of problems students bring to school. Additionally, this study offers tips for bridging the gap between school and community in an effort to build positive assets in youth. We suggest that you review the entire study to learn more about how positive influences fortify young people.

Web Site
For more information, contact the Search Institute at 1-800-888-7828 or visit their web site at http://www.search-institute.org.

AssessYourself

What are your beliefs about resiliency?

Do you know of cases in which individuals were able to rebound from adverse circumstances to become well-adjusted and self-sufficient members of society?

What developmental assets do you think they possessed that made them resilient?

Would you consider yourself to be a resilient person?

What positive assets do you have that have given you strength and endurance to overcome seemingly impossible odds?

Familial Challenges and Implications for Teachers

What are some of the societal problems that negatively affect students? Specifically, what can teachers do to alleviate some of the problems students face? It is important to recognize that teachers are not to blame for the circumstances of their students; most of the time teachers are relatively powerless to change their students' situations outside of school. However, teachers are responsible for what happens to children while at school under their care. Teachers can make the classroom a refuge for students, in addition to making it a place where students can feel worthy and important. Ensuring that your students experience personal and academic success in the classroom will equip them with the self-worth and confidence they need to cope with situations outside of school.

As you recall from Unit 1, teachers' attitudes and behaviors can improve student morale, motivation, achievement, and self-esteem. Caring and concerned teachers attempt to make every exchange among those in the classroom edifying for every student and to make every learning activity enjoyable, practical, and achievable. During the school day, teachers have many opportunities to bolster students' self-image. One effective and efficient way to make students feel worthy is to greet every student you pass in the hallway, playground, lunchroom (or wherever) with a friendly "hello."

Let's begin by listing problems students face that begin in the family and home and then discuss the implications for teachers.

Changes in Family Structure

As you are aware, family structure today has changed considerably over the past few decades, which (for better or worse) has affected young people. Today's "typical" family bears little resemblance to those portrayed in television shows of the mid-1950s and early 1960s. The families of Ward and June Cleaver and Ozzie and Harriet Nelson were much different from the typical family of the 21st century. The "traditional" family unit is becoming increasingly uncommon in American society. The spiraling divorce rate has transformed many conventional families into blended family units, or stepfamilies. Additionally, grandparents are raising more children, which is certainly a change from the traditional nuclear family unit. (Sociologists define a **nuclear family** as one in which both parents live in the home.)

nuclear family

A family unit with both parents living in the home.

Implications for Teachers

Because modern households come in various forms we cannot sketch a "typical" family profile. What you must understand as a teacher is that your students might come from any kind of family configuration: nuclear, extended, blended, or single-parent or from homes where grandparents or foster parents assume parental responsibilities. You must be careful not to stereotype or prejudge a family (regardless of the arrangement) until more is known about the functionality of the unit.

What does a healthy, functioning family look like? Well, it depends. Fortunately, many seemingly "non-traditional" family structures have been found to be functional. But what is more surprising and unfortunate is that we cannot assume that all "traditional" units are necessarily "functional." In other words, just because a child lives in a nuclear family with both biological parents, we cannot conclude that the family unit is functional. It may be, but it may not be. There are no longer definite guidelines as to what is the best living arrangement for a child.

To illustrate, in a nuclear family one parent (or both) could be emotionally distant from the child or physically and/or psychologically abusive. Likewise, we cannot presume that because a child lives with a foster family or in an orphanage that he or she will automatically have adjustment problems resulting from this living arrangement. Fortunately, many atypical living environments produce well-adjusted individuals.

Unhealthy family units are not always discernible to the "untrained" eye; therefore, when differentiating "functional" homes from "dysfunctional" ones, many factors must be considered. There is no such entity as a "completely" functional family; rather, there are degrees of functionality. Few people can claim they were raised in a totally healthy or totally dysfunctional family.

Nonetheless, some family structures can contribute extra stress that could precipitate problems for family members. For example, in a single-parent home the sole parent has no one with whom to divide family chores and responsibilities, which can certainly evoke additional pressure. But again, we should not prejudge. There are cases in which single parents have been remarkably capable of handling the extra stress that comes from being the sole provider. The ability to cope depends on the individual. Many single-parent households have support teams (extended families) that provide children with appropriate role models to emulate. The bottom line is that each family unit must be assessed individually to determine its degree of functionality.

Another family unit in today's society is composed of children being raised by gays and lesbians. Because homosexuality is not uniformly accepted in all communities, these families also may face additional stress. You should not assume that children raised by homosexuals have adjustment and/or behavioral problems. To date there is no evidence to suggest differences in children's adjustment, or sexual orientation, based on the sexual orientation of the parent(s) (Falk, 1989). Thus living with a homosexual parent(s) is not an indicator that a child will have psychological problems or that the family unit is not functional. Teachers may find, however, chiefly because of prevailing biases, that some children may need support to cope with possible ridicule and rejection from their peers. Teachers must be willing to give extra support to children in this situation.

Unreasonable Parental Expectations: Diana Baumrind's Theory

One family problem that negatively affects classrooms is the inordinate number of children being raised in homes where expectations are unreasonable. To simplify this, there are basically two extremes with regard to unreasonable parental expectations: either too much is expected from children or too little is expected. In homes where parents expect too much from children, punishment is likely to be frequent, harsh, and arbitrary. In contrast, in homes where parents expect too little from their children, punishment is lax, inconsistent, or nonexistent. As is the case with most extremities, neither of these two attitudes or approaches is healthy or productive for the development of children.

To explain this conceptually, we selected Diana Baumrind's theory on child-rearing practices (1967; 1971) to describe the various modes of parenting and their effect on children's adjustment. In the 1960s Baumrind began studying parenting styles to determine those child-rearing practices that produced the most competent children. From her research, three fundamental parenting styles emerged: *authoritarian, permissive,* and *authoritative.*

You may be wondering what parenting styles have to do with teaching school. Over the years Baumrind's research on parenting styles has been applied to classroom settings and teacher-student relationships, which makes her studies quite relevant to future teachers (Baumrind, 1967; 1971). From our teaching experiences, we agree with Baumrind that the way you were raised will affect not only your approach to parenting but also how you will respond to your students.

Authoritarian Parents

authoritarian parents
Parenting style in which parents exercise absolute control, have unreasonably high expectations, are unresponsive, and lack warmth toward their children's needs.

Authoritarian parents are demanding; they exercise absolute control over their children. Children are not consulted regarding family matters; these parents make all the decisions. Authoritarian parents lack warmth and are unresponsive to their children's needs and feelings.

One study revealed that authoritarian approaches tend to magnify a child's feelings of alienation and accelerate instances of misbehavior (Dornbusch, Ritter, Leiderman, Roberts, & Fraleigh, 1987). Baumrind found that children from authoritarian homes were insecure, anxious, and resentful (Baumrind, 1967; 1971). Steinberg (1990) found children raised in authoritarian homes lacked social competence. In adolescence, males tended to lack confidence and initiative (Baumrind, 1991). Overall, these children were compliant at home (but mainly out of fear); however, in their interactions with peers they were found to be aggressive (Weiss, Dodge, Bates & Pettit, 1992).

Permissive Parents

permissive parents
Parenting style in which parents are disorganized, inconsistent, and insecure; fail to set limits or enforce rules; and demand very little from their children.

Permissive parents, the extreme opposite of authoritarian, are disorganized, inconsistent, and insecure. Being unsure themselves, these parents fail to set limits or enforce rules; they demand and expect very little from their children. Unlike authoritarian parents, permissive parents are warm and responsive in their interactions with their children. Children are loved unconditionally—in spite of what they do or don't do. This tends to give children an inflated sense of self that can evoke conflict when feedback from others (not family) does not validate their glorified image.

Baumrind (1967; 1971) found children raised by permissive parents, because of lack of structure and excessive indulgence, were often confused about their identity and worth and had difficulty setting and pursuing goals. In turn, they became overly dependent on adults to take care of them. Later studies suggest that these children tend to have substance abuse problems in addition to school-related problems (Steinberg, 1990).

Authoritative Parents

authoritative parents
Parenting style between authoritarian and permissive in which parents are confident and secure; set reasonable, challenging goals; set limits; enforce rules; and are responsive.

Authoritative parents, who fall between authoritarian and permissive on Baumrind's continuum, are confident and secure about who they are as persons and thus as parents. These parents set reasonable (although challenging) goals for their children. They set limits and enforce limits, in addition to explaining the purpose of the restrictions. They encourage their children to think independently and critically. Furthermore, they solicit feedback from children when making many family decisions and weigh those opinions when making final plans. Authoritative parents were found to be warm and responsive when interacting with their children (Baumrind, 1967).

Baumrind (1967; 1971) found that children raised by authoritative parents were more secure and confident in their abilities than those raised by authoritarian or permissive parents. Moreover, they were energetic, socially well adjusted, and high achievers. As adolescents, these children continued to exhibit prosocial behaviors and social competencies. Later studies substantiate Baumrind's original research suggesting that children raised in authoritative homes are psychologically healthier and more prosocial in their interactions than those raised in authoritarian or permissive homes (Dornbusch et al., 1987; Darling-Hammond, 1997).

REFLECTION QUESTIONS

- As you read, think about your family of origin and the parenting skills of your parents. Some of us want to emulate our caregivers, and sometimes we may need to modify our approach. The purpose of this exercise is not to blame, but to understand and learn from our past. We can change or break the cycle if we so desire.

- Do you see a connection between how you were treated by your parents and how you respond to young people now?

- To what extent do you predict your teaching style will be influenced by early life experiences in your family?

- Do you want to do things the same or differently from the way you were taught by significant others in your formative years?

AssessYourself

Which of the three parenting styles comes closest to the type of parenting you received as a child?

Were you raised in an authoritative home, an authoritarian home, or a permissive home? Perhaps it was a combination of the three types.
Can you see how one's teaching style could take on the characteristics of one or more of these parenting styles? Which style do you lean toward?

Toward which style do you see yourself: more autocratic or democratic? Perhaps you are a lackadaisical person, and thus a laissez-faire style suits you better. What can you do to change your style if desired?

Authoritarian parents

OFTEN
YIELD

- Insecurity.
- Alienation.
- Social anxiety.
- Resentfulness.

Authoritative parents

OFTEN
YIELD

- Security.
- Confidence.
- Social maturity.
- High achievement.

Permissive parents

HAPPY
BIRTHDAY
SON.

OFTEN
YIELD

- Confusion.
- Self-indulgence.
- Inflated sense of self.
- Inconsistent behavior.
- Overdependence.

Implications for Teachers

By examining this parenting style model carefully, teachers can find practical ways to enhance classroom management skills and interpersonal skills (Baumrind, 1967). Students raised in authoritarian homes give up on their studies because parental expectations are impossible to meet. On the other hand, some may push themselves almost beyond human limits in an effort to please and/or avoid punishment from home. Teachers can bolster students' confidence by providing achievable (although challenging) tasks.

Furthermore, students raised in authoritarian homes may need help from their teachers in learning how to manage anger and resolve conflicts. Dealing with angry students can be very intimidating to a new teacher (or any teacher for that matter). Fortunately, in most schools there are support staff for teachers to consult, such as the school counselor, social worker, or psychologist. These specialists may be in a better position to know what kind of approach would be therapeutic for a child.

In contrast, children from permissive homes may need assistance adhering to classroom rules and procedures. These children may need the teacher's guidance in learning basic management skills, such as organization, discipline, and goal setting. Teaching students skills such as forethought, frugality, persistence, and patience may be necessary. Some children have learned how to manipulate parents and caregivers to get their way. For example, some children learn at an early age that throwing a temper tantrum is a way to control adults or that doing a chore poorly will get them out of doing household chores.

Depending on the extent of the child's problems, teachers may need to consult the school counselor or psychologist for ideas on how to handle the lack of impulse control. In some cases the child may need to be referred for counseling, because impulsiveness can lead to high-risk behaviors such as drug and alcohol abuse, sexual promiscuity, recklessness, and other unhealthy lifestyle choices.

Many respected educators believe that teachers should adopt authoritative attitudes and practices, which they consider facilitate communication with children. Authoritative teachers encourage students to talk about their ideas and opinions (Darling-Hammond, 1997), which promotes the exchange of ideas—a practice that is key to democratic living. Later in the text we will frequently return to the concept of the authoritative teacher.

Lack of Adult Supervision

Many parents today, because of economic necessity, must work late shifts or second and third jobs to make ends meet. Therefore they are unavailable when their children come home from school in the afternoon. Returning to an empty house puts children at physical and emotional risk. Not only is this an unsafe practice, but most children need adult guidance and supervision. Many "latchkey kids" (as they are commonly called) have to assume adult responsibilities for younger siblings, such as cooking, bathing, and supervising homework. What problems can you foresee for these children who come home to an empty house or who have to stay late at daycare facilities? Were you a latchkey kid? What effect, if any, did this have on you?

Implications for Teachers

Preschool and elementary teachers should find out which children are unsupervised after school. As custodians of children, it is our responsibility to protect them. If you ascertain that a child in your class is in danger when he or she leaves school, action should be taken. Consulting with your school counselor or social worker is possibly the first move. Or you could ask the building principal or vice-principal how to proceed in this matter. Of course, your intention is to offer assistance (not make parents feel unworthy or irresponsible). Many times parents are unaware of free or discounted programs and services available in the community. Informing parents of these services will most likely be appreciated. The majority of parents and guardians are concerned about their children's welfare and should be receptive to information that could remedy the latchkey dilemma.

Lack of Parental Interest in Children

Regrettably, not all parents and guardians are concerned about the welfare of their children; in fact, some parents are unaffected by and oblivious to their children's needs. In research conducted by Maccoby and Martin (1983), a fourth type of parenting—the **uninvolved parents** was added to Baumrind's theory. Uninvolved parents are permissive, unresponsive, and lack concern for the well-being of their children. These parents permit their children "to engage in unsupervised behavior without apparent concern for their welfare" (Horton-Parker, 1998, p.70). These parents neither try to control their children nor hold expectations for them. Studies have shown that these children are more prone to skip school, drop out of school, abuse drugs and alcohol, become sexually active, and engage in criminal activity than children whose parents are involved (Lamborn, Mounts, Steinberg, & Dornbusch, 1991).

It is alarming to realize the number of parents today who are uninterested in their children's academic performance. A 10-year study conducted by Steinberg (1996) found that more than half of the 20,000 students surveyed believed that their parents would not be upset by a grade of C or less; one fourth of the sample reported their parents would not be upset by a grade of D or worse. But the most troubling finding was that nearly one third of the students reported that their parents "had no idea how they were doing in school" (Steinberg and associates, 1996, p. 19). Are you surprised by this finding?

uninvolved parents
Parenting style in which parents are permissive and unresponsive, showing a lack of concern for their children.

Implications for Teachers

As discussed in Chapter 3, there are many ways to enlist the help of parents in the education of their children. Refer to Chapter 3 for specific ways to increase parental involvement. Chapter 5 offers additional advice for soliciting parental participation. The best tip is to persevere with parents.

Lack of Student Interest in Schoolwork

Generally, "disengaged" and "uninvolved" parents produce children who are also "disengaged" and "uninvolved" in their schoolwork. Laurence Steinberg and associates (1996) studied students who were "engaged" in their studies and compared them with students who were "disengaged." Steinberg (1996) defined **engaged students** as those who were "psychologically connected to what is going on in their classes" (p. 15). **Disengaged students** were defined as those who performed at "bare minimum to get by." They put little effort or energy into school or school activities—they were merely "going through the motions" (p.15). Steinberg's study (1996) revealed that one third of the student sample showed signs of being emotionally disengaged from school. Half of the students found their classes to be boring. Students' lack of involvement in school was directly related to absenteeism and attrition. What is most disturbing about this study is that the student sample came from "average" schools as opposed to schools in high-crime areas.

engaged students

Students who are psychologically connected to what is going on in their classes.

disengaged students

Students who are uninvolved in their schoolwork.

Implications for Teachers

To reiterate, don't give up on your students! This textbook abounds with ideas on how to engage students in learning. Effective teachers continually look for ways to help students connect to school. Teachers who actively seek solutions to problems are those who eventually find answers. Be prepared to become surrogate parents to your students, especially if you choose to teach in the lower grades. The Latin term *in loco parentis* translates to "in place of parents." Prospective teachers may not have considered this aspect of teaching. Some teachers are surprised to discover they have to compensate for indifferent and uninvolved parents. Of course, this is not specifically spelled out in your contract, but involved teachers have made a critical difference in many students' lives.

in loco parentis

A Latin term meaning "in place of parents."

> ## ❝ NOTABLE QUOTE
>
> Although it is less visible, less dramatic, and less commented upon than other social problems involving youth—crime, pregnancy, violence—student disengagement is more pervasive and in some ways potentially more harmful to the future well-being of American society. *(Laurence Steinberg)*

REFLECTION QUESTIONS

- From your experiences, what are the implications of "disengaged" youth?
  ....

- Were you ever a "disengaged" student? If so, how did you turn it around? Did a teacher or some other adult help you, or did you do it on your own?
  ....

- Describe how you will go about "engaging" your students so they will be more interested in school and academic achievement.
  ....

Societal Challenges and Implications for Teachers

To introduce this section, we allude to an article written by the editor of *Phi Delta Kappan*, Pauline Gough, in the April issue (1997). Of the 16 indicators that the Fordham Institute uses as an index of the status of our nation's social health, 11 indicators showed a dramatic decline since the 1970s. Indicators of particular concern to educators include (1) an increase in the number of teen suicides, (2) children living in poverty, (3) child abuse, and (4) families with inadequate health coverage. Evidence indicates that the chasm between the rich and the poor continues to widen, which suggests a poor prognosis.

Let's now consider a few of the many societal conditions that negatively affect students' mental and physical health, school achievement, motivation, and behavior.

Poverty

It is estimated that one out of five children in America lives in poverty. Poor children live in substandard housing, lack nutritious diets, lack adequate health care, and may have physical and dental problems. According to the U.S. Department of Commerce, Bureau of the Census, in 1970, 14.9% of children under 18 lived in poverty. In contrast, in 1994, 21.2% lived in poverty. Of the 21.2% living in poverty, 43.3 % are African-American, 41.1% are Hispanic, and 16.3% are Caucasian (U.S. Bureau of the Census, 1991). Research consistently finds a link between poverty and children's health, achievement, and behavior. Simply, the effects of poverty place children at risk mentally, intellectually, and physically. Our nation's poverty rate is higher than that of any other industrialized nation. Does that statement surprise you? Does it concern you?

Homelessness

Linked to poverty is the number of children who live on the streets. Homelessness is a disturbing social problem many of us would like to forget. It is

Web Site
The Southern Poverty Law Center has a web site that offers suggestions for curriculum and classroom activities. Check it out at http://www.splcenter.org/teaching tolerance/tt-index.html.

inconceivable to imagine that you might be teaching a child who has no home to return to at the end of the day. Many children who are homeless are being deprived of an education because families try to conceal their circumstances from authorities; many families live on the run or in seclusion. Some youth are "runaways" and survive by joining gangs of homeless kids. For these reasons, it is naturally hard to arrive at precise figures on the numbers of children who are homeless. It is estimated that over 40% of the homeless population are families; and about one million children are homeless.

The McKinney Education of Homeless Children and Youth Act (EHCY) was established by Congress in 1987 to respond to reports that as many as 50% of homeless children were not attending school. The McKinney program funds state and local educational agencies to provide access to schooling to homeless children. As a result, attendance has increased over the years. However, because of budget cuts, only about 3% of local agencies receive McKinney funds. If you would like more information, contact your state's coordinator for the education of homeless children and youth.

Web Site
To receive current information on the McKinney Education of Homeless Children and Youth program contact Barbara Duffield at nch@ari.net.

Implications for Teachers

Teachers can help students who live in poverty or are homeless by being sensitive to their situations. These students need a safe and supportive environment; schools can offer stability and hope. Sometimes, however, school personnel do not handle these issues delicately. Insensitivity could cause a child to detest coming to school. As you might surmise, many homeless children experience feelings of depression, alienation, and defeat. For example, completing homework assignments in a timely manner may be difficult for them.

Teachers should try to find out the living arrangements of their students so they can help students. One way to help is by informing the school's social worker, school counselor, or principal to discuss concerns about specific students. By the teacher informing the proper officials, the student and family might be able to get the assistance they need.

Sensitive teachers also make a point of finding out the living arrangements of their students so as not to embarrass a child needlessly. Let's say that a fourth grade teacher is unaware that one of her students is living in a homeless shelter and one day she asks the students to draw a picture of their house or bedroom. You can imagine the emotional pain this type of assignment would create for that child.

Caring teachers are careful not to show shock, pity, or disgust for a child's poverty. An excellent book written by Martin Haberman (1995) entitled *Star Teachers of Children in Poverty* describes attributes and practices of exemplary teachers who work with urban children. According to his research, successful teachers who work with children in poverty are "nonjudgmental" and "not moralistic"; they are not easily shocked by horrific events (p. 93). Star teachers continually ask themselves, "What can I do about this?" (p. 93).

Haberman (1995) recommends that new teachers confront their own biases about poverty and neglect before stepping into the classroom. Those individuals who do not want to work with impoverished children may need to reconsider teaching as a field.

Negative Peer Pressure

In accord with psychosocial development, adolescence is a time for experimentation. As students enter adolescent years, they are likely to try on new "adult" behaviors. Adolescents are encouraged to find their own identity during these teen years. However, many troubled and insecure youth, especially those who are not firmly grounded in their values and beliefs, may link up with the wrong crowd and become susceptible to peer pressure in order to gain acceptance.

A student, for example, might choose to conform to the expectations of peers rather than to school or parental expectations. One concern in today's society is the availability of illegal drugs. Substance abuse can be very destructive for young people who are struggling with identify issues. Drugs and alcohol can be highly dangerous and in some cases addictive. When teens are trying to fit into a group, they probably are not thinking about whether they could be vulnerable to addictions. Teens are prone to think they are "invincible" and nothing can hurt them, thus an innocent flirtation with alcohol or drugs could be the beginning of an addiction.

The bottom line is that when children are experimenting, they are gambling with high stakes. One never knows what combination of heredity and environment will leave them susceptible to addictive lifestyles and substances. The list of addictions is unlimited: eating disorders, gambling, alcohol, and drugs. A lack of impulse control can lead to reckless behavior such as speeding, driving under the influence of alcohol or drugs, refusing to use a seat belt, running stop signs, unprotected sex, and promiscuity (having sex with many partners). As expected, teens who are battling addictive behaviors will have little time or energy left for school-related activities. It should be noted, however, that not all peer pressure is negative. Some peer groups or cliques have many positive aspects; the degree of positive or negative influence mainly depends on the motives or purposes of the group.

Reflections from the Field

A high school art teacher from Poplar Bluff, Missouri, observed that in the past few years she has seen a marked change in students' attitudes. She attributes this positive attitude change to the fact that her school now allows a Christian youth organization to meet on school premises. Overall, this type of "peer influence" has helped many students who were aimless and unmotivated. She surmises that school morale improved significantly when restrictions against religious groups were lifted.

What do you think about the comments of the art teacher in *Reflections from the Field?* What about students in the school whose families are not Christian, such as children from Jewish families? Would these children feel left out if the "in group" belongs to the Christian organization? Would students feel pressured to join an organization, just to "fit in"? The bottom line is that peer pressure can be very powerful.

Implications for Teachers

To be safe, teachers who suspect that students may be associating with the wrong crowd, experimenting with illegal substances, or engaging in other dangerous behaviors should probably refer them to the school counselor. It may be prudent to talk over your concerns about a particular student with the counselor before speaking with that student. Older students may, for example, resist and perhaps resent a teacher's effort to help. However, a counselor can summon any student for consultation without informing the student of the referral source or the suspected concern. Depending on the circumstances, a report to social services may need to be made if a student's behavior is life threatening. The counselor or psychologist is trained to know what to do at this point.

Teen Pregnancy

Although the statistics indicate that teen pregnancy is lower today than in earlier decades, it is still considered a social problem that demands attention. In the 1950s, a teen mother was more likely to be married, and her husband was more likely to be able to support a family without a formal education. In contrast, today's teen mother is less likely to be married and is at greater risk for poverty. Health care is a critical issue for young mothers living in poverty. Proper prenatal and postnatal care may be non-existent for some teen mothers.

Implications for Teachers

The primary aim is to keep teen mothers in school. Some schools offer parenting classes for young mothers, and some offer day care and nurseries for the children of their students in an attempt to keep the mother in attendance.

Life skills training and sex education programs are prevention programs that can prepare young people for adult roles and responsibilities. Later in this chapter we address ways that the schools and community can link to provide better health care to young mothers.

Youth Violence and Anti-Social Behaviors

Youth violence is a major concern today. The National School Boards Association (1993) surveyed over 700 school districts and found that inadequate family guidance, glamorization of violence by the media, easy access to guns, substance abuse, and poverty were instrumental in aggravating crime. Young people who exhibit anti-social behavior are aggressive, disobedient, and defiant and will challenge social norms and mores (Walker, Colvin, & Ramsey, 1995).

Web Site
For more statistics regarding youth violence, check out http://www.aacap.org/.

Implications for Teachers

Fortunately, more than 78% of schools today have instituted school violence prevention programs (National Center for Educational Statistics, 1998), and the figure is climbing. To assist students who may become victims of violence or who are potential offenders, teachers and schools are beginning to solidify ties with the local police, juvenile detention officers, and social services representatives. Teachers can include conflict resolution as part of the curriculum they teach.

Web Site
There are many resources and web sites that attempt to teach non-violence and conflict resolution. For example, a student pledge against using guns as a means to settle disputes can be found at http://www.pledge.org/home.htm.

A caveat for future teachers may be in order here: Try not to take students' anti-social behavior personally; they are not angry at you (even though it feels like they are). Separate the behavior from the person. Do not show fear. Lastly, remember you did not cause the student's problems, so you must not accept the blame. Your primary responsibility lies in helping the child to feel safe, secure, and supported while under your care.

Depression: Teen Suicide

Excessive hopelessness and despair in children if left untreated can lead to clinical depression and sometimes to death. Teachers must be alert for signs of depression in their students. Regrettably, many children who are depressed go untreated because families either do not recognize the signs, or if they do, they are unable to provide proper assistance to their children. Parents may not know where to go for psychological services for their children. In addition, medical health insurance policies do not always provide equal benefits for mental health needs; often mental health coverage may be limited by managed care. Also, antidepressants are expensive.

Some depressed children go untreated because they were never properly diagnosed. Many adults tend to equate child pain with adult pain and fail to recognize the extent that a child is suffering. To a pubescent, the break-up of a relationship can be overwhelming; the loss of a pet may likewise cause distress for a child. A child's loss should not be judged by an adult's perceptions.

Depression sometimes goes untreated because some individuals believe that depression is a sign of personal weakness and can be overcome through sheer willpower. A limitation to this kind of thinking is that the person experiencing the depression may become even more despondent—thinking he or she is to blame for the condition. Believing depression is a character flaw or the sign of a weak person can heap more guilt on an already disheartened spirit.

Implications for Teachers

Do not judge a student's loss in terms of your own experiences with loss. For example, if a child returns to school after the funeral of a sibling, the teacher should not expect the same level of student performance as before the death. It is important to recognize the feelings the child is experiencing. Teachers need to acknowledge a child's grief and respect the pace of the child's grieving process—students and adults grieve differently and progress through different stages. Therefore teachers must be sensitive to students' concept of loss.

Teachers must also be sensitive to distinguish when a student's actions are pleas for help. All teachers need ongoing training about detecting suicidal behaviors. Teachers will need to feel comfortable asking students about their feelings. They must not assume that small children are immune from taking their own lives. If a teacher has reason to suspect a child is in imminent danger, he or she must report this immediately to the school principal or school counselor. The ethical and legal implications of this situation are discussed in Chapter 13.

Teachers must be watchful for the following warning signs in students and notice the extent to which these behaviors are exhibited:

❑ Depressed mood, lack of emotion

❑ Changes in sleep and/or appetite

❑ Limited coping skills

❑ Withdrawal from peers or few friends

❑ Lack of family support

❑ Difficulty interacting with teachers

❑ Excessive alcohol and substance abuse

❑ Overwhelming feelings of hopelessness, sadness, and despair

❑ Preoccupation with death

❑ Previous known suicide attempt(s)

❑ Risk-taking behaviors

❑ Psychosomatic illnesses

A final note: many homosexuals feel isolated and rejected by peers and family; therefore this group of students is at great risk for suicide. Some figures estimate that lesbian and gay students are two to six times more likely to attempt suicide, and they account for 30 percent of all successful suicide attempts. The bottom line is that teachers must be sensitive to signs of hopelessness in their students.

A CASE STUDY ....

A first-year teacher, Pedro, is worried about the behavior of one of his most promising students, June. June had always been very conscientious about grades. But now Pedro wishes she would challenge him over every incorrect test item (as she had consistently done in the past). Instead, she has lost interest in her grades and also in her appearance. It is unlike her to not care about her performance and grooming. One day Pedro overhears June boasting to her friends, "I don't care about that anyway; nothing matters to me anymore! What difference does it make?" In private, he asks June's friends if they have noticed a change in her attitude. They likewise voice similar concerns. They share with him that June has been making remarks such as, "My parents will be sorry when I'm gone" or "I'll show them." They assumed, however, these comments stemmed from her anger over her parents' pending divorce.

What would you do if you were this teacher? Do you think you should get involved, or is June just trying to get attention? Should we take seriously threats that appear to be idle? Do people who commit suicide talk about it in advance, or do they keep such suicidal thoughts to themselves? How would a teacher assess the degree of seriousness of June's remarks?

Classroom Teachers' Strategies

There are, of course, many school-age children who come from "relatively" healthy families, live in "relatively" healthy neighborhoods, and perhaps are less affected by societal pressures. But whether this is the norm or the exception to the rule is really a moot question; beginning teachers must acknowledge that not all of their students will arrive at school ready and eager to learn. If you are planning to teach, you should realize the "ideal" school with the "ideal" students may exist only in your imagination. Granted, some schools come *closer to* the ideal than others, but it is not smart to expect that your entire teaching career will be spent in those schools.

Over the last several years most of the schools where shootings have taken place were not in locales with high rates of violence. Quite the contrary, Westside Middle School, where two students killed four children and a teacher, is a small school in a quiet, rural community outside of Jonesboro, Arkansas. This is why we prefaced "healthy" with "relatively"—to note that there are no guarantees that violence will not erupt in the school you choose. Teachers must be willing to assist in efforts to reduce the impact of societal problems on young people.

Before moving on to consider what schools and communities can do as partners, we would like to summarize what things all teachers can do individually to make a difference in the personal and social lives of their students. Of course, there are no easy answers to problems students face, but there are many ways in which you can help.

Respecting Students

Respecting all students regardless of income, family background, gender, sexual orientation, minority status, or disability is imperative to empowering your students. In Chapter 3, we discussed the importance of developing caring relationships with students and how these positive interactions can reap positive student outcomes. Murphy (1997) suggests that one way to show respect for your students is "by enlisting students as consultants on their own school problems" (p. 161). Asking the student his or her opinion might improve the problem, makes the student responsible for the solution, and demonstrates that you think the student is capable of solving his or her own problems (Murphy, 1997). Even if it is cognitively beyond a student's ability to offer alternatives or solutions, the point is that the child was shown respect by the teacher.

Empathizing with Students

Empathizing with students dovetails with respecting students. However, do not confuse empathy with sympathy. Being sympathetic can be interpreted by the student as pity (which connotes defeat). For example, a teacher who continually rescues a child may inadvertently be giving the message that the child is incapable of overcoming adversity. Or a teacher who overly identifies with a student's distress may overcompensate by being too easy on the child. The student could misconstrue this to mean he or she is incapable and that the situation is truly hopeless. To illustrate, let's say that a teacher happens to know that one of his students lives with an alcoholic parent. Having been a child of an alcoholic parent, the teacher shelters this child and expects less from him. This teacher is fostering dependency by being overly protective, which is not constructive.

Some teachers, however, err on the side of being too hard on students who come from disadvantaged backgrounds or who are experiencing pain.

These teachers hold all students to the same measure of accountability, regardless of circumstances. They rigidly hold to the belief that all children must be treated the same. Thus they fail to make exceptions or accommodations for individual needs. In the case above, this teacher expects the student to perform just like the other children and does not make allowances for the situation. He expects the student to be in a good mood every day because that is what he demands for all students. Taking this position is also not helpful because it discounts the student's feelings.

Taking a Positive, Preventive Approach to Discipline

Taking a positive, preventive approach to discipline, as discussed in Chapter 9, will avert most behavioral problems and foster student responsibility. Simply put, when teachers focus on positive instead of negative student behaviors, fewer discipline problems arise. Preventive, positive strategies have been shown to work even with the most challenging students. Therefore a proactive approach rather than a reactive approach is the optimal way to teach students self-management skills.

Modeling Self-Discipline

Modeling self-discipline for students helps them learn the basic life skills they will need to be self-sufficient and productive citizens. As previously mentioned, many children who are being raised in chaotic homes and neighborhoods do not observe good examples of responsible behavior. By default then, teachers become role models to their students. Therefore they must demonstrate self-discipline and responsibility in their actions. Many children do not learn these life skills at home; therefore teachers must be willing to help students acquire essential behaviors.

Consulting with the School Counselor

Working with the school counselor is a viable way to assist students who may need counseling services and guidance. Because of the enormous societal pressures on young people, in addition to high counselor to student ratios, it is impossible for one mental health professional to meet the full range of psychological needs present among today's children. Hence, an efficient and effective approach is for the counselor and teacher to work collaboratively to help those children whose cognitive, social, and behavioral problems interfere with their ability to learn. One effective plan for making this happen is to set up a comprehensive developmental guidance program in a school that designates all school personnel as playing a critical role in the personal, social, and academic lives of students (Myrick, 1993).

We will return to this concept shortly in the discussion of teacher advisory programs.

Adopting a Constructivist Teaching Approach

Adopting a constructivist approach to teaching focuses on the learner's developmental needs, interests, and abilities when planning and delivering instruction. The teacher's role becomes more of a facilitator than a dispenser of knowledge. Constructivist teachers encourage students to find meaning in what they are being taught. Teaching students higher-order thinking skills such as critical thinking and problem solving can be beneficial to students as they deal with peer pressure and other societal demands.

Teaching Character Education

character education

Movement that encourages schools to teach good character traits and values to students.

Teaching **character education** to students is an important affective goal. A study published in 1999 entitled: *Teachers as Educators of Character: Are the Nation's Schools of Education Coming Up Short?* underscored the importance of "developing teachers as character educators" (Jones, Ryan, & Bohlin,1999, p. 20). Over 90% of teacher educators in the sample supported "character education" and agreed that "core values can and should be taught in schools" (Jones, Ryan, & Bohlin, 1999, p. 7).

The Character Education Partnership (CEP) is a national nonprofit coalition of more than 600 organizations and individuals whose aim is to encourage teachers to instruct and model positive character traits to their students. It does not promote a single curriculum or pedagogy for character education. The aim is to create a new generation of "character educators" in schools. You may want to join CEP as a way to lend support to its mission. To learn more about character education, we suggest you read *Teachers as Educators of Character: Are the Nation's Schools of Education Coming Up Short?* (Jones, Ryan, & Bohlin, 1999).

 **Web Site**
To order copies of this report, e-mail the Character Education Partnership at geninfo@character.org or call 1-800-988-8081.

 You can contact the Center for the Advancement of Ethics and Character, Boston University, at 605 Commonwealth Avenue, Boston, Massachusetts 02215. Or visit the Center's web site at: http://education.bu.edu/charactered.

> ❝ **NOTABLE QUOTE**
>
> . . . [A] child who is sick, tired, hungry, or abused will find it difficult, even perhaps impossible, to be a confident, self-directed learner. And responding to the physical and emotional needs of children is both the educational and ethical thing to do. *(Ernest Boyer)* ❞

Collective Strategies: Schools and Community

The next section considers how schools can help students deal with problems in their homes and neighborhoods. Fortunately, for the school that adopts a proactive attitude there are many positive interventions that can be used with its students. The strategies we suggest can help students be better prepared to handle societal pressures and cope with personal problems they may have.

Promoting Partnerships with Parents

As discussed in Chapter 3, the need to involve parents in the schooling of their children is paramount. A school that has had great success involving parents in the education of their children is the Comer School initiated by James Comer in 1968. As director of the School Development Program at the Yale Child Study Center, Comer is a leading child advocate and prolific writer on child development. Comer was raised in an East Chicago black community, in a family with neither money nor education. Despite these obstacles, Comer became a professor and an associate dean of the Yale Medical School. When Comer was asked to collaborate with the New Haven Public Schools to reform inner-city schools, he drew from his experience as a student.

Since its inception the Comer School Development Program, more recently called the Comer Project for Change in Education, has become a model for other schools to emulate. The Comer model demonstrates the importance of collaborating with parents, teachers, school staff, officials, and community members to successfully operate a school. Comer believes that the key to successful schooling is the cooperative relationship between the parent and the teacher (Comer, 1988). From his experiences, Comer concludes that all children can experience success if adults in their lives take the time to create a healthy climate.

The school designed for the special needs of disadvantaged children quickly became recognized as a prototype that would work with children from all socioeconomic backgrounds. Today, James Comer's School Development Program is the model used in many schools across the nation. We suggest that you read, *Rallying the Whole Village: The Comer Process for Reforming Education* (Comer, Haynes, Joyner, and Ben-Avie, 1996) for information on the success of the Comer's School Development Program on educational reform.

Another model worth emulating is The Basic School, which is an idea about how elementary schools should function. Ernest Boyer, in his book, *The Basic School: A Community for Learning* (1995), outlines priorities for effective elementary education: community, curriculum coherence, climate, and character. A vital connection is made to embrace parents in the education of their children; this partnership starts during the preschool years and continues through fifth grade. The conclusions drawn by The Carnegie Foundation for the Advancement of Teaching suggests a minimum of four parent-teacher conferences per year. Another idea is a "parent place," where parents are free to meet. Schools should keep a current list of parents who have skills or expertise that can be drawn upon to benefit the school's program. If you are contemplating elementary education, we suggest you read Boyer's book, *The Basic School: A Community for Learning* (1995).

Supporting a Multicultural Curriculum

As we will see in the coming chapter, the prevalence of culturally diverse classrooms in the 21st century indicates a need to develop a curriculum that reflects the makeup of our society. If school officials fail to acknowledge this need, the curricula will probably remain predominately Euro-American (i.e., monocultural), which could result in some students feeling estranged from the educational system. Feeling like outsiders, they could dissociate from the activity of the classroom. It is essential that all ethnic and cultural groups are able to identify in some way with the content that is being taught. Students need to feel a kinship to what is being taught in schools. One way teachers can do this is by selecting poems for the poetry unit from a diverse group of authors. Furthermore, the curriculum should avoid perpetuating gender biases. In fact, any group bias or form of negative stereotyping should be eliminated.

Using Students as Peer Facilitators

peer facilitators

A concept in which students help other students solve problem situations.

The idea of peers helping peers is not really a new concept, but the increase in the number of programs of its kind has been rather recent. These programs use a variety of names for student helpers, such as **peer facilitators**, peer mediators, special friends, group leaders, tutors, and guidance assistants. What we call these peer assistants is not nearly as important as what they do. Basically, students are selected, trained, and supervised by teachers and counselors to provide assistance to other students who are in need. Once prepared, these helpers can be invaluable to teachers and counselors who cannot find the time to work individually with all students.

Students learning from each other has proven to be an effective way to teach.

© Michael Newman/PhotoEdit

By the way, using peers to help peers benefits both parties. Most students consider it an honor to be chosen to be a peer helper; it demonstrates that those students can handle major responsibilities. Peer helpers take on leadership roles; for example, they can orient new students to the school and help current students who are having difficulty with their schoolwork or with personal demands.

The time spent coordinating these kinds of programs is time well spent. Peer assistance programs have been found to be effective with all ages and in all grades. Even the most disruptive and non-compliant students have benefited from being selected to assume leadership roles such as peer facilitators (Glasser, 1990). The literature is replete with fine programs to emulate. Or teachers, administrators, and counselors could collaboratively design a program tailored to their students' needs.

Implementing a Teacher Advisory Program

A noteworthy trend in middle schools today is the number of teacher-advisor programs (TAP) being implemented. Teacher-advisor programs are known by a variety of names such as advisor/advisee, home base, or home room (Mauk & Taylor, 1993). It should be noted that teacher-advisor programs can be instituted at any grade level. The premise is that every student needs an adult friend at school who will advocate for him or her; the teacher plays that role. These teacher-advisor programs have been endorsed by the National Middle School Association and the National Association of Secondary School Principals (NASSP, 1996) and are frequently cited in the respective professional journals (Galassi & Gulledge, 1997).

Teacher-advisor programs are rooted in the belief that counseling is everyone's job in a school and that teachers are critical to the success of any developmental guidance program (Galassi & Gulledge, 1997). Myrick (1993) recommends the school counselor as the one to coordinate this program. Counselors in the school provide the leadership, inservice training, and relevant materials to teachers.

A teacher-advisor program is organized around a guidance curriculum, with the ultimate goal to help students learn more effectively and efficiently (Myrick, 1993). The teacher implements the comprehensive developmental guidance program. The school counselor and the classroom teacher combine their talents and skills to assist as students negotiate developmental issues. Comprehensive school guidance programs can help children develop social skills through group counseling and classroom guidance activities (Horton-Parker, 1998). School counselors can provide curriculum assistance geared toward helping students resist violence and learn peaceful means to resolve conflict.

Enlisting Volunteers from the Community

Another way that schools can help students is by reaching out to the community for help. There are many untapped sources that could aid in this

Volunteers from the community have an array of talents to offer to schools.

venture. For example, many elderly people would love the opportunity to make a difference in schools today, but they do not know how. Because longevity has increased, there are many mentally alert and physically active senior citizens who would be glad to help if they were asked. Schools need to seek out those people in the community who would like to volunteer as mentors and teaching assistants.

Reciprocating Services with the Community

Having established the need for schools to reach out to the community (private and public sectors) for help, we also must realize that this is a two-way street: we need the community and the community needs us. Schools must strengthen their neighborhood ties with local mental health agencies and other community-based outreach programs and facilities that provide assistance to school-age children.

Some schools have already developed elaborate networks with community agencies that serve their children. Many children today need individualized instruction and intensive counseling in a structured, therapeutic milieu in order to survive. Some private hospitals and public clinics offer inpatient and outpatient services to these students. Alternative schools and residential treatment settings can offer assistance to students who are unable to function in a regular school setting.

School personnel are increasingly being asked to serve on youth boards, action groups, and other grassroots coalitions that are combating societal problems. The unique talents and skills schools can bring to these efforts are indispensable. Solving the problems children bring to the classroom requires a cooperative, collaborative effort that is school-wide and community-based. This leads to the next section, which addresses specific ways schools can become actively involved in community efforts that target young people.

Civic leaders are beginning to become more aware of the important role teachers and schools can play in community-based projects aimed at helping young people. In recent years "a coordinated school health initiative has emerged in response to the state of affairs in children's health and education" (Tyson, 1999, p. 3). The underlying goal of a comprehensive health program is to improve the health and well-being of students and develop social competencies and skills that will help students function successfully in life. Every child should have knowledge of and access to health-related services such as nutritional experts, counselors, psychologists, social workers, physicians, nurses, and dentists.

school health programs

Partnership between school and community that provides comprehensive health services to schoolchildren.

School health programs must solicit assistance from the community in order to achieve a successful comprehensive enterprise. School administrators must spearhead the movement by asking school personnel, parents, community leaders, and health services staff to participate. The purpose of a school health program is to improve the overall mental and physical health of the students through a dynamic partnership with the community.

The school environment must be conducive to good health. For example, the cafeteria should offer nutritious and appetizing foods that meet U.S. Dietary Guidelines for Americans. The school facility should promote health. This means, for example, that the physical environment is free from toxic chemicals such as lead, noxious odors, excessive noise, inadequate lighting, and extremes in temperature.

full-service community schools

An outgrowth of school-based health clinics that expands health services for children.

Many states have initiated the creation of **full-service community schools.** This concept grew out of the school health clinics, or school-based clinics, in the 1980s (Dryfoos,1994). Full-service implies a broader definition of the concept of school health programs (Dryfoos,1994). The full-service model naturally depends on the good will of community agencies. To illustrate, in areas where parents are least likely to be able to afford good health care for their children, community health agencies would set up clinics in schools. You may be familiar with these clinics; they may be called school-based clinics or primary health care centers (Dryfoos, 1994). Educational reform efforts (which we discuss in more depth in later chapters) has incorporated "access to health services" as an integral part of school change.

Implications for Teachers

Along with the obvious benefit of improved health care for students, there are other advantages to full-service schools. The overall health of all participants will likely be improved by this community effort. Any attempt to promote healthy living yields positive results for all involved. For example, healthy teachers are happier, are more energetic, and exhibit more favorable attitudes and behaviors. Simply, those teachers who are healthy are in a better position to help their students enhance the quality of their lives.

NOTABLE QUOTE

If all socializing systems in a community share a commitment to a vision of healthy development, each can see its own niche in the larger vision. Everyone doesn't have to do everything, but all recognize that they are on the same team, working for the good of young people, rather than vying for attention for their particular agenda. *(Peter L. Benson)*

By including parents in this venture, some otherwise "disengaged" parents may become involved. When the community is involved, public relations should improve. Taxpayers may appreciate the school's interest in the health of its students. Alliances with private and public sectors can provide much needed resources and services. Individuals from the community can be appointed to committees or serve on boards which influence policies.

A cautionary note is needed here: Turf issues can be detrimental to the overall goal of improving the plight of children. In-fighting about whose responsibility it is to address students' emotional needs is a no-win proposition. When professionals draw rigid lines and claim that only "they" have the credentials and training to help distressed youth, the student is not helped but hurt. We should work as a team; we need as many dedicated persons as possible to aid in this endeavor. Let's welcome any professional group who has the welfare of children at heart, including custodians, cafeteria workers, security officers, and so on.

AssessYourself

As we have seen, teachers need to be socially attuned to the needs of the communities where their students live. To be socially attentive demands time, effort, and commitment. Do you think you would be willing to help students negotiate problems stemming from their homes or neighborhoods?

How do you feel about volunteering service to the community? Would you respond if asked? Or would you be too exhausted at the end of a day to even consider volunteering your time?

Federal Government's Response to At-Risk Students

compensatory education
Federal programs to help schoolchildren overcome social and economic barriers.

Many federal programs have been developed to better serve the special needs of "at-risk" students. Generally these programs designed to help schoolchildren overcome social and economic barriers are referred to as **compensatory education.** Compensatory programs try to "compensate" for the ill effects of

GREAT TEACHERS

Ernest L. Boyer

Ernest Boyer was born in Dayton, Ohio on September 13, 1928, and died on December 8, 1995. Boyer earned his Ph.D. from the University of Southern California in 1957. During his career he held many positions in education and served as chancellor of State University of New York from 1970 to 1977. Boyer became well known as Commissioner of Education under the Carter Administration. He left that position to become president of the Carnegie Foundation for the Advancement of Teaching. Boyer was named Educator of the Year by *U.S. News and World Report* in 1990.

In 1995, Boyer laid the foundation for school reform in a report that focused on elementary education: *The Basic School: A Community for Learning.* He named the school "basic" because its program pushes for educational reform to begin in the early years of schooling. "And in the Basic School, the circle of community, which begins with the principal, teachers, and students, quickly extends outward to embrace the family" (Boyer, 1995, p. 47). Boyer's Basic School designates four priorities for quality education: (1) the school as a community, (2) a climate for learning, (3) a curriculum with coherence, and (4) a commitment to character.

Head Start

A federally funded preschool program that provides enrichment opportunities to children of low-income families.

bilingual education

Instructional method that allows non–English-speaking students to receive instruction in their native language while learning English.

Bilingual Education Act

Law passed by the U.S. Congress in 1968 that allocates funds to schools to establish English as a Second Language (ESL) programs.

poverty, neglect, and other forms of deprivation. The goal is to ensure that all children have access to equal educational opportunities. To make up for cultural and economic disparity, federal compensatory programs such as Head Start, Title I, free lunch programs, and school-to-work programs have been developed to target at-risk children. Many of these programs are discussed in detail in later chapters.

Compensatory education programs are based on the premise that disadvantaged children can learn if they are provided with interventions that will remedy (remediate) an inadequate beginning. **Head Start** is a familiar preschool program that has met with success over the years. Funded by the federal government in the mid-1960s, this project was designed to give students from low-income families a "head start" that they might have missed because of a limited environment. Of course, it does not give them an advantage over children from enriched environments, but it does attempt to decrease the disparity.

Bilingual education is another type of compensatory educational program implemented in schools to teach non–English-speaking students. Students whose native language is not English will clearly be at risk in the classroom. Thus in 1968 the U.S. Congress passed the **Bilingual Education Act**,

Children learn basic skills at a Head Start program.

© Elizabeth Crews

English as a Second Language (ESL)

An instructional method of teaching English to non–English speaking students.

which allocates funds to schools to set up **English as a Second Language (ESL)** programs to assist bilingual students. There is some debate as to the best way to teach English. Some believe that keeping students in the regular classroom is the most effective way for them to learn English; this is called the "submersion model." The "English as a second language model" keeps students in a regular class with peers most of the day, but perhaps pulls them out for special instruction during certain periods. (There is a shortage of ESL teachers; you might want to consider becoming proficient in another language.)

By far the most comprehensive federal legislation that helps children compensate for the adverse effects of social and economic deprivation is the **Elementary and Secondary Education Act (ESEA).** Much of the ESEA's budget is reserved for schools in low-income areas that are willing to offer compensatory programs to disadvantaged students. Students from low-income families are labeled as "educationally deprived" and are entitled to compensatory programs such as **Title I** of ESEA. Schools that qualify under federal guidelines can receive funding if they agree to provide these services to disadvantaged students. Compensatory education is discussed further in Chapter 7, Historical Perspective.

Elementary and Secondary Education Act (ESEA)

Legislation passed in 1965 for federal funding for schools; it provides for compensatory programs in low-income areas.

Title I

Federal assistance for schools with a large number of children from low-income families.

The National Institute on the Education of At-Risk Students (At-Risk Institute) was established by the Educational Research, Development, Dissemination and Improvement Act of 1994. Housed in the Office of Educational Research and Improvement at the U.S. Department of Education, the At-Risk Institute attempts to improve the education of students at risk because

Threats to cut education programs—especially bilingual programs—have triggered protests.

© Mary Kate Denny/PhotoEdit

Web Site
Visit the At-Risk Institute's web site at http://www.ed.gov/offices/OERI/At-Risk.

of limited English proficiency, poverty, race, geographic location, or economic disadvantage.*

> " **NOTABLE QUOTE**
>
> Whenever there is a disparity of power between groups . . . the group with the most power must make the greatest effort to overcome the real and potential obstacles to creating a desirable relationship. *(James Comer)*
> "

Conclusion

As we have seen, students bring a host of problems to school today. In this chapter, we examined how individual teachers can make a difference in the lives of their students. You were cautioned, however, against becoming too involved with or too detached from your students' problems. Either extreme can be ineffectual and counterproductive in bolstering a child's confidence and willpower. Conversely, a more helpful response is to believe that a child can overcome even an adverse situation by drawing on personal strengths and resources. Recognizing that you are not responsible for your students'

*Contact U.S. Department of Education, OERI/At-Risk, Room 610, 555 New Jersey Avenue, NW, Washington, D.C. 20208-5521.

situations outside of school is the first step to their empowerment. Our responsibility lies in being willing to prepare our students to handle life's adversities and supporting them in the process. A teacher can begin by treating every child in class with respect and kindness. And a teacher can provide relevant instruction that will equip students with practical skills for handling life's challenges.

In this chapter, we explored how teachers can join forces with other concerned individuals and groups to make a difference in the community. For example, a coordinated school health program and full-service school were presented as ways to improve students' mental and physical health and consequently their performance. Other suggestions showed how concerted efforts can help make a difference in community problems.

Our intention is to portray a realistic picture of the effects society and family have on students and how this in turn affects your job as a teacher. In the process we hope we did not discourage you from pursuing teaching as a career. We believe that knowledge is power, and if you are fully aware of the impact of outside influences on student behavior and learning, you will be in a better position to combat these problems.

KEY TERMS

at-risk students

authoritarian parents

authoritative parents

bilingual education

Bilingual Education Act

character education

compensatory education

disengaged students

Elementary and Secondary Education Act (ESEA)

engaged students

English as a Second Language (ESL)

full-service community schools

Head Start

in loco parentis

nuclear family

peer facilitators

permissive parents

resilient

school health programs

Title I

uninvolved parents

SUGGESTED READING

Benson, P. L. (1997). *All kids are our kids: What communities must do to raise caring and responsible children and adolescents.* San Francisco: Jossey-Bass

Dryfoos, J. G. (1994). *Full service schools: A revolution in health and social services for children, youth, and families.* San Francisco: Jossey-Bass.

Jones, E. N., Ryan, K., & Bohlin, K. E. (April 1999). *Teachers as educators of character: Are the nation's schools of education coming up short?* Washington, D.C.: Character Education Partnership.

REFERENCES

Baumrind, D. (1967). Child care practices anteceding three patterns of preschool behavior. *Genetic Psychology Monographs, 75,* 43–88.

Baumrind, D. (1971). Current patterns of parental authority. *Developmental Psychology Monograph, 4,* 1–103.

Baumrind, D. (1991). The influence of parenting style on adolescent competence and substance use. *Journal of Early Adolescence, 11,* 56–95.

Benson, P. L. (1997). *All kids are our kids: What communities must do to raise caring and responsible children and adolescents.* San Francisco: Jossey-Bass

Boyer, E. L. (1995). *The basic school: A community for learning.* Princeton, NJ: The Carnegie Foundation for the Advancement of Teaching.

Comer, J. P., Haynes, N. M., Joyner, E. T., & Ben-Avie, M. (1996) *Rallying the whole village: The Comer process for reforming education.* New York: Teachers College Press.

Comer, J. P. (1988). Is "parenting" essential to good teaching? *NEA Today, 6,* 34–40.

Darling-Hammond, L. (1997). *The right to learn: A blueprint for creating schools that work.* San Francisco: Jossey-Bass.

Dornbusch, S., Ritter, P., Leiderman, P., Roberts, D., & Fraleigh, M. (1987). The relation of parenting style to adolescent school performance. *Child Development, 58,* 1244–1257.

Dryfoos, J. G. (1994). *Full service schools: A revolution in health and social services for children, youth, and families.* San Francisco: Jossey-Bass.

Falk, P. J. (1989). Lesbian mothers: Psychosocial assumptions in family law. *American Psychologist, 44*(6), 941–947.

Galassi, J. P., & Gulledge, S. A. (1997). The middle school counselor and teacher-advisor programs. *Professional School Counseling, 1*(2) 55–60.

Glasser, W. (1990). *The quality school: Managing students without coercion.* New York: Harper-Collins.

Gough, P. B. (1997). Editor's Page: A transfusion for democracy. *Phi Delta Kappan, 78*(8), 590.

Haberman, M. (1995). *Star teachers of children in poverty.* West Lafayette, IN: Kappa Delta Pi.

Hendren, R. L. (1994). *HealthWise: A Bulletin for School Health, 13*(2), 1–2.

Horton-Parker, R. J. (1998). Teaching children to care: Engendering prosocial behavior through humanistic parenting. *Journal of Humanistic Education and Development, 37,* 66–77.

Jones, E. N., Ryan, K. & Bohlin, K. E. (April 1999). *Teachers as educators of character: Are the nation's schools of education coming up short?* Washington, D.C.: Character Education Partnership.

Lamborn, S. D., Mounts, N. S., Steinberg, L., & Dornbusch, S. M. (1991). Patterns of competence and adjustment among adolescents from authoritative, authoritarian, indulgent, and neglectful families. *Child Development, 60,* 25–39.

Mauk, G. W., & Taylor, M. J. (1993). Counselors in middle level schools: Issues of recognition, reclaiming, redefinition and rededication. *Middle School Journal, 24*(5), 3–9.

Maccoby, E. E., & Martin, J. A. (1983). Socialization in the context of the family: Parent-child interaction. In P. H. Mussen (Series Ed.) & E. M. Hetherington (Vol. Ed.), *Handbook of child psychology: Vol. 4, Socialization, personality, and social development* (4th ed.) (pp. 1–101). New York: Wiley.

Murphy, J. J. (1997). *Solution-focused counseling in middle and high schools.* Alexandria, VA: American Counseling Association.

Myrick, R. D. (1993). *Developmental guidance and counseling: A practical approach* (2nd ed.). Minneapolis, MN: Educational Media Corporation.

National Association of Secondary School Principals. (1996). *Breaking Ranks: Changing an American Institution.* Reston, VA: Author.

National School Boards Association. (January 1993). Report of the National School Boards Association on Violence in Schools. *The Los Angeles Times.*

Search Institute. (1997). *The asset approach: Giving kids what they need to succeed.* Minneapolis, MN: Author.

Steinberg, L. (1990). Interdependence in the family: Autonomy, conflict, and harmony in the parent-adolescent relationship. In S. S. Feldman & G. R. Elliot (Eds.), *At the threshold: The developing adolescent* (pp. 255–276). Cambridge, MA: Harvard University Press.

Steinberg, L., Brown B. B, and Dornbusch, S. M. (1996). *Beyond the classroom: Why school reform has failed and what parents need to do.* New York: Touchstone Book, Simon & Schuster.

Tyson, H. (1999). A load off the teachers' backs: Coordinated school health programs. *Phi Delta Kappan, 80*(5), 1–8.

U.S. Department of Commerce, Bureau of the Census. (1991). *Characteristics of the Population Below the Poverty Level.* Current Population Reports, Series P-20. no. 181.

U.S. Department of Education. (1997). *Meeting the needs of homeless children and youth: A resource for schools and communities.* U.S. Department of Education, Compensatory Education Programs Office of Elementary and Secondary Education. Washington, D.C.

Walker, H. M., Colvin, G., & Ramsey, E. (1995). *Antisocial behavior in schools: Strategies and best practices.* Pacific Grove, CA: Brooks/Cole.

Weiss, B., Dodge, K. A, Bates, J. E., & Pettit, G. S. (1992). Some consequences of early harsh discipline: Child aggression and a maladaptive social information processing style. *Child Development, 63,* 1321–1335.

© Bruce Forster/STONE

At the end of this chapter, you will be able to

● Define terminology associated with cultural diversity.

● Identify minority groups and other underrepresented groups and distinguish commonalities.

● List major categories of student diversity and implications for teachers.

● Describe attitudes, competencies, and strategies needed to work well with diverse student populations.

● Describe ways you might differ from your students and identify personal biases that could affect your effectiveness working with students.

CHAPTER 5

Diversity in Schools

A bird's eye view of what to expect in this chapter

It has been projected that in the 21st century the minority student populations will be the majority, particularly in urban schools. In light of this projection, future teachers must be receptive to learning all they can about the diversity (pluralism) that exists in modern classrooms. When we speak of "diversity," we tend to think of ethnicity or race. And although these are factors of diversity, it is a rather limited view of the range of diversity found in today's schools and communities. In actuality, teachers must be prepared and willing to work with a myriad of differences, including differences in language, learning style, gender, sexual orientation, social class, and disability.

Of course, it would be impossible to discuss in a single chapter all the categories of student diversity teachers will face in schools, nor discuss ways to adequately address those variations. However, we hope that the information presented here will help you recognize and plan for student diversity. As you become more aware of and sensitive to individual differences, we ask that you reflect on attitudes and competencies that teachers should develop. Pertinent questions for you to answer might be: In what ways might you be perceived as "different" from the students you teach? How might this affect your ability to work with them? And lastly, what would you do about it?

Differences among students make teaching interesting. Student differences are not the problem; rather it is how differences are perceived that counts. To those who see differences in a positive light, the notion of diversity is exciting and educational. We hope that by the end of this chapter you will have a greater understanding of and appreciation for students who are different.

As you read this chapter consider these questions: What attitudes and competencies are required to be effective with students? How does your cultural background enter into this picture? How does one become culturally sensitive to the needs of students? With this in mind, read the following case study to gain an understanding of why it is important for prospective teachers to learn all they can about cultural and ethnic differences before their first classroom experience.

A CASE STUDY ....

Alicia is a "typical" graduate of a typical teacher education program in the United States: Caucasian, middle class, female. Graduation was an exciting event for Alicia as she looked forward to entering the teaching arena as a certified professional. The job search was not too stressful for her because she had the foresight to begin the process early. Before graduation, she interviewed for a teaching position in a school near her hometown. She received stellar recommendations from her field placement teachers and university supervisors.

Two weeks after the interview, however, Alicia was informed she did not get the job. Disappointed, but not defeated, Alicia began pursuing other job possibilities. Three weeks before the end of summer, she was hired as a fifth-grade teacher in an urban school located four hours from her hometown. She accepted the position even though this meant moving to an unfamiliar area. Despite the inconvenience, she eagerly anticipated her first teaching experience.

During orientation she is informed that she will teach a fifth-grade class of 24 students (14 boys and 10 girls). Ten of the students are African American, three Asian, five Hispanic, two Native American, and four Caucasian. On the surface, Alicia is not disturbed or deterred by this mix. She is, however, conscious of the fact that she has had few (if any) encounters with students who are not like her. "I can do this," she repeats silently to herself, as her students file into the classroom on that very important first day. She greets her students with a smile and notices immediately that some do not respond. She later realizes that two of her Asian students are struggling with the English language. She also observes that the Native American students distance themselves from the other students in the room.

During lunch Alicia confides to her mentor, "Perhaps this will be harder than I anticipated. I really don't know much about my students. I wish I had more experience working with culturally diverse students." Apparently Alicia was not sufficiently prepared for the challenges of a culturally diverse classroom.

The Need for Culturally Sensitive Teachers

A multitude of differences is found among students today. Liberal immigration laws have resulted in an influx of school-age children who speak languages other than English (Table 5-1). It has been estimated that there

Table 5-1	Percentage Distribution of Enrollment in Public Elementary and Secondary Schools by Race/Ethnicity: 1976-1995									
Race/ Ethnicity	1976	1984	1986	1988	1990	1992*	1993*	1994*	1995*	1976–1995 (Change in percentage points)
Total	100.0	100.0	100.0	100.0	100.0	100.0	100.0	100.0	100.0	—
White, non-Hispanic	76.0	71.2	70.4	70.7	67.8	66.7	66.1	65.6	64.8	−11.2
Total minority	24.0	28.8	29.6	29.3	32.1	33.3	34.0	34.4	35.1	11.1
Black, non-Hispanic	15.5	16.2	16.1	15.2	16.2	16.5	16.6	16.7	16.8	1.3
Hispanic	6.4	9.1	9.9	10.1	11.5	12.3	12.7	13.0	13.5	7.1
Asian/ Pacific Islander	1.2	2.5	2.8	3.1	3.4	3.5	3.6	3.6	3.7	2.5
American Indian/ Alaskan Native	0.8	0.9	0.9	0.9	1.0	1.0	1.1	1.1	1.1	0.3

— = Not applicable.

*Data are from the Common Core of Data (CCD) survey.

NOTE: Data shown in this table are taken from surveys other than the Current Population Surveys (CPS) and are not comparable to the data in other tables of this analysis. Enrollment includes kindergarten students and a small number of pre-kindergarten students. Details may not add to totals because of rounding.

Source: U.S. Department of Education, Office for Civil Rights, Elementary and Secondary School Civil Rights Survey, 1976, 1984, 1986, 1988, and 1990; National Center for Education Statistics, Common Core of Data survey, 1992; and Digest of Education Statistics, 1995, 1996, and 1997, Table 45.

are more than 150 different languages spoken among students in the United States (Wiseman, Cooner, & Knight, 1999). Figures such as this demonstrate the significance of teachers being "culturally sensitive." Each day students come to school with "invisible baggage," which Bennett and LeCompte (1990) label *cultural capital* (e.g., unique background, knowledge, and skills passed from one generation to the next, which varies based on the economic and social status of the family). Some of these students will discover that their capital (*stock*) is undervalued, depending on the cultural norms of a particular school and the attitudes of teachers they encounter.

The majority of those entering teaching represent white, middle-class America, therefore "cultural clashes" are inevitable (Segall & Wilson, 1998). Many teachers, like Alicia, may have had limited field experience in multicultural settings. Without this exposure, a European-American teacher might make erroneous, possibly harmful, assumptions about students. For example, Alicia might mistakenly conclude that those students who respond in short phrases or speak in dialects are less capable than the other students. Or she may infer that students who avoid eye contact with her are less cooperative and respectful. All of these mistaken assumptions have the potential to undermine her students' success.

However, if teacher candidates are open to learning about the cultural backgrounds of their students, these kinds of misconceptions are less likely to occur. Hopefully, this chapter will remind you of the importance of these issues, and you will begin to prepare for and seek out opportunities that will broaden your understanding of diversity.

REFLECTION QUESTIONS

- Field experiences in multicultural settings would be the best place to expand your current knowledge base and develop cross-cultural skills. To do this you might begin by contacting peers in your education program who have had field experiences in multicultural settings. Then compile a list of possible field-based sites and student teaching sites.

- Identify those school settings you believe would offer optimal exposure to students who are culturally different from you. Explain your rationale for choosing those school settings.

- What specifically do you plan to do now that will better prepare you for diversity among your students?

- In what ways can you widen your lens to encompass a world view instead of a monocultural view?

Interpreting Diversity in America

Diversity, in and of itself, is certainly not new to America. Historically, from the early entrance of European explorers to this continent there has been a cultural mix. Even among Native Americans, tribal differences are prevalent in customs and languages. As a nation we have interpreted this diversity in various ways.

Melting Pot Metaphor

melting pot metaphor
An interpretation of diversity which suggests that various ethnic groups allowed their cultures to be absorbed into a single "American" culture.

Initially a **melting pot metaphor** was used to describe the cultural interaction in the United States (Glazer & Moynihan, 1970). This metaphor suggests that the various ethnic groups allowed their culture to become absorbed into a single "American" culture. As you can see, this is not exactly accurate because many ethnic groups resisted assimilation and tried to retain old-world customs, traditions, languages, and dialects. Jewish, Italian, and Irish immigrants in New York City are examples of cultural groups who resisted becoming "Americanized." Furthermore, endorsing a melting pot theory suggests that each ethnic group or nationality lost its identity to some degree. Yet by all indications, the European-American culture has remained virtually unchanged and continues to be the dominant culture.

Salad Bowl Metaphor

salad bowl metaphor
An interpretation of diversity that suggests that various ethnic groups live side by side without compromising unique cultural differences.

Some believe that a more accurate descriptor of American diversity is the **salad bowl metaphor** (McCormick, 1984). This metaphor suggests that varied ethnic groups live side by side but maintain individual differences specific to their culture. This perspective embraces "differences" as positive traits that enrich our American society (Manning & Baruth, 1996). But critics of the salad bowl metaphor claim it fails to acknowledge inevitable and subtle changes in cultural patterns that occur over time through interaction.

Kaleidoscope Metaphor

kaleidoscope metaphor
An interpretation of diversity that describes the "American" culture as dynamic, fluid, and evolving.

Consequently a more recent interpretation describes American diversity using the **kaleidoscope metaphor** (Fuch, 1990). This metaphor describes American culture as continually shifting and splintering, producing dynamic and evolving patterns like those viewed through a kaleidoscope. American diversity is pictured as the patterns reflected in the kaleidoscope, with every nuance and twist producing a new and beautiful configuration. Both the kaleidoscope and salad bowl metaphors underscore the need to develop teachers who are sensitive, flexible, and capable of appreciating and adapting to the various cultural and ethnic groups found among our people (and our children).

Definitions of Culture, Ethnicity, and Race

culture

Patterns of behavior and customs including knowledge, beliefs, values, art, and morals.

It is important to distinguish among culture, ethnicity, and race. Anthropologists define **culture** in terms of patterns of behavior and customs (Bennett, 1995), as well as a complex whole that includes knowledge, beliefs, values, art, and morals. Social reconstructionists (discussed in Chapter 6) define culture somewhat differently than anthropologists. They believe culture is an adaptation to life's circumstances resulting from group competition for resources. Culture is a group's effort to function within a shared set of circumstances. When seen this way, culture becomes dynamic; it is continually recreated as people face daily challenges in their environment (Suzuki, 1984).

When defining culture, you may overlook the various subcultural groups found in schools, with which students align for intended purposes. Teachers need to be aware of these cultural groups and the implications of certain labels on individuals. These groups go by many names; some groups are assigned more derogatory names, such as geeks or nerds, compared with more acceptable names, such as preppies or jocks. Joining groups can be a way to provide students with identity and approval. For better or worse, it is part of the socialization process of discovering who they are as individuals separate from their families. Sororities, fraternities, and gangs all have unique cultures. Socially concerned teachers learn about the different cultural groups in their school in an effort to better understand the needs of their students. What cultural groups were you a member of in junior high and high school? Were you stigmatized because of your associations with particular cultural groups? Or were you affiliated with groups that were more socially accepted by your peers?

James A. Banks, a widely recognized authority in the field of multicultural education, says that defining culture is not easy; not everyone agrees on a universal definition (Banks, 1997). However, even though the definition is ambiguous, culture is still an important concept to understand, especially for those who become teachers. In addition to acquiring an understanding of culture, you need to consider the distinction between ethnicity and culture. Banks (1994) defines **ethnicity** as a shared feeling of common identity, derived in part from a common ancestral origin and a common set of values and experiences. Banks (1997) distinguishes an ethnic minority group as one with "unique physical and/or cultural characteristics that enable individuals who belong to other ethnic groups to identify its members easily, often for discriminatory purposes" (p. 66). Keeping this definition in mind what are some minority ethnic groups in America that have experienced the sting of discriminatory attitudes and practices?

ethnicity

As defined by James Banks, a shared feeling of common identity, derived from a common origin and a common set of values and experiences.

race

A classification scheme that identifies humans based on biological traits and physical characteristics.

Of the three terms, the most misunderstood and controversial is **race.** Anthropologists use the term race to distinguish among humans on the basis of biological traits and characteristics. In today's racially mixed society, this type of classification scheme has obvious drawbacks (Banks & Banks, 1997). For example, in contemporary Puerto Rican society, individuals with a wide range of skin color are regarded as white (Banks & Banks, 1997). It is important that teachers be sensitive to how classifying children by race is often misleading. For example, it has been estimated that over 3 million school-age children are racially mixed (this is a conservative estimate). Certain physical characteristics that once differentiated race in America are now less apparent because of interracial marriages.

Clearly, defining race is complicated and applying the definition of race is even more difficult. It is probably a good idea to refrain from using "race" when describing a person or group of people. The complexities and incongruities found when defining culture, ethnicity, and race merely highlight the need for reflection and further study into cross-cultural differences.

Cultural and Ethnic Differences: Barriers, Characteristics, and Learning Styles

As discussed earlier, future teachers need to acquire a knowledge base and a repertoire of skills for helping students experience academic success in their classrooms. Like Alicia, in the case study, teachers who come from mainstream backgrounds need to know what is appropriate and what is not appropriate when working with culturally different students. Certain attitudes and practices could impede student progress if one is not culturally aware. Alicia (like most well-meaning people) had good intentions, but sometimes good intentions are not enough.

In Chapter 7, Historical Perspectives, you will see that many ethnic minority groups have historically been discriminated against in terms of quality education. In this section, we briefly look at four cultural and ethnic groups who historically have been underrepresented and discriminated against in mainstream education: African Americans, Hispanic Americans, Native Americans, and Asian Americans. We also identify common characteristics found among these groups, including prevalent learning styles.

Please understand that these four cultural groups are certainly not the only groups that have felt the sting of discrimination in our schools. On the contrary, there are many groups who have been oppressed or overlooked, but because of space and time limitations, we narrowed our selection to these main groups. Also, although we discuss each of the four ethnic groups individually, you must realize there are more differences among individuals who compose a group than there are differences among groups. Therefore we must be cautious about overgeneralizing when referring to an individual student. Every student is a unique person, different from all the others. When looking for commonalities, we must never lose sight of the uniqueness of each person.

Let's begin by examining barriers that impede students' academic progress. Considerable insight can be gained by educators if they try to understand the characteristics and preferred learning styles of their students. The following section presents a brief summary of these distinctive traits and implications for instruction and learning.

A typical African-American school, circa 1940.

© Archive Photos

African-American Students

Obstacles such as racism, discrimination, poverty, crime, unemployment, and underemployment have prevented many African Americans from receiving an education and enjoying a quality life. It is important, however, to note that in spite of these barriers, not all African-American children are deterred by them. A significant percentage of African Americans are members of the middle and upper classes and have fared quite well in mainstream society (Banks & Banks, 1997).

Let's consider some academic needs of African-American children that should be addressed. Manning and Baruth (1996) suggest that teachers understand that not all students in a class will be amenable to European-American standards and expectations. Also, teachers who habitually group students by ability will discourage African-American children, particularly if grouping leads to segregation by culture and social class.

To encourage African-American children, teachers should integrate culture-specific materials with basic school textbooks when possible. Also teachers should use cooperative learning instead of competitive learning when appropriate. Research suggests that African-American students favor group instruction in which students help each other reach mutual learning goals (Aronson & Gonzalez,1988). Thus teaching strategies that foster cooperation among students rather than competition may result in higher achievement levels among African-American children.

Bennett (1995) finds that African-American students learn better through oral activities, such as reading aloud or listening to audiotapes, because many children grew up hearing stories told by family members. It is usually facilitative when teaching African-American children to encourage them to draw from their cultural backgrounds whenever possible. Families can also be invaluable sources to teachers as they try to understand language, achievement levels, unique learning styles, and personal identities of individual students (Manning & Baruth, 1996).

Teachers should not assume that each African-American student will fit the specific characteristics identified. The most important thing to remember is that there are differences within groups that preclude us from making sweeping generalizations. Each student, regardless of ethnicity and cultural background, is unique and should be treated as an individual. It is important to remember that there are more differences among groups than between groups; therefore we will reiterate this message after each section.

Hispanic-American Students

The Hispanic population is the fastest growing ethnic group in the United States. It is predicted that by the year 2020 the number of Hispanics will surpass African, Asian, and Native Americans. By the year 2050, 23% of the population will be of Hispanic origin. Classifying all people of Spanish descent as Hispanic is far from accurate. Many ethnic groups, such as Columbian, Cuban, Mexican, and Puerto Rican, are classified as Hispanic Americans (Lasley & Matczynski, 1997). Hispanics have faced many obstacles in our society that have deterred them from obtaining an education; Hispanic-Americans are the most undereducated group of citizens in the United States (De La Rosa & Maw, 1990).

Alicia and other European-American teachers may need to understand that many Hispanic children are taught that European Americans are untrustworthy. For these children, believing that teachers are sincere and concerned about their welfare may be difficult (Fitzpatrick, 1987). The irony is that although Hispanic children are more prone to avoid eye contact, they are more likely to want "personalism," or individualized attention, from teachers or other adult models. Hispanics are known to be devoted to the extended family and show a deference to males (Fitzpatrick, 1987; Christensen, 1989).

Prior knowledge of these commonalities might help teachers plan instruction better suited for the cognitive and affective needs of Hispanic students (Manning & Baruth, 1996). For example, knowing that Hispanic students have a propensity for group work of a noncompetitive nature, teachers might plan fewer classroom activities that foster competitiveness and more that promote cooperation among students. A teacher who acknowledges that "personalism" is desired by many Hispanic students might increase personal interaction with Hispanic students.

Manning and Baruth (1996) suggest teachers avoid overwhelming Hispanic students with verbal instruction, particularly those with limited English skills. Hispanic children and adolescents are loyal to Spanish as their native language; consequently prohibiting or punishing students for speaking in Spanish could create a chasm that would further impede academic progress. It is essential to create an accepting environment that fosters rather than hinders the academic success of Hispanic students.

You should not assume that because a student is Hispanic the above characteristics will be exhibited. Again we caution against applying cultural characteristics in a generic manner. Be wary of labeling or fostering stereotypical attitudes toward students, because every child is different.

Asian-American Students

It is estimated that there are 10 million Asian Americans, and by the middle of the 21st century this group will make up 6.4% of the population (Bennett, 1995). Asian-American students represent an increasingly diverse population. To illustrate, the three largest Asian-American groups—Chinese, Japanese, and Filipinos—have recently been joined by people from Southeast Asia, South Asia, and the Pacific Islands (Banks, 1997). This "diversity within diversity" merely underscores how important it is for teachers not to stereotype Asians.

Manning and Baruth (1996) have delineated some teacher practices that have the potential to impede Asian Americans' progress in school: emphasizing verbal teaching and learning, providing unclear oral directions, and expecting students to share in class. Manning and Baruth also suggest that certain behaviors that could suggest disinterest or indifference are, in fact, quite appropriate for Asian-American learners. For example, Asian-American children are taught by their culture to respect adults and to listen more than speak. Educators should also be aware of the tendency of these learners to be reluctant to reveal their opinions or abilities voluntarily in class discussions, even when they may know the answer (Yao, 1985).

Asian-American learners tend to need teacher reinforcement. They tend to work more efficiently in well-structured, quiet learning environments in which teachers have established definite goals. West (1993) suggests that reprimands and disciplinary actions are more effective with Asian-American learners if done privately rather than publicly. (This is practical advice regardless of students' cultural background).

One common stereotype many of us hold is that all Asian-American students are model students (Sue & Sue, 1990). This assumption may cause teachers to hold unrealistically high expectations of these students. Not all Asian students are model students; in the Asian community there are students who are at risk, just as in any student population (Manning & Baruth, 1996). Teachers who cling to this misconception might overlook warning signs of academic and/or emotional distress in their Asian students.

To avoid overgeneralizing, one must consider each Asian-American student as an individual. By clinging to stereotypical profiles of Asian students, a teacher could easily miss an opportunity to refer a child to the proper authorities for help.

Native-American Students

Native Americans (American Indians) represent about 1% of the total U.S. population (U.S. Bureau of the Census, 1993). Extreme diversity characterizes Native-American culture; for example, there are more than 500 tribes and bands—representing hundreds of languages and distinct cultures (Manning & Baruth, 1996; Banks, 1997; U.S. Bureau of the Census, 1993). Although physical and cultural diversity exists among Native Americans, there are some similarities that might help educators become more aware of their learning needs.

Overall, Native-American children, like Asian children, are taught respect for their elders. They are also taught to be in harmony with nature and to be self-sufficient. Native Americans have an abiding respect for the rights and dignity of individuals. Native Americans are taught to be patient, to demonstrate passive temperaments, to control emotions, and to avoid overreacting to trivial matters (Nel, 1994). Teachers may find that Native-American children tend to speak softly, show unconcern with regard to time or schedules, expect few rules, and avoid looking authority figures in the eye (Manning & Baruth, 1996). In the classroom these behaviors may be misinterpreted by teachers who have little knowledge of Native-American culture as laziness, indifference, or insubordination.

Teacher practices that could impede the academic progress of Native-American students, for example, would be forcing children to talk about themselves, fostering competitiveness among students, expecting eye contact, and relying heavily on verbal participation.

Providing an environment that is emotionally and academically supportive for Native-American students requires recognition of the range of diversity that exists among the more than 500 identified tribes. But the first step is refraining from forming negative opinions about students based on your views of what constitutes "appropriate" classroom attitudes and behaviors. Each child's behavior should be assessed individually to determine its meaning; every child is a unique person in his or her own right.

Emerging as a Multicultural Teacher

The bottom line is that all teachers, regardless of whether they are a member of a minority or the majority, need to develop cultural awareness and sensitivity in order to relate to and work with students. Let's take a minute to summarize ways to develop a greater sensitivity to cultural differences among students.

- Teachers need to understand how diversity is interpreted in this country in order to determine the best ways of addressing it in the school environment.

- Teachers in culturally diverse settings should acquire a vocabulary that includes relevant terminology.
- Teachers must acquire knowledge of the cultures and distinctive characteristics of students representing each culture in their classrooms.
- Teachers should cultivate working relationships and friendships with people who are culturally different from them.

Teaching today requires more than new models and theories; it requires cultural sensitivity resulting from deliberate efforts to become more knowledgeable about the cultural heritage of all students. Irvine (1990) reminds us that teachers who pretend not to notice students' racial and ethnic identities and deny or minimize cultural differences are indeed setting themselves up for difficulty and conflict.

So where do we begin? Admittedly, becoming a multicultural teacher is a daunting challenge. What does it take to become a multicultural teacher? What knowledge base is required? What skills must be developed? How do we integrate and reflect a multicultural component in the curriculum?

This section of the chapter focuses on questions related to preparing oneself to become an "emerging" multicultural teacher. We use "emerging" to point out that this is a process, no one can really claim to have "arrived" as a multicultural teacher. Emerging as a multicultural teacher is truly a lifelong endeavor. We all start this journey at a different place, depending on our life experiences until now. If you do not care about becoming a multicultural teacher, perhaps you should reconsider becoming a teacher.

Defining Multicultural Education

multicultural education

A compilation of teaching and learning approaches that fosters an appreciation and respect for cultural pluralism.

To begin this section, let's define **multicultural education.** Here are two possibilities:

- An approach to teaching and learning that is based upon democratic values and beliefs, and seeks to foster cultural pluralism within culturally diverse societies in an interdependent world" (Bennett, 1995, p. 13).
- A concept and a deliberate process designed to (1) teach learners to recognize, accept, and appreciate cultural, ethnic, social class, religious, and gender differences and (2) instill in learners during crucial developmental years a sense of responsibility and a commitment to work toward the democratic ideals of justice, equality, and democracy" (Manning & Baruth, 1996, pp. 2–3).

As these definitions suggest, there are various ways to define multicultural education. Be careful not to get bogged down in definitions and semantics. Instead, begin incorporating these and other definitions into your developing conceptualization of what multiculturalism means to you.

Multicultural Curriculum

Banks (1997) believes that the "current school curriculum is not preparing students to function successfully within the ethnically and culturally diverse world of the future" (p. 28). Banks (1997) also contends that the multicultural curriculum should encourage students to do the following:

- View historical and contemporary events from diverse ethnic perspectives.
- Understand their own ethnic identities so they can relate to others who are culturally and ethnically different.
- Learn how to function effectively with other cultures and how to interact in positive ways.
- Evaluate any given culture within its context.
- Find solutions to national and international racial and ethnic conflicts (pp. 25–27).

These goals do not call for developing a different curriculum for each student, but rather building a curriculum that transcends a narrow, monocultural focus.

Multicultural Teaching

Admittedly, it is not easy for a new teacher to incorporate cultural knowledge in curriculum and instruction. The first step is to find out who you are in relation to others. Until you are secure in your own culture, you will have problems validating the legitimacy of your students' cultures. For successful teaching in a diverse society, Banks (1997) recommends that teachers continually assess their own cultural attitudes, beliefs, and values and by doing this discover that people are more alike than they are different. In short, self-knowledge depends on developing an attitude of lifelong learning about self and others.

Sleeter and Grant (1999) offer the following list of principles identified by advocates of multicultural education as guides for prospective teachers. Multicultural teachers exhibit the following behaviors:

- Realize all students are innately curious.
- Believe all students are capable of learning complex material and performing at high skill levels.
- Foster cooperation among students, particularly those with limited English proficiency.
- Treat boys and girls equally and in nonsexist ways.
- Strive to develop positive self-concepts in all students (pp. 169–171).

How does multicultural teaching become a reality? What skills are necessary? What instructional methods and models need to be employed? Teaching that is genuinely multicultural requires that educators not only possess knowledge of culturally diverse learners, but also have the ability to recognize individual and cultural needs of their learners and demonstrate genuine concern (Manning & Baruth, 1996).

Culturally Appropriate Learning Models

Multicultural teaching requires skill in planning and implementing instruction that is culturally appropriate. Gollnick and Chinn (1994) observe that multicultural teaching requires weaving cultural diversity throughout the learning process. For example, a unit on the Civil War could include not only issues regarding slavery, but also the impact the war had on women, the poor, and other minority groups in this country.

The next section presents teaching methods and approaches from the professional literature that should be considered when attempting to meet the special needs of culturally different learners.

Cooperative Learning

cooperative learning

A teaching method that provides peer interaction and promotes cooperation rather than competition among students.

One teaching method that is effective with culturally diverse students is **cooperative learning**. Tyler (1989) found that cooperative learning reinforces the efforts made by culturally diverse students to complete their learning tasks. Slavin (1983) reported that cooperative learning provides opportunity for peer interaction, establishes group cohesiveness, and engages students in pleasant activities that require teamwork. A synthesis of research finds that cooperative learning encourages students to work together and contributes to successful learning for specific ethnic groups (Manning & Baruth, 1996). For example, research by Slavin (1987) indicates that working in cooperative learning situations appears to be particularly effective with both Hispanic-American and African-American students.

Constructivism

Constructivism is a teaching approach that tends to complement the unique learning needs of many culturally diverse students. Actually, constructivism is not a teaching method per se, but more a philosophical orientation about how learning occurs. In essence, the theory postulates that learning occurs when a schema (prior knowledge) is activated and new knowledge is constructed by the learner. This paradigm places responsibility on the learner as the constructor of knowledge and the teacher as "the scaffold" and "the guide" in this interaction (Levin & Nolan, 1996).

Constructivist teaching requires that the teacher provide opportunities for student inquiry, discussion, debate, and various other interactive activities such as role-playing. Constructivists' methods tend to be compatible with the learning needs of many African-American, Hispanic-American, and

Native-American students. For example, cultural groups that generally like expressive movement and demonstrative behavior, as in the case of many African-American children, will respond well to constructivist methods, which allow for group interaction (Levin & Nolan, 1996). (Constructivism is discussed further in Chapters 6 and 8).

Howard Gardner's Theory of Multiple Intelligences

multiple intelligences

A theory that contends that intelligence is not a single entity but is multifaceted.

Howard Gardner's (1983) theory of **multiple intelligences** (MI) offers an approach that accommodates the needs of culturally diverse students. Gardner explains that an intelligence involves the ability to solve problems or fashion products that are of consequence in a particular cultural setting. Based on this definition of intelligence, a person is intelligent if he or she is able to solve personal problems and produce outcomes that are of value to a particular culture (Lazear, 1991). A person does not have to be "book smart" to be intelligent. According to Gardner's theory, intelligence is multifaceted. There are many ways to manifest intelligence.

Gardner (1983; 1993) identified seven categories of human intelligence: *linguistic intelligence* (the capacity to use words effectively orally or in writing); *logical-mathematical intelligence* (the capacity to use logic in math and science); *spatial intelligence* (the ability to perceive the visual-spatial world accurately); *bodily-kinesthetic intelligence* (the ability to use the body to express feelings, create products, or play sports and games); *musical intelligence* (the capacity to recognize and use rhythmic and tonal patterns); *interpersonal intelligence* (the ability to work cooperatively with others in a group and communicate verbally and nonverbally with others); and *intrapersonal intelligence* (capacity for self-knowledge and the ability to act on that knowledge). Gardner has recently added *naturalist,* as an eighth intelligence to this list. According to Gardner, a naturalist has the ability to recognize, appreciate, and classify plants, minerals, and animals, which includes rocks and all types of flora and fauna.

Gardner (1983; 1993) asserts that no intelligence exists by itself and intelligences always interact with each other. "We do not wish to imply that in adulthood intelligences operate in isolation. Indeed, except for abnormal individuals, intelligences always work in concert..." (Gardner, 1993, p. 17).

Armstrong (1994) makes the following four specific points relative to Gardner's theory:

- Everyone possesses each of these types of intelligences to some degree.
- Most people can develop each intelligence to a sufficient level of competency, given appropriate instruction, encouragement, and enrichment.
- The intelligences work together in complex ways.
- There are multiple ways to be intelligent within each category. For example, one may be unable to read but have a sophisticated oral vocabulary (pp. 11–12).

Traditionally, logical-mathematical and verbal-linguistic intelligences have been the basis of most systems of Western education and standardized

> ## ❝ NOTABLE QUOTE
>
> Prospective teachers must understand that a class of twenty-five students is made up of twenty-five unique individuals. Each student has different strengths, weaknesses, abilities, interests, and learning styles. Curriculum planning must address the differences in students and offer components for all students. *(Bonnie C. Bumpers, Horace Mann Arts and Science Magnet Middle School, 16 years' experience* ❞

tests (Lazear, 1991). An obvious limitation is that those children who do not perform well in these areas could develop self-esteem problems regarding their abilities. Teachers must help students develop those intelligences they possess so they can "feel more engaged and competent, and therefore more inclined to serve the society in a constructive way" (Gardner, 1993, p. 9).

Armstrong (1994) suggests that educators avoid the trap of referring to specific racial or ethnic groups in terms of only one intelligence. Every culture has and uses all the intelligences, although one or more may be more highly developed and valued because of the context in which that culture has relied on that skill for survival.

According to Hervey, Calhoun, & Holmes (1997), implementing the multiple intelligences theory in the classroom requires an instructional paradigm shift—one that will hasten teachers' emergence as "multicultural" teachers. In contrast to traditional methods (e.g., lecturing at the front of the classroom), the teacher makes an instructional shift by alternating from one of the intelligences to another. In this way, the teacher goes beyond the textbook and the blackboard to awaken students' minds. By using an eclectic repertoire of teaching strategies, teachers are in a better position to effectively meet the diverse needs of all their students (Hervey, Calhoun, & Holmes, 1997).

Parents as Partners

Parental involvement is such a critical factor when working with culturally different students that we would be remiss if we failed to acknowledge it again in this chapter. As we learned in Chapter 3, current research, successful practice, new legislation, and educational reform efforts have all indicated the need for greater parental involvement (Winzer & Mazurek, 1998). A family's cultural beliefs are among the most fundamental components of the family. The family's ethnic, racial, cultural, and linguistic identity significantly influences their values and beliefs, as well as their attitudes toward school.

Winzer and Mazurek (1998) found that the educational literature consistently shows a link between parental involvement and student achievement. The more involved parents are in their child's school work the better the child performs in school. Parents can be indispensable allies. As well as bridging the gap between school and home, parent-teacher exchanges also facilitate the teacher's understanding of cultural differences.

Culturally and linguistically diverse parents tend to be less involved than mainstream parents in their children's education. But teachers should not conclude that lack of involvement translates to lack of concern (Winzer & Mazurek, 1998). As discussed in Chapter 3, there are numerous factors—in addition to previous unpleasant school experiences—that might dissuade parents from becoming involved in their children's education. For example, work schedules, financial pressures, poor health, and lack of transportation are a few reasons that could prevent parental participation (Sleeter & Grant, 1999; Winzer & Mazurek, 1998).

Because public schools could be a past source of alienation for low-income and minority parents, the need to break this cycle is critical (Calabrese, 1990). For the sake of their students, teachers must do whatever it takes to make parents feel comfortable (Epstein, 1987). There are many ways to make parents feel welcome, as we learned in Chapter 3. The first priority is to communicate trust and respect to parents. Teachers should recognize that parents send their best to school (i.e., their children); therefore teachers need to convey a genuine appreciation for the children (Grant & Gomez, 1996).

Grant and Gomez (1996) recommend that teachers learn as much as they can about a child's family and culture before the initial meeting with his or her parents. If possible, teachers should meet with parents in homes and/or community settings, which might make the exchange easier and less threatening. Teachers must not assume that culturally diverse parents do not want to be involved in their children's education (Chavkin, 1989); it may only be a matter of not knowing how to proceed. It is the teacher's responsibility to find ways to make these vital connections happen.*

AssessYourself

How will your cultural heritage or ethnicity affect how you will relate to students? Have your cultural experiences been minimal or broad?

Have you had the opportunity to travel extensively or perhaps live in various places?

What attitudes will you need to cultivate to effectively meet the needs of a wide range of culturally diverse students?

What should you do now to broaden your world view?

*To learn more about ways to increase parental involvement, contact Partnership for Family Involvement in Education (PFIE), U.S. Department of Education, 400 Maryland Ave. S.W., Washington, D.C. 20202-8173 or e-mail: Partner@ed.gov. Also visit http://pfie.ed.gov.

GREAT TEACHERS

James P. Comer

Born on September 25, 1934, in East Chicago, Indiana, Comer earned his B.A. from Indiana University in 1956 and his medical doctorate from Howard University in 1960. He pursued child psychiatry as his specialization at Yale University. Comer remained at Yale to work as a professor of child psychiatry and associate dean of the Yale School of Medicine. In 1968, he became the director of the Yale University Child Study Center School Development Program, a program designed to assist low-income, low-achieving schools. Basically, Comer believes that the fostering of a family-like atmosphere in a school will improve achievement scores of inner-city children. His model, the Comer Project for Change in Education, has been replicated in more than 600 schools in 82 districts in 26 states. Comer's model has been effective with all types of schools and with students from all income levels. Comer has received numerous awards and honors as a leader in school reform.

Courtesy of Dr. James Comer

Web Sites
Check out these web sites to learn more about establishing partnerships with parents: www.napehq.org (National Association of Partners in Education); www.pta.org/ (National Parent Teacher Association); or http://www.cisnet.org (Communities in Schools).

Diverse Learning Abilities

In this section we explore diversity among students regarding their ability to learn. Special needs students are typically those who possess cognitive and/or physical disabilities that hinder their ability to learn. The number of children receiving special services in federally funded programs has increased from 8% percent in 1977 to 12% in 1996 (U.S. Department of Education, National Center for Education Statistics, 1997). These figures suggest challenges for classroom teachers; they must not only learn how to adequately meet the cognitive and physical needs of these students, but also be knowledgeable about the laws that affect special education.

Federal Legislation

Vocational Rehabilitation Act

A federal law passed in 1973 to ensure that the civil rights of handicapped persons are not discriminated against in the workplace.

Education for All Handicapped Children Act (PL 94-142)

A federal law passed in 1975 providing federal funding to schools to ensure all children receive a free and appropriate education.

Individuals with Disabilities Education Act (IDEA)

A federal law passed in 1990 extending the provisions of the Education for All Handicapped Children Act of 1975.

least restrictive environment (LRE)

Under federal law, students who qualify for special education are to receive instruction in regular classrooms with peers as much as possible.

individualized education program (IEP)

A provision of the Individuals with Disabilities Act that requires schools to write a customized plan for each child who receives special education.

Two important pieces of legislation were enacted by Congress in the 1970s relevant to special education. Briefly, Section 504 of the **Vocational Rehabilitation Act** of 1973 stated that public school students with disabilities cannot be denied access to education. The second law, **Education for All Handicapped Children Act (PL 94-142),** passed in 1975 and amended in 1990 by the **Individuals with Disabilities Act (IDEA),** mandates that free appropriate public education must be made available to all children with disabilities between the ages of 3 and 21. Special education and related services must be provided in the **least restrictive environment (LRE),** which means that the child should be included in the regular school setting as much as possible (i.e., inclusion), rather than be segregated in resource rooms or separate schools. Furthermore, each child is provided with an **individualized education program (IEP),** which is developed and maintained in collaboration with parent(s) or guardian(s), teacher(s) and school principal, counselor, psychological examiner, or other related parties.

The Individuals with Disabilities Education Act (IDEA) was amended in 1995 and 1997. The 1995 amendment was based on the following six principles identified by the U.S. Department of Education:

1. Align IDEA with state and local educational reforms.

2. Improve student performance through higher expectations and access to the general curriculum.

3. Address individual needs in the least restrictive setting.

4. Provide families and teachers with knowledge and training to support students' learning.

5. Focus resources on teaching and learning.

6. Strengthen early intervention to ensure that every child starts school ready to learn.

Major issues addressed by the 1997 amendment are IEPs and general curriculum, state- and district-wide assessments, regular education and teacher involvement, discipline, and graduation with a regular diploma.

Reflections from the Field

Ralph Calhoun, Special Educator, North Little Rock School District, when asked to respond to the impact of IDEA regulations on regular classroom teachers, made these remarks: "With changes in legislation, the Individuals with Disabilities Act (IDEA) has made inclusion in public education more common. Not only have I seen enhanced academic opportunities for children, but also a greater acceptance of these children by their peers. When placed in an inclusive setting and given appropriate instruction, students with disabilities have made significant gains in the regular classroom. As a teacher in an inclusive classroom, I have seen that these opportunities have benefited not only students with special needs, but all students as well."

Gifted and Talented Students

gifted and talented students

Students who have demonstrated a high level of performance in intellectual, creative, artistic, leadership, and/or academic areas.

A second category of students with special needs are **gifted and talented students.** To date, there is no uniform definition of gifted and/or talented. Because of this, state programs have differing criteria to describe a "gifted" or "talented" student. Most states develop their program according to some agreed upon definition. In Arkansas, we have adopted Renzulli's (1977) three ring definition that characterizes "giftedness" as an interaction of (1) above average intellectual ability, (2) creativity, and (3) task commitment. An advantage of using these criteria is that more students can be included in gifted programs compared with those programs that focus exclusively on intellect.

Giftedness exists in all cultures and across all economic strata, yet difficulty arises when identifying and selecting those students. There is no uniform identification process, and therefore many school districts identify students for their programs based on standardized tests scores and grades, especially those programs that define "giftedness" in cognitive terms only. The problem with this is that minimum cut-off scores and grade emphasis have limited participation by many students, particularly those students from underrepresented groups.

Recognition of these disparities has led the U.S. Department of Education to develop a new, more inclusive definition. Gifted children demonstrate high performance in intellectual, creative, and/or artistic areas; unique leadership qualities; or excellence in specific academic content areas. If equity is to be achieved in the process of identifying students with special needs, the identification process must be as inclusive as possible. To do this, there must be multiple means of assessing the types of gifts served by these programs. In addition, teacher and parental recommendations and other forms of evidence should be assessed to determine eligibility.

Reflections from the Field

Marilyn Larson, Director of Gifted and Talented Education for the Conway School District, Conway, Arkansas, reflects on the impact of diversity on gifted education in her work setting. "Fourteen years ago, the state recommended that we 'cast the net widely' when identifying students for our program. By doing this, we were able to include students from diverse ethnic backgrounds that might otherwise have been overlooked. Our job has been to maintain the balance and integrity of gifted and talented education while serving the strongest students from all populations."

Bilingual Differences

As discussed in Chapter 4, liberal immigration laws have resulted in an influx of students who speak languages other than English. Children whose native language is not English pose a challenge for the regular classroom teacher. Hernandez (1997) describes a classroom in which there is diversity in language and culture as a "multilingual" classroom. Within this context, teachers must work with the diverse language abilities of students while being mindful of the need to promote development of English language skills. The teacher must not equate lack of English proficiency with intelligence or ability. For example, a non–English-speaking student who qualifies for the school's gifted and talented program could be overlooked if a teacher can't separate language from ability.

Reflections from the Field

When asked "How has student diversity affected you as a teacher?" Anita Cegers-Coleman of Bob Courtway Middle School, with four years' teaching experience, replied, "Before I started teaching I was unaware of the extent to which I would have to modify students' work. I did not realize the amount of work involved in planning and accommodating for students with special needs. To illustrate, I was not aware of how many special education conferences I would have to attend or that I would have to change the number of choices on a multiple choice test, highlight important items in textbooks, or rearrange seating charts so certain students can see, hear or 'act' better in class. Not only have I had to modify for students who may be working below their grade level, but I have even had to find enrichment activities for those students who seem to be more advanced than everyone else. So far I have not taught any students whose native language is not English, nor any students with hearing impairments, but I know of other teachers who have. I think that student diversity has really opened my eyes as a teacher; it is much clearer that not all students learn as easily as others. I now have a greater tolerance for student differences, and I try to work more closely with other teachers such as the special education or gifted and talented teachers to maximize a student's learning."

An ESL teacher providing English instruction to a non–English speaking child.

© Mary Kate Denny/PhotoEdit

Differences in Learning Styles

When you begin teaching you will shortly realize the range of differences your students have in how they process information. Because students learn differently, teachers must be attuned to diverse learning styles. Brain-based research suggests that some students are more right-brain dominated, whereas others are more left-brain dominated. As mentioned earlier, Gardner contends that individuals have "multiple intelligences." Effective teachers try to apply these findings to instruction.

Reflections from the Field

Bonnie Bumpers, from Horace Mann Magnet Middle School, helps us get a better idea of how teachers can make use of knowledge about various learning styles. "The recognition and acceptance of individual differences in a classroom helps students gain confidence and feel good about themselves. Thus one of my first lessons each year is on learning styles. Using a learning style inventory, my students determine their preferred learning style. From this activity, they learn that we are all different and differences are okay. I share my own learning style, which works for me in my graduate studies. This lesson always leads to a wonderful discussion about how we process information differently. I also tell my students how I design class activities to offer varying approaches that cross learning styles. Throughout the year I am amused at how my students respond to this kind of information. 'Ms. Bumpers, you hit all the learning styles today.' The students' awareness of different learning styles encourages them to determine what is the best approach for them. The recognition of differences allows students the freedom to be themselves and appreciate the differences in others."

The observations of the teacher in *Reflections from the Field* illustrate the wide range of diversity among students. Regrettably, we cannot discuss here all categories of students with special needs; our aim is to illuminate the diversity of student populations. If you stay in education you will probably take other courses that will explore in more depth the needs of students with diverse learning needs. If you become a teacher, you should prepare for such diversity so you can help *all* of your students succeed.

Discrimination Based on Negative Stereotypes

So far, we have discussed taking into account individual differences when responding to students. What happens, for example, when a student or group of students is treated differently based on an unfavorable bias or negative stereotype? In this case, acknowledging differences could work against that student or group, particularly if treatment of one group puts another group at a more favorable advantage. The purpose for recognizing student differences is to promote positive outcomes, not place certain students at a disadvantage. If this is confusing, consider the example in the next section.

Gender Bias

Let's take a look at gender differences, for example. Do we treat male and female students differently because of their gender? Does differential treatment benefit both parties? Or does it benefit one sex but not the other?

To illustrate, a mathematics teacher acknowledges gender differences between males and females in aptitude for math. In her advanced calculus class, she honors those differences by expecting less from female students and more from males. When this teacher was observed by a colleague (as part of her yearly evaluation), it was noted that she reacted differently to boys' responses than to girls' responses. Specifically, the teacher encouraged males in class by bestowing more attention on them. She would call on boys more in class and reinforce their responses (even incorrect answers). For example, she tended to coach a male student until he came up with a more satisfactory response. Whereas, when a female student gave an incorrect response she would move on to the next student.

This example demonstrates what research has shown—that boys are encouraged in school more often than girls are (Sadker & Sadker, 1986; 1994). Sadker and Sadker (1994) studied over 100 classrooms in five states and found that gender bias exists in American schools; educational opportunities are not the same for males and females. Research also reveals that sexual bias occurs regardless of the teacher's gender. In other words, female teachers are just as likely as male teachers to favor boys over girls in the classroom. Why do you think this occurs?

One indicator of sexual bias is the salary discrepancy between males and females. Despite the narrowing of the gap in math and science scores between genders over the past few years, males continue to be overrepresented in fields of mathematics and science (Tavris, 1992). And with more males in these technological positions, the wage earning gap remains (i.e., males earn considerably higher salaries than women in the workforce).

Web Sites
To explore this topic further, you might want to visit the web site of the American Association of University Women at http://www.aauw.org.

Research conducted by the American Association of University Women (1992) found that girls' self-esteem regarding academic ability decreased with years of schooling, whereas boys' confidence increased over time. To learn more about how girls fare with regard to education, we suggest that you read *How Schools Shortchange Girls* (1992). This cites research findings from a study commissioned by the American Association of University Women (AAUW) and conducted by the Wellesley College Center for Research on Women.

REFLECTION QUESTIONS

- We suggest that you be attentive to how your instructors respond to classmates based on gender.

- Do you think teachers have differentiated their actions toward you based on your gender? In what ways?

- Do you think our society in general favors men over women? How?

Have you ever caught yourself making a "sexist" comment?

If you think you might have a tendency to do this, begin sensitizing yourself to this practice. Being aware of "unfavorable" teacher practices is clearly the first step to correcting for them.

Sexual Orientation Bias

One group of students who continue to be overlooked and in most cases ostracized or harassed are gays and lesbians. This minority group is subjected to negative discrimination because some heterosexuals have trouble empathizing with a homosexual orientation. Also, many Christian denominations and other religious sects condemn homosexual behavior. The climate in some communities is so hostile that gay students have been targeted strictly because of their sexual orientation. Gay students have two choices: to hide their orientation or to "come out" and face ridicule, rejection, and open hostility. In the media we have heard and read of instances where homosexuals were targets of hate crimes. Some homosexuals have actually been killed because of their sexual orientation.

Because it is difficult in a homophobic society to develop a positive identity, gay and lesbian youth are considered an at-risk population (Cooley, 1998). Gay adolescents are two to three times more likely to attempt suicide. They are more likely to run away from home and drop out of school. In some communities the hatred is so great that many gays fear for their lives.

Regardless of a teacher's views about homosexuality, the issue is that treating people who are different in ways that hurt them is not right. To allow children to taunt and tease gay students in your class or school is to condone harassment. It is unethical, immoral, and in most cases illegal to malign or mistreat people. Teachers are in the business of helping children (all children). They must model appropriate behavior so their students can learn civility through emulation.

In 1988 the National Education Association (NEA), recognizing the responsibility teachers have for protecting gay and lesbian children, adopted a resolution which took an unequivocal stand on this issue. The resolution stated that the National Education Association believes that all persons, regardless of sexual orientation, should be afforded equal opportunity within the public education system and that every school district should provide counseling by trained personnel for students who are struggling with their sexual/gender orientation (NEA, Resolution C-13: Student Sexual Orientation).

In 1997 the policy in the *NEA Handbook* was slightly revised to read: "The National Education Association believes that all persons, regardless of sexual orientation, should be afforded equal opportunity within the public education system. The Association also believes that, for students who are struggling with their sexual/gender orientation, every school district and educational institution should provide counseling services and programs that deal with high suicide and drop-out rates and the high incidence of teen prostitution. These services and programs shall be staffed by trained personnel" (NEA Resolution C-29: Student Sexual Orientation, *National Education Association Handbook,* 1999–2000, p. 301).

AssessYourself

Multicultural teachers perceive differences in a positive light; they develop attitudes and skills that reflect their accepting and edifying views about diversity. Do you perceive differences this way?

Do you think you could work with students who are different from you? How would you feel about working with children from disadvantaged backgrounds?

Are you flexible enough to deal with the diversity you will find among your students? Would you be willing to make accommodations for students who need adjustments because of a learning or physical disability? Would you welcome mentally and physically challenged students to your class?

What about students who are gay—would you stand up for these students against peer ridicule or scorn?

❝ NOTABLE QUOTE

Adolescence by itself is a difficult developmental stage, fraught with change and turmoil. It is only made further complicated by being gay or lesbian. *(Jonna Cooley)* ❞

Overcoming Dissimilar Backgrounds

A critical question Corey, Corey, and Callanan (1998) pose to prospective counselors and therapists is: "Can you help people whose life experiences, values, and problems...differ from yours?" (p. 77). They take the position that if a therapist is relating on a feeling level, "cultural and age differences can be transcended" (Corey, Corey, & Callanan, 1998, p. 78). Does their answer apply to teachers? Will you need to have had the same background as your students in order to teach effectively? By believing that only members of the same racial and/or ethnic group can teach a particular student population, you could undermine the success of your teaching. If you want to overcome differences and relate to your students, you can—it is a choice you make.

Even though teachers and students do not have to be identical to one another in order to relate, they should be able to harmonize with one another. Levin and Nolan (1996) refer to this as "cultural synchronization," which they define as the ability to be in step with your students regarding expected behavior. Cultural synchronization can only happen when understanding of backgrounds, values, and perceptions is achieved between teacher and student. A teacher's goal then should be to provide each student with an equal opportunity to learn under conditions that facilitate rather than impede progress and success. If this goal is to be realized in an increasingly pluralistic society, teachers must be educated and trained to be multicultural persons.

Differences in life experiences between teachers and students should be viewed positively, and can make teaching more exciting and educational for everyone involved.

REFLECTION QUESTIONS

● Although teachers do not have to be of the same cultural background to be effective with students, this does not take away from the need to ensure that today's teaching force mirrors diversity.

....

● What do you think U.S. Secretary of Education Richard Riley (1998) meant when he made the remark, "... students today need to see themselves in the faces of their teachers. We need teachers from different backgrounds to share different experiences and points of view with colleagues. This sharing enriches and empowers the entire profession and students from all backgrounds" (p. 19)?

....

● How can teacher education programs recruit persons of diverse ethnic and cultural backgrounds to the profession?

....

Conclusion

In this chapter, we discussed the importance of beginning teachers' developing a heightened sensitivity and awareness to the cross-cultural differences in today's student population. Indeed, an understanding of generic cultural characteristics and implications for teacher practice is necessary if equality in educational opportunity is to be achieved. Novice teachers will be more adept at meeting the needs of their students if they cultivate an appreciation for students' unique cultural backgrounds. Teacher candidates must become more culturally literate in order to negotiate effectively the challenges of teaching in a culturally diverse educational setting.

To be effective in a culturally diverse classroom, teachers should broaden their knowledge base to understand student differences. Deliberate effort should be made to integrate the cultural heritage of students into the curriculum. Multicultural teaching requires a deliberate instructional paradigm shift. In effect, becoming a multicultural teacher requires the development of a repertoire of non-traditional teaching strategies designed to meet the needs of a diverse student population. Some strategies found to be particularly facilitative with minority students are cooperative learning, constructivist teaching, and recognition of multiple intelligences. The multicultural teacher is aware of the importance of parental involvement and seeks to enlist parents as partners in the education of their children.

In this chapter we also explored the idea that diversity includes more than culture. There are differences in students' languages, learning styles, socioeconomic status, gender, sexual orientation, and disabilities. Socially sensitive teachers must continually engage in reflection and lifelong learning in order to stay attuned to differences found among their students. Along with reading and studying about diversity, prospective teachers should experience as much diversity as they can in order to transcend prejudicial thinking. We believe that even though dealing with student diversity is an additional task for new teachers, it is also a source of reward and satisfaction.

KEY TERMS

cooperative learning

culture

Education for All Handicapped
  Children Act (PL 94-142)

ethnicity

gifted and talented students

individualized education program (IEP)

Individuals with Disabilities Education
  Act (IDEA)

kaleidoscope metaphor

least restrictive environment (LRE)

melting pot metaphor

multicultural education

multiple intelligences

race

salad bowl metaphor

Vocational Rehabilitation Act

SUGGESTED READING

Banks, J. A. (1997). *Teaching strategies for ethnic studies* (6th ed.). Boston: Allyn and Bacon.

Ladson-Billings, G. (1994). *The dreamkeepers: Successful teachers of African American children.* San Francisco: Jossey-Bass.

Sadker, M., & Sadker, D. (1994). *Failing at fairness: How our schools cheat girls.* New York: Simon & Schuster.

REFERENCES

American Association of University Women (1992). *How schools shortchange girls.* Washington, D. C: Author.

Armstrong, T. (1994). *Multiple intelligences in the classroom.* Alexandria, VA: Association for Supervision and Curriculum Development.

Aronson, E., & Gonzalez, A. (1988). Desegregation, jigsaw, and the Mexican-American experience. In P. A. Katz & D. A. Taylor (Eds.), *Eliminating racism: Profiles in controversy.* New York: Plenum Press.

Banks, J. A. (1994). *An introduction to multicultural education.* Boston: Allyn & Bacon.

Banks, J. A. (1997). *Teaching strategies for ethnic studies* (6th ed.). Boston: Allyn & Bacon.

Banks, J. A., & Banks, C. M. (1997). *Multicultural education: A cultural perspective* (3rd ed.). Boston: Allyn & Bacon.

Bennett, C. I. (1995). *Comprehensive multicultural education: Theory and practice* (3rd ed.). Allyn & Bacon.

Bennett, K. P., & LeCompte, M. D. (1990). *How schools work: A sociological analysis of education.* New York: Longman.

Calabrese, R. L. (1990). The public school: A source of alienation for minority parents. *Journal of Negro Education, 59*(2), 148–154.

Chavkin, N. F. (1989). Debunking the myth about minority parents. *Educational Horizons, 67*(4), 119–123.

FOUNDATIONS OF LEARNING

© Ken Whitmore/STONE

At the end of this chapter, you will be able to

- Explain core philosophical questions and issues that provide a foundation for the study of philosophy.

- Describe four schools of philosophy and explain their relationship to education.

- Identify four educational philosophies derived from those schools of philosophy and explain their impact on curriculum development and teacher practices.

- Identify three psychological perspectives that have influenced curriculum development and teacher practices.

- Articulate a personal educational philosophy.

Philosophical Orientations

A bird's eye view of what to expect in this chapter

In this chapter you will be introduced to major schools of philosophy that have shaped and influenced education. Second, you will discover four educational philosophies emanating from those schools of philosophy. Third, you will see the influence that three psychological perspectives have had on educational philosophies. Last, and most important, you will begin to see how an individual's approach to teaching is based on personal philosophical beliefs. Curricular decisions and teaching practices, for example, are heavily influenced by personal values and beliefs held by individuals.

Some questions raised in this chapter are: What is the purpose of education? Is the aim of education to maintain a strong and safe nation? Or is the aim to ensure that our children grow into secure and independent adults who are happy? Is it for society's good or the good of the person that we mandate school attendance? Is knowledge constant or fluid? How does one's philosophy of education affect teacher practice and the function of schooling?

These and similar questions will be raised as we explore the philosophical legacy of education. As you read this chapter, examine your own views regarding these theoretical questions and contemplate what education has meant to you. The principal objective is to stimulate you to begin formulating your personal philosophy of education. Perhaps by the end of this chapter, you will want to learn more about the philosophical heritage at the base of American education.

n your teacher education program you may be required to take a course in educational philosophy. In the meantime, this chapter (albeit abbreviated) will expose you to the major philosophical traditions that underlie current educational systems. Please note, the philosophies we selected are not inclusive; there are other recognized and respected philosophies from which to draw when developing your own personal philosophy. Furthermore, many of the philosophies we selected have branches or subdivisions that we do not discuss in this chapter because of space and time constraints. Narrowing our discussion to Western philosophies should not in any way minimize or negate the positive influence of Eastern philosophies or other philosophical frameworks, such as Native American or African American, on education.

As you look for meaningful answers to the rather abstract and speculative questions raised in the chapter, you will be developing your personal philosophy. Because a single philosophy of education does not exist, the possibilities are limitless. Whatever stance you take, we suggest you try it out on your instructor and peers. Exchanging philosophical beliefs with others is an excellent way to clarify your beliefs about the purposes of education. By the way, a class discussion on which philosophy has more merit could trigger a lively and thoughtful debate.

What is the purpose of education? Your approach to teaching will reflect your personal values and beliefs.

© Don and Pat Valenti/STONE

Influences on Personal Philosophy

What is your personal philosophy about the role of education? You may be thinking that it's premature to ask such a question at this time, particularly if this is your first teacher education course. We believe, however, that you already have a core set of beliefs from which you operate. After all, you have been a consumer (client) of the educational system for years, which means that you have had ample experience from which to draw. As you progress in your teacher education program, the ideas you hold will naturally unfold and take shape.

Philosophies are not fixed entities, and personal philosophies change proportionately to how you change as a person. Whatever your current philosophy of education is now, it emanated from your life experiences up to this point. Beliefs, attitudes, values, and experiences influence a person's personal philosophy of education and life in general. Let's pause for a moment to assess your current beliefs and values about what is important in education.

AssessYourself

This is your first school board meeting since the election. The superintendent has come to ask the board's opinion on how to trim the budget for next year. It is obvious that some courses and positions must be eliminated.

The superintendent recommends that the high school's art program be cut, in addition to the elementary school counselor's position. Further, she proposes that Latin be eliminated from the curriculum.

What opinion would you voice about these proposed budget cuts? Do you think your opinion about the proposed budget reflects your philosophical beliefs and assumptions about the purposes of education?

Identify life experiences you have had that you think may have affected your response to the budget dilemma.

Core Philosophical Questions and Issues

The following fundamental questions precede any serious study of philosophy:

- What is of value?
- How do you know what you know?
- What is reality?
- What is logical?

From these questions, axiology, epistemology, metaphysics, and logic emerge. A brief description of these core philosophical issues follows, accompanied by examples of teacher practices.

Axiology

axiology

Philosophical questions about what is of value. There are two branches: ethics (morality and conduct) and aesthetics (beauty and art).

Axiology poses questions about the nature of values. What do we value as individuals and as a society? There are two branches of axiology: ethics and aesthetics. **Ethics** is concerned with personal and societal standards of morality. **Aesthetics** is concerned with developing an appreciation for beauty and art. (We will discuss the ethical dimensions of teaching in more depth in Chapter 13, Ethical and Legal Issues)

ethics

A branch of axiology concerned with personal and societal standards of morality.

Teacher Application

Assist students to develop character traits by posing ethical dilemmas for them to solve.

aesthetics

A branch of axiology concerned with developing an appreciation for beauty and art.

- Example: Ask students this question: "If you observed another student cheating on a test, what would you do?" How will you as a teacher respond when a student cheats?

Help students discern differences in the fine arts by exposing them to various artistic modalities and learn to appreciate beauty and art.

- Example: Play classical music in the background while students are reading silently. Later ask students: "Which music did you like the most, the Mozart selection or the Beethoven selection? Why?" How will you as a teacher decorate your classroom to reflect what you see as "beauty"?

Epistemology

epistemology

Philosophical questions about the nature of and origin of truth and knowledge.

Epistemology seeks answers to questions about the nature and origin of truth and knowledge. Are truth and knowledge absolute (objective) or relative (subjective)? Can truth be known independently of sensory experiences? There are primarily five sources of knowledge, as follows:

- Empirical knowledge is based on knowledge acquired through the senses. Experiential learning is an example of empirical knowledge.

- Revealed knowledge is based on knowledge acquired through the supernatural realm. Christians consider the Bible the revealed word of God; Jews look to the Torah for guidance; and Muslims view the Koran as sacred.

- Authoritative knowledge is based on knowledge from experts or tradition. A person acquires this authoritative knowledge by reading literary works and studying masterpieces.

- Rational knowledge is knowledge acquired through reasoning. Engaging in logical thinking is an example of rational knowledge.

- Intuitive knowledge is knowledge derived from being attuned to one's emotions. Being perceptive to one's feelings can result in knowledge based on insight.

Teacher Application

Ask students to identify the source of their knowledge.

- Example: "How did you come up with that solution to the math equation?"
- Example: "So your group agreed that the Golden Rule is something we should abide by in our conduct with each other. Let me ask you, where did that wisdom come from? What is the basis for your premise?"

As a teacher, what sources of knowledge will you use in teaching? Do you see the textbook as infallible?

Metaphysics

metaphysics

Philosophical system concerned about the nature of reality, such as the origin of the universe and the nature of God and man.

Metaphysics poses questions about the nature of reality. Why are we here? What is our purpose in the universe? Because human knowledge is limited, we can only speculate about the nature of man and our existence in the cosmos. Metaphysics asks questions about the following:

- The origin and evolution of the universe *(cosmology)*
- God and faith *(theology)*
- The study of man *(anthropology)*
- One's existence *(ontology)*

Teacher Application

Ask students to speculate about metaphysical questions. Following are examples:

- "Are criminals bad or good, or do they have elements of both?"
- "Do alcoholics choose to drink (free will), or is it beyond their control (heredity)?"
- "How did the universe begin?"

As a teacher, what motivates student behavior?

logic

A branch of philosophy that asks questions about how humans reason.

Logic

inductive reasoning

A type of reasoning that moves from the facts (specifics) to an understanding of general principles (generalizations).

Logic asks questions about how humans reason. Logic also defines rules of reasoning. Basically, there are two types of reasoning: inductive and deductive. **Inductive reasoning** moves from the facts (specifics) to an understanding of general principles (generalizations). For example, Judy wants to

To a pragmatist, reality is in a state of flux. Truth in one situation may not be the same in another. Because education is constantly changing, pragmatists contend that the knowledge base should be broad rather than narrow. Education is seen as a process; therefore its knowledge base must be flexible and accommodating. The curriculum should take an interdisciplinary approach, which means that subjects interface with each other in an effort to arrive at practical solutions (Newman, 1990).

GREAT TEACHERS

John Dewey

© Archive Photos

Born in 1859 in Burlington, Vermont, John Dewey was an influential philosopher, educator, social critic, and author. Dewey was a professor at the University of Chicago from 1894 to 1904 and at Columbia University from 1904 to 1930. He died in 1952. As an educational philosopher, Dewey is associated with progressivism, pragmatism, and experimentalism.

At the University of Chicago, Dewey and his wife opened a Laboratory School to test progressive tenets. He considered the classrooms to be laboratories for experimentation and cooperation. Dewey's focus was more on experience and action than on a purely academic approach to philosophy. His book *Democracy and Education* (1916) claims that students should learn to apply the scientific method to every area of life. His methodology is based on active, creative student learning.

Because of his dedication to academic freedom, Dewey is often credited with beginning the progressive education movement. Late in life, he was also a proponent of scientific and technological progress, as he extended his influence into social and political arenas. Toward the end of his life, he experienced personal attack from critics. Although his progressive ideas were controversial, Dewey has remained one of the most influential figures of the 20th century. As a prolific writer, he left an indelible mark on ethics, aesthetics, epistemology, logic, and political philosophy for seven decades.

Teacher Practices

A pragmatist encourages students to think for themselves. Experiential learning is integrated whenever possible. Students are given ample opportunities to solve problems. Students are helped to see how knowledge and skills learned in school can be applied to real-life situations. Pragmatist teachers recognize the value of out-of-class experiences, such as field trips.

Existentialism

existentialism

A philosophical attitude that perceives reality to be nothing more than what is perceived to be real from an individual's perspective.

Although **existentialism** is considered a modern philosophy, its roots can be traced to ancient Europe. Existentialism emanates from the writings of 19th-century philosophers such as Soren Kierkegaard and Nietzsche. Other influential existentialists are Jean-Paul Sartre, Van Cleve Morris, A. S. Neill, and Carl Rogers. Existentialism is more an attitude than a philosophy. Nevertheless, it has had considerable impact on schools of philosophy.

An existentialist perceives a quest for truth as futile, because life to the existentialist has no absolute meaning. If meaning does exist, it is a product of one's creation. Finding meaning in one's life is an individual choice. Reality, then, is nothing more than what is perceived to be real from that person's perspective. Because reality is an individual interpretation, no one can give meaning to another person. Each individual fabricates a personal reality for self. The existentialist believes that you can choose to see meaning in your life or not; it is really up to you. Regarding responsibility, Jean-Paul Sarte (1957) wrote that " . . . existentialism's first move is to make every man aware of what he is and to make the full responsibility of his existence rest on him" (p. 16).

Existentialist educators might suggest an array of electives that would encourage self-expression in students. A pure existentialist would challenge the notion of required subjects for graduation, claiming that it robs students of choice. An existential curriculum would be thought provoking—it would afford students an opportunity to question and find personal solutions to problems. In 1921, A. S. Neill founded Summerhill, a school that epitomizes an existential philosophy of freedom and choice. To get an idea of how a student-centered school works, you might want to read Neill's (1960) book, *Summerhill: A Radical Approach to Child Rearing*.

Teacher Practices

An existentialist teaches personal responsibility by having students pay consequences for their actions. For example, an existentialist would not lecture students on the merits of using study hall to "study." Instead, students who waste valuable time at school would earn lower grades. In due time, students begin to understand that teachers don't give grades—students earn marks by their actions. Existential teachers help students make good decisions in the future by allowing them freedom to make poor choices now. Existential teachers assist students to find individual meaning from their experiences. They understand that each child's interpretation will be a unique rendition.

Would you consider yourself an existentialist?

Do you think students have choices and are responsible for those choices?

Does the following adage apply here: "You can lead a horse to water, but you can't make it drink"?

> **NOTABLE QUOTE**
>
> Man is nothing else but what he makes of himself. *(Jean-Paul Sartre)*

Educational Philosophies

From the above-mentioned schools of philosophy, four educational philosophies emerge: perennialism, essentialism, progressivism, and social reconstructionism. We will describe each separately and show how it was influenced by one or more of the previous schools of philosophy.

Perennialism

perennialism

An educational philosophy in which truth is absolute and that seeks to develop student intellect and appreciation for classical literature, humanities, and the fine arts.

Perennialism, emanating from the philosophies of idealism and realism, deems truth to be absolute and human nature constant. Along these lines, perennialism espouses a liberal education with an emphasis on Western philosophy and European classics. The purpose of education is to develop rational thought in students to enable them to adopt traditional values that will perpetuate the European-American culture. Robert M. Hutchins (1899-1979) was a central figure in American perennialism. Hutchins believed that extracurricular activities were diversions to the real purpose of education—scholarship.

In the 1930s Robert Hutchins and Mortimer Adler, in an effort to revive classical education, developed a list of "Great Books" from European and American literature that they designated as required reading (Hutchins, 1954). In 1982 Adler published *The Paideia Proposal,* espousing a liberal arts education for all students. A perennialist curriculum stresses the basics—subjects such as reading, writing, and mathematics, in addition to literature and humanities—with minimal choice (electives).

Teacher Practices

A perennialist would have students select books from the list of "Great Books" in an effort to improve their intellect and character. Students would be taught how to reason logically and ethically. Teachers would assume a "take charge" kind of approach in their classrooms, and students would not be allowed to undermine a teacher's authority.

Essentialism

essentialism

An educational philosophy in which education focuses on core scholastic subjects that will develop students' intellectual abilities and produce good citizens.

Essentialism, like perennialism, is influenced by the philosophies of idealism and realism. Essentialism stresses the importance of sharpening students' intellectual abilities so they can become rational, upstanding members of society. In the 1930s, William C. Bagley, a leading spokesperson for essentialism, proposed that the "essential" purpose of education is to help students acquire basic knowledge required to be successful in a democratic nation.

As you can see, essentialism and perennialism are similar, yet there are distinctions. An essentialist takes a more practical approach. An essentialist curriculum goes beyond the basics and the "Great Books" to include skills necessary for competing in a technologically advanced, global economy. The curriculum and the classroom are controlled by the teacher (Bagley, 1941). Teachers, as the authority, are expected to enforce rules and administer punishments for misbehavior.

Fueled mainly by the report "A Nation at Risk" (National Commission on Excellence in Education, 1983), many critics argued that education had become too "soft," resulting in poor achievement scores. Public pressure demanded that schools return to the three R's: reading, writing, and arithmetic. This rallying cry for the back-to-basics move was heard (loudly) in the 1980s; proponents of essentialism took a major role in this call for reform.

Teacher Practices

An essentialist would provide a highly structured curriculum with very few electives. The lecture approach would be the predominant pedagogy. Class discussions would be infrequent. Students would be given ample drill and

> **❝ NOTABLE QUOTE**
>
> There are certain basic facts, ideas, and ideals that are common to all people ... the task is to give each pupil that which is recognized as essential.... *(William C. Bagley)* **❞**

practice to memorize important facts. An essentialist curriculum emphasizes the practicality of certain courses such as accounting and computer science.

Progressivism

progressivism

An educational theory that considers the whole student and contends the way to prepare children for a democratic society is to teach independent thinking.

Progressivism, based on the philosophy of pragmatism, contrasts sharply with perennialism and essentialism. Progressivism takes a holistic approach to education—the whole student with all of his or her interests and abilities must be taken into account when planning the curriculum or delivering instruction. Progressivists believe that education should prepare children for independent thinking in a democratic society.

John Dewey and William H. Kilpatrick were progressivist educators who contended that students learn best when actively participating in their own learning. Dewey describes several progressive schools in his book, *Schools of Tomorrow* (1915). Although there are differences among progressive schools in how to "connect" a child with his or her environment, Dewey contends that in general these schools and teachers are "working away from a curriculum adapted to a small and specialized class" to one that is more "representative of the needs and conditions of a democratic society" (Dewey, 1915, p. 288). All children should be prepared for democratic living not just those who are college bound.

With the publication of the *Cardinal Principles of Secondary Education* (National Education Association, 1918) the role of the secondary schools was expanded to better prepare students for adulthood. After this report, progressivism gained strength in numbers and influence. Progressivism was most popular during the 1920s, 1930s, and 1940s. However, by the end of World War II (1945), it came under attack. Critics pointed to declining test scores as evidence of its inability to prepare students academically. Many supporters, fearing a loss of credibility, distanced themselves from progressivism.

Teacher Practices

Progressivists believe people are basically good. Thus a progressivist teacher would try to bring out the best in students. Classrooms would be open and inviting places with minimal structure. Children would be encouraged to think critically and solve problems. Progressivism supports

Social reconstructionist philosophy is reflected in a curriculum that encourages community service as a way to erase social injustices.

an interdisciplinary approach to curriculum and a constructivist teaching approach.

A progressivist would encourage students to develop unique talents and skills. Open-ended questions would be posed to facilitate higher levels of cognitive thought in students. Progressivist educators embrace a student-centered approach to curriculum and instruction. The constructivist point of view is consistent with this type of thinking. In effect, the process of learning (or the search) is more important than the final outcome.

Social Reconstructionism

social reconstructionism

An educational philosophy that seeks to ameliorate societal ills.

Social reconstructionism developed in the 1920s and 1930s among a faction of progressivists who lost patience with the delayed efforts to implement school and societal reform. This subgroup separated from progressivism and founded reconstructionism (i.e., social reconstructionism). Social reconstructionists view society as being in need of reform and believe schools are the means for making those changes. Social reconstructionists include George S. Counts, Harold Rugg, John Childs, and Theodore Brameld. George Counts (1934) contended that education must address inequities found in schools, because it is apparent that the notion of ". . . free tuition does not guarantee equality of educational opportunity" (p. 264).

Social reconstructionists would include objectives in the curriculum that would instill noble ideals and would erase social injustices such as prejudices and discrimination. Because most human prejudices are rooted in misinformation or inadequate knowledge, students would be offered opportunities to mingle with people who are culturally different. Community service projects would be viewed as optimal ways to increase students' exposure to a wide range of people.

To teach this, many high schools in the 1990s began experimenting with the concept of community service as a way to expand students' world view beyond self. Working in soup lines, for example, would give students a chance to see homeless people as real people with real problems. They would then be encouraged to be more proactive as citizens and work to solve societal problems.

Teacher Practices

Social reconstructionists design projects for students to stir them to become incensed by inequities in the system. Teachers would object to any form of literature that perpetuates negative or harmful stereotypes and explain to their students why the material is offensive. Students would be encouraged to protest societal and political wrongs. Students would be permitted to challenge the status quo by freely expressing their opinions in class. Creative and unconventional thinking would be rewarded.

REFLECTION QUESTIONS

What do you think George S. Counts meant when he said, "Now, if we but have the wisdom, we can make life rich and abundant for all. There should no longer be the slightest rational justification for the continuation of the age-long struggle of classes and nations over bread" (1945, p. 72)?

Do you agree with Counts? Why or why not?

Psychological Perspectives Affecting Education

There are three perspectives emanating from psychology that have influenced and shaped educational philosophy: behaviorism, constructivism, and humanism. These psychological perspectives offer another dimension to philosophical thought and teacher practice.

Behaviorism

behaviorism

A psychological theory and perspective on learning involving rewards and punishments that has influenced educational philosophy and teacher practice.

Behaviorism is a theory of learning that focuses on the observable effect of the environment on human behavior. B. F. Skinner and other behaviorists contend that "free will" does not exist. Instead, they argue that although we think we act as independent agents, our behavior is actually merely a response to a stimulus or stimuli in the environment. To change student be-

Giving out stickers or stars to students is a behaviorist technique that reinforces positive behavior.

havior, a behaviorist would suggest teachers change the classroom environment to one that would reward students for desirable behavior. Behaviorists use a system of rewards and punishments to elicit desirable responses.

J. B. Watson (1878–1958) introduced behaviorism to the United States in 1913. Watson's research studied reflexive responses to certain stimuli. His research suggests setting up positive classroom settings that will facilitate success for children (Watson, 1925).

E. L. Thorndike (1874–1949), another contributor to behaviorism, studied trial-and-error learning with cats in laboratory cages. In training animals to press levers to receive rewards, he discovered that appropriate behaviors could be learned if the desired actions were followed by satisfying outcomes. For example, teachers should reward children who raise their hands before speaking with comments such as "Thank you for obeying class rules."

B. F. Skinner (1904–1990), a famous behaviorist, developed a model of learning called **operant conditioning.** Skinner's (1953) research found that reinforced behaviors are more likely to increase in frequency and duration. In contrast, behaviors that are ignored or punished will likely decrease in frequency and strength. Thus, when students learn that certain responses will be reinforced (either positively or negatively), they tend to increase those responses accordingly. The application of behavioral concepts to education is known as *applied behavior analysis (ABA)* or *behavior modification.*

operant conditioning

A model of learning that postulates that reinforced responses likely increase in frequency and duration, ignored or punished responses likely decrease in frequency and strength.

assertive discipline

A structured, teacher-centered approach to classroom management that applies basic principles of operant conditioning.

A well-known behavioral modification management program developed by Lee Canter is **assertive discipline,** which applies basic principles of operant conditioning to student behavior. According to Canter, "The key to assertive discipline is catching students being good, recognizing and supporting them when they behave appropriately, and letting them know you like it, day in and day out" (Canter, 1989, p. 58). Assertive discipline is discussed further in Chapter 9, Create Environments That Engage Learners.

Teacher Practices

Behaviorists use reinforcement techniques such as positive reinforcement and shaping to modify student behavior. Reinforcement is provided whenever a student's behavior approximates the target goal. For example, a teacher compliments a highly disorganized student every time he observes her making an attempt to become more organized. The ultimate goal is to get the child organized without having to rely on reinforcement. Teachers who apply behaviorism to the classroom try to manipulate the environment to reinforce desirable behaviors. Behavioral principles appeal to many teachers because they can be applied readily to students, notably in the area of classroom management and discipline, and results can be observed.

Constructivism

constructivism

A philosophical approach to learning that grew out of cognitive psychology, in which individuals connect new learning to familiar experiences to gain personal insight.

Constructivism is a view of knowledge and an approach to instruction, embedded in cognitive theory, that is gaining popularity among educators. Constructivists view the student as the creator of his or her knowledge (Brooks & Brooks, 1993). A constructivist teacher believes that knowledge is fluid and in flux, which means that students must discover meaningful patterns, themes, and relationships for themselves. This approach to learning draws heavily on the work of cognitive psychologists, notably Jean Piaget and Lev Vygotsky. Although behaviorists focus on student behavior, a constructivist teacher is interested in how students process information. Even though the internal processes of how we think cannot be easily observed or studied scientifically, researchers continue to look for explanations.

In the 1980s researchers became interested in the thought processes that a person goes through to arrive at an answer or solution. Thinking about one's thinking is a cognitive approach to learning. The constructivist approach can be seen as a philosophical perspective similar to progressivism in which students are capable of finding meaning out of personal experiences.

Teacher Practices

Constructivist teachers would encourage students to find solutions for themselves. They would ask students questions about how they processed internally their answers to problems. Students would be asked to share those cognitions with others. A constructivist teacher asks questions rather than tells information. Students' dialogue will, in turn, improve oral communication skills. An objective for a constructivist teacher would be to expand students' thinking via open dialogue and social interaction with classmates, to allow students to see problems from different angles. As society becomes more diverse, students will benefit from being able to view the multiple perspectives of a situation. The constructivist teacher tries to make the material meaningful to students so they can see connections between what they already know and new information they receive.

Humanism

humanism

A philosophical and psychological approach to teaching that emphasizes the intrinsic worth and dignity of all human beings.

Humanism is a philosophical approach to teaching and curriculum development. In the 1960s and 1970s humanism grew out of existential philosophy. Its historical roots can be traced to secular humanism in Western Europe during the Renaissance and Reformation periods, when people began to question the authority of the Catholic Church. Individuals began to choose for themselves what was in their best interest, rather than deferring to the authority of clergy or divine intervention.

Humanism emerged in the United States as a reaction to fear that schools were becoming sterile and aloof places emphasizing academic achievement at the expense of student needs. Adherents of humanism perceive students' personal needs and feelings as a critical component of the learning process. A humanistic teacher would emphasize affective education—education that acknowledges students' attitudes, feelings, and values in addition to their cognitions and behaviors in the learning process. By the 1970s humanism had gained a considerable following.

Humanism has been considered by many as a branch of existentialism because of the apparent similarities. They both emphasize personal choice, free will, and responsibility. The main distinction is that existentialists see no meaning to life other than that which a person creates, whereas humanists believe that meaning lies within an individual and that the individual must extract that meaning to fulfill or "actualize" his or her potential.

Although modern humanism stems from the human potential movement in psychology, its foundation in education is in the writings of Arthur Jersild, Arthur Combs, and Donald Snygg (Ornstein, 1982). In Chapter 3, we discussed contributions made by Carl Rogers and Arthur Combs to humanism. Abraham Maslow (1908–1970) also contributed to humanism.

According to Maslow (1954), individuals are motivated to satisfy basic needs (called *deficiency needs*). Once these basic deficiency needs (e.g., food, clothing, shelter, and safety) are met, individuals seek gratification of higher-level needs (e.g., belonging and self-esteem) (Maslow, 1954; 1968). Maslow arranged these human needs in ascending order; he called this the **hierarchy of needs.**

hierarchy of needs

Maslow's pyramid of affective needs that must be gratified for a person to ascend to the next level.

Teachers help students satisfy basic deficiency needs so they can reach higher levels of growth. Students whose deficiency needs are unmet tend to be at risk for academic failure. According to Maslow's theory, the ultimate goal for

self-actualized

The pinnacle of Maslow's hierarchy of needs in which all deficiency needs have been met and one has realized his or her full potential.

any person is to become **self-actualized,** which means that one's human potential had been realized. Although most people strive to become self-actualized, Maslow speculates fewer than 1% will achieve this state (Maslow, 1968).

Teacher Practices

Humanism views the teacher-student relationship as essential to student motivation and learning. A humanist teacher, like a progressivist, embraces a holistic approach to motivational learning, which means that all aspects of a student's life are considered when deciding what is the best course of action to take with that individual. Simply, humanistic educators are interested in developing the "whole" student, not just the intellect. The curriculum incorporates affective goals with cognitive and behavioral goals. Humanist teachers are student advocates; they believe in the worth and dignity of each student and value the uniqueness of each individual. The teacher would support students in their quest to improve and affirm themselves. Humanistic instruction would include cooperative learning activities in which group effort is emphasized. Academic goals could be met by group work, which would simultaneously foster good relations among students and improve their confidence and self-worth.

A CASE STUDY

A new teacher came into the lounge one morning to grab a cup of coffee before class and was surprised by the intense conversation among several teachers. Ms. Birdsong was arguing that students today are not given enough choices. "This core curriculum we have to follow is about a mile long and an inch deep. It robs students of creativity. My students don't have time to think critically. They are so busy memorizing facts that they must know to pass the basic skills assessments prescribed by the state legislature." Mr. DeSalvo replied that students would pass state exams if teachers would simply focus on developing each student's intellect. Ms. Holland retorted that those students who knew how to measure the physical world and apply the scientific method to problem solving would have the academic edge over students who were counting on memorized facts and figures. About this time, Ms. Abby spoke up and said, "What we need to be concerned about is equipping our students for the real world. Have you driven through your students' neighborhoods lately? That's what we should be addressing. What is our state doing about these glaring inequities in schooling?" Mr. Morgenstein quipped, "We need to think about the health of our children. They can't pass tests when they are hungry or sick."

Try to label the appropriate philosophical stance of each of the teachers in the case study. Is there an overlap in their ideologies?

Reflections from the Field

Patty considers herself an idealist at heart. She believes in the power of ideas that are timeless. The teacher's role is to connect students' minds to these ideas. As an idealist, she emphasizes the importance of role modeling. "The teacher as well as the subject matter has much to offer in terms of building students' character. A primary purpose of education is to shape students into responsible citizens who think about and cherish perennial ideas."

Lynda believes that education should emphasize problem-solving skills to prepare students for the demands of the work place. Furthermore, schools should prepare students for life so they will be happy, content, and self-sufficient. According to her, teaching social skills and life skills are as critical as vocational skills. "The 'whole' child should be taken into account when we are developing curriculum and delivering instruction. Additionally, students should be taught empathy and responsibility. I want my students to be outraged by injustices in the system and be willing to involve themselves in causes that promote a healthier and more humane society. I think community service is a prime way to expand students' understanding and interest in the welfare of others."

Developing a Personal Philosophy of Education

When you apply for a teaching position, you will probably be asked: What is your personal philosophy of teaching? This may be asked during the face-to-face interview or on the application or both. You could be asked, for example, to elaborate on what you have written in your application. The key is to be prepared. Start now developing your philosophy of education. At the end of the semester go back and see if your ideas have changed and in what ways.

As you have seen, there is a great deal of overlap among many of the philosophies. To illustrate, throughout this book we have asked you to search for personal meaning when deciding whether teaching is right for you. When we took this position, does this mean we subscribe to existentialism, progressivism, humanism, or constructivism? Or is it a blend of all four? Perhaps we are just "pragmatic" people who believe we should think for ourselves to find the truth. Pragmatists see education as a process (i.e., truth depends on your unique experiences). The bottom line is that as individuals we are complex, and our philosophies usually reflect this depth.

Further, it is rare to find someone who subscribes "purely" to one orientation or perspective. You will borrow from many philosophies when you construct your personal philosophy. Your philosophy of education will more than likely be eclectic. A method or system for freely choosing from a variety of ideas or sources is called **eclecticism.**

eclecticism

A method by which individuals choose ideas based on what they think is the best approach under the circumstances.

Another thing to remember is that whatever your philosophy is now, it probably will change over time. We are complex human beings, and therefore our philosophies will be altered periodically. Every revision reflects growth. Sometimes we doubt our own growth, until we review something we wrote earlier. It is such a pleasant surprise when we are able to observe maturity! Not only is it interesting to watch our ideas unfold (and change), but it is equally interesting to notice themes that remain unchanged. However, it may be reassuring to some to know that fundamental values generally do not vary greatly over time. The point is that those patterns or themes that define us also differentiate us from others. You are unique, and your philosophy will reflect that distinctiveness.

One last tip: In the 1970s, when we were applying for teaching positions, the word "diversity" was rarely used. In those days, we expounded on our philosophies of education without ever mentioning individual differences. But today we are more knowledgeable about children and how they learn. We do not expect all children to learn in the same way. Therefore, when you are developing your philosophy of teaching, we suggest you take individual differences into account.

REFLECTION QUESTIONS

With experience, you may have to rethink many preconceived ideas and assumptions you hold, especially as you move from being a student to being a teacher. It is important to articulate often what one believes about the profession he or she has chosen.

From your experiences as a student, what is your philosophy of education?

As a teacher, what do you foresee your philosophy of education will be?

Is there congruence between your philosophy as a student and as a teacher? If not, what are the differences? To what do you attribute this discrepancy?

Conclusion

In this chapter we examined major schools of philosophies that have shaped and defined education philosophies. You were exposed to the rich philosophical heritage that supports education. By studying varying philosophical positions, we are compelled to rethink our own values and beliefs, particularly with regard to how we perceive the world and our place in that world.

The study of philosophy gives education a spiritual dimension that is sometimes overlooked or neglected. We are all philosophers on life, even if we do not specialize in this discipline. Specifically, reflective teachers constantly question their purposes and motivations. Why I am here? What is the meaning of this? What is the plan for my life? How can I be of service? What part do I play in the overall scheme of life? Inquiring people are always contemplating the meaning of the universe and the purpose for their existence.

If you become a teacher, what you do in the classroom will exemplify your personal philosophy of education. Simply put, your philosophical beliefs will drive your behavior. To illustrate, you will interpret school policy and class rules and develop curriculum largely based on the philosophical ideas that guide you. Of course, your philosophy of education is not set in stone, but this is what makes the process of living so exciting. This inevitable change is what keeps us always anticipating the next new lessons coming our way. Thus personal philosophies are always under construction, which is a sign of authentic growth and development. What is most important is to be receptive to new ideas so you won't miss opportunities for growth.

We hope this chapter has piqued your curiosity to learn more about philosophy as a subject that will help you crystallize your own beliefs. As is the case with most topics in an introductory book, we have barely scratched the surface of this large body of knowledge. There is much more to learn if you so desire.

KEY TERMS

aesthetics	humanism
assertive discipline	idealism
axiology	inductive reasoning
behaviorism	logic
constructivism	metaphysics
deductive reasoning	operant conditioning
eclecticism	perennialism
epistemology	pragmatism
essentialism	progressivism
ethics	realism
existentialism	self-actualized
hierarchy of needs	social reconstructionism

SUGGESTED READING

Reed, R. F., & Johnson, T. W. (2000). *Philosophical documents* (2nd ed.). New York: Addison-Wesley Longman.

Tanner, L. (1997). *Dewey's laboratory school. Lessons for today.* New York: Teachers College Press.

REFERENCES

Adler, M. J. (1982). *The paideia proposal: An educational manifesto.* New York: Macmillan.

Bagley, W. C. (1941). The case for essentialism in education. *NEA Journal, 30*(7), 201–202.

Brooks, J. G., & Brooks, M. G. (1993). *The case for constructivist classrooms.* Alexandria, VA: Association for Supervision and Curriculum Development.

Canter, L. (1989). Assertive discipline: More than names on the board and marbles in a jar. *Phi Delta Kappan, 71,* 57–61.

Counts, G. S. (1934). *The social foundations of education.* New York: Charles Scribner's Sons.

Counts, G. S. (1945). *Education and the promise of America.* New York: Macmillan.

Dewey, J. (1915). *Schools of tomorrow.* New York: E. P. Dutton.

Dewey, J. (1916) *Democracy and education: An introduction to the philosophy of education.* New York: Macmillan.

Hutchins, R. M. (1954). *Great books: The foundation of liberal education.* New York: Simon & Schuster.

Maslow, A. H. (1954). *Motivation and personality.* New York: Harper & Row.

Maslow, A. H. (1968). *Toward a psychology of being* (2nd ed.). Princeton, NJ: Van Nostrand.

National Commission on Excellence in Education. (1983). *A nation at risk: The imperative for educational reform.* Washington, D.C.: Author.

National Education Association, Commission on Reorganization of Secondary Education (1918). *Cardinal principles of secondary education.* Bulletin 35. Washington, D.C.: U.S. Bureau of Education.

Neill, A. S. (1960). *Summerhill: A radical approach to child rearing.* New York: Hart.

Newman, J. W. (1990). *America's teachers: An introduction to education.* New York: Longman.

Ornstein, A. C. (1982). Curriculum contrasts: A historical overview. *Phi Delta Kappan, 63*(6), 404–408.

Sartre, J. P. (1957). *Existentialism and human emotions.* New York: Philosophical Library.

Skinner, B. F. (1953). *Science and human behavior.* New York: Macmillan.

Thorndike, E. L. (1913). Educational psychology. In *The psychology of learning,* Vol. 2. New York: Teachers' College Press.

Watson, J. B. (1925). *Behaviorism.* New York: W. W. Norton.

© Kevin Fleming/CORBIS

At the end of this chapter, you will be able to

- Trace the influence of religion on American education and schools.
- List in chronological order and by topic major historical events affecting contemporary schools.
- Recognize flaws from the past that must be addressed to ensure that the current education system is representative and responsive to all our nation's children.
- Identify past educational issues that remain unresolved and controversial.
- Recognize trends that will change the traditional school of the 21st century.

Historical Perspectives

A bird's eye view of what to expect in this chapter

Before embarking on any new career, it is advantageous to study that profession's historical roots to gain a perspective of its present and its future. By studying the history of American education, we glean not only an understanding of its current status but a glimpse of its future as well. Of course we are not implying that anyone can accurately predict the future for teachers, but we are suggesting that an understanding of events, themes, and issues can give clues as to what *might* happen.

As you read, you will notice that many educational issues and challenges facing us today are similar to those of our ancestors. For example, we still wrestle with the proper role of the federal government in education, as well as the appropriate role religion should play in our schools. Underlying these unsettled issues is the question: How do we ensure that each child in America receives the best possible education?

In spite of these and other unresolved issues, American education over the years has made tremendous progress. However, as a nation we cannot afford to rest on our laurels. It would be shortsighted to become complacent on issues as vital as education. And besides, we still have a long way to go before every child receives the quality education he or she deserves. As you view American education from a historical context, you will observe changes in the making for modern schools. If the idea of reform evokes excitement, this could be an opportune time for you to join the ranks of our profession.

This chapter traces the history of American schools by highlighting some important milestones from its inception to its current status. Several of the major themes, trends, and issues affecting schools then and now have been identified. As you read this chapter, think about how education has evolved over the years and differentiate those changes that were for the better and those that were for the worse.

When writing this chapter on the history of American education, we tried to be objective; although we admit our biases may have prevented us from being totally neutral (which is expected and desirable). Even historians are not neutral in their interpretations of the past, which serves to remind us that our perceptions of events are tempered by our personal histories. What is most important, then, is not what others think, but what you think. While you search for personal meaning from the past, we suggest you also look for solutions to these complex issues that challenge and elude us even to this day.

Western European Influences

This chapter begins in medieval Europe around 500 AD. We will show you how American education was influenced and shaped by people, ideas, and events in Europe during the Renaissance and Reformation. This chapter could just as easily begin in ancient Greece in 500 BC, with the study of great teachers such as Socrates, Plato, and Aristotle. However, because of space and time constraints, we begin in the Middle Ages. Bear in mind that the ancient Greeks and Romans also made considerable contributions to our educational heritage.

The Middle Ages

Historians aptly refer to the *Middle Ages* in Europe (from roughly 500 to 1300 AD) as the "Dark Ages," primarily because the vast majority of people were illiterate, making progress virtually nonexistent during these years. Before the invention of the printing press in 1445 by Johannes Gutenberg, Bibles and other reading materials were too costly for the average person to afford (Segall & Wilson, 1998). The masses depended on the Roman Catholic clergy for spiritual and personal guidance in all areas of their lives. Education was basically in the hands of the Catholic Church.

The Renaissance

The next era, from roughly 1300 to 1500, was called the *Renaissance* and was a period of "rebirth" of interest in Greco-Roman art and literature. It was during this rebirth of interest in learning that clergymen lost their grip over their parishioners. The once "indisputable" power of the Roman Catholic Church was being challenged and weakened as "man" sought control over his own destiny. The idea that "man" (not the Church) is in charge of private and public life is called *secularism*. Simply stated, secularism separates church and state. As you may recall, Chapter 3 introduced the concept of secular humanism.

Reformation

The era after the Renaissance was called the *Reformation*. The Reformation began in 1517 when Martin Luther (1483–1546), a German monk, posted his *Ninety-five Theses* on the door of a German church; these tenets contradicted specific Catholic beliefs and practices. In short, Luther disputed the Roman Catholic Church's interpretation of how a person is saved. According to Luther, a person is saved by God's grace, and forgiveness is granted by praying directly to God. Converts to Luther's protest of the Catholic Church were called *Protestants*. In general, Protestants believed that all children, regardless of social and economic class, should receive an education. Thus the Protestant Reformation laid the foundation for the concept of universal education.

Colonization of the Americas

During this time the Americas were a vast continent inhabited by an estimated 5 million Native Americans (Lyons & Mohawk, 1992). According to Segall and Wilson (1998), insinuating that America was founded by Spanish and other European explorers in the 1600s, "merely fosters a Euro-American myth" (p. 50). In reality, various nations of Native Americans, living in harmony with nature, were the original residents of the Americas.

The Native Americans' respect for and peaceful coexistence with the land was incompatible with European priorities. The early explorers and settlers were interested in the land for what it could do for them: basically acquiring large tracts of land as property for colonization and economic gain. The idea that land could be bought and sold (traded) was incomprehensible to Native Americans, who regarded land as free from acquisition (Spring, 1997). Other value-clashes such as this convinced Europeans that their culture was superior. It was their duty, therefore, to educate and convert these "savages" to Christianity and to a "civilized" culture.

Believing that one's culture or way of life is superior to other cultures is called **ethnocentrism.** From all historical accounts, European explorers and settlers were predominately ethnocentric in their thinking (Spring, 1997). Unfortunately for all parties, this narrow-mindedness prevented early settlers from fully appreciating the customs, traditions, and values of the Native American people (Lyons & Mohawk, 1992; Segall & Wilson, 1998; Spring, 1997).

ethnocentrism

A belief that one's culture or way of life is superior to other cultures.

A seminary for the education of Cherokee girls in Tahlequah, Oklahoma (1875).

© Superstock

REFLECTION QUESTIONS

- Are Anglo-Saxon Protestants the dominant group in America today?

- Do you think ethnocentrism is a prevalent attitude in contemporary schools and society? Why or why not?

- What evidence exists that those students whose cultural roots can be traced to Western Europe are the "favored" ones?

- When international students come to our schools, do we try to learn from them about their culture or do we expect them to acclimate to our way of life?

AssessYourself

What experiences have you had with ethnocentrism?

In what ways are you ethnocentric?

Do you foresee your views about your own culture interfering with your effectiveness as a teacher working with diverse students?

Colonial Schools

The first colonial schools in America were established by immigrants who left Europe in the 17th and 18th centuries in search of a better life. These early settlers came to the North Atlantic seaboard for various reasons. As you remember, the United States began as 13 colonies. These colonies were divided into three geographic areas: *New England Colonies, Middle Colonies,* and *Southern Colonies.* Each region perceived the role of education somewhat differently, mainly depending on the reasons for settling there and the environmental conditions the settlers encountered.

New England Colonies

By the 1600s the Church of England had replaced the Roman Catholic Church. In England, any individuals or groups who criticized Church doctrine or refused to convert were held in suspicion. The Puritans, who were ardent followers of the religious teachings of John Calvin, were considered insubordinate to the Church of England. Consequently the Puritans fled to the New World to find a refuge to practice their religious beliefs free from persecution. (Keep in mind that the Puritans did *not* come to the Americas to promote religious tolerance; on the contrary, their intent was to establish *their* church as the rightful one.)

In the New England colonies, particularly Massachusetts Bay Colony, the Puritan religion became the dominant force in government and education. Puritans strongly believed that the aim of education was to teach children to read the Bible so they could learn "proper" conduct (which was deemed mandatory for salvation). The curriculum consisted of the basics: reading, writing, and arithmetic (the "three R's") and righteous conduct. Most children in colonial America were schooled at home. However, some women opened **dame schools** in their homes that could provide basic instruction to boys and girls for a small fee. These schools offered much-needed day care to parents at a reasonable cost.

In the 1600s, particularly in New England, local schools, called town schools, were started. A **town school** was usually a one-room schoolhouse built on land donated by the town. Colonial teachers were usually male. Discipline in these town schools was harsh and frequent (particularly by today's standards). Schoolmasters used fear, intimidation, ridicule, and corporal punishment to guarantee students' conformity and obedience. Teaching methods were mainly memorization and recitation. For example, students would stand in front of the class and recite lengthy passages from memory (can you imagine how unpleasant this exercise must have been?). It should be noted that girls were often excluded from education because Puritan elders (who were males) failed to see merit in educating young girls whose destiny was marriage and motherhood. Girls could, however, enroll in dame schools.

Textbooks in colonial days were a far cry from those of today. The **hornbook** was a small piece of wood in the shape of a paddle, which could be

dame school

In colonial America, a coeducational school run by a woman in her home; a rudimentary education was provided for a small fee.

town school

A New England colonial school built on land donated by the town. Typically this was required for areas with 50 families or more.

hornbook

The first primary text used in colonial America. It contained the alphabet, numbers, and the Lord's Prayer.

Color engraving of a New England dame school, which offered colonial children the rudiments of an education for a small fee.

© Bettmann/CORBIS

hung around the student's neck. It contained the alphabet, numbers, and the Lord's Prayer. The hornbook was laminated with a transparent sheet made from a cow's horn. After students mastered the basic skills from the hornbook, they advanced to the *New England Primer,* which contained various lessons with a moral intent, such as, "The idle fool is whipt at School." The first publication of the *New England Primer* was in 1690; it remained the main reading text until the turn of the 19th century.

Massachusetts Act of 1642

A law passed by the Massachusetts Bay Colony that made parents responsible for educating their children.

Massachusetts Act of 1647

A law passed by Puritan elders that deemed local communities responsible for the education of their youth.

Latin grammar school

A secondary school to prepare young men for advanced education in seminaries or universities by offering them a curriculum steeped in the classics.

The Massachusetts Bay Colony passed the **Massachusetts Act of 1642,** which made parents responsible for educating their children. This piece of legislation is considered the first educational law in our country's history. Five years later the church elders passed a second law, the **Massachusetts Act of 1647,** referred to as the *Old Deluder Satan Act,* to ensure children were receiving adequate instruction to resist the cunning tricks of the Devil. The following year the first property tax was levied to support local education. The Old Deluder Satan Act made local communities responsible for the education of their young people. This law specified that each town of 50 households must hire a schoolmaster, who would agree to teach a curriculum steeped in Puritan values.

In addition, towns of 100 households or more were expected to provide **Latin grammar schools** for local boys planning to attend seminaries or universities. The first Latin grammar school was founded in Boston in 1635. The aim of Latin grammar schools was to provide a classical background to young men preparing to compete at choice institutions of higher education,

A one-room schoolhouse.

mainly Harvard and Princeton. Today's prep schools are similar in philosophy to early Latin grammar schools.

By the early 1700s colonial leaders began to question whether an elementary education was sufficient to prepare young men in the community for adult roles. To better serve civic needs, **English grammar schools** were established. The major distinction between an English grammar school and a Latin grammar school was the curriculum: English grammar schools offered applied courses such as engineering and accounting, whereas Latin grammar schools offered classical courses in Greek and Roman literature.

English grammar school

In colonial America, a school emphasizing applied courses in adult civic roles to prepare young men not planning to attend college.

Middle Colonies

The Middle Colonies—Pennsylvania, New Jersey, New York, and Maryland—were inhabited by people from various ethnic and religious backgrounds, which meant that their reasons for migrating to America (unlike their Puritan neighbors) were mixed. Settlers came from Portugal, Spain, Belgium, France, Italy, and England. Numerous faiths and sects were found among the colonists: Jews, Roman Catholics, Quakers, Dutch Reformed, Baptists, and Lutherans. Perhaps because of this diversity, settlers in the Middle Colonies tended to be more tolerant of differing religious beliefs and practices of other people.

parochial schools

Schools established and controlled by a religious denomination or faith.

It is not surprising that schools in the Middle Colonies were as varied as their residents. Because populations were less concentrated throughout the Middle Colonies as opposed to New England towns, community schools were rare. As a result, many denominations established schools based on their religious faith, called **parochial schools**. For example, The Dutch Reformed Church created a network of private schools in the colony of New York. By the 18th century, the Society of Friends (Quakers) in Philadelphia had set up coeducational schools for their children. In Quaker schools, unlike most other parochial schools, children of all faiths were welcomed. Native-American and African-American children were also accepted in Quaker schools.

academy

A school providing an education beyond elementary, with an academic track for students preparing for college and a vocational track for those preparing for work.

Along with parochial schools in the Middle Colonies, there were Latin grammar schools, English grammar schools, and academies, which provided students with education beyond an elementary level. Benjamin Franklin established the first **academy** in Philadelphia in 1751. Academies offered a full range of courses that satisfied the academic requirements for those students who were going to college and those who were not. By providing two curriculum tracks in one school (e.g., academic and vocational), academies eliminated the need for separate Latin and English grammar schools.

In the latter half of the 18th century, academies—based on Franklin's model—grew in number. These original academies became the forerunners of today's secondary schools. In time academies became more classical than practical in orientation. In spite of this, the concept of vocational education (school-to-work) has remained a major component of modern secondary school curricula.

Southern Colonies

The lifestyle found in the Southern colonies, contrasted with that of the other colonies, closely resembled the stratified social system existing in England. The relationship between the Mother Country and the southern colonists was more conciliatory because most English settlers came to the New World for economic, not political, reasons. Colonists in the Southern Colonies engaged in commerce or farming for their livelihoods. Wealthy landowners began importing slaves from Africa to work the fields.

Sprawling southern plantations placed neighbors at a distance, which made local schooling impractical. As a result, generally only children from affluent families received formal education. To illustrate, the sons of planters were either taught by tutors or sent to private boarding schools. In terms of higher education, wealthy landowners usually sent their sons to European universities or to Harvard College, which was founded in 1636 in Boston.

By the 18th century a few Latin grammar schools and English grammar schools could be found in the South; however, tuition fees prevented children from middle- or low- income families from attending. Also, African-American children were excluded from education. In fact, in many locales it was illegal to teach slaves to read. The concept of public education for all children was clearly not a consideration in the Southern colonies.

In colonial America, education was usually reserved for boys whose parents could afford tuition costs for private schooling.

Events Shaping the Republic

The era of the 1700s in Europe was called the "Enlightenment" and the "Age of Reason" because new ideas were being proposed and discussed by liberal intellectuals and philosophers of the day. Lofty (yet radical) ideas, such as "government by the consent of the people," "reasoning solves human problems," and "all men are created equal," were being earnestly advanced by scholars and civic leaders of the day. Although these beliefs do not seem radical by contemporary standards, they were radical during the 1700s. To illustrate, beliefs such as "all men are created equal" and "rule by the people" were in direct opposition to the "divine right of kings" (the prevalent political belief that monarchs ruled by the will of God).

One famous "enlightened" philosopher—who debunked the idea of "divine right of kings" and who profoundly influenced American education—was Jean-Jacques Rousseau (1712–1778). Rousseau contended that human nature was inherently good (not evil). This meant that children's innate tendencies are good and therefore teachers must give children freedom to explore and discover truths. Rousseau advocated universal education; he believed that education was key to eradicating poverty and other social and political ills of the era.

Once "rule by the people" was articulated, the concept quickly spread throughout Europe and even to the shores of the Americas. Thomas Jefferson was inspired by the writings of John Locke (1632–1704), an English philosopher and scientist who expounded on many of the "enlightened" European beliefs. Jefferson concurred with Locke's philosophy that governments should derive their authority from the consent of their constituents, and thus citizens must be educated to make sound political decisions.

Thomas Jefferson not only provided astute political leadership, he also provided leadership in education. Jefferson believed that children, regardless of socioeconomic status, should receive a "practical" education in order to be self-sufficient. A classical background in Latin and Greek was therefore meaningless for most children, who would be preparing for work and citizenship. Benjamin Franklin, also a renowned Founding Father, held beliefs about education that were remarkably similar to those of Jefferson. He also believed that the curriculum should offer applied subjects with a vocational emphasis.

The Federal Government's Role in Education

Unquestionably, the Founding Fathers were inspired by the "enlightened" views of European contemporaries in the 18th century. Many of those ideas and ideals became the basis for the U.S. Constitution (1788). Ironically, however, although the authors of the constitution understood quite well that the strength of a democracy depends on educated voters, they failed to mention education directly in the constitution. Many historians have speculated that because of adverse experiences with powerful governments in Europe, the constitution's authors may have been nervous about creating a strong centralized government that would diminish the role of the states. When the U.S. Constitution was amended with the Bill of Rights in 1791, it was the 10th Amendment that gave to the states powers not specifically delegated to the federal government. At that point, the responsibility for education resided with the individual states.

Although the states were granted authority over education, the federal government retained an interest in education. To illustrate, under the nation's first constitution, the *Articles of Confederation*, the federal government passed the Land Ordinance Act (1785) and the Northwest Ordinance (1787) to ensure that children living in the western territories would receive an education. To accomplish this, the federal government surveyed the land west of Pennsylvania and north of the Ohio River and divided it into townships. Each township was further divided into sections, and the 16th section of every township was designated for schools. This concern about the schooling of children on the frontier accentuated the central government's interest in education.

Throughout American history, the federal government continued to show interest in matters regarding education. In fact, at certain times the central government and the federal courts have been extremely involved in education, as you will see later in this chapter. The extent of involvement is usu-

> ## " NOTABLE QUOTE
>
> The task is clear. We need to make children's learning—and therefore, quality teaching—our top priority. *(Richard Riley)* "

ally contingent on the prevailing political, economic, and social climate of the nation.

Some have speculated that the omission of education in the constitution was a deliberate effort by the Founding Fathers to curb the sovereignty of the federal government. Do you think it was a wise decision? In hindsight, would a centralized educational system have been more efficient? Would having national standards from the start have yielded higher test scores? Would there have been fewer inequities in education and inequalities in facilities if the national government had assumed greater responsibility for schooling? Or do you think schools are more sensitive to community needs when they are run by state and local governments?

REFLECTION QUESTIONS

- How have events in Western Civilization shaped the history of America's system of education?

....

- In what ways did the ideas and ideals of certain Europeans inspire the authors of the U.S. Constitution?

....

Exclusion of Minorities from Mainstream Education

So far we have observed that poor children in colonial America were typically excluded from mainstream education. For example, even though academies opened their doors to all children, most youngsters were excluded because of tuition costs. Even town schools in the New England colonies relied on tuition. Clearly, the idea of universal education at the public's expense was not a reality for the majority of children.

In addition to children from low-income families, most minorities in America were excluded from receiving a formal education. For example, Native Americans, African Americans, Hispanics, and females for the most part were denied equal access to education.

Girls were usually excluded from education because the dominant view (held by men) was that women would have their husbands to take care of them and motherhood did not necessitate extensive schooling. In the 1700s, however, girls were permitted to enroll in English grammar schools.

Native Americans received a rudimentary education from the early missionaries and colonists. Nevertheless, the underlying reason for education was to assimilate Native Americans into the European-American culture and convert them to Christianity.

Hispanic children were educated mainly in Catholic schools and missions. Because most parochial schools were established in low-income areas, facilities were inadequate and instruction limited.

African-American children fared poorly with respect to education. Before the Civil War many Southern statutes prohibited schooling for the children of slaves. For those African-American children who were able to obtain an education, it was usually only in the basic subjects.

This mistreatment of minority children is so blatant and offensive by today's standards that it is difficult to even imagine how it could have happened. But before we become too indignant, we need to honestly appraise where we are now with regard to minority education. As you may recall from Chapter 5, even in today's schools many minorities are being shortchanged and discriminated against based on color, religion, culture, gender, sexual orientation, income, or disability. We still have a long way to go in this regard.

19th-Century Schools

By the beginning of the 19th century, changes were taking place in America that would subsequently reform the educational system. The United States was moving from being an agrarian nation to being an industrial nation. Industrialization, coupled with an influx of immigrants during the 1840s and 1850s, prompted Americans to rethink the purposes of education. It became apparent that to ensure that people would be gainfully employed and properly acclimated into the "American" culture, schooling would have to be more accessible. Americans began to comprehend the benefits of having an educated populace. Education was perceived as the vehicle to successfully assimilate children of immigrants into the dominant culture.

Common School Movement

The time was ripe for a reformer like Horace Mann (1796–1859) to gather support for his ideas that would eventually improve the educational system. Mann was trained in law and served in the Massachusetts state legislature. He was instrumental in establishing the state's first board of education; in

1837, Mann became secretary of the Massachusetts Board of Education. Mann persuasively argued that education is an inalienable right of every citizen and that it is the states' responsibility to make it available to children at the public's expense. In effect, Mann advocated that every child be provided with free schooling at the elementary level.

common school movement

A network of elementary schools that exposed students to a "common" culture and curriculum.

Mann's dynamic ideas became the backbone of what was known as the **common school movement.** During his career, Mann worked diligently to create a network of elementary schools that would expose all children to a *common* culture. Mann believed that a public school system driven by a *common* curriculum would be the best means to ensure that children from various religious, ethnic, and cultural backgrounds were appropriately assimilated into the uniquely "American" culture.

With the election of Andrew Jackson to the White House in 1828, the middle class had scored a victory. Because Jacksonian Democrats endorsed public education, Mann gained federal support for his crusade. Mann and like-minded proponents believed public education would lessen the gap between the rich and the poor. They contended that an "educated" workforce would stimulate the economy, create jobs, and reduce unemployment (which, in turn, would reduce crime). It was presumed that public education had the potential to remedy a myriad of political, social, and economic problems plaguing America.

REFLECTION QUESTIONS

- **Has public education lived up to the expectations held by Mann and his devotees? Why or why not?**

- **Did the common school philosophy uphold its intended promises? Cite evidence to support your position.**

- **Has universal education mitigated class distinctions found in America? Why or why not?**

Opposition to the Common School Movement

Despite the compelling arguments of Mann and others, not all Americans favored common schools. Questions were voiced, such as: Who would control these schools? Where was the money coming from to support these schools? Were they practical? Many argued that universal education in theory was a misuse of allocated resources, because most children would work in factories or on farms upon graduation. Further, when it became known that local taxes would be the primary source of revenue, public opposition against common schools intensified. Some argued the unfairness of taxing childless couples and elderly people to defray educational costs. Because of the obvious disparities in personal income among certain regions and locales, many forewarned that this disproportional income tax base would create inequities in education.

Finally, common schools were resisted by some religious leaders, particularly Catholics, who perceived public education as a threat to parochial control. Even though Mann did not espouse a single denomination for the schools, common schools tended to promulgate "Protestant" values, which naturally offended Catholic sensibilities. With an influx of Catholic immigrants in the mid-19th century, Catholics began establishing a large network of private schools throughout the nation for their children.

Despite the apparent opposition to common schools, the number of schools grew between 1830 and 1865. And in the ensuing decades after the Civil War, enrollments continued to climb steadily. As towns became more populated, smaller schools were combined into larger school districts, which proved to be more cost-effective. Individual states began passing laws making school attendance compulsory.

REFLECTION QUESTIONS

Based on your experience, have you found that some schools are better than others depending on the locale? What is the answer to this dilemma?

Have you found that public schools tend to promote Protestant values? If so, in what ways?

Education for African Americans

During Reconstruction and chiefly as a result of the efforts of the Freedman's Bureau, schools for blacks were established in the South. However, these schools were perceived as "Northern meddling" and therefore were not endorsed by most whites. Schools in the South were segregated by race; after the Civil War, whites and blacks continued to attend separate schools according to Jim Crow laws. **Jim Crow laws** were state laws intended to keep races apart in public facilities. The white community contended that schools, although "separate," were "equal." In reality this was hardly the case. Jim Crow laws prevented African Americans from advancing economically and participating fully in a quality life.

In 1896 the legality of Jim Crow laws was challenged in *Plessy v. Ferguson*. The U.S. Supreme Court upheld the "separate but equal" doctrine of Jim Crow laws as constitutional. Although *Plessy* v. *Ferguson* centered on segregated railroad cars, the court's decision was used by white school boards to

Jim Crow laws

State statutes segregating the races in public facilities and in schools.

Plessy v. *Ferguson*

An 1896 U.S. Supreme Court decision that upheld "separate but equal" accommodations for blacks and whites.

Booker T. Washington

W. E. B. DuBois

justify the continuance of segregated schools. This fateful court decision was a major setback for African-American students, who continued for another 60 years to be segregated in so-called "separate but equal" schools.

Two Distinct Viewpoints on Education for African Americans

In the latter half of the 1800s a few colleges and universities allowed blacks to attend. Two African-American men who greatly influenced the education of blacks during the end of the 19th century and into the 20th century were Booker T. Washington and W. E. B. DuBois. Philosophically speaking, these men could not have been further apart with regard to views on education for black Americans.

Booker T. Washington (1856–1915), born a slave, educated at Hampton Institute, and the founder of Tuskegee Institute in Alabama, believed the aim of education was to prepare black children "for work." In this vein, Tuskegee offered vocational education for blacks. Washington surmised that the two races could live in harmony if blacks would not threaten the economic prosperity held by whites.

On the other hand, W. E. B. DuBois (1868–1963), a Ph.D. graduate of Harvard, rejected the notion that blacks were to be educated solely "for work" in blue collar, semi-skilled jobs. Instead, he favored a liberal arts education for those African Americans who would be competing with whites as equal partners in the workplace. DuBois became an active leader in the National Association for the Advancement of Colored People (NAACP), founded in 1909. DuBois assumed a high profile in the struggle for political equality. The majority of whites, however, were not ready at that time in history to accept African Americans as peers.

Early Childhood Education

Early childhood education in America did not become a recognized specialty area until the latter half of the 19th century. To trace its roots we would have to look back to Europe during the 18th century. As you may recall, Rousseau had definite ideas about the education of young children; his ideology influenced a Swiss educator named Johann Heinrich Pestalozzi (1747–1827). Pestalozzi hypothesized that children learned best through sensory manipulation and experimentation. To test his theory, he started a preschool on a farm; children were given freedom to actively explore their environment and learn by doing.

kindergarten

A preschool for children rooted in the ideas of the German educator Friedrich Froebel.

Friedrich Froebel (1782-1852), a German educator influenced by Rousseau and Pestalozzi, introduced the concept of a **kindergarten,** "a child's garden," to Europe in 1837. Froebel is referred to as the "father of the kindergarten." According to Froebel, kindergarten teachers should be kind and nurturing, and schools should be warm and inviting with lots of sensory experiences. (This is rather commonsense to us, but obviously was not in those days, when children were seen as nothing more than "miniature adults.")

When Germans immigrated to the United States in the mid-19th century, the concept of kindergarten came with them. In 1856 the first German-speaking kindergarten was established by Margarethe Schurz in Watertown, Wisconsin. Four years later, Elizabeth Peabody established the first English-language kindergarten in Boston. In 1873 the first public kindergarten was founded by Susan Blow in St. Louis.

Another important person who left a permanent mark on early childhood education was Maria Montessori (1870–1952), the first female physician in Italy. Montessori became interested in the educational needs of disadvantaged and challenged children. Refuting the notion of a fixed intelligence, she sought to enrich her students' world by designing environments that offer ample tactile and sensory stimulation. She believed that the curriculum should encourage children to "work" and learn with minimal adult supervision. With the exception of a brief decline in popularity in the 1930s and 1940s, Montessori instruction has been endorsed by many preschools and schools in America. To this day, Montessori education remains a major force in early childhood education.

> ## ❝ NOTABLE QUOTE
>
> Education consists of example and love—nothing else. *(Heinrich Pestalozzi)* ❞

Maria Montessori

© Hulton–Deutsch Collection/CORBIS

20th-Century Schools

At the turn of the 20th century, questions were being raised about the quality of the teaching force and there was an emerging interest in how to improve the training of our teachers. Researchers commenced to systematically examine the best teaching practices so that colleges of education could improve teacher education, which resulted in courses in pedagogy (Wiseman, Cooner, & Knight, 1999). **Pedagogy** is a term widely used in education that basically means the systematic study of teaching and the application of teaching methods and instruction. Training in pedagogy led to further scientific inquiry by scholars to determine the best teacher practices. (More will be said about how the quality of teacher education has improved over time in Chapter 12, Teaching as a Profession.)

pedagogy

An educational term that means the systematic study of teaching and the application of teaching methods and instruction.

Secondary Education

By 1920 mandatory school attendance laws were in effect in every state. Indeed, Horace Mann's dream of offering an elementary education to all children had become a reality. But what about high school education? What was the status of secondary education by the turn of the century? Let's backtrack a moment to the latter half of the 19th century to address this question.

During the 1800s a high school education at public expense was not a reality. However, this would change in 1874 with *Stuart* v. *School District No.1 of the Village of Kalamazoo*. In the famous *Kalamazoo* case, a Michigan court upheld a school district's decision to use tax money to support a high school. This case would establish a precedent for public funding of secondary schools.

Up to this point, secondary education catered to capable students who were preparing for college. In 1892 the Committee of Ten was formed by the National Education Association to study secondary education. This group recommended that secondary schools offer a traditional and classical course of study with few electives. Each course should meet 1 hour four to five times per week for a year and would earn one credit unit—a **Carnegie unit**. A certain number of units would be required for graduation and admission to college. As you can see, the focus was on entry to higher education.

Carnegie unit

A credit earned by a high school student for having successfully completed a course. Units are accrued for graduation and admission into college.

The scope of the high school curriculum would change dramatically in the 1900s from its original emphasis. To illustrate, in 1918 the National Education Association (NEA) assembled a group of educators to study the current state of high school education in America. A report was published, called the *Cardinal Principles of Secondary Education* (National Education Association, 1918). The following goals were set for inclusion in the curriculum:

- Health
- Command of fundamental academic skills
- Worthy home membership
- Vocational preparation
- Citizenship
- Worthy use of leisure time
- Ethical character

From this report, we see how high school curriculum was broadened to include teaching personal and social skills in addition to academic skills. Public high schools with a comprehensive curriculum spread during the 20th century as enrollments in secondary education increased.

When trying to determine the grade that would be the cutoff from elementary school to high school, many arrangements were tried in an effort to find the best division. In the 1920s the junior high emerged as a solution to this dilemma. Junior high would include grades 7 through 9. By the 1960s, another concept, called the "middle school" (typically grades 6 through 8), emerged to challenge the traditional junior high pattern. More will be said about school organization by grade levels in Chapter 15.

Progressive Era (1920–1945)

One of the most influential educators of the first half of the 20th century was John Dewey (1859–1952). Born in Burlington, Vermont, Dewey taught at the University of Chicago and later at Columbia University. In 1896, Dewey established a laboratory school at the University of Chicago to test his experimental ideas that classrooms were learning laboratories. A prolific writer and educator, Dewey has had a tremendous impact on education in

> **NOTABLE QUOTE**
>
> The modes of freedom guaranteed in the Bill of Rights ....Freedom of belief and conscience, of expression of opinion, of assembly for discussion and conference, of the press as an organ of communication ...are guaranteed because without them individuals are not free to develop and society is deprived of what they might contribute. *(John Dewey)*

the 20th century. Dewey supported a child-centered curriculum that takes children's needs into consideration. His belief that students learn by doing (i.e., experiential learning) was a central tenet to his progressive and pragmatic philosophy.

During the 1920s and 1930s, the laboratory school became the prototype of progressive education for many suburban and city schools. Dewey proposed a child-centered curriculum with instruction geared to children's interests; instruction was less teacher-directed and more student-directed. Class participation and experiential learning was paramount to learning how to function in a democracy. As you might guess, students became active (rather than passive) participants in their own learning. Dewey's followers founded the Progressive Education Association, which heavily influenced education. In sum, Dewey's brand of progressivism favored the scientific approach to learning, and the child's role in the context of society.

By the beginning of World War II, progressivism came under attack by conservative groups who claimed that schools had abdicated their role by allowing students too much freedom and autonomy over their own learning. By the 1950s, critics blamed progressive educators for too much emphasis on social adjustment and not enough on academic rigor; which many claimed was the cause of declining student achievement. Progressives were accused of watering down academic standards by offering a lax curriculum that resulted in poor test scores nationally. Some right wing groups branded "progressives" as anti-American or communists. Although the influence of Dewey may not be as strong today as it was in its heyday, many progressive ideas have survived. To illustrate, group work, student projects, self-discovery activities, and field trips are a few progressive ideas that are still used in today's classroom. (For more information on progressivism, turn to Chapter 6).

Web Sites

To learn more about John Dewey, visit http://www.siu.edu/-deweyctr/index2.html. In addition, the Center for Contemporary Education provides information and materials on progressive education at http://www.parkcce.org/edres/prog.html.

Post–World War II

Earlier in the chapter we remarked that the federal government has become more or less active in education depending on the circumstances and political climate. An example was the Servicemen's Readjustment Act in 1944, commonly called the **G. I. Bill of Rights,** passed by Congress to provide

G. I. Bill of Rights

A federal law providing funds for college education to veterans.

federal funding for the education of veterans returning from World War II. Similar educational benefits were extended to veterans from the Korean and Vietnam conflicts.

A major turning point for American education was in 1957 when the Soviet Union launched the satellite *Sputnik*. Americans became alarmed that the Communists had advanced further in technology, which would give them an edge in the Cold War. In response to this U.S. Congress in 1958 passed the **National Defense Education Act (NDEA)**, which poured massive amounts of money into education. Students who showed promise in science, mathematics, and foreign languages were identified and encouraged to pursue advanced courses in these areas. Money earmarked for specific educational programs for "gifted and talented" students was made available. Institutions of higher education received grant money to improve teacher and counselor education.

National Defense Education Act (NDEA)

Passed by the U.S. Congress, this act allocates funds to enhance mathematics and science programs and encourages gifted students to pursue majors in the hard sciences.

Civil Rights Legislation

In the late 1960s, social conditions in America shifted our attention to children who were being overlooked in education. One development during this time was an increased awareness that children, especially minority children, were receiving inferior education. As mentioned earlier, Jim Crow laws allowed separation of races in public facilities, including schools. These laws continued to be upheld as constitutional until the 1954 landmark U.S. Supreme Court decision *Brown* **v.** *Board of Education of Topeka,* which struck down the "separate but equal" clause as unconstitutional. The schools were instructed by the Court to desegregate at "deliberate speed." Many school districts, particularly in the South, attempted dilatory tactics to resist compliance. Subsequently, many black children remained in inferior schools for many years following the 1954 court decision. The delay to desegregate, along with other apparent inequities in the system, became the impetus for legislation over the next two decades to redress social and political injustices.

Brown v. Board of Education of Topeka

The landmark 1954 U.S. Supreme Court decision that "separate but equal" was unconstitutional, paving the way for school desegregation.

As part of Lyndon Johnson's "War on Poverty" campaign, compensatory programs, such as Head Start and other work-study and on-the-job training programs, were funded by Congress to help disadvantaged youngsters overcome educational barriers. The 1960s saw legislative acts targeted at children from low-income families and children with special needs. Compensatory programs help students with special needs "compensate" for deficits and/or barriers they may experience, such as poverty, physical and mental disabilities, or language.

In 1965 the U.S. Congress passed the Immigration Act, which eliminated earlier restrictions based on quotas. Before that time, many ethnic groups and nationalities had to wait for permission to immigrate; access was based on the percentages of persons currently living in the United States. By eliminating quotas, immigrants who had traditionally been underrepresented in the total population were now free to enter without delays. As a result, there was an influx of people immigrating to the United States, which meant our schools witnessed an increase of school-age children who could not speak English. In 1968 the U.S. Congress passed the Bilingual Education Act, which allocates funds to schools to establish English as a Second Language (ESL) programs to assist these children whose native language is not English.

By far the most comprehensive federal legislation to date is the Elementary and Secondary Education Act (ESEA) passed in 1965. Through amendments and reauthorizations over the years, this law has become a substantial source of income for the nation's public schools. A sizable portion of ESEA's budget is reserved for schools in low-income areas. Those students from low-income families labeled as "educationally deprived" are entitled to compensatory programs under Title I of ESEA. Schools that qualify under federal guidelines can receive funding if they agree to provide these programs to disadvantaged students.

In an effort to protect the civil rights of handicapped individuals in public schools, Congress passed the Vocational Rehabilitation Act (1973), which declares that handicapped people in the United States should not be excluded or denied benefits from any program or activity receiving federal assistance. To ensure persons with disabilities were not discriminated against in the workplace, reasonable accommodations had to be made. Students with disabilities attending public schools are protected under Section 504. Any public school failing to comply with the federal guidelines stands in danger of losing federal monies.

In 1975 the Education for All Handicapped Children Act (PL 94-142) was passed to provide federal funding to schools to ensure that all students receive a "free and appropriate education." In October 1990 PL 94-142 was superseded by the Individuals with Disabilities Education Act (IDEA), which specifically protects the civil rights of handicapped children. Under the law, each child receives an individualized education plan (IEP) that spells out educational programs and services appropriate for that particular child's special needs. It should be noted that although IDEA protects children with disabilities in public schools, the **Americans with Disabilities Act (ADA)**—passed by Congress in 1990—covers all citizens with disabilities in the workplace. Thus the rights of disabled children attending private schools are protected as well.

Americans with Disabilities Act (ADA)

Federal legislation to ensure that all citizens with disabilities are treated fairly.

When identifying children who qualify for special services, due-process procedures must be strictly followed to safeguard students' personal rights. Students who are eligible for special assistance receive instruction in the least-restrictive environment (LRE). Simply put, these children should remain in the regular classroom as much as possible (inclusion) rather than be segregated from peers in resource rooms or separate schools.

Students with acquired immunodeficiency syndrome (AIDS) are special-needs children who have not always been welcome in schools. In recent years the court system has had to intervene to ensure that these children are not discriminated against in public schools. Under the provisions of Section 504 of the Vocational Rehabilitation Act and the Individuals with Disabilities Act (IDEA), courts have ruled that children with AIDS cannot be denied access to a public school education. (This is discussed again in Chapter 13, Ethical and Legal Issues.)

As noted, many compensatory programs in the 1960s and 1970s were funded with federal dollars. However, by the 1980s many of these compensatory programs, such as Title I, bilingual education, school-to-work transition programs, and free lunch programs for disadvantaged students, came under public scrutiny by policymakers who questioned whether these programs were cost-effective. Was there sufficient evidence to justify that compensatory programs and other entitlements were making a measurable difference in students' learning?

Excellence In Education

In the 1980s an alarming report issued by the National Commission on Excellence in Education—*A Nation at Risk: The Imperative for Educational Reform* (1983), evoked an onslaught of criticism aimed at education. To summarize, this report claimed that American students were performing below other countries in mathematics, science, reading, and other academic areas. This report ignited a **back-to-basics movement,** which demanded educational reforms that included setting higher performance standards and developing a more rigorous curriculum for students and teachers alike. The rallying cry, which resonates to this day, calls for **excellence in education.** Simply put, students who work hard for their grades will achieve self-worth through their efforts.

Religion in American Schools

Undoubtedly one of the most pervasive and controversial themes in American history has been (and is) the proper role of religion in education. Religious groups have influenced American culture and schools throughout the centuries. In colonial America, notably in the New England colonies, religion and instruction were inseparable. In the Puritan colonies, schooling was church-dominated.

Two cases in particular determined the destiny of religion in America's public schools. In 1962, in *Engel* v. *Vitale,* the U.S. Supreme Court prohibited prayer in public schools. The following year, in *Abington School District* v. *Schempp* (1963), the U.S. Supreme Court ruled that reading from the Bible in public schools violated the constitution's "separation of church and state." The Bible could be read as prose in a literature class, but not as part of school instruction.

The right wing accused the U.S. Supreme Court of "undermining the moral and spiritual forces of public schools" (Spring, 1997, p. 386). In response there has been a considerable increase in the number of children attending private religious schools (estimated to be 1 million). Minority families are among those who are choosing parochial schools for their children, and Roman Catholic families are turning to church-supported schools (Alexander, 1993). Although the Christian schools have the largest student enrollments, there are religious schools representing many faiths, including Islam, Jewish, Mennonite, and Amish. It looks as if private religious schooling will remain an alternative to public school education in the 21st century.

Another alternative for parents who are frustrated with the secular nature of public education is **home schooling.** As mentioned earlier, colonial education for the majority of the children usually occurred in homes because public education was unavailable. Ironically, after all this time, home schooling has made a comeback. In effect, home schooling creates yet another challenge for the future of public education. What do you think about home schooling? What are the advantages and the limitations to this type of instruction? Do you think the benefits of this type of instruction outweigh the disadvantages?

home schooling

An alternative to public education in which parents teach their children at home.

School Choice

An alternative for parents who want more input in how schools are run, yet want their children to remain in public schools, is the option of **charter schools.** Charter schools are established through a contract or "charter" with the state or local governing agency that authorizes teachers, administrators, concerned community leaders, and parents to establish a school (Wallis, 1994). Although charter schools are less restrained by state regulations than public schools, they are still held accountable for student achievement.

charter schools

Public schools that place the authority for governance with parents and teachers.

School choice for parents will continue into the 21st century as a debated and contentious issue. In a nutshell, Democrats and the National Education Association tend to favor choice as long as it is within public schools. On the other hand, Republicans tend to favor choice across the board, contending that families should be given assistance to send their children to whatever school they choose, whether private, parochial, or public. Assistance can be in the form of a tax credit or an allocation that could defray the costs of schooling. (Charter schools and school choice are discussed further in Chapter 14, Organization, Governance, and Financing of Schools; and in Chapter 15, Schools in the New Century.)

Teacher Power: Site-Based Management

Not only are parents today being given a greater voice in school governance, teachers are as well. This trend is called **site-based management,** school-based decision making, or school-based leadership. Traditionally, decisions affecting teachers and students were made by the central administration. Site-based management is a reform movement that gives teachers shared decision making at the level of the individual school rather than at the state or district level. (This is discussed further in Chapter 14, Organization, Governance, and Financing of Schools.)

site-based management

A reform effort in which teachers and parents are involved in the daily operation of schools.

REFLECTION QUESTIONS

● Reflect on this 1945 quote from George S. Counts: "We have had unsurpassed faith in the worth and power of learning ... And the great champions of democracy throughout our national history have insisted that the survival of our free institutions requires an educated people ... Today, when confronted with difficult personal or social problems, we are inclined to turn to education as an unfailing solution. This disposition is manifest at the present time." (Counts, 1945, p. 17).

● What do you think Counts was referring to when he made this assertion in 1945?

● Does his assertion apply to us today? What personal and social problems do we face?

● Should we expect schools and education to take up the slack when things are not going well in society? Why or why not?

What Does the Future Hold?

What is the future for American education? In conclusion, we summarize specific educational issues that remain unsettled and controversial. Many of the issues raised and debated in the 1990s will take center stage in the 21st century. As you read the list, think about where you stand on these issues. Keep in mind that the following list of issues is not exhaustive:

- Whether or not local schools should be accountable to parents and the community for test scores and achievement levels of students.
- Whether or not parents should have a stronger voice and role in the governance of local schools.
- Whether or not parents and guardians should be given a choice in deciding what schools their children attend.
- Whether or not inner-city schools can afford to offer quality education for students when increasing numbers of affluent parents vacate urban areas for suburban schools.
- Whether or not children schooled at home will receive education comparable to that of their peers.
- Whether or not charter schools will be a solution to current problems evident in public schools.
- Whether or not we can afford as a nation to allow some children to be computer literate while others do not have the same exposure to advanced technology.

As you reflect on these and related questions, you could easily become discouraged (if you let yourself). However, there is some good news here: Leading politicians in both national parties are actively seeking ways to improve American education. And most people will agree that (1) schools need to be restructured in ways that better prepare students and society for working and living successfully in an industrial and technological world, and (2) teachers and students must be held accountable to high standards. The trend is definitely for a call to excellence.

Of course, the bad news is that the means to accomplish excellence in education goals are not always apparent. And differences in ideologies keep policymakers from arriving at immediate solutions to problems. As we all know, to build consensus takes time—consequently educational reform comes slowly. On the other hand, this prevents lawmakers from making uninformed and impulsive decisions. In sum, it is heartening to know that many groups and individuals are actively involved in the reform effort to restructure education.

Equal Educational Opportunity

As we conclude this chapter, we see there have been apparent flaws in our educational system. Our nation must accept responsibility for being neglectful of the educational rights of minorities, such as females, Native Americans, African Americans, Hispanic Americans, immigrants, poor children, and others who have been excluded from full participation in the educational system. Efforts must be made to ensure that all children receive equal educational opportunities so they can reach their full potential. Schools must assume responsibility for ensuring that children from underrepresented groups or minority groups are no longer denied a quality education. Minorities, who have historically been alienated from the mainstream of American education, cannot be overlooked any longer.

Fortunately, in spite of many budget cuts, the federal government remains interested in helping economically disadvantaged children and children who are physically or mentally challenged. Confronting social problems such as crime, violence, and social injustice is still perceived by many as a necessary function of schools. In 1998, Richard Riley, U.S. Secretary of Education, recommended a continued commitment to compensatory education programs such as Head Start, Title I, and before- and after-school programs, especially in low-income areas.

John Dewey once said that election "campaigns are certainly not always as educational as they might be, but by and large they do serve the purpose of making the citizens of the country aware of what is going on in society, what the problems are, and the various measures and policies that are proposed to deal with the issues of the day." (Dewey, 1958, p. 34). Do you agree with Dewey that elections alert us to the critical issues that must be addressed?

As you have seen, teachers must be committed to improving the educational system for young people. They continually search for ways to ensure that all children receive quality education. Obviously this will demand a reflective and responsible individual. Are you that person?

Would you be interested in deciding the future of our educational system? Are you willing to fight the battles facing education today?

Are you prepared to put yourself in the line of fire? Or do you feel that the prognosis for American education is too precarious?

Would you rather find a profession with more certainty and greater public trust and support? Without a doubt, these questions are worth considering.

REFLECTION QUESTIONS

History is basically a perceptual (not a literal) interpretation of what transpired in the past. Historians (like authors) select events and gather facts and decipher them based on their personal histories.

What is your interpretation of the history of American education? Should we be proud of our heritage, or has it failed to live up to democratic values and ideals?

What can we do to increase educational excellence for all students?

Conclusion

Looking into the past hopefully gave you insight into the present situation facing American schools. As you can see, America has made tremendous progress over the centuries with regard to education. In spite of this growth, however, we must not be content with former achievements; undeniably, there is ample room for educational reform and improvement. For example, in this chapter you were reminded that our educational system has not been responsive to all groups of Americans. Many populations were denied rights from the beginning, and many of those same minority groups continue to be treated unfairly by the system. Ways to remedy this are being publicly discussed and debated; the future's outcomes are unclear.

In this chapter you observed how differing political, economic, and social ideologies vied for control of education. Admittedly this is nothing new; conflict is inevitable and necessary for a democracy to flourish. It behooves us, as citizens of a free nation, to vocalize our opinions by actively supporting like-minded candidates or by running for political office ourselves. The direction education takes in the future depends on the goodwill of concerned and informed citizens. Education needs committed people with good ideas.

Reflections from the Field

A foreign language teacher in high school voiced the following concerns: "One concern I have is whether we will be able to supply a qualified teacher in every American classroom. Changes in education and teacher shortages are rapidly increasing. I fear that we will be unable to provide the most qualified individuals to meet the needs and demands of our schools. A second concern is the creation of positive school climates. The pressures in society reflected in diverse family structures and the prevalence of violence are making it more challenging to provide a safe environment in schools. I think smaller schools and classes and better prepared teachers are important factors in making schools positive places. My hope is that we will achieve excellence in education without sacrificing equal access to opportunities."

KEY TERMS

academy

Americans with Disabilities Act (ADA)

back-to-basics movement

Brown v. Board of Education of Topeka

Carnegie unit

charter school

common school movement

dame school

English grammar school

ethnocentrism

excellence in education

G.I. Bill of Rights

home schooling

hornbook

Jim Crow laws

kindergarten

Latin grammar school

Massachusetts Act of 1642

Massachusetts Act of 1647

A Nation at Risk: The Imperative for Educational Reform

National Defense Education Act (NDEA)

parochial school

pedagogy

Plessy v. Ferguson

site-based management

town school

SUGGESTED READING

Noll, J. W. (Ed.). (1999). *Taking sides: Clashing views on controversial educational issues*. Guilford, CT: Dushkin/McGraw-Hill.

Spring, J. (1998). *American education*. Boston: McGraw-Hill.

REFERENCES

Alexander, L. (1993). School choice in the year 2000. *Phi Delta Kappan, 74*(10), 762–767.

Counts, G. S. (1945). *Education and the promise of America*. New York: The Macmillan Company.

Dewey, J. (1958). *Philosophy of education (problems of men)*. Totowa, NJ: Littlefield, Adams.

Lyons, O., & Mohawk, J. (Eds.). (1992). *Exiled in the land of the free: Democracy, Indian nations, and the U.S. Constitution*. Santa Fe: Clear Light Publishers.

National Commission on Excellence in Education. (1983). *A nation at risk: The imperative for educational reform*. Washington, D.C.: Author.

National Education Association, Commission on Reorganization of Secondary Education. (1918). *Cardinal principles of secondary education*. Bulletin 35. Washington, D.C.: U.S. Bureau of Education.

Riley, R. W. (1998). Our teachers should be excellent, and they should look like America. *Education and Urban Society, 31*(1), 18–29.

Segall, W., & Wilson, A. (1998). *Introduction to education: Teaching in a diverse society*. New York: Prentice Hall.

Spring, J. (1997). *The American school* 1642–1996 (4th ed.). New York: McGraw-Hill.

Wagner, T. (1996). Bringing school reform back down to earth. *Phi Delta Kappan, 78*(2), 145– 149.

Wallis, C. (1994). A class of their own. *Time, 144*(18), 53–63.

Wiseman, D. L., Cooner, D. D., & Knight, S. L. (1999). *Becoming a teacher in a field-based setting*. Belmont, CA: Wadsworth.

WHAT TEACHERS DO

© Superstock

At the end of this chapter, you will be able to

- Describe four cognitive stages of teaching and recognize respective decisions.
- Contrast a teacher-centered approach and a student-centered approach to teaching.
- Describe and contrast behaviorism and cognitivism and identify teacher applications.
- Cite the advantages and limitations of behaviorism and cognitivism.
- Articulate your beliefs about how individuals learn best.

Making Decisions About Instruction

A bird's eye view of what to expect in this chapter

Teachers play numerous roles in schools; however, their principal role is to provide instruction so students can learn. Effective teachers continually look for optimal ways to deliver instruction to students. In this chapter, you are introduced to the thought processes (cognitions) involved in making decisions regarding instruction. Second, you will consider the extent to which teachers are involved in and responsible for student learning. We conclude by re-examining two major learning theories: behaviorism and cognitivism. Although discussed earlier in the chapter on philosophy, we revisit them to provide a conceptual framework with which to compare our ideas about how students learn. When teachers are deciding how to deliver instruction most efficiently and effectively, their decisions are usually affected by their ideas about how students learn.

You will find, however, that no single theory or model can adequately explain the complexities of human learning. Every instructional approach has both strengths and limitations. In the final analysis, there are numerous variables to consider when deciding which model to use. Should you become a teacher, you must be willing to experiment with a variety of approaches to maximize learning. You likely already have views about how people learn; we hope this chapter will clarify and refine those beliefs. Regardless of what those beliefs are, they will affect the kind of instruction you will provide should you become a teacher.

Children working in groups on mathematical concepts fosters cooperative learning.

authentic assessment

An approach that measures students' learning by having them perform tasks that resemble actual problems and situations.

students' performance with that of other students. In addition to normative data, an **authentic assessment** can be used. Authentic assessment is sometimes referred to as *performance assessment;* it generally requires that students engage in higher-order thinking such as analysis and integration. Students are asked to solve problems that closely resemble real problems they will face later.

Using portfolios to assess students' performance is a good example of authentic assessment. In this text we provide reflection questions that can be used as entries in your portfolio. Along with reflective questions, many other kinds of activities can be used to measure a student's abilities. The point is that teachers should try to conceptualize assessment as much more than ordinary evaluative measures such as multiple-choice and true-false tests. In your teacher education courses you will learn various methods for evaluating students' performance.

As you can see, during the preactive stage the teacher is expected to make numerous complex decisions. The preactive stage is the foundation on which the other stages rest (Costa & Garmston, 1985). Consequently its decisions are crucial.

interactive stage

The second cognitive stage of teaching in which the live classroom action takes place.

Teaching: Interactive Stage

The second cognitive stage of teaching **(interactive stage)** is probably the most familiar one because of your first-hand experience as a student. In this stage the "live action" of teaching takes place. Plans made during the preactive stage are now carried out or revised. However, lesson plans must be perceived as tentative because considerations such as weather, students' moods, and other factors can result in a swift change in plans. Hunter (1982) calls this need to change plans as being able to "monitor and adjust." Decisions made in the preactive stage are not fixed; therefore teachers must "monitor and adjust" classroom conditions to accommodate these changes.

You may be surprised by the number of decisions teachers make in the course of their classroom interactions with students. The interactive stage requires teachers to make quick, on-the-spot decisions. Teachers then must be able to "think on their feet." The quintessential question of the interactive stage is: What shall I do now? Other questions raised by the teacher at this time may include: Am I being clear enough? How could I explain this concept more fully? Should I give this handout now or wait until the end of the lesson? How can I increase students' interest and participation? The list of decisions goes on as the dynamics within the classroom change.

The *immediacy* of classroom action demands responsiveness and spontaneity on the part of the teacher. Kounin (1970) found good classroom managers were able to juggle many demands at once, which is called *overlapping*. Adept teachers appear to know what is going on at all times in their classrooms, which is described as **withitness** (Kounin, 1970). It is as if these teachers who are "withit" have a second set of eyes (in the back of their heads). Kounin's research is discussed further in Chapter 9, Creating Environments That Engage Learners.

Because there is scant time to think during this phase, teachers must act quickly when change is imminent. Occasionally, in mid-sentence a teacher realizes that a major change in plans must be made. For example: A teacher passes out the test and reminds the students to look over the test first before they begin. Ten minutes into the test the principal announces that all students must immediately report to the auditorium for an important assembly. As you can see, this teacher will have to "monitor and adjust" quickly. Interruptions such as this happen often, and although the interruption is annoying, you must respond quickly.

withitness

A term that describes adept teachers who appear to know what is going on in their classrooms at all times.

AssessYourself

Can you act quickly and "think on your feet," or do you foresee trouble with the immediacy present in classroom interaction?

Do you have the ability to attend to several dynamics simultaneously, or do you think this would be too overwhelming and distracting?

Analyzing and Evaluating: Reflective Stage

reflective stage

The third cognitive stage of teaching, analyzing and evaluating, in which the teacher processes what transpired during instruction and adjusts accordingly.

The analyzing and evaluating stage **(reflective stage)** is probably the one with which you are the least familiar, unless you have had actual teaching experience. During this phase the teacher recalls the lesson and assesses outcomes. Teachers engage in self-evaluation by asking such questions as: What worked? What did not work? Why or why not? Only by asking such questions can teachers modify and improve their practices. Engaging in the reflective phase of teaching is like holding up a mirror to examine what just transpired.

What are some characteristics of reflective teachers? Zeichner and Liston (1996) describe a reflective teacher as one who examines and solves classroom dilemmas, questions assumptions and values brought to the classroom, attends to the cultural context of a specific school setting, participates in curriculum development and school reform, and assumes responsibility for professional development (p. 6). Dewey (1933) described reflective teachers as open-minded individuals who attempt to see both sides of an issue. Reflective practitioners are sincere (Dewey, 1933); they earnestly seek answers to the questions they ask. Moreover, reflective teachers are not threatened by what they may discover. Reflective teachers are dedicated students who want to learn all they can about theory and practice to improve their teaching skills (Cruickshank, 1987). Thus the goal in the reflective stage is to improve one's teaching practice.

Are you introspective? Do you like to analyze your decisions and actions? Beginning teachers will need to consciously set aside time for the reflective stage and may even want to keep a record of their thoughts and assessments. For example, keeping a teaching journal is an ideal way to track one's reflections. As you become more seasoned, you will ease into this reflective mode almost automatically. It is second nature to an experienced teacher.

Sometimes the teacher will have a markedly different agenda than students might have. When you begin student teaching, you will have ample opportunity to consult with your cooperating teacher about what transpired during this stage. Use these experiences to learn more about the reflective stage from a teacher's perspective. During your field experiences, ask your classroom teacher at the end of each lesson what he or she thought about the lesson's effectiveness. Note discrepancies between your observations and those of the classroom teacher.

Applying: Projective Stage

projective stage

The final cognitive stage of teaching, based on prediction and commitment, in which teachers try to predict the outcome if an alternative method were used.

During the final stage **(projective stage),** the teacher engages in abstract and hypothetical thinking. A key component here is being able to predict student responses to different approaches. The teacher asks, What would have happened if I had used another approach? Underlying most of the questions asked during this phase is "What if?" Future plans are made depending on what the teacher learned from the previous experience. Basically, the teacher tries to imagine what might have happened differently if an alternative approach had been used. Thus the teacher projects about possible outcomes.

As a result of projective thinking, a teacher generates guiding principles for future teaching. During the projective phase the focus is on "next time." You may say that most things we learn come through trial-and-error experiences, and although this is true, the main difference in this cognitive stage is that good teachers will take learning one step further. They learn what worked (and what did not), and they *commit* to doing it differently the next time. Learning in the projective stage translates to commitment, which requires a high level of intrinsic motivation on the teacher's part.

Postscript on Cognitive Stages

There are infinite decisions involved in teaching. Thinking about teaching and planning in your mind is clearly desirable and necessary for effective teaching. There is a fine line between thinking about teaching and being consumed by thoughts about teaching. One could become preoccupied with teaching. Obsessing could be problematic for both you and your loved ones. Finding a healthy balance is the trick.

As you review the four cognitive stages of teaching and the decisions involved with each, remember that stages can and do overlap. Decisions at one stage can occur simultaneously with decisions at another stage. Consequently, stages are not distinct nor do they operate independently of each other.

Reflections from the Field

When asked what her most difficult stage of teaching was, Patty answered this way: "Sometimes the preactive stage consumes too much of my time and energy. Nonetheless, I have found that spending time planning helps eliminate many "surprises" that were more frequent during my earlier years of teaching. The stage I find the most challenging, however, is the reflective stage. It is not so much my forgetting to engage in this stage as it is questioning the accuracy of my own feedback as I recall what transpired in a lesson. I have found that videotaping a lesson provides the most accurate picture of what occurred in a classroom, but of course that is not always practical. Recalling all that happened in the interactive stage and judging whether it worked is not easy for me. I tend to be very hard on myself and overly analytical. Thus moving on to the next stage poses a real challenge because I tend to get bogged down in the reflective stage."

As for me (Lynda), the most difficult stage is interactive, because I tend to get caught up in the moment (immediacy) and sometimes forget what I had planned to cover that day. I am to blame for this because I encourage students to ask questions and make comments if something is bothering them. On days that a student gets me off track, I am never sure if the "spontaneity of the moment" was helpful. (It was probably helpful to the student with the issue, but less likely for the others.)

When we asked teachers in the field to describe their most difficult stage of teaching, these comments were generated: A middle school teacher, Dionne Bennett, considers planning how to evaluate students' performance as the most difficult part of teaching. "I have trouble assessing the extent to which my students have acquired the knowledge presented. This can lead to problems developing accurate measurements (i.e., tests) that are related to student learning."

A second-grade teacher made this comment: "I am a structured person, so I like the feeling of having a lesson planned and prepared. Therefore, when I find myself in the midst of a lesson and a teachable moment arises, I am hesitant to grasp that opportunity. My tendency is to stick with what is written in my lesson plan. My advice to new teachers is not to let your "plans" get in the way of your "teaching.""

Levels of Teacher Involvement

Another decision teachers make is the extent to which they become involved in or responsible for student learning. To answer this question try to picture a continuum from *teacher-centered* to *student-centered*. As you read, think about where your views fall along that continuum.

Teacher-Centered Approach

The teacher-centered approach, at one end of the continuum, deems the teacher mainly responsible for student learning. The teacher, as the "all-knowing" expert, is considered the one most qualified for imparting knowledge to students. The teacher-centered approach is analogous to the medical model. In the field of medicine, it is the physician who is perceived as all-knowing. The patient shows deference to the doctor, who is considered to be the authority on medical matters. The patient waits passively (sometimes nervously) for the physician's opinions and directives. The doctor, like the teacher, assesses a situation, prescribes appropriate treatment, and evaluates progress.

John Locke (1632–1704), an English philosopher of the 17th century, described a child's mind as a blank tablet ("tabula rasa") waiting to be filled with knowledge imparted by authority figures. This theory suggests that students' minds are basically "empty" until teachers and other adults fill

Delivering a lecture to students is a teacher-centered approach to learning.

© Elizabeth Crews

them with appropriate life experiences. This approach underscores the significant role of the teacher as dispenser of relevant knowledge.

Examples of instructional methods that are basically teacher-centered approaches are lecture, demonstration, lecture with demonstration, and modeling (Moore, 1998). Generally the teacher stands in front of the class and delivers and directs instruction while students sit at their desks. At times students are requested by the teacher to participate by responding to questions or emulating what they observed from the teacher's demonstration (Moore, 1998).

direct instruction

A systematic approach to learning basic skills and knowledge in a sequential manner.

A model of instruction based on the teacher-centered approach is **direct instruction.** Direct instruction is a systematic approach to learning basic skills and knowledge; the teacher organizes and presents the content or skill in a step-by-step (sequential) manner. Students are provided opportunities to practice new learning. In their book *Models of Teaching*, Joyce, Weil, and Showers explain that direct instruction, although empirically based, is theoretically derived from behaviorism. "Behavioral psychologists address the interaction between teachers and students . . . such as modeling, reinforcement, feedback, and successive approximations" (Joyce, Weil, & Showers, 1992, p. 308).

Madeline Hunter's (1982) approach to direct instruction is the *mastery teaching model.* This instructional model emphasizes the need to develop an objective (or a learning outcome) for the lesson in terms of what the student will learn. The lesson begins with an anticipatory set (or focus) that captures students' attention. The "body" of the lesson consists of providing examples, checking for understanding (CFU) through questioning, and providing guided practice followed by independent practice (an opportunity for students to "try out" new learning under the teacher's direct supervision).

Another teacher-centered model, proposed by Rosenshine and Stevens (1986), is called *explicit instruction.* This model identifies six teaching functions of direct instruction: (1) daily review, (2) presentation of material through demonstration and modeling, (3) guided student practice (performance supervised by the teacher), (4) feedback and correctives during guided practice, (5) independent work, and (6) weekly and monthly reviews.

Keep in mind that theorists and researchers use different names for their particular models. Good, Grouws, and Ebmeier (1983), for example, call their model *active teaching.* Regardless of the name used, there is growing evidence suggesting that these teacher-centered instructional approaches work well for basic skill instruction and for learning that can be broken down into parts (Good & Brophy, 1994). The use of reinforcement, sequential learning, and review of previous learning demonstrates the influence of behaviorism on student learning. (Behaviorism is discussed later in this chapter).

Advantages

As mentioned, research has found the teacher-centered approach to be effective when teaching students basic skills such as reading and math. It is also effective when teaching students specific terminology for the first time.

Younger children in the primary grades seem to benefit from a teacher's guidance, especially when being presented with unfamiliar material. Also, students who need additional assistance grasping a concept may need a direct approach.

Many times teachers use the teacher-centered approach in an effort to protect students and resources. For example, the first time students are asked to use a microscope they will need direct modeling from a teacher who is familiar with the equipment. In a chemistry lab, a teacher could be held liable for failing to provide adequate instruction to students regarding the danger of mixing certain chemicals and the importance of attention to details when working with dangerous chemicals. Thus a teacher-centered approach would be prudent in this case.

Limitations

Although the teacher-centered approach is the one most frequently used by teachers, it does have limitations. Some critics believe it relies too heavily on behaviorism, which stresses product (performance) over process (understanding). Some students may become overly dependent on the teacher and expect the teacher to do all the work. Constructivists would argue that it is better for students to find their own meaning in order to learn anything of lasting value. Furthermore, some believe that using a teacher-centered approach fails to take into account various learning styles existing among students and fails to accommodate for diversity. And lastly, research has suggested that other approaches may be better for teaching abstract thinking, creativity, and problem-solving (Joyce, Weil, & Showers, 1992).

Student-Centered Approach

At the other end of the continuum, the student-centered approach deems the individual student more responsible for his or her own learning. With the focus on the student, the teacher's role is de-emphasized. The teacher's approach is non-directive as opposed to directive. The student, rather than the teacher, is responsible for personal learning. Although the student is at the center of instruction, this does not negate the role of the teacher. Teachers play the role of facilitator or consultant as they supervise and guide the instruction to meet the performance objectives.

The student-centered approach contradicts John Locke's theory that students' minds are empty slates waiting to be filled with knowledge only teachers or other adults possess. In contrast, students are encouraged to actively interact with their environment to promote learning. Students are provided with experiential activities and situations conducive to students' making discoveries themselves. Examples of student-centered instructional approaches are as follows: small group discussions, student debates, role playing, cooperative learning activities, individualized instruction, and

In contrast to the teacher-centered approach, a student-centered approach places responsibility for learning more on the student; the teacher assumes the role of facilitator.

© Myrleen Ferguson/PhotoEdit

independent study (Moore, 1998). In the student-centered approach, students learn by activities that involve "telling" or "doing," such as interacting with peers; explaining, discussing, modeling, and role-playing; or working alone (independent of others) to answer questions or solve problems (Moore, 1998).

The foundation for the student-centered approach is cognitive theory in general and constructivism in particular. (Cognitivism and constructivism are discussed later in this chapter). On the other hand, this approach is also linked to Carl Rogers (1982) and other non-directive counseling adherents who perceive the teacher's role to be that of a facilitator—one who encourages and guides a student to make discoveries.

Advantages

The major advantage of the student-centered approach is that it places the responsibility of learning squarely on the students' shoulders, which prepares them for a lifetime of learning. The period of formal schooling in a person's life is quite brief. The ultimate goal is to instill students with a love and passion for learning so they will engage in its pursuit for the rest of their adult lives. Thus a student-centered approach encourages students to value learning, which becomes its own reward. Students who are internally motivated will not have to rely on teacher incentives, because their motivation comes from within. Cognitive psychologists argue that meaningful learning is more likely to be remembered and thus used. Research has shown that indirect instruction is effective at teaching students higher-level skills of problem-solving, inquiry, and creativity (Joyce, Weil, & Showers, 1992).

Limitations

The primary limitation of the student-centered approach is that the learning of certain material and skills demands the assistance of a teacher. When a teacher is introducing unfamiliar material, such as new vocabulary words or basic motor skills, it is probably better to use a teacher-centered approach. For example, a teacher may have to model changing a spark plug or adding two-digit numbers to students before they can perform the skill independently. The teacher-centered approach, as mentioned, is more effective at teaching students factual information that may be necessary to build a strong knowledge base.

Inevitably there will be situations in which the student-centered approach is impractical. In times of impending crisis, for example, the maturity teachers possess is needed to act quickly to avert danger. When time is of essence, students must forfeit the luxury of coming up with their own solutions to a problem, because student-centered learning often takes longer. The same content taught via cooperative learning could take twice as long to learn contrasted to direct instruction.

Choosing: Teacher-Centered or Student-Centered?

The question of which is better—teacher-centered or student-centered—often has evoked intense debate. Hlebowitsh and Tellez (1997) suggest that we avoid thinking in "dual terms" of "either-or" because it could lead to narrow-mindedness and stagnation. Most authorities acknowledge the value of both approaches to teaching. Our rationale for presenting the teacher-centered versus student-centered continuum is to demonstrate the range teachers have in presenting information. In reality, versatile teachers can move comfortably along the continuum as needed.

When a teacher decides on an approach, many variables are considered, such as subject matter, performance objectives, students' abilities, individual learning styles, and the teacher's personality. Research indicates that teachers who use a variety of instructional methods have higher levels of student achievement (Rosenshine & Furst, 1973). By using different strategies, a teacher can capture and maintain students' attention, increase motivation, and accommodate the varying abilities existing among students (McIntyre & O'Hair, 1996).

Beginning teachers are inclined to assume a teacher-centered role initially because it is less threatening and thus more comfortable. But as soon as you can, we suggest you start experimenting—moving further along the continuum. Growth results when we take risks. Furthermore, not knowing which approach you will use will keep your students "on their toes." Varying your approach will also help you avoid boredom. The bottom line is that being open to flexibility will prevent you from becoming blasé to students as well as to yourself.

What is your theory on learning? How do students learn best?

© Paul Conklin/PhotoEdit

REFLECTION QUESTIONS

- Toward which direction on the teacher-centered/student-centered continuum do you prefer your instructors to lean?

- As a student, what do you like and dislike about each extremity? Explain.

- As a teacher, which direction on the teacher-centered/student-centered continuum do you predict you will lean and to what extent? Why?

Community of Learners

Progressive educators suggest an integrated approach to student learning. John Dewey and other progressive leaders contend that learning takes place in the *context* of society, among people. Accordingly, most contemporary educators and teachers perceive learning as a social endeavor that involves teachers, students, parents, and community partnerships (Prawat, 1992). Learning in the classroom is a partnership between the teacher and students, who mutually learn from interactions with each other. In the literature, this dynamic is often referred to as creating a "community of learners." In the orientation to this textbook we first introduced this concept as a way to encourage readers to consult with peers and others when determining whether teaching would be a good career match.

If you become a teacher, you will want to model this idea to your students. Teachers who make it a point to show their students how much they learn every day from interacting with them, model the importance of life-long learning to personal growth and development. As a result, students begin to see that life is full of interesting people whose personal experiences can enhance their own learning. The goal is to get students to embrace the notion that living life is a process of learning. We are never too old to learn new things or to see life in new ways.

For example, as we reflect at the end of each semester, it never ceases to amaze us how much we learned about ourselves, others, and the subject. If you accept this "partnership in learning" view, you will be less likely to experience burnout. Your excitement about learning can be contagious. Your students will probably adopt your enthusiasm regarding learning when they see how stimulated you are by it. We look forward to every new term because we never know what new things we will learn with each new group of students.

And lastly, striving to create a community of learners in one's classroom is not only an optimal way to promote positive attitudes about learning, but it also creates respectful attitudes about each child's heritage and cultural background. Teachers who create a sense of community in their classroom give the message that each child's contribution is important; it can be an excellent way to handle diversity because every cultural view represented in a class is given an equal voice (Garcia, 1994).

Research Findings Regarding Effective Instruction

Regardless of which approach you use, your goal as a teacher is student achievement. To conclude this section we would like to summarize some salient research to keep in mind when deciding which teaching approach to use.

- The more time allocated for academic instruction, the greater student achievement will be (Stallings & Kaskowitz, 1974).
- The more students are actively engaged in learning, the greater student achievement will be (Rosenshine & Furst, 1973).
- The clearer the teacher's presentation, directions, instructions, questions, and organization, the more likely it is that students will learn (Rosenshine & Furst, 1973).
- The enthusiasm displayed by a teacher affects students' learning (Rosenshine & Furst, 1973).

As you can see, there are many things to consider when planning and implementing instruction. In sum, whether using a teacher-centered or student-centered approach, effective teachers use class time judiciously, speak with clarity, and exude excitement about learning and their subjects.

> ❝
> **NOTABLE QUOTE**
>
> Nothing great was ever accomplished without enthusiasm. *(Ralph Waldo Emerson)*
> ❞

Learning Theories

By now you may be wondering how students learn. As you can imagine, there are many theories and models from which to choose. Those of you who pursue education will probably take other courses that examine more fully how students learn. In this introductory textbook, we highlight two major theories of learning in an abbreviated form: behaviorism and cognitivism. We also identify important theorists associated with each and their respective contributions to the field.

learning theory

An attempt to systematically organize complicated human phenomena in an effort to better understand, explain, and predict behavior.

We begin by defining theory. Basically, a **learning theory** explains and makes predictions about human behavior. The primary purpose for developing theories is to make sense out of complicated phenomena to identify ways to handle human problems. A learning theory then provides a framework to test hypotheses about human behavior. The worth of a learning theory lies in its ability to help teachers better understand how students learn so they can deliver instruction more effectively. Researchers strive to describe, explain, and predict outcomes in any given situation (Rothstein, 1990).

Beginning teachers often complain that theories taught in teacher education courses are not applicable to real-life problems in today's schools. However, in this textbook, we provide concrete examples that are relevant to each learning theory. By doing this, we hope to bring meaning to somewhat abstract concepts and give life to what could otherwise be rather dry technical information.

learning

Any relatively permanent change in behavior or mental associations resulting from experiences.

One way of introducing behaviorism and cognitivism is to examine differences in how these two theories define **learning.** Behaviorists define learning as any relatively permanent change in behavior resulting from experiences, whereas a cognitivist defines learning as any relatively permanent change in mental associations resulting from experience (Ormrod, 1998). How do you define learning? To answer the question of how people learn, let's turn to psychology for possible explanations offered by some of the leading theorists in the field.

The book *Educational Psychology,* authored by Pamela Rothstein (1990), provides a concise, clear overview of psychological principles applicable to teaching. This book was extremely helpful to us as we wrote this chapter, and we recommend it for further reading on this topic.

behaviorism

A psychological theory of learning characterized by rewards and punishments that has widely influenced educational philosophy and teacher practice.

Behaviorism

Behaviorism, a theory with a strong research base, seeks explanations for how organisms learn by observing behavior that can be measured. Behaviorists are interested in responses made by interaction with the physical envi-

ronment. A behavioral psychologist views learning as a response to stimuli; behavior is shaped by one's environment. In light of this, teachers should provide students with appropriate learning experiences in a positive environment that reinforces correct student responses. Behavioral principles appeal to many teachers because, as we have seen earlier in this chapter, teacher-centered instruction can be broken down into discrete tasks that can be taught directly and the results can be quantified more easily. Many times, teachers use behavioral techniques to treat symptoms of student misbehavior.

Contributors to Behaviorism

Ivan Pavlov. If you have studied psychology, you are probably familiar with Ivan Pavlov (1849–1936), a Russian physician and researcher who studied reflexive behavior of organisms. Pavlov's research laid the foundation for learning known as **classical conditioning.** Although Pavlov's original studies were with animals, many of the behavioral principles apply to humans as well.

classical conditioning

A theory on learning that demonstrates how emotional responses stem from past associations.

While studying the digestive system of dogs, Pavlov observed that the dogs would salivate reflexively (an unconditioned response) at the sight of food (an unconditional stimulus). In time the mere sight of the laboratory assistants who fed them would elicit salivation (a conditioned response). This raised the question: Could dogs learn to salivate to other stimuli not ordinarily associated with a primary reinforcer such as food? To test this hypothesis, Pavlov ran a series of experiments.

In one experiment a bell was rung before feeding the dogs. As expected the dogs did not secrete saliva at the sound of a bell, but after pairing the bell tone with food for a number of times (trials), dogs did learn to salivate (a conditioned response) at the sound of the bell alone (a conditioned stimulus). Even when food (the unconditioned stimulus) was withheld, the dogs would salivate. The dogs had learned to respond (conditioned response) to the sound of the bell (a conditional stimulus) by association (repeated trials) with the primary reinforcer (food). Also as expected, after a certain number of trials without being reinforced, the dogs stopped salivating at the sound of the bell (referred to as *extinction*). Simply put, when learned responses to stimuli are not reinforced, they become less frequent.

At first glance, you may question how this research of a physiological nature relates to teaching. Consider how your own emotional responses to persons, things, or events stem from past associations. Pavlov's research provides us with an understanding of how some emotional responses are learned through conditioning. For example, personal likes and dislikes may also be the result of unconscious learning from associations with pleasant or unpleasant reinforcers. Have you ever met someone and instantaneously took a dislike to that person? Maybe that person reminds you of someone from your past, someone you associate with painful or unpleasant memories. On occasion, teachers will find certain students particularly annoying, yet cannot explain why, or students may instantly dislike a teacher before getting to know that person.

In addition to personality conflicts, there are other learned associations that influence our attitudes and behavior. For example, why do some children come to school more eager to learn than others? Could it be that those youngsters who are most excited have already experienced pleasant learning under the guidance of a nurturing caregiver?

As teachers we must be sensitive to the emotional responses students learn from the school environment and related experiences. Students can learn negative or positive attitudes about subjects, teachers, peers, or school in general as a result of classical conditioning. Peer harassment can contribute to a student's aversive responses to school. Teachers need to be sensitive to students' fears and try to locate the source of the fear. Caring teachers strive to make schooling as pleasant and safe as possible for their students.

John B. Watson. John B. Watson (1878–1958) introduced behaviorism to the United States in 1913 with an article entitled: "Psychology as the Behaviorist Views It" in the journal *Psychological Review* (Watson, 1913). Watson was interested in studying reflexive responses elicited by certain stimuli in order to predict and thus to control human behavior. His research found that individual differences were the result of variations in environment. This view, called environmentalism, highlights the importance of arranging a classroom setting to produce desired student outcomes. Watson believed all children could succeed if given appropriate learning experiences in their environment (Watson, 1925).

Edward L. Thorndike. Edward L. Thorndike (1874–1949), a researcher at Teachers College at Columbia University, was also curious about how behaviors are acquired. Using trial-and-error learning with cats in laboratory cages, Thorndike (1913) trained the animals to press levers to receive rewards (food). These seemingly simple conditioned responses paved the way for educational behaviorism. In effect, a teacher could get students to make appropriate responses by following desired behaviors with satisfying outcomes, such as rewarding children who turn homework in early with stickers or bonus points. (Naturally the efficacy of a reinforcer will depend on the developmental and personal interests of the individual student.)

B. F. Skinner. B. F. Skinner (1904–1990) developed a model of learning called **operant conditioning.** Skinner (1953) found that reinforced behaviors are more likely to increase in frequency and duration. In contrast, behaviors that are ignored or punished will likely decrease in frequency and strength. Thus, when students learn that certain responses will be reinforced (either positively or negatively), they tend to increase those responses accordingly. Notice that the student is the "operator" because he or she does something deliberate to elicit a desired response. Behaviorists sometimes use the term *instrumental learning* to describe this type of learning, because the person (student) is instrumental in bringing about a desired outcome.

To change student behavior, a teacher elicits desirable behaviors by using positive or negative reinforcement (Skinner, 1953). Positive reinforcement is the presentation of a pleasant stimulus after desired behavior to increase the likelihood of that response. For example, the teacher smiles at James every time she sees him cleaning out his desk; the smile (a positive reinforcer) will elicit future acts of tidiness from the child.

Negative reinforcement is the removal of an unpleasant stimulus to increase the likelihood of desired responses. For example, every time Josh forgets his textbook, his teacher lectures him about being irresponsible. The student starts bringing his textbook to class just to avoid the negative consequences of hearing his teacher harp about how irresponsible he is. In another example a self-conscious teenager arrives early to class every day to escape the unpleasantness of coming in late and being stared at by others.

Negative reinforcement is sometimes confused with punishment. Punishment is the presentation of a stimulus or the removal of a stimulus after an undesirable student response to decrease the likelihood of undesired responses in the future. When a teacher adds extra math problems to a child's homework assignment because he acted up during math class, a stimulus has been added; the intent of the punishment is to decrease further a misbehavior on the part of the student during math instruction. When a teacher takes away a student's privileges, such as hall monitoring, because he failed to do his homework, a stimulus is removed. The purpose of the punishment is to decrease the likelihood of this student being delinquent again with homework.

Behavior Modification

The application of behavioral concepts to education is known as **applied behavior analysis (ABA)** or behavior modification. Applied behavior analysis uses reinforcement techniques such as positive and negative reinforcement and shaping to modify student behavior. **Shaping** is an operant

---

operant conditioning

A model of learning postulating that reinforced responses increase and ignored or punished responses decrease.

applied behavior analysis (ABA)

The application of behavioral concepts and techniques such as positive and negative reinforcement to shape and modify student behavior.

shaping

An operant learning technique that reinforces any response or effort that comes close to the desired behavior.

learning technique used frequently by teachers to change students' more complex responses. The goal is to teach a student new behavior by reinforcing any behavior that comes close to the desired response. Reinforcement is provided whenever a student's behavior approximates the target goal. For example, a teacher compliments a highly disorganized student every time he observes her making an attempt to get more organized. The ultimate goal is to get the child organized without having to rely on reinforcement.

Application of Behaviorism

To make behaviorism more meaningful to teachers, this section briefly defines some of the core principles. In addition, we will offer concrete examples to make its application to the classroom more understandable.

Positive reinforcement. Provide a pleasant response after a desired student behavior has occurred. By associating pleasant outcomes with certain behaviors, a student will more likely repeat those actions or similar ones. Look for opportunities to praise students for desirable behavior. The following are examples:

- "Thank you, Jacob, for raising your hand before you answered the question."
- "I liked how you did not speak out of turn; I knew you already had the answer."

Negative reinforcement. Remove an unpleasant stimulus after a desired behavior has been exhibited. A student will likely increase a desirable response to escape an aversive reinforcer. The following is an example:

- "Anne, you are not going out to recess until your desk is cleaned out." (Consequently Anne, wanting to avoid losing her cherished break, begins to throw out the rubbish.)

Punishment. Provide negative consequences for undesirable behavior by either presenting or removing a stimulus in order to decrease the frequency of the unwanted behavior. The following is an example:

- "Anne, because you did not clean out your desk as I requested, you will stay in at recess." (Next time, because missing recess was so aversive, Anne will do what the teacher wants her to do without being told.)

Shaping. Reinforce any student response or effort that comes close to the desired behavior. In doing this, a student is rewarded for effort expended toward the desired goal. Shaping approximations toward the goal is reinforcing, which encourages the student to keep trying. The following is an example:

- "Well, Maria, that's certainly a good introduction to your paper. I am looking forward to seeing where you go with that idea."

Feedback. Give students specific information about their performance at scheduled times and within reasonable timeframes. Teacher feedback should be frequent and as close to the task as possible. When students finish a test, quiz, or work sheet, have the key available so they can have immediate feedback on the results; this permits students to know what they missed and how to avoid future errors. The following is an example:

● "When you finish your test, you may come up to my desk, one at a time, to look at the answer sheet."

Computer-Assisted Instruction (CAI)

In a perfect world, teachers provide students with regular and prompt feedback regarding their responses and behavior. But, as we know, this is not an ideal world. Considering all the demands on a teacher's time, not to mention large class sizes, it is not practical to expect this promptness. Fortunately, the presence of a teacher is not mandatory for all student learning. Some instruction that is individualized and self-paced can be presented. Students can work independently until they have sufficiently mastered the material. In the 1940s and 1950s, this type of instruction, called *programmed instruction,* was developed by behaviorists; it was the predecessor of today's computer-assisted instruction (Ryan & Cooper, 1998).

With the advent of computers in the 1970s and 1980s, programmed instruction was vastly improved. This type of instruction is called **computer-assisted instruction (CAI)** or computer-based instruction (CBI). These new software programs have many benefits for students and teachers. Computer programs can reduce rather detailed information into manageable frames, and students' responses to the stimuli presented are immediately reinforced. Therefore, like programmed instruction, CAI allows students to work at their own pace and receive prompt and consistent feedback regarding performance. CAI tutorials are effective for providing drill and practice to students in basic skills, such as mathematics, and foreign languages. A teacher might suggest, for example, that a student go to the computer lab for additional drill in multiplication tables. Computer-assisted instruction is discussed further in Chapter 11, Integrate Computer Technology.

computer-assisted instruction (CAI)

A type of programmed instruction in which detailed information can be reduced to manageable frames and student responses to stimuli can be immediately reinforced.

Social Learning Theory

social learning theory

A theory of learning postulating that students learn by observing and imitating others who serve as models of behavior.

A product of behaviorism is **social learning theory,** sometimes referred to as observational learning. In the 1940s, Miller and Dollard (1941) found that students learn by observing and imitating models. Bandura (1977) noted that "most behavior is learned observationally through modeling; by observing others one learns how new behavior is performed" (p. 22). Teachers' behaviors represent models for students to emulate and learn. By modeling virtues such as honesty, justice, and openness, teachers can build character in their students. The bottom line is that teachers must monitor their actions to serve as good examples.

Modeling provides students with feedback; the goal is to expose students to positive role models so they can imitate appropriate behavior instead of inappropriate behavior. The bottom line is that teachers should monitor words and actions in an effort to model behavior worthy of emulation. We will return to social learning theory later in the chapter.

Advantages of Behavioral Theory

As we see from the examples above, there are many advantages to using behavioral theory in the classroom. Recognizing the impact of associations, teachers can strive to ensure that students' experiences at school are positive and help avert any negative associations formed. Teaching students relaxation skills might help those individuals who suffer from test anxiety alleviate some of the fear they experience when taking examinations.

Behavioral theory has widespread application to classroom management. By being clear about expectations and providing consequences for misbehavior, students are taught which behaviors are acceptable and which ones are not. Behavioral techniques can be effective when teaching students self-control. Specifically, behavior modification has been shown to be effective with students who are mentally disabled or learning disabled. Autistic children also benefit from behavioral management techniques. Positive reinforcement and shaping can improve learning, motivation, and conduct in most children regardless of age or ability.

Computer-assisted instruction has proven to be invaluable for several obvious reasons. Computer programs reduce difficult material into distinct, manageable components or frames that prevent students from becoming overwhelmed by too much information. A student then works at his or her own speed when learning new material. The built-in reinforcement of responses tends to reduce students' errors and sustains interest. Also, specific computer software programs are invaluable instructional tools, primarily for those skills requiring ample repetition and drill. Lastly, students typically like using computers; it gives them a sense of mastery over their learning. And aside from that, it makes learning interesting (and even fun!).

In the section on teacher-centered approaches to learning, such as direct instruction and explicit models, we discussed the fact that many students benefit from review, modeling, and feedback from teachers. In effect, active teaching works well, especially for those students who need more direction and supervision from an adult.

Limitations of Behavioral Theory

Behavioral learning has been criticized for its simplistic approach to teaching new skills and behaviors. Critics argue that most learning requires higher-order thinking such as analysis, synthesis, and evaluation. Higher-order thinking must be acquired in context rather than in isolation. Subsequently, critics argue that learning reduced to a simple stimulus-response action overlooks the process of learning. Further, not all information can be compressed so neatly into a few discrete steps (or frames) as behaviorists contend.

Educators who profess experiential learning and other kinds of hands-on learning activities will naturally object to behaviorism. Experiential learning is based on the premise that learning is a complex mental activity, and to have meaning to the learner it must be discovered by that person. Critics contend students should seek answers and draw conclusions for themselves if real learning is to occur.

Another frequently cited limitation of behavioral theory is that it treats symptoms of misbehavior (not causes); therefore results are usually short term (Palardy, 1992). These critics maintain that real changes in a child's behavior demand an examination of underlying causes that must be identified and dealt with before permanent change can occur for an individual.

Lastly, a teacher who rigidly uses reinforcers to entice student learning may be inadvertently decreasing student motivation by rewarding a student for doing something that is intrinsically satisfying (Steinberg, 1996). Also students who are externally motivated may be dependent on reinforcers and refuse to work unless there is a known reward for doing so (Steinberg, 1996).

To illustrate, students who expect rewards (e.g., tokens, points, or grades) every time they exert effort may have lost sight of the joy that comes from learning for the sake of learning. For example, in the middle of a very stimulating class discussion, a student inquires, "Is this going to be on the test?" Realizing it is not test material, he tunes out and starts thinking about other things. In this particular case, the student has learned to attend only to those things that are reinforced. At any rate, teachers should use incentives sparingly and cautiously in an effort not to deter or inhibit learning.

Teachers need to discern when and with whom to use rewards. They should notice when rewards have been overused and have lost efficacy. Overkill can be counterproductive; in other words, using reinforcers excessively may discourage rather than encourage learning. Also, teachers should make sure the incentives are individualized (because each student has preferences with respect to what is reinforcing and what is not).

cognitivism

A theory of learning that attempts to explain human learning by studying internal processes of the mind.

Cognitivism

Cognitivism, derived from cognitive psychology, is a learning theory that examines the intellectual and mental dimensions of learning. Cognitivism was a move toward understanding the complexities of human behavior by

> ## NOTABLE QUOTE
>
> Rewards and high marks are at best artificial aims to strive for; they accustom children to expect to get something besides the value of the product for work they do. *(John Dewey)*

examining the mind's internal processes. Whereas behaviorists focus on student behavior, cognitivists focus on student thinking (cognitions). Even though the internal processes of how we think cannot be easily observed or studied scientifically, researchers continue to look for explanations.

Cognitive learning theory provides a conceptual framework to test hypotheses related to learning, specifically how the mind processes information. Cognitive psychologists and educators are interested in how students think, learn, and remember and how they process information. **Information processing theory,** as it is aptly labeled, examines how individuals input, store, and retrieve information when needed.

A name given to one's awareness of his or her own learning processes is **metacognition.** Metacognition involves "thinking about one's own thinking." Basically we ask ourselves questions as we solve a problem. Identifying what strategies work best, for example, when studying for a test, will help one be more efficient and effective. This is an example of metacognition. As we grow, we become more knowledgeable about how we learn; thus the potential to improve our learning is ever present. Those who think about how to apply metacognitive strategies to personal learning can become better problem-solvers.

As discussed earlier in the text, *constructivism* is a view of knowledge and an approach to instruction, embedded in cognitive theory, that is gaining popularity among educators. Constructivists view the student as the creator of his or her knowledge (Brooks & Brooks, 1993). Constructivists believe that knowledge is fluid or in flux, which means that students must discover meaningful patterns, themes, and relationships for themselves. This approach to learning draws heavily on the work of cognitive psychologists, notably that of Jean Piaget and Lev Vygotsky.

Contributors to Cognitivism

To understand cognitive psychology and constructivism, let's begin with Jean Piaget and Lev Vygotsky. If you take further education courses, you will learn more about these remarkable theorists and their work. Here we will summarize those findings that shaped cognitive theory.

Jean Piaget. Jean Piaget (1896–1980), a Swiss cognitive psychologist, was interested in how humans process and derive meaning from information. Piaget was so fascinated by the subject that he devoted his entire professional career to studying the intellectual development of children.

A fundamental concept of Piaget's theory on cognitive development is the schema; schemas are mental representations a person holds of the abstract world. As children interact with their environment, they confront new information; this new information builds and expands existing schemas. However, when new information conflicts with old learning, an individual has essentially two choices, the new information is adapted either (1) by fitting the new learning into an existing schema (called assimilation) or (2) by changing the original schema (called accommodation) (Piaget, 1954). Ac-

---

information processing theory

A theory that attempts to explain how individuals take in, store, and retrieve information.

metacognition

The knowledge people possess about how they learn best.

Web Sites

To learn more about metacognition visit the following web site: http://www.ncrel.org/sdrs/areas/issues/students/learning/lr1metn.htm. Information on constructivism can be found at: http://carbon.cudenver.edu/myrder/itc_data/constructivism.html (University of Colorado at Denver, School of Education).

cording to Piaget, these internal processes of assimilation and accommodation provide balance (called equilibrium) for the student. However for real learning to occur it is imperative to upset equilibrium, creating conflict or discord (called disequilibrium).

A teacher's job, then, is to introduce problems or new information that contradicts what students already know, forcing them to adapt by either expanding or changing existing schemas. To create disequilibrium, for example, teachers can design situations that produce internal conflict for students. To illustrate, one teacher challenges the negative stereotypes held by some of her Caucasian students by bringing in guest speakers—specifically she invites ethnic minorities who obviously refute prejudicial beliefs and notions.

Piaget (1952) postulated a theory of intellectual development in which a child's development progresses through four stages: sensorimotor, preoperational, concrete operational, and formal operational (Piaget, 1952). Each stage builds on the preceding one (children cannot skip a stage). Different types of learning are associated with each stage. The rate of progression through the stages varies with the individual.

In the *sensorimotor stage* (birth to 2 years of age) an infant learns through physical interaction with his or her environment via the five senses. By age 2, the child can see simple relationships and understand basic symbols. During the *preoperational stage* (2 to 7 years), children learn language and how to manipulate symbols. Thinking in this stage becomes more sophisticated, less illogical, and less dependent on motor skills. In the third stage, *concrete operations* (7 to 11 years), children can reason logically, although only in concrete terms. Learning is primarily derived from real experiences. For example, if you asked children in this stage what they want to be when they grow up, they will likely select an occupation of someone they know personally or have seen in the media. By the last stage, *formal operations* (11 years and older), children begin to think hypothetically and solve abstract problems. For example, teachers can encourage students to think about possibilities by posing ethical dilemmas that do not have concrete answers. To illustrate, the teacher poses this hypothetical question: "What would happen if the U.S. Supreme Court declared public education unconstitutional and closed down all public schools?"

The goal is to help students advance to the next cognitive stage by providing opportunities to think critically and problem solve.

Lev Vygotsky. Lev Vygotsky (1896–1934), a Russian psychologist, focused on how language and social interaction are critical to cognitive development in children. A child's cognitive abilities are enhanced through dialogue and activity with others. According to Vygotsky, children's language skills can be developed through self-talk and imaginary play (Cole, John-Steiner, Scriber, Souberman, & Vygotsky, 1978). Vygotsky's work has influenced the development of cooperative learning techniques.

Vygotsky postulated that learning occurs when students are working within their **zone of proximal development.** The zone of proximal development is an area, or range, between a child's current level of ability and

zone of proximal development

A range between current level of ability and potential level of ability that is the place most conducive for learning.

Web Sites
To learn more about Vygotsky, Piaget, and Bruner, try these web sites: http://www. ncrel.org/sdrs/areas/issues/ methods/instructn/in5lk2-4.htm or http://www.pbs.org/wgbh/ aso/databank/entries/dh23p.html.

potential level of ability. In this zone a child is capable of learning new material if presented by an adult or experienced peer. As the student becomes more capable of learning on his or her own, outside assistance is gradually decreased. A teacher's goal would be to move a child into a higher zone, where new learning is acquired.

Remembering: Key to Learning

Modern cognitive theory emerged in the 1950s and 1960s as cognitive psychologists became more interested in questions regarding how individuals learn and remember. As mentioned, information processing theory examines how a person encodes, stores, and retrieves information. Educators are likewise interested in how information is processed and remembered. Cognitive research found that remembering was key to learning. Therefore finding ways to help students commit information to memory for easy access later is a cognitive goal of interest to teachers. Memory aids and tricks are cognitive tools that can help students store information in long-term memory, where it can be retrieved.

Meaningful Learning

Many cognitive psychologists maintain that the foremost way to access information is to make new learning meaningful to the individual; this approach is referred to as meaningful learning. To ensure meaningfulness, material should be presented in a way that captures students' attention. Learners must be able to see connections between what they already know and the new information that is being introduced to them.

reception learning

An instructional method in which teachers begin by describing main ideas to be taught, so students can connect new information to familiar knowledge.

In the 1970s, David Ausubel introduced **reception learning** as an instructional method for teachers. To illustrate, a teacher begins a lesson by describing the main ideas and concepts to be taught (advance organizers) (Ausubel, Novak, & Hanesian, 1978). The objective for advance organizers is to structure information in an orderly fashion to prevent students from feeling overwhelmed by too much information. Advance organizers help students connect new knowledge to familiar knowledge. Visual aids such as diagrams, figures, charts, maps, and concrete examples can be used by the teacher to foster student understanding. The examples teachers select, however, must be perceived by students as relevant if they are to make connections to existing knowledge (Ausubel, Novak, & Hanesian, 1978).

You may be thinking that reception learning sounds like direct instruction, in which the teacher is active and the student is passive. Advocates of reception learning take exception to this; reception learning does not equate with student passivity. When students pay attention, they are actively learning, even when they are listening to a teacher's lectures, viewing videos, or reading textbooks. In fact, Ausubel and others (1978) contend that students can be highly engaged mentally while taking part in activities such as these.

NOTABLE QUOTE

Activity calls for the positive virtues—energy, initiative, and original-ity—qualities that are worth more to the world than even the most perfect faithfulness in carrying out orders. *(John Dewey)*

Discovery Learning

Like Ausubel, Jerome Bruner believes that new learning should be linked to familiar knowledge to make it more meaningful. In contrast though, Bruner de-emphasizes the teacher's role and emphasizes the student's role in learn-ing. His approach, **discovery learning,** based on Piaget's views, contends that instruction should be delivered in ways that allow students to make connections and find meaning for themselves—instead of being told by a teacher or other authority.

An example of discovery teaching is as follows: The teacher introduces a lesson or unit of study with specific examples that motivates students to rec-ognize principles and relationships for themselves (Bruner, 1966). Although teachers provide initial examples, the students are the ones to "discover" those relationships. Bruner (1966) emphasizes the use of examples, con-cepts, and relationships to facilitate learning. As you can see, Bruner's views on learning overlap with the student-centered approaches of progressivism and constructivism.

Application of Cognitive Theory

Again we will make cognitivism more meaningful by identifying core prin-ciples and providing specific examples of classroom application.

The zone of proximal development. Find the range of development for each stu-dent where they can optimally learn with the assistance of a teacher or peer. Study skills can be taught by having students work cooperatively in small groups. The following are examples:

- Have students read a passage, underline the main ideas with a highlighter, and then compare notes with others in the group.
- Have students generate possible test questions from the text and share with peers.

Disequilibrium. Provide students with activities that create disequilibrium in students' thinking, which will compel them to restore equilibrium by either adapting the new knowledge to fit old schemas (assimilation) or modifying existing schemas (accommodation). The following is an example:

- "After our trip to the courtroom yesterday and after hearing the defen-dant's testimony, did you change your mind about what you think the verdict should be?"

discovery learning

A method of delivering instruction in such a way that students are able to make connections and find meaning for themselves.

Metacognition. Help students to become aware of how they learn and how they remember and retrieve knowledge. Teachers can model thinking by talking aloud so students can "hear" how they cognitively work through a problem. Use strategies and memory tricks to assist students to remember new information. Use visual and verbal mnemonics when teaching unrelated bits of information or complicated terms. The following is an example:

- Point out recognized acronyms (e.g., acquired immune deficiency syndrome [AIDS]) to help students retain information. Encourage students to create their own mnemonic devices.

Meaningful learning. Make learning more meaningful to students so they will remember it by organizing and presenting new information clearly or by allowing students to discover relationships. Get students' attention by introducing information in such as way that students can see the usefulness of learning for later in life. The following is an example:

- Show how learning simple computations is essential to adult activities such as balancing a checking account, building a bookcase, and cutting fabric to exact specifications.

Advantages of Cognitive Theory

As you can see from the examples above, there are many practical applications of cognitive theory to student learning in the classroom. In a nutshell, cognitive theory and constructivism attempt to make learning more meaningful to students so they will remember and use the information more readily. In finding personal meaning, one's understanding of the material has greater depth (Brooks & Brooks, 1993).

Metacognition suggests that teachers encourage students to think about and talk about how they learn best and share these thought processes with others. Students can be taught how to store, retain, and access information. A cognitive approach allows students to have more control over their own learning and to become responsible for it. Taking a cognitive approach can help improve students' language skills by arranging activities in which they can interact socially and converse with peers and teachers. A constructivist teacher asks students questions rather than telling them information. Students' dialogue will, in turn, improve oral communication skills.

Last, but important, cognitivism embraces the premise that a single answer for every question raised does not always exist. Expanding students' thinking, via open dialogue and social interaction with classmates, allows students to see problems from different angles and through different lenses. As our society continues to become more diverse, it will be beneficial for students to see multiple perspectives; thus this is an important asset for both teachers and students to cultivate.

Limitations of Cognitive Theory

In spite of its appeal to educators, cognitive theory and constructivist practices have apparent limitations. Many teachers are reluctant to try experiential (hands-on) learning because it is innovative. They may be more comfortable with the familiar approach of telling students what they need to know. Additionally, teachers who dislike change will tend to stay with traditional approaches to teaching (Brooks & Brooks, 1993). Furthermore, not all subjects or skills are amenable to discovery learning. Some material may be far too complex to learn without the direct assistance of a teacher or adult. Also, there may not be sufficient time for students to discover relationships for themselves. Obviously problem-solving activities take time (and patience) to implement.

The effectiveness of using constructivist approaches has been difficult to measure scientifically. Therefore some teachers are reluctant to employ cognitive methods when they realize these methods are difficult to assess objectively (Brooks & Brooks, 1993). Critics contend that qualitative learning is rarely measured by standardized achievement tests. Gordon (1998) notes that because real-life problem-solving is not always compatible with "mandated curricula, textbooks, standardized tests, state standards, and the seven period day" (p. 391), many teachers are skeptical about using such strategies. In summary, many educators consider cognitive approaches, especially discovery learning activities, impractical for present-day realities in school systems.

Web Site

For information about Albert Bandura's social learning theory, you may want to check out this web site: http://www.richmond.edu/%7Epsych/tvagslt.html.

social cognitive learning theory

A theory of learning postulating that students form expectations about consequences that motivate them to behave in certain ways.

Social Cognitive Learning Theory

Earlier we considered the social learning theory from a behaviorist perspective. Behaviorist teachers reinforce behaviors they want students to emulate by providing appropriate models. Albert Bandura and other cognitive psychologists began to investigate the "cognitive" aspects of observation, the mental processes involved when students observe models and imitate behaviors (Lefrançois, 1997). Their approach, called **social cognitive learning theory,** retains basic operant behavioral principles, such as reinforcement and shaping.

Social cognitive learning theorists interpret reinforcers differently from behaviorists. For example, they believe that individuals form *expectations* about consequences, and those expectations (cognitions) motivate the person to behave in certain ways. If students are exposed to people who have successfully transcended disadvantaged backgrounds, they too might *expect* that this could happen to them through similar attitudes and work habits. For obvious reasons, teachers should expose students to positive and successful role models from diverse cultural backgrounds, representing both genders, in addition to successful persons who have overcome significant mental and physical disabilities.

REFLECTION QUESTIONS

Which theory resembles the way you learn the best? Explain.

Which theory do you think would facilitate student learning the most? Why or why not?

An Eclectic Approach

If you become a teacher, you will be constantly looking for those approaches that improve student learning and thinking. Deciding which theory or strategies to use under what conditions can be very confusing, especially for a beginning teacher. In reality most teachers draw from all the theories; they borrow from those models that are most suitable for their specified purposes. In Chapter 6 we called this system or approach *eclecticism*. An eclectic teacher, being familiar with many theories and models of learning, will recognize inherent strengths and limitations and then proceed to select the optimal approaches or methods for the situation at hand.

Simply stated, adhering rigidly to one theory or model could limit your effectiveness as a teacher. Being willing to experiment with a wide range of approaches will enhance your effectiveness. As our student bodies become more diverse and we learn more about individual learning styles, teachers will have to be more discriminating when selecting appropriate modes of instruction.

On a final note, individuals perceive and process information differently; we found one model of learning, called *4MAT* (developed by Excel, Inc.), to be helpful in describing this idea.*

Web Site
To learn more about the 4MAT system model, visit Excel Incorporated's web site at http://www.excelcorp.com.

AssessYourself

This chapter suggests that teachers need to constantly seek ways to help students learn more efficiently and effectively.

Do you like to try new things, or do you tend to resist change?

Would you be willing to use new strategies even if initially you were uncomfortable using them?

*For more information about the 4MAT model, you can write to Excel Incorporated at 23385 Old Barrington Road, Barrington, IL 60010; or call 1-800-822-4628.

Conclusion

In this chapter you are given a chance to go "behind the scenes" and examine the thought processes teachers experience as they decide how to optimally deliver instruction to students. Because teachers make countless decisions on a daily basis, the ability to make sound decisions and act quickly is central to a teacher's success in the classroom. Reflective teachers evaluate their decisions and actions to determine how they can improve instruction. Learning from mistakes and adjusting instruction requires reflection, commitment, and flexibility on the teacher's part.

This chapter also considers that attitudes about how students learn can greatly affect a teacher's choice in how instruction is delivered. If you believe your role is chiefly to transmit a body of knowledge, then you might lean more toward a teacher-centered approach to instruction. Or if you believe that students are ultimately responsible for their own learning, then you may adopt a more student-centered approach. The ability to slide back and forth along this continuum increases a teacher's versatility that enhances effectiveness.

In this chapter, two theories of learning, behaviorism and cognitivism, are presented; both are applicable to classroom instruction. Each theory has advantages and limitations that must be taken into account. Although accomplished in slightly different ways, both theories stress the importance of positive role modeling in student learning.

Prospective teachers should become familiar with the various learning theories and models so they can choose those that work best under certain conditions. Teachers, in addition to being good role models, must be knowledgeable about how students learn and open to the idea of choosing instruction that considers the diversity found among learners.

KEY TERMS

applied behavior analysis (ABA)

authentic assessment

behaviorism

classical conditioning

cognitivism

computer-assisted instruction (CAI)

direct instruction

discovery learning

information processing theory

interactive stage

learning

learning theory

metacognition

operant conditioning

preactive stage

projective stage

reception learning

reflective stage

shaping

social cognitive learning theory

social learning theory

withitness

zone of proximal development

SUGGESTED READING

Brooks, J. G., & Brooks, M. G. (1993). *The case for constructivist classrooms.* Alexandria, VA: Association for Supervision and Curriculum Development.

Jensen, E. (1998). *Teaching with the brain in mind.* Alexandria, VA: Association for Supervision and Curriculum Development.

Rothstein, P. R. (1990). *Educational psychology.* New York: McGraw-Hill.

REFERENCES

Ausubel, D. P., Novak, J. D., & Hanesian, H. (1978). *Educational psychology: A cognitive view* (2nd ed.). New York: Holt, Rinehart & Winston.

Bandura, A. (1977). *Social learning theory.* Upper Saddle River, NJ: Prentice Hall.

Brooks, J. G., & Brooks, M. G. (1993). *The case for constructivist classrooms.* Alexandria, VA: Association for Supervision and Curriculum Development.

Bruner, J. (1966). *Toward a theory of instruction.* New York: Norton.

Cole, M., John-Steiner, V., Scriber, S., Souberman, E., & Vygotsky, L. S. (1978). *Mind in society: The development of higher psychological processes.* Cambridge, MA: Harvard University Press.

Costa, A. L., & Garmston, R. (1985). Supervision for intelligent teaching. *Educational Leadership, 42,* 70–80.

Costa, A. L., & Garmston, R. J. (1994). *Cognitive coaching: A foundation for renaissance schools.* Norwood, MA: Christopher-Gordon Publishers.

Cruickshank, D. R. (1987). *Reflective teaching: The preparation of students of teaching.* Reston, VA: Association of Teacher Educators.

Dewey, J. (1915). *Schools of tomorrow.* New York: E. P. Dutton.

Dewey, J. (1933). *How we think.* Boston: Heath.

Garcia, E. E. (1994). *Understanding and meeting the challenge of student cultural diversity.* Boston: Houghton Mifflin.

Good, T. L., & Brophy, J. E. (1994). *Looking in classrooms* (6th ed.). New York: Harper Collins.

Good, T. L., Grouws, D. A., & Ebmeier, H. (1983). *Active mathematics teaching.* New York: Longman.

Gordon, R. (1998). Balancing real-world problems with real-world results. *Phi Delta Kappan, 79*(5), 390–393.

Hlebowitsh, P. S., & Tellez, K. (1997). *American education: Purpose and promise.* Belmont, CA: West/Wadsworth.

Hunter, M. C. (1982). *Mastery teaching.* El Segundo, CA: TIP Publishing.

Joyce, B., Weil, M., & Showers, B. (1992). *Models of teaching* (4th ed.). Needham Heights, MA: Simon & Schuster.

Kounin, J. S. (1970). *Discipline and group management in classrooms.* New York: Holt, Rinehart and Winston.

Lefrançois, G. R. (1997). *Psychology for teachers* (9th ed.). Belmont CA: Wadsworth.

Lortie D. (1975). *School teacher: A sociological study.* Chicago: University of Chicago Press.

McIntyre, D. J., & O'Hair, M. J. (1996). *The reflective roles of the classroom teacher.* Belmont, CA: Wadsworth.

Miller, N. E., & Dollard, J. C. (1941). *Social learning and imitation.* New Haven, CT: Yale University Press.

Moore, K. D. (1998). *Classroom teaching skills* (4th ed.). Boston: McGraw Hill.

Ormrod, J. E. (1998). *Educational psychology: Developing learners.* Upper Saddle River, NJ: Prentice Hall.

Palardy, J. M. (1992). Behavior modification: It does work, but... *Journal of Instructional Psychology, 22,* 127–132.

Piaget, J. (1952). *The language and thought of the child.* London: Routledge and Kegal Paul.

Piaget, J. (1954). *The construction of reality in the child.* New York: Basic Books.

Prawat, R. S. (1992). From individual differences to learning communities: Our changing focus. *Educational Leadership, 49*(7), 9–13.

Rosenshine, B., & Furst, N. (1973). The use of direct observation to study teaching. In R. M. Travers (ed.), *Second handbook of research on teaching.* Chicago: Rand McNally.

Rosenshine, B., & Stevens, R. (1986). Teaching functions. In M. C. Wittrock (Ed.), *Handbook of research on teaching* (3rd ed.) (pp. 376–391). New York: Macmillan.

Rothstein, P. R. (1990). *Educational psychology.* New York: McGraw-Hill.

Ryan, K., & Cooper, J. M. (1998). *Those who can, teach* (8th ed.). Boston: Houghton Mifflin.

Skinner, B. F. (1953). *Science and human behavior.* New York: Macmillan.

Stallings, J., & Kaskowitz, D. (1974). *Follow through classroom observation evaluation, 1972– 73.* Menlo Park, CA: Stanford Research Institute.

Steinberg, L. (1996). *Beyond the classroom: Why school reform has failed and what parents need to do.* New York: Simon & Schuster.

Thorndike, E. L. (1913). Educational psychology. In *The psychology of learning* (Vol. 2). New York: Teachers College.

Watson, J. B. (1913). Psychology as the behaviorist views it. *Psychological Review, 20,* 158– 177.

Watson, J. B. (1925). *Behaviorism.* New York: W. W. Norton.

Zeichner, K. M., & Liston, D. P. (1996). *Reflective teaching: An introduction.* Mahwah, N.J.: Lawrence Erlbaum Associates.

At the end of this chapter, you will be able to

- Explain what it means to manage a classroom.

- Identify six features of classrooms that make management challenging.

- Describe effective strategies for managing the classroom.

- Differentiate between teacher-centered and student-centered classroom management approaches.

- Assess yourself in terms of qualities needed to manage a classroom.

CHAPTER 9

Creating Environments That Engage Learners

A bird's eye view of what to expect in this chapter

To be concerned about managing student behavior is not unusual. Many prospective teachers worry about whether they will be able to handle student behavior. In this chapter you will learn what is involved in managing a classroom. You will explore the relationship between instructional and managerial skills, and you will learn that many classroom problems can be averted by positive teacher attitudes and proactive strategies.

As you read this chapter, formulate your ideas about what it means to manage a classroom, develop classroom rules, set up your classroom, and respond to student misbehavior. After you read this chapter, we hope that many of your concerns about classroom management will be alleviated and that your confidence level is increased. Classrooms are complex places that require leadership in solving the problems of management. It is our hope that you will become leaders in the classrooms of the future.

f you are like most beginning teachers, you associate classroom management with student behavior. In particular, you probably think about misbehavior and how you will handle various incidents. However, it is important to understand that classroom management entails much more than responding to student behavior. As Weinstein (1996, p. 28) notes, it means "gaining student cooperation and promoting their involvement in learning activities." The challenge of managing a classroom lies in balancing the needs of individuals with those of the group so that all students can learn.

What Does Managing a Classroom Mean?

Understanding what it means to manage a classroom begins with knowing the reason for it. This includes knowing what the purpose of classroom management is *not*. The reason for a well-managed classroom is not so that quiet prevails. It is not to maintain your peace of mind. Its purpose is not even to control student behavior. As Good and Brophy (1994) emphasize, classroom management should be directed toward developing students' self-control rather than promoting teachers' control over students. Managing a classroom effectively means to create the conditions that facilitate learning. Simply, **classroom management** involves teacher decisions and actions intended to create an environment conducive to learning.

classroom management

Teacher decisions and actions intended to create an environment conducive to learning.

To illustrate this idea, let's assume you have invited guests over to your home for a meal. Although you cannot control their reactions to your preparations, you can determine how you will best use the time, space, and materials at your disposal. As a result of your planning efforts, you can achieve a successful event. Again, you will not be able to control the guests but you will be able to arrange the conditions under which your dinner party will occur. The same is true in managing a classroom. Much of what it means to manage a classroom takes place behind the scenes, before interacting with the class. Managing a classroom involves making many decisions, requires exceptional organizational skills, and is a skill that is developed over time.

As Kohn (1996) in *Beyond Discipline: From Compliance to Community* points out, community rather than compliance should be the teacher's goal in managing a classroom. Likewise, Glasser (1990) in *The Quality School* indicates that boss-managers try to control others, whereas leader-managers desire to empower others. Classrooms managed by authoritarian teachers have a different look and feel than those managed by authoritative teachers. In managing behavior, there is a definite trend of moving from teacher control to student self-control (Evertson & Harris, 1992).

Most people associate discipline with classroom management. However, as we examine the meaning of classroom management, it is important to

Good classroom managers can juggle many classroom demands at once.

© Elizabeth Crews

view it as more than discipline. We usually think of discipline in terms of correcting behavior, but the origin of the word "discipline" literally means "instruction" or "training." Thus, teaching itself is "discipline." Whether we realize it or not, we are always teaching behavior through modeling. In his review of research on classroom management, Doyle (1986) emphasized the notion of "order." He further defined this concept of "order" as "a harmony of action with structure and purpose" (Doyle, 1986, p. 424). Classroom management decisions affect how this harmony is established and maintained.

Teachers' skills in classroom management are closely related to their instructional skills (Doyle, 1986). In fact, one of the best off-task preventive measures is a well-organized, interesting lesson (Martin, 1997). When students are engaged in the learning activities, they are less likely to cause discipline problems. As you think about managing a classroom, consider the impact of the following three variables (Allen, 1995, p. 178):

● *Students' aptitudes*—Who are the students in our classrooms and what do we know about them?

● *Instructional treatments*—What are the most effective ways to instruct students so they will learn and will want to learn?

● *Learning outcomes*—What do we want students to learn, and how will we evaluate their progress?

As you can see from the list above, it is difficult to separate effective instruction from management because they overlap so much. Giving attention to all three of these variables will greatly influence how well you are able to manage the classroom. Often, management challenges are actually instructional problems. Once the teacher makes a change in method or gives greater attention to students' needs, management difficulties diminish. Planning lessons that are focused on desired learning outcomes for students will help you prevent many classroom problems. Yet, it is vital that you not forget that problems pervade the practice of teaching. Haberman (1995) found that star teachers (i.e., those who successfully teach children of poverty) hold this view and search for ways to solve problems and engage students in learning.

You should remember that management is "a means to an end" (Ralph, 1993, p. 64). It is very possible for a classroom to be well managed and yet no learning takes place. "Whereas good classroom management is necessary for learning, it does not stand alone" (Evertson & Harris, 1992, p. 77). Your need for order should not take precedence over the creation of meaningful instruction (Weinstein, 1996). For example, imagine that you have discovered an exciting approach to helping students learn the names and locations of the 50 states, but this new method has the potential for student rowdiness. Teachers who have a strong need for order will not even attempt the activity for fear of losing control.

Teachers who take a proactive approach to management know how to adapt strategies to their learners and will find a way to structure the activity in such a way to allow its use. Proactive classroom management, according to Ralph (1993, p. 60), is defined as "a process of establishing and maintaining the conditions under which effective teaching and learning will occur." This is what it means to manage a classroom.

AssessYourself

What is your simile for classroom management? To help identify your simile, try completing this statement: "Managing a classroom is like ..." (what object or event?). Share your simile with a classmate. What does your simile tell you about yourself and what you value?

What in a classroom is under your control? What in a classroom is outside your control?

What does "losing control" mean to you?

Why Is Managing a Classroom Difficult?

To answer this question, let's zoom in for a look inside Mr. Spencer's ninth-grade English class.

A CASE STUDY

The 90-minute period has just begun. Students are getting out their notebooks and the paperback novel they will discuss today. Mr. Spencer notes that his students are especially talkative today. He remembers that the dress rehearsal for the school play is tonight and that several of his students have roles. In addition, he is aware that most students have a major social studies project due on Friday. Mr. Spencer tries to stay aware of all the demands placed on his students and anticipate the impact of these external forces.

Today's lesson includes time for peer editing of essays and a chance to watch a video biography on the novel's author. As Mr. Spencer is telling the class what they will be doing today, two students come in late, three students begin digging in their backpacks, and an office worker brings Mr. Spencer a note. Mr. Spencer nods to the latecomers, positions himself closer to the "diggers," and accepts the delivered note. He does this without missing a beat or saying a word. Once students get settled, Mr. Spencer opens the discussion about the novel's major conflict.

Before long, Mr. Spencer notices that it's time to allow students to exchange rough drafts and edit each other's work. Just as he's ready to announce this plan, the intercom sounds; Mr. Spencer is asked to send those in the play to the auditorium for a photograph. If this was printed on the announcement sheet in his mailbox, Mr. Spencer overlooked it, because he was not expecting the interruption. He dismisses the eight students involved in the play and quickly regroups the peer editing teams. He has learned to think quickly on his feet, although today's adjustment is not the best plan.

Once students are working on reading and editing each other's papers, Mr. Spencer circulates among them to offer assistance. He finds one team that is totally off-task and asks them what they are supposed to be doing. Two other teams really wanted to talk about going to the play but change their minds when they witness Mr. Spencer's interaction with the other team.

When the peer editors are done with their work, they return their desks to their original locations. They know the routine in Mr. Spencer's room. They also know that the video segments he selects are usually both informative and enjoyable, and they are looking forward to watching the one today.

Walter Doyle (1986) describes six features of classrooms that were evident in Mr. Spencer's classroom. These features will help us understand the complexity involved in managing a classroom. First, classrooms are characterized by *multidimensionality,* that is, they are complex social systems where many things are going on at several different levels. Anyone who has ever

Walter Doyle views classrooms as multidimensional—i.e., various activities occur simultaneously yet on different learning levels.

entered a classroom cannot help but notice what a busy place it is. As Mr. Spencer observed, his students were excited about activities outside his classroom and there were interactions within his classroom that were unrelated to the lesson. He is keenly aware that all his students have different needs, interests, and abilities. This quality of multidimensionality makes teaching and managing a classroom challenging.

Not only does much activity occur in a classroom, but everything also happens at the same time. Doyle labeled this quality as *simultaneity.* If you have ever prepared a three (or five) course meal, you have experienced this feature. Juggling events in the classroom is a similar experience. Because of simultaneity teachers must operate along several tracks at once. To manage the classroom well, teachers must be able to attend to multiple events at the same time.

A third feature of classrooms is *unpredictability.* Much of what goes on in classrooms is hard to predict. Mr. Spencer had no idea that several students would be called from his classroom for a photograph. This unpredictability in teaching demands the ability to "monitor and adjust" (Hunter, 1982).

Additionally, because *immediacy* characterizes life in classrooms, teachers must be able to respond quickly. Because of the fast pace of classroom action, there is little time to stop and think about situations. Teachers must be ready to act as they draw upon their past experiences and knowledge of students. The immediacy of events in the classroom and the rate at which things happen call for fast decisions and actions.

A fifth feature of classrooms is *publicness.* The publicness of classrooms involves the teacher's lack of privacy when interacting with students. Students witness the teacher's every word and action. This publicness can be a difficult adjustment for new teachers. It's like being on stage or living in a fishbowl. Just keep in mind that whatever you say and do with one student is seen by other students. Your behavior toward one or a few students can sometimes greatly affect your relationship with other students who have observed the interaction. This can work to your advantage as well as to your disadvantage.

Finally, classrooms have a *history*. The past influences the present and the future in classroom life. Students learn how you will respond and what you expect. Mr. Spencer's students understand the precedent he has set in how he handles interruptions and how he overcomes unexpected events. They also know the procedures to follow when they are finished with peer editing. Consistency is critical if you expect history to work in your favor.

All classrooms have Doyle's (1980) six features. The presence of these features makes managing a classroom a challenge. We also know that social forces spill over into the classroom. The influence of drugs, violence, teen pregnancy, homelessness, and other social problems contribute to the wide range of needs among students. This composition in the nature of students makes managing a classroom an even greater challenge today. Where else are so many people with such diverse needs and backgrounds crowded into such a small space to achieve a single purpose?

AssessYourself

Which of Doyle's classroom features do you think will pose the greatest challenge to you? Why?

What can you do to prepare yourself to handle this particular aspect of classroom life?

How Do Effective Teachers Manage the Classroom?

The classic study of what effective teachers do when it comes to managing the classroom was published in 1970 by Jacob Kounin. Because of the impact of his work, some have called Kounin the "father of classroom management." Kounin's studies involved the analysis of numerous hours of videotaped segments from classrooms at various grade levels. Through his research, Kounin contributed a rich vocabulary of terms. In this section we shall learn some of Kounin's concepts that emphasize preventive approaches to managing the classroom.

A CASE STUDY

Ms. Bennett is a fifth-grade teacher who frequently uses cooperative learning techniques. Today she plans to begin her math lesson with the use of manipulatives and a small group activity. Ms. Bennett arranges the desks and sets out the students' nameplates before her class returns from recess. As the students come into the classroom, she points to the directions on the board: "Please find your nameplate, be seated with your group, and select a reader, writer, reporter, and manager." As soon as the bell rings, Ms. Bennett instructs the designated managers from each group to collect the supplies and instruction sheet from the front table, return to their groups, and begin work while the reader begins sharing the contents of the instruction sheet. As students are getting organized, Ms. Bennett notices that Ashley has stopped to visit with another group. Ms. Bennett moves toward Ashley, catches her attention, and then points to the materials table. Ashley quickly retrieves the materials and returns to her group. Ms. Bennett now moves around the classroom to make sure that every group is on task. When Jimmy raises his hand, Ms. Bennett goes over to respond while keeping an eye on Ashley's group to see whether they have started. After eight minutes have passed, Ms. Bennett sees that some students have almost completed their work. She provides the class with a two-minute warning: "Class, in two minutes I will collect your sheets, and we will begin the whole-group activity."

Maintain Activity Flow

Ms. Bennett exhibited what Kounin (1970) has called "withitness." She was aware of, or in tune with, what was going on in her classroom and her students knew it. Teachers most often communicate their withitness in nonverbal ways. Recall Ms. Bennett's interaction with Ashley. Kounin's research found that "withit" teachers anticipate potential difficulties, and they are able to "nip things in the bud." Withit teachers act as if they have eyes in the back of their heads. You can begin now to develop withitness by being observant of all that goes on in a classroom.

Ms. Bennett also possessed the ability to overlap, that is, to do more than one thing at a time. By overlapping, Kounin meant the teacher's ability to handle two or more simultaneous events. For example, a teacher who can overlap can answer a student's question and hand another student a hall pass without neglecting the first student. Situations continually arise in the classroom that call for the teacher to overlap.

Kounin (1970) also discovered that effective classroom managers are conscious of momentum and aim to achieve smoothness. Momentum refers to the rate or pace of the lesson, and smoothness involves the lesson's flow. Ms. Bennett carefully watched students for signs of boredom or frustration and

intervened appropriately. She was aware of the lesson's momentum and planned ahead for transitions, knowing that these are troublesome in the classroom. As a way to enhance lesson smoothness, teachers can use group alerting. *Group alerting* includes what the teacher does to "keep students on their toes." For example, teachers who wait to call on a particular student after giving all students a chance to think about a question are using group alerting. In addition, a teacher who says "Everyone look up here" is also using group alerting as a way to focus the class' attention.

Along with exhibiting specific behaviors, maintaining activity flow also means that the teacher does not engage in certain behaviors. Kounin (1970) used some colorful terms for these behaviors. One such teacher behavior that leads to what Kounin called jerkiness is *overdwelling* in which the teacher goes over the same point or direction repeatedly. When a teacher overdwells, students lose interest, become frustrated, and may take advantage of opportunities to misbehave. Another teacher behavior to avoid is what Kounin labeled *stimulus-boundedness.* This occurs when the teacher is distracted by some external stimulus (e.g., the teacher may comment on something she sees in the hallway and thus cause the students to redirect their attention). A teacher who is stimulus-bound is easily drawn off track; the result is confusion on the part of students.

Use Time Effectively

Evertson and Harris (1992) highlighted this research finding as basic to effective classroom management. A well-known educational research study, the Beginning Teacher Evaluation Study (BTES) (Fisher, Berliner, Filby, Marliave, Cahen, & Dishaw [1980]) demonstrates that teachers' use of time matters when it comes to learning. This finding should not be at all surprising. Just think about your own life and how investing time in something usually pays off positively. For example, when you spend time exercising, you get results. In the same way, when teachers devote as much classroom time as possible to instructional activities, students learn more of that knowledge or skill area. In classrooms where time is valued, there is little "down" or lost time, but also there is not a sense of excessive pressure. The productive use of class time demands organizational skills and an investment in planning time. Haberman (1995) discovered that star teachers plan in terms of what the students (not the teacher) will be doing, with whom, for how long, and under what conditions. This kind of orientation to planning will result in more engagement in the learning tasks.

To use time effectively, you will need to establish routines to streamline non-instructional tasks such as returning papers, checking roll, and making announcements. Effective time managers find ways to check attendance without wasting time. For example, the use of a seating chart can streamline this process, as can having students place their personalized clothespin on the lunch count chart. The less time teachers spend on non-instructional duties, the more time is available for learning to occur.

In addition to implementing classroom routines, teachers can also productively use time by minimizing transition time. This is the time between two activities. For example, after the bell rings there is a transition period. The shorter this time is and the more structured, the less likely it is that time will be wasted. Emmer, Evertson, and Worsham (2000) recommend a beginning of class activity or routine, because it is essential to capture student attention during the first few minutes of class so that this time is not a lost learning opportunity. Arlin's (1979) research revealed that twice as many disruptions occur during transition times than during non-transition times in classrooms. Teachers can help students get through transitions more smoothly by giving them warnings (e.g., "You have two minutes to complete this task." or "In three minutes we will begin watching the videotape.")

We can also carefully plan for transitions and find ways to facilitate the movement to the next lesson segment. For example, by having the vocabulary words already written on the chalkboard under the overhead projector screen, the teacher can finish showing a chart on the overhead projector and then lift the screen to reveal the words to be discussed. When we make students sit and wait, they are more likely to find other opportunities for engagement. Cutting down on transition time requires advance preparation on the teacher's part.

academic learning time (ALT)
The amount of time students are engaged in learning and achieving a high rate of success.

Teachers who use time wisely look for ways to maximize academic learning time. This term **academic learning time (ALT)** was coined by the BTES researchers (Fisher et al., 1980) to describe the amount of time students were engaged (on task) with the learning at a high level of success. Achieving greater ALT means that you understand the needs and abilities of your learners and you are able to design activities at the right level of difficulty—neither too easy nor too hard. Targeting the appropriate level is especially challenging for new teachers, who tend to teach at a higher level (often college) than is appropriate for students. Our goal as teachers should be to make as much of the class time as possible to be academic learning time.

Keeping students engaged in academic learning spells success for students and teachers.

We suggest that you start collecting ideas from teachers on time savers in the classroom and recording them in a notebook. You may be able to find some excellent tips on the Internet. Find a lesson plan on the Internet and evaluate its effectiveness for a particular group of learners you may teach. For what level of students do you think it is most appropriate? What preparations would be required before teaching the lesson that would help you use class time most effectively?

Pay Attention to the Physical Setting

The creation of a learning environment begins with setting up your classroom. You will make many decisions about the layout and decor of your room. These decisions will affect how students think and act. Weinstein (1996) stresses the teacher's role as environmental designer and advocates personalization of classroom space. You can personalize your classroom by including photos of your students; displays of student work, especially art work; newspaper clippings that contain students' names; and calendars of students' birthdays. Your classroom should communicate information about you, your students, and your subject matter (Weinstein, 1996). Your classroom space should be attractive and inviting. Students should feel welcome there.

In making decisions about the layout of your classroom, you should follow several guidelines. Emmer, Evertson, and Worsham (2000, pp. 2–3) provide the following five keys to good room arrangement:

1. Use a room arrangement consistent with your instructional goals and activities.

2. Keep high-traffic areas free of congestion.

3. Be sure students are easily seen by the teacher.

4. Keep frequently used teaching materials and student supplies readily accessible.

5. Be certain students can easily see instructional presentations and displays.

Some teachers ignore (or are unaware of) these guidelines, and thus, either through neglect or oversight, they contribute to a poorly managed learning environment. Of the five keys, the first one is the most important. Your decisions about the look and feel of your classroom should be determined by what you are trying to accomplish. Thus, before arranging your classroom, you will need to spell out your long-term goals for students. For example, a high school business education teacher who desires to prepare students for the workplace might decide to arrange her classroom to resemble an office. Similarly, a third-grade teacher who wants students to learn how to work cooperatively and plans to use small groups frequently may place students' desks in pods of four. And finally, a teacher at any grade level who wants to provide easy computer access for Internet research would set up the classroom so that computer usage could be monitored and so that those students on the computer would not disturb other students.

The major work of preparing your classroom takes place during the few days before students arrive. However, changes can and should be made throughout the year in response to students' needs and on the basis of instructional changes. You should not view arranging your classroom as a one-time event. Whenever behavior problems arise, look for signs that the physical environment could be the source.

REFLECTION QUESTIONS

Start imagining the way you would like the layout of your future classroom to look.

What kinds of furnishings and materials will you select for your room?

Begin noticing classrooms. Walk through several classrooms. What are your observations having visited these classrooms?

What impressions do these classrooms make according to how they are designed?

What does the room setup tell you about the teacher's goals?

Hold Students Accountable

In a well-managed classroom, teachers hold students responsible for the work assigned. Emmer, Evertson, and Worsham (2000) present three ways teachers can promote greater student accountability. First, teachers should clearly communicate assignment expectations and requirements. This can be done both verbally and in writing. Directions must be clearly stated. It is also helpful to provide students with the grading criteria at the time an assignment is given. These criteria can be presented in the form of a scoring rubric.

Second, in order to hold students accountable, teachers should monitor their progress. During class this can be accomplished by circulating around the classroom and giving corrective feedback. For assignments completed outside the classroom, the teacher can monitor students' work by scheduling progress checks.

Third, students are more accountable when teachers provide regular and prompt feedback. When students know where they stand, what they are lacking, and how closely they have hit the mark, they are more motivated to perform.

Note how this feedback mechanism already exists in most sports. For example, kids know immediately whether they have hit an archery target and can see where they need to aim next time. Teachers need to provide students with a similar kind of feedback in order to keep them focused on learning tasks. They also need to help students learn how to self-evaluate.

An issue related to helping students be accountable is raised by Kohn (1996, p. 19) when he suggests that a key question to ask when students are off task is "What's the task?" Sometimes students do not follow through with the work assigned because they do not see the purpose of it; they may perceive it as busy work or may question its relevancy. When Glasser (1993) talks about teaching useful skills, he is addressing the same issue. Thus teachers should make sure that what they are asking students to do has value. Can you provide a reason for students to do what they are asked to do? Is the task itself interesting, relevant, and meaningful? If not, then recognize that students may not engage in the work.

AssessYourself

What helps you to be accountable in a learning situation?

How can you incorporate these principles into your own teaching?

What's your view of the ideas of Kohn and Glasser relative to meaningful learning tasks?

Have Clearly Defined Limits

Effective teachers implement a management system at the beginning of the school year (Doyle, 1986; Evertson & Harris, 1992). Rules and procedures are important components of this management system (Emmer, Evertson, & Worsham, 2000). Whether set by the students or the teacher, **rules** are clearly stated expectations that guide student behavior. If rules are unclear or "fuzzy," students are likely to push or test the limits so that they can figure out what is expected. As Good and Brophy (1994, p. 134) point out, "Students are likely to follow rules that they understand and accept." Of most importance when it comes to classroom rules is a rationale for each one. You need to be able to state why and how a particular rule creates a learning environment (Good & Brophy, 1994). If you cannot do so, then consider eliminating the rule.

Just as we have "rules of the road," we also need classroom rules. When driving, rules prevent accidents and promote orderly movement of traffic. When learning in a group, rules also protect students from harm (both physical and psychological) and assist in the smooth operation of the class so that learning can result. In developing rules, teachers should create a small number (generally 3 to 5), phrase them clearly, and use positive statements (i.e., tell students what to do rather than what not to do). Teachers must not just present the rules but should spend time directly teaching them (Doyle, 1986). The younger your students, the more opportunities they will need to practice following rules.

The difference between rules and procedures is often unclear. Wong and Wong (1998) make this distinction, as do Emmer, Evertson, and Worsham (2000). A classroom typically will have many more procedures than rules; **procedures** are routines for accomplishing tasks and allowing for efficient use of time. They "consist of approved ways of taking care of various duties and privileges in classrooms" (Doyle, 1986, p. 410). Procedures direct students in heading their papers, sharpening pencils, going to the restroom, obtaining a hall pass, and so forth. You should begin designing a set of procedures that you wish to use in your classroom. Devoting careful thought and attention to the development of your classroom rules and procedures will make them easier to explain and implement with students (Good & Brophy, 1994).

Some teachers allow student input on class rules. Those who value the preparation of students to function in a democracy often give students opportunities to develop rules. Lickona (1991) and Kohn (1996) support the participation of students in rule development. Consulting students on rules can take several forms. One idea is to let students make rules for the teacher. Another approach is asking students to discuss the reason for rules set by the teacher. In a study conducted by Williams and Kennedy (1993), high school students who constructed the rules made rules very similar to ones the teacher had formulated.

rules

Stated teacher expectations that guide student behavior.

procedures

Routines developed and taught by teachers to students in an effort to facilitate order and save instruction time.

REFLECTION QUESTIONS

● Formulate a list of rules for your classroom. For each rule, develop a rationale (i.e., how you would explain its value to your students).

● Select one classroom activity for which you would establish a procedure and describe that specific procedure.

Use Appropriate Methods

In the past the most frequent response teachers had to behavior problems was punishment. Punishment is designed to make someone else feel bad (or suffer) in order to learn a lesson. It is a reactive response to another person's behavior. In recent years the use of punishment has been criticized (Gordon, 1989). Kohn (1996) challenges teachers to consider the messages sent to students about learning when punishment is the method of correction. He suggests that teachers need to examine why they use punishment. Among the reasons that he outlines are the following:

● Punishment is expedient—it's fast and easy (for the teacher).

● Teachers may know no other strategies.

● The use of punishment makes teachers (and other adults) feel powerful.

According to Kohn (1996, p. 31), one of the primary reasons that teachers use punishment is because we falsely reason: "I must punish or do nothing." As teachers we need to recognize that this type of reasoning sets up a false dichotomy and that there really are alternatives. Whereas punishment usually results in temporary compliance, it does not teach better behavior. A problem-solving approach, on the other hand, helps the offender learn better behavior.

Kohn (1996, pp. 27–28) presents an analysis of what is wrong with punishment. Following are three problems with punishment: (1) it teaches a disturbing lesson (i.e., "might is right"); (2) it warps the relationship between the punisher and the punished; and (3) it impedes the process of ethical development. Thus in response to disruptive behavior, we need to find strategies that preserve the relationship and that teach self-responsibility.

As schools and classrooms become more democratic organizations and environments (Evans, 1996), teachers are including students more in the process of learning more responsible behavior. In the book *How to Talk so Kids Can Learn at Home and in School,* Adele Faber and Elaine Mazlish (1995) identify alternatives to punishment, such as pointing out ways to be helpful and giving students choices. These strategies promote self-discipline by involving students.

logical consequence

An action imposed by the teacher that is connected to the student's behavior.

When teachers view rule enforcement as a "teachable moment" (Lickona, 1991), they are more likely to use logical consequences instead of punishment. A **logical consequence** is an action that is connected to the student's behavior. In many situations, natural consequences already exist in the world. For example, if you fix dinner while you are wearing nice clothes, the natural consequence is that your clothes will become soiled. Should this unfortunate outcome happen once, chances are you will change clothes before cooking in the future. Logical consequences can also be powerful teachers. These are brought into existence by the intervention of a teacher (or some other authority). For example, should you leave a messy work station in science lab, the logical consequence would be for you to clean up the area.

Wong and Wong (1998) emphasize that students cooperate more readily when they understand that consequences logically follow their behavior. In selecting consequences, teachers should follow three guidelines (MacKenzie, 1996; Nelsen, Lott, & Glenn, 1993):

1. The consequence should be related to the behavior.

2. The consequence should be reasonable.

3. The consequence should be delivered in a respectful manner.

When consequences are related, students see the connection between what they have done and its outcome. For example, if a student leaves paper on the floor, a related consequence would be to pick up the trash. Teachers can formulate reasonable consequences by making sure their decisions do not seem arbitrary to students. And finally, consequences that are respectful are administered in a way that does not seem overly harsh; respectful consequences have well-defined beginnings and endings (MacKenzie, 1996).

In addressing problems that arise in classrooms, teachers can use class meetings. A class meeting is an interactive discussion among the members of a class. Teachers who hold such meetings can involve students in decision making, build a sense of community, and model the problem-solving process (Lickona, 1991; Nelsen, Lott, & Glenn, 1993). Lickona (1991) presents examples of different types of class meetings and lists the steps for conducting class meetings. Nelsen, Lott, and Glenn (1993) discuss the building blocks of effective class meetings. Common to both sources is the use of brainstorming as a part of the problem-solving process and the inclusion of positive affirmations as a way to build students' respect and appreciation for each other.

The use of encouragement is an effective strategy for working with students (Evans, 1996). By using encouragement, teachers express belief in the student's ability to improve. Encouraging statements focus on the process more than the product; praise statements, on the other hand, stress the product (i.e., what the student has done). For example, these words of encouragement: "I can tell that you have been practicing your Spanish" send the message to students that you value their efforts and reinforces their focus and attention on future behavior. Additionally, words of encouragement are less judgmental and controlling.

When teachers use encouragement, they can influence student behavior in positive ways. For example, the teacher who says, "I know you will make the right choice about how to act while we watch a video" is more effective than the one who states, "I doubt your ability to sit still and listen during the program." As you think about assuming the role of teacher, you can look for opportunities to send messages of encouragement to others now. This ability will serve you well in the classroom as you interact with students and their families.

What Classroom Management Approaches Do Teachers Use?

Before we examine different management approaches that teachers use, it may be helpful to gain a perspective on student behavior. According to Curwin and Mendler (1988, p. 28), an "80-15-5 rule" defines the reality teachers face in the classroom. This "rule" suggests students statistically fall into one of three groups: 80% of students rarely break rules and are motivated to learn; 15% of students break rules on a regular basis and need the structure of clear expectations; and 5% of students are chronic rule breakers who may be caught in a cycle of failure. It's often easy for teachers to focus their management plans on the problem 5% and overlook the majority. However, it is vital that we keep the whole spectrum in mind as we also consider the diverse needs of individual students.

Creating a positive learning environment begins by establishing relationships with students. Drawing on the works of Kohn (1996) and Fried (1995), we offer the following set of general strategies:

- Enjoy being with your students. Assume the attitude that you can learn from them. Show that you value their perspective. Ask what they think and then demonstrate interest in what they say. When students speak, avoid interrupting them, and listen carefully.

- Care about individual students. Remember the details of their lives. Periodically ask specific questions (or make comments) to show your concern. For example, "I noticed that you have an Atlanta Braves notebook. Are you a fan?"

- Acknowledge students outside of class. Greet them in the hallways and cafeteria and at the mall.

- Be available to students. Tell them when and how they can contact you. Respect students' personal space and watch for nonverbal signs of discomfort. It is important not to distance yourself from students. For example, try not to refer to yourself in the third person, such as: "Coach Jones doesn't like to see paper all over the floor."

● Strive to make your classroom embarrassment proof. Sarcasm will poison your relationships with students.

● Have a sense of humor, and be able to laugh at yourself.

Inevitably, students will act inappropriately. When this happens, teachers can respond in several ways. According to Emmer, Evertson, and Worsham (2000, p. 135), teachers can use one of four general ways to respond to inappropriate behavior:

1. Make eye contact and use proximity.

2. Give a reminder or ask the student "What are you supposed to be doing?"

3. Redirect the student's attention (e.g., "You should be working on the problems on page fifty-three.").

4. Issue a direct command by telling the student to stop the behavior.

These strategies illustrate how implementing the least disruptive intervention is often a teacher's best choice. You want to be as unobtrusive as possible, so that your intervention is not more disruptive than the student's behavior itself.

Kounin (1970) found the use of lower-level desist strategies were more effective than higher-level ones. This means you should try the lowest level of intervention first. This is one that is private (between you and the student) and low in terms of force and form of communication (the nonverbal method). Curwin and Mendler (1988; 1997) talk about PEP (privacy, eye contact, and proximity) as a guiding principle for intervention. Responding to misbehavior can be effectively handled through meeting the student's eye, moving closer to the student, and/or making a remark to the student privately.

Jim Fay and David Funk (1995), co-authors of *Love and Logic*, propose a "love and logic" approach to managing student behavior based on the idea of shared thinking. Fay and Funk believe that teachers need to involve students more in finding solutions. When the teacher and the student are in an emotional state, problems are not resolved. One way to engage students in thinking is to ask questions such as "What do you think might work?" or "How would you rate that decision?" The teacher's asking questions coupled with desiring to understand can eliminate many discipline difficulties.

Meeting with students one-on-one is often an effective strategy to use when dealing with behavior problems. The following list provides tips for interacting with a student privately in a non-threatening way.

The optimal way to resolve a classroom conflict with a student is to meet in private with that student.

© Dennis MacDonald/PhotoEdit

Tips for a Productive Private Session with a Student

1. Greet the student warmly and express your appreciation for meeting with you. Make the session as inviting as possible.

2. Frame your observations and comments in a positive light, so that the student leaves with hope that things will get better and knows that you will not hold a grudge.

3. Ask open-ended questions first to get the student to talk about the problem ("How do you perceive what's going on?")

4. Ask if there is something you can do to help.

5. Conclude by brainstorming with the student to identify ways the problem can be remedied.

6. Leave with a plan of action that is mutually agreeable.

One outcome of an individual meeting with a student can be an action plan (Wong & Wong, 1998). The action plan may be in written or oral form. Either way, the student defines the problem and identifies a solution to implement. There is a commitment on the part of both the student and the teacher to resolve the difficulty and to stick with the agreed upon action plan.

 NOTABLE QUOTE

Punishment hardens and numbs, it sharpens the consciousness of alienation. It strengthens the power of resistance. *(Nietzsche)*

Teacher-Centered Approach

Martin (1997) contrasts teacher-centered with student-centered classroom management approaches. In a teacher-centered classroom, the teacher's needs prevail. Methods of extrinsic control are used. The teacher takes an authoritarian stance. Communication is typically one-way—from teacher to students. All students are treated the same. Students depend on the teacher for discipline direction. The teacher's goal is student compliance. Curwin and Mendler (1988) label the teacher-centered approach an "obedience model," which is often more expedient. In a student-centered classroom, the individual needs of students are taken into consideration. The teacher values an intrinsic approach to managing behavior and sees misbehavior as an opportunity to teach better behavior and instill self-discipline.

assertive discipline

A structured, teacher-centered approach to classroom management that applies basic principles of operant conditioning.

Assertive Discipline is a structured, teacher-centered approach to classroom management developed by Lee Canter (1988, 1992). Central to Assertive Discipline are teachers' rights to establish optimal learning environments and rights to receive support from parents and administrators (Canter & Canter, 1992). Canter emphasizes that teachers have the right to teach without disruption. In effect, the teacher who uses Assertive Discipline holds the belief that "I care too much about my responsibility as a teacher to allow disruptive behavior to stop me from teaching" (Canter & Canter, 1992, p. 15). He presents techniques to help teachers efficiently respond to student behavior and to take charge of their classrooms. In addition, Canter stresses the importance of teaching behaviors to students.

The primary goal in Assertive Discipline is order. It is based on behaviorism, which assumes that students act in response to what happens in their environment. This stimulus-response view of student behavior affects how teachers respond. According to Charles (1996), more than 1 million teachers have been trained in Assertive Discipline, which has been criticized for being harsh, impersonal, and based on extrinsic rewards and punishments. In recent years, Canter's approach has become more positive and student-focused. Previously, he recommended placing the names of disruptive students on the chalkboard followed by check marks to indicate multiple offenses. Now he suggests that names be privately recorded on a clipboard. Canter also stresses how teachers' negative expectations about their ability to deal with inappropriate behavior affects their ability to deal with it (Charles, 1996).

Student-Centered Approach

In a student-centered classroom the teacher-student relationship is paramount. Curwin and Mendler (1988, p. 25) characterize the student-centered approach as a responsibility model that fosters critical thinking by teaching students to make responsible choices.

cooperative discipline

A "hands joined" style of teaching in which teacher and student have joint responsibility for improved, goal-directed behavior.

Linda Albert's (1989) **Cooperative Discipline** is a student-centered approach to classroom management. In contrast to Assertive Discipline, Cooperative Discipline advocates what Albert (1989) has called a "hands-joined" style of teaching because teacher and student have joint responsibility for improved behavior. Based on the work of Dreikurs, Grunwald, and Pepper (1982), behavior is seen as goal-directed. According to this view, students are not merely reacting to the environment but are actively choosing their behavior.

The strongest need that students have is to belong. Thus student misbehavior can best be understood in terms of finding ways to meet this need. According to Dreikurs, Grunwald, and Pepper (1982), when students do not feel a sense of importance (or belonging), they will assume a mistaken goal, which often results in misbehavior. The four most common mistaken goals are attention, power, revenge, and inadequacy. When teachers understand the goal of students' behavior, they can respond more appropriately.

In determining what this goal might be, knowing how the teacher feels is a clue. For example, when the teacher feels threatened by the student's behavior, most often the student's goal is power. Albert (1989; 1995) presents numerous strategies teachers can use once they know the goal of the student's behavior. This approach teaches student responsibility for actions and categorizes behavior according to its intended goal. Thus Cooperative Discipline assumes a more individualized approach by capitalizing on the student's strengths and by not treating all students the same. This approach relies on the use of encouragement and logical consequences (Dreikurs & Cassel, 1972; Dreikurs, Grunwald, & Pepper, 1982).

As Martin (1997) points out, moving to a student-centered classroom management system requires much introspection. She indicates that many teachers want to be student-centered but have difficulty moving from theory to practice. Jerome Freiberg (1996) recommends that teachers create classrooms that are person-centered. His approach is to help students feel more like "citizens" of classrooms and less like "tourists" by sharing leadership with students and giving them jobs of responsibility. Thus the management function becomes a joint responsibility of teacher and students. Although beginning teachers frequently assume a more teacher-centered approach, it is important to use an approach that matches your personality and style and that best meets the needs of your learners.

AssessYourself

Which type of classroom appeals most to you? Why?

What classroom decisions and/or tasks would you feel comfortable turning over to students?

Reflections from the Field

We asked four teachers to describe their approaches to managing the classroom. Anita Cegers-Coleman of Bob Courtway Middle School (who has four years' experience teaching keyboarding and math) describes her approach this way: "I try not to stand in one place for very long during class discussions or tests or when students are working in class. As I teach I walk around the room, and I try to pay attention to what the students are doing. I like for the seating arrangement to be such that no matter where I stand, I can see most, if not all, of what happens in the classroom. As I am talking, if I feel that students are not paying attention, I may ask them a question or maybe even walk closer to where they are and stand there for a while to redirect their attention. If the student is doing something unrelated to the class, I try to continue doing whatever I am doing and at the same time politely take away the object the student may be using or motion for the student to put something away. We talk about respect for each other and the equipment in the classroom at the beginning of the year and throughout the semester so that the students know what I expect of them."

Dionne Bennett of Horace Mann Arts and Science Magnet Middle School in Little Rock (who has three years' experience as a science teacher) describes her approach this way: "I place classroom management in the hands of my students. We begin the year by establishing respect for adults and peers. Once this respect is established and understood, I begin assigning classroom tasks to students. By the fourth week of school, each student knows his or her responsibilities. By making my students responsible for various tasks, I have the opportunity to spend most of my time teaching. This also gives my students a sense of responsibility for their behavior and the behavior of others. Because they feel responsible for behavior, they often work to correct their classmates' inappropriate behavior before I have to do so."

Frank Baker of Horace Mann Arts and Science Magnet Middle School in Little Rock (who has 19 years' experience) describes his approach this way: "It's fairly easy for me to manage my class because I respect who I am. Having offered that as a premise, it's not much of a task to demonstrate respect for others, including my students. When the students realize that I'm genuinely concerned about them and respect them as real people, they usually govern themselves. Initially I do model the behavior I expect them to exhibit in class. And, when attitudes have to be adjusted, including mine, it's executed in a tenor that will not breach our relationship. I have discovered that my students will operate on the level that I anticipate."

Bonnie Bumper of Horace Mann Arts and Science Magnet Middle School in Little Rock (who has 16 years' experience) describes her approach this way: "I teach in a middle school where students move from room to room for 50-minute classes. Classroom management is achieved through organized planning for the entire 50 minutes. I begin by greeting students at the door as they enter the room. This allows me to set the tone for class immediately. The students have been taught the beginning procedure for class. They are to copy the day's objective, agenda, and homework assignment in their class notebooks. This information is on the board and serves as a reference for the students. The agenda allows the students to see exactly what we are going to do during the class period. This organization allows us to move from task to task in an orderly manner, with the students aware of what we're doing. Through careful planning for the entire period, students are engaged the entire time we are together. This leaves no time for the problems that can arise when a teacher's plans are inadequate. Organization of time and assignments and clear directions eliminate confusion and frustration for the students."

What Teacher Qualities Contribute to a Well-Managed Classroom?

A *caring* stance contributes to an effectively managed classroom. Teachers who care about students are genuinely interested in helping them succeed. A caring attitude toward students will affect student behavior. As Noddings (1988) asserts, the importance of establishing caring relationships with students cannot be underestimated. Miller (1998), in her book *Enhancing Adolescent Competence: Strategies for Classroom Management*, contends that positive teacher-student relationships lead to effective classroom management. Furthermore, Curwin and Mendler (1997) discuss the importance of warmth in relating to students who may be potentially violent. They suggest that teachers confront their underlying fears of students and extend empathy toward these students. Teacher practices that project warmth include greeting students by name, smiling, welcoming students to the classroom, and getting to know them on a personal level.

Glasser (1993, p. 32) reminds teachers to let students get to know them by sharing the following information:

- Who you are
- What you stand for
- What you will ask them to do
- What you will not ask them to do
- What you will do for them
- What you will not do for them

One condition of quality schoolwork is a warm, supportive classroom environment (Glasser, 1993, p. 22). It is the teacher who sets the classroom's tone.

Good classroom managers are perceived as caring, credible, consistent, and persistent.

© Superstock

Credibility is another important quality for teachers to possess (Good & Brophy, 1994). This quality resides in students' minds and basically determines whether they find us trustworthy. A teacher who has credibility does what he or she says (i.e., words and actions are congruent). Teachers who make idle threats and empty promises lack credibility. Credibility is enhanced when teachers are reliable, set forth reasonable expectations, and model the same behaviors they expect. In identifying the "disciplines" of credibility, Kouzes and Posner (1993) include affirming shared values, sustaining hope, and appreciating constituents. Therefore credibility is gained when our constituents (i.e., students) believe that we have their best interests at heart (Kouzes & Posner, 1993, p. 53). Teachers who build a sense of community and hold optimistic views also have greater credibility.

Closely related to credibility is *consistency*. Emmer, Evertson, and Worsham (2000) cite the following three sources of inconsistency: (1) unreasonable or

> ## NOTABLE QUOTE
>
> A teacher who has to resort to repeated calling his school to order by tinkling the bell or by speaking, lacks the art of good management.
> *(Abbie G. Hall, 1891)*

inappropriate rules or procedures, (2) failure to monitor student behavior; and (3) a lack of strong support on the teacher's part for a rule or procedure. Students are keenly aware when teachers lack consistency. As teachers we need to self-monitor our actions to check for consistency and deal with any signs of our inconsistency. Sometimes this may mean changing a rule or procedure.

Finally, *persistence* is important when it comes to teaching and managing. Haberman (1995) found this function among star teachers. As they continually search for "what works," teachers who persist do not give up. Persistence is shown by repeatedly asking, "What do I do next?" and looking for ways to improve one's teaching practice so that learning for all is achieved.

REFLECTION QUESTIONS

Write a self-introduction that you would give as a teacher before a class.

How would you rate yourself on the dimensions of caring, credibility, consistency, and persistence? Which qualities need further development and how can you work on these areas?

Web Sites

Check out the following web sites related to classroom management:

www.kdp.org/lounge

www.teachnet.com

www.teachers.net/mentors/ classroom_management

www.proteacher.com030001. shtml

www.new-teacher.com

www.spa3.k12.sc.us/newteacher. htm

www.responsiveclassroom.org

Conclusion

Perhaps this chapter has broadened your view of what classroom management entails. We hope that you now see your task as one of designing an environment conducive to learning and that you understand how preventive strategies can make a positive difference in the classroom. There are multiple effective ways to manage a classroom. What works for one teacher may not work for another teacher. And what works with one student may be ineffective with another student. The individuality of students and teachers is particularly evident when it comes to management issues and strategies.

We encourage you to remain open to new ideas and to seek the insight and advice of other teachers. You should know that effective managers are sensitive to the use of class time, invest energy and thought in planning, and

GREAT TEACHERS

William Glasser

Born in 1925, William Glasser's first career at age 19 was as a chemical engineer. By the age of 28, he had graduated from medical school at Case Western Reserve University. During his psychiatric training at the Veterans Administration Center in West Los Angeles, he began to notice that the traditional Freudian model of psychotherapy had limitations. In 1965, Glasser published *Reality Therapy: A New Approach to Psychiatry,* which explained his belief that people must be personally responsible for their behavior. He contends that people cannot achieve a high level of mental health if they blame the past or outside forces for their choices. His focus was on behavioral change.

The educational community welcomed Glasser's contribution and asked him to apply his therapeutic concepts to managing student behavior. Glasser wrote *Schools without Failure* (1969) to explain how his ideas could be used in large group settings, called "class meetings," as well as with individuals. In *The Identity Society* (1972), Glasser described the theoretical basis of reality therapy and laid the foundation for control theory to explain human behavior.

In 1990, Glasser conceptualized a school where all students were doing competent work and many actually accomplishing "quality" work. This led to the publication of *The Quality School: Managing Students Without Coercion* (1990), now in its third edition (1998), which applies control theory to school administration. Since the first publication of this book, Glasser has changed the name from control theory to choice theory, which more appropriately describes his approach, and over 200 schools have been working in the Quality School Consortium. Choice theory suggests that the only behavior a person can control is his or her own.

Glasser expounds on his new theory in his latest book, *Choice Theory: A New Psychology of Personal Freedom* (1998). Glasser continues to give lectures and workshops nationally and internationally.*

*For more information about Choice Theory and how it applies to schools, contact The William Glasser Institute, 22024 Lassen Street, Suite 118, Chatsworth, CA 91311.

value positive relationships with students. They also develop rules, procedures, and consequences that teach better behavior and enhance student responsibility. Finally, they understand that, even though classrooms are complex places where many demands for attention exist, their effectiveness in management is closely connected to their effectiveness in instruction.

Web Site
Visit the William Glasser Institute online at: http://www.wglasserinst.com.

KEY TERMS

academic learning time (ALT)

assertive discipline

classroom management

cooperative discipline

logical consequence

procedures

rules

SUGGESTED READING

Faber, A., & Mazlish, E. (1995). *How to talk so kids can learn at home and in school.* New York: Simon & Schuster.

Fay, J., & Funk, D. (1995). *Teaching with love and logic: Taking control of the classroom.* Golden, CO: The Love and Logic Press.

Wong, H., & Wong, R. (1998). *How to be an effective teacher: The first days of school.* Sunnyvale, CA: Harry R. Wong.

REFERENCES

Albert, L. (1989). *A teacher's guide to cooperative discipline.* Circle Pines, MN: American Guidance Service.

Albert, L. (1995). Discipline: Is it a dirty word? *Learning, 24*(2), 43–46.

Allen, J. D. (1995). Classroom management: Creating a positive learning climate. *Kappa Delta Pi Record, 31*(4), 178–181.

Arlin, M. (1979). Teacher transitions can disrupt time flow in classrooms. *American Educational Research Journal, 16*(1), 42–56.

Canter, L. (1988). Assertive discipline and the search for the perfect classroom. *Young Children, 43*(2), 24.

Canter, L. (1989). Assertive discipline: More than names on the board and marbles in a jar. *Phi Delta Kappan, 71*(1), 57–61.

Canter, L. (1992). *Assertive discipline: Positive behavior management for today's classroom.* Santa Monica, CA: Lee Canter & Associates.

Canter, L. (1996). First the rapport—then, the rules. *Learning, 24*(5), 12, 14.

Charles, C. M. (1996). *Building classroom discipline* (5th ed.). White Plains, NY: Longman.

Curwin, R. L., & Mendler, A. N. (1997). *As tough as necessary: Countering violence, aggression, and hostility in our schools.* Alexandria, VA: Association for Supervision and Curriculum Development.

Curwin, R. L., & Mendler, A. N. (1988). *Discipline with dignity.* Alexandria, VA: Association for Supervision and Curriculum Development.

Doyle, W. (1986). Classroom organization and management. In Wittrock, M. C. (ed.), *Handbook of research on teaching* (pp. 392–431). New York: Macmillan Publishing.

Dreikurs, R., & Cassel, P. (1972). *Discipline without tears.* New York: Hawthorn.

Dreikurs, R., Grunwald, B. B., Pepper, F. C. (1982). *Maintaining sanity in the classroom* (2nd ed). New York: Harper & Row.

Emmer, E. T., Evertson, C. M., & Worsham, M. E. (2000). *Classroom management for secondary teachers* (5th ed.). Boston: Allyn & Bacon.

Evans, T. D. (1996). Encouragement: The key to reforming classrooms. *Educational Leadership, 54*(1), 81–85.

Evertson, C. M., & Harris, A. H. (1992). What we know about managing classrooms. *Educational Leadership, 49*(7), 74–78.

Faber, A., & Mazlish, E. (1995). *How to talk so kids can learn at home and in school.* New York: Simon & Schuster.

Fay, J., & Funk, D. (1995). *Teaching with love and logic: Taking control of the classroom.* Golden, CO: The Love and Logic Press.

Fisher, C. W., Berliner, D. C., Filby, N. N., Marliave, R., Cahen, L. S., & Dishaw, M. M. (1980). Teaching behaviors, academic learning time, and student achievement: An overview (pp. 7–32). In D. Denham & A. Lieberman (Eds.), *Time to learn.* Washington, D.C.: U.S. Department of Education.

Freiberg, J. (1996). From tourists to citizens in the classroom. *Educational Leadership, 54*(1), 32–36.

Fried, R. (1995). *The passionate teacher.* Boston: Beacon Press.

Glasser, W. (1965). *Reality therapy: A new approach to psychiatry.* New York: Harper & Row.

Glasser, W. (1969). *Schools without failure.* New York: Harper & Row.

Glasser, W. (1986). *Control theory in the classroom.* New York: Harper & Row.

Glasser, W. (1990). *The quality school.* New York: Harper & Row.

Glasser, W. (1993). *The quality school teacher.* New York: HarperCollins.

Glasser, W. (1998). *Choice theory: A new psychology of personal freedom.* New York: HarperCollins.

Glasser W. (1998). *The quality school: Managing students without coercion.* Revised edition. New York: Harper Perennial.

Good, T. L., & Brophy, J. E. (1994). *Looking in classrooms* (6th ed.). New York: HarperCollins.

Gordon, T. (1989). *Discipline that works: Promoting self-discipline in children.* New York: Penguin Books.

Haberman, M. (1995). *Star teachers of children in poverty,* West Lafayette, IN: Kappa Delta Pi.

Hunter, M. (1982). *Mastery teaching.* El Segundo, CA: TIP Publications.

Kohn, A. (1996). *Beyond discipline: From compliance to community.* Alexandria, VA: Association for Supervision and Curriculum Development.

Kounin, J. (1970). *Discipline and group management in classrooms.* New York: Holt, Rinehart & Winston.

Kouzes, J. M., & Posner, B. Z. (1993). *Credibility: How leaders gain and lose it, why people demand it.* San Francisco: Jossey-Bass Publishers.

Lickona, T. (1991). *Educating for character: How our schools can teach respect and responsibility.* New York: Bantam Books.

MacKenzie, R. (1996). *Setting limits in the classroom.* Rocklin, CA: Prima Publishing.

Martin, N. K. (1997) Connecting instruction and management in a student-centered classroom. *Middle School Journal, 28*(4) 3–9.

Miller, D. (1998). *Enhancing adolescent competence: Strategies for classroom management.* Belmont, CA: West/Wadsworth Publishing Company.

Nelsen, J., Lott, L. & Glenn, H. S. (1993). *Positive discipline in the classroom.* Rocklin, CA: Prima Publishing.

Noddings, N. (1988). An ethic of caring and its implications for instructional arrangements. *American Journal of Education, 96*(2), 215–230.

Ralph, E. G. (1993). Beginning teachers and classroom management: Questions from practice, answers from research. *Middle School Journal, 25*(1), 60–64.

Weinstein, C. S. (1996). *Secondary classroom management: Lessons from research and practice.* New York: McGraw Hill.

Wong, H., & Wong, R. (1998). *How to be an effective teacher: The first days of school.* Sunnyvale, CA: Harry R. Wong.

© Michael Newman/PhotoEdit

At the end of this chapter, you will be able to

- Define curriculum in several ways.
- Identify the major types of curriculum.
- Identify sources for developing curriculum.
- Describe ways the curriculum can be organized.
- List and describe forces that shape and affect the curriculum.
- Recognize the value of community support for school curriculum.
- Express your beliefs concerning curricular content.

CHAPTER 10

Designing and Implementing Curriculum

A bird's eye view of what to expect in this chapter

On a daily basis teachers make important decisions about what students should learn. However, they do not do so in a vacuum. In this chapter you will examine the meaning of curriculum, the forces that shape it, the process of curriculum development, and various ways in which the curriculum is organized. You will have an opportunity to reflect on curriculum as it relates to your own school experiences.

Some of the questions raised in this chapter are: Is there a curriculum that all students must learn? What should a relevant curriculum include? Should the curriculum promote a single European-American culture or a pluralistic society? Do students learn lessons in school that are unrelated to the formal curriculum? How much input should parents have regarding what schools teach?

Soon you will discover that deciding what students should learn is not an easy task. It is further complicated by the influence of several groups. In short, a school's curriculum must conform to the expectations of more people than just teachers. Expectations range from standards set by the state legislature to recommendations espoused by professional organizations. In the midst of all these influences, the teacher is and will remain a pivotal player in making curricular decisions. This chapter will help you understand the process of designing and implementing curriculum.

For the last four decades English teachers have been stressing the importance of including writing assignments in every discipline to ensure that students are learning basic language skills. This concept is referred to as "writing across the curriculum." As you read the following chapter and case study (below), you will see more examples of how curriculum can be interdisciplinary.

Carol, a third-grade teacher, wishes to create more of a community spirit in her classroom and has decided to incorporate character education into her curriculum. Rather than plan a separate unit on character traits, she and the other third-grade teachers decide to integrate science, language arts, and social studies. Carol has begun to gather materials and to plan activities. She has several resource books that she purchased at a recent conference where she attended a session on character education. The third-grade teacher team has discussed several novels to read as a class. Carol believes that writing assignments can be designed that reinforce these character traits. The other third-grade teachers are gathering additional ideas to bring to the next team planning session.

If you were one of these teachers, what suggestions and sources would you bring to the meeting? What is your initial reaction to integrating content across the curriculum? What are some assignments and class activities you might bring to the planning session that would help students improve their writing skills while acquiring good character traits?

What Is Curriculum?

Mom: "What did you learn in school today?"

Child: "I learned not to eat candy for breakfast."

Mom: "Oh, did Mrs. Jones teach a lesson on healthy eating?"

Child: "No. Susan threw up before school started, and it looked like she had eaten chocolate for breakfast!"

This brief exchange (based on a true story) illustrates that "what we teach" (and what students learn) is not so simple to pinpoint. Sometimes the curriculum that parents expect and that teachers intend is not the curriculum students experience. Let's begin our study of this critical dimension of teaching by examining several definitions of curriculum.

Curriculum is one of the most difficult educational concepts to define. In fact, the *American Educators' Encyclopedia* (Dejnozka & Kapel, 1991) states that curriculum is "a complex term that has no agreed upon definition" (p. 151). The word *curriculum* comes from the Latin verb *currere,* meaning "to run a course." Thus the original meaning of the word was a course of study. (Note: This Latin derivation explains why the plural form of *curriculum* is *curricula.*) Curriculum was originally conceived as a set of courses that students would complete in a manner similar to running around a track. Completing a course (i.e., passing an examination) was analogous to reaching the finish line. Many still view curriculum in this manner. Perhaps you see your own college program of study in this way. Yet this traditional definition overlooks other aspects of the school curriculum. Therefore the term *curriculum* has come to mean much more than the courses students take.

How diverse are the definitions of "curriculum"? Here is a sampling offered by various authorities:

- "A plan or program for the learning experiences that the learner encounters under the direction of the school" (Oliva, 1988, p. 20)
- "A series of planned events that are intended to have educational consequences for one or more students" (Eisner, 1994, p. 31)
- "The planned interaction of students with instructional content, instructional resources, and instructional processes for the attainment of educational objectives" (Shafritz, Koeppe, & Soper, 1988, p. 138)
- "The learning experiences shaped by committed teachers for their own students who use appropriate materials and actions in their classrooms" (Ben-Peretz, 1990, p. 24)

As you examine these definitions, what common elements do you notice? We noted four common elements of curriculum embodied in the above definitions:

- *Planning:* Curriculum results from the planning efforts of educators. A well-designed curriculum does not just happen. Forethought must be given to various curricular components (i.e., content, methods, and assessment tools).

- *Purpose:* The intended outcome of any planned curriculum is for learning to occur. A simple way to conceive of learning is as a change in some behavior, attitude, knowledge, or skill. Thus the curriculum is designed to bring about some kind of change. Although learning is the primary goal, more specific objectives (or intended outcomes) also are part of curriculum development. What a school or individual teacher is trying to accomplish drives the curriculum. The basic question in creating curriculum is "What do students need to know and be able to do?"

- *Focus:* Students are the focus of curriculum—they are the intended "audience." Thus a language arts curriculum for 6-year-old learners will be

---

curriculum

Learning experiences under the school's direction; a written plan of what students will be taught.

markedly different from that for 16-year-old students. Developmental needs and abilities of students are a major consideration when thinking about curriculum.

- *Fluidity:* Curriculum comes to life when it is enacted in the classroom. However, the curriculum on paper and the curriculum in action may differ somewhat. For example, two teachers can take the same curricular content and implement it in their own unique way. Individual teaching styles (and students' learning styles) have a major impact on how a particular area of the curriculum is delivered.

What Are the Major Types of Curriculum?

Most of the time we associate the word "curriculum" with its traditional meaning, which consists primarily of the formal, stated skills and content that schools teach. Nevertheless, it is important to note that schools have more than one kind of curriculum. Eisner (1994) identified the following three types of curriculum: explicit, implicit, and null. Let's take a look at each of these types.

Explicit Curriculum

explicit curriculum

The stated or adopted set of learning outcomes (knowledge, skills, and attitudes) students are expected to be taught.

The **explicit curriculum** is that which is publicly stated (Eisner, 1994). This "formal curriculum" consists of the courses of study, the curriculum guides, the content of adopted textbooks, and the standardized tests used to measure student achievement. This explicit curriculum is that which exists "on paper"; it is the official curriculum of a school or school district. It is also made up of teachers' lesson plans and statements about what they intend to teach. For example, a teacher's presentation to parents at the annual "Back to School" night concerning what their children will learn that year would constitute the explicit curriculum.

Implicit Curriculum

implicit curriculum

The unstated teachings of a school that derive from its practices.

The **implicit curriculum**, which some call the "hidden curriculum," or "informal curriculum" consists of what is indirectly taught. The implicit curriculum is what a school teaches "because of the kind of place it is" (Eisner, 1994, p. 93). Goodlad (1984), in his exhaustively researched book, *A Place Called School,* noted that labeling this curriculum as "hidden" is a misnomer (p. 197) because it is fairly easy to spot. He notes that it is obvious what we want students to learn when we ask them to sit quietly in rows and copy notes from the teacher's lecture. Some would say that schools teach compli-

Does today's curriculum include the fine arts?

ance, rather than independence, by the way rooms are designed and by the structure in general.

The implicit curriculum includes those messages "conveyed by the ways the explicit curriculum is presented" (Goodlad, 1984, p. 197). Thus students who are frequently exposed to cooperative activities learn the importance of working together without the teacher giving them a lesson on collaboration. A question to consider, then, is: What do students learn from the predominance of "teacher talk," which Goodlad (1984, p. 229) found to outnumber student talk by three times?

Null Curriculum

null curriculum

Nonexistent or neglected curriculum that is content that schools do not teach.

The **null curriculum** is "what schools do not teach" (Eisner, 1994, p. 97). Eisner pointed out that what schools do not teach often has a more powerful effect than what they do teach. In particular, he expressed concern about the lack of attention schools give to the "cultivation of imagination," as well as the neglect of such subjects as law, anthropology, and the fine arts (Eisner, 1979). Therefore the null curriculum is that which is absent or overlooked. For example, based on the large number of individual bankruptcies listed in the newspaper weekly, it seems that schools are not addressing the issues and skills of personal finance or consumer math. What examples of the null curriculum have you noticed?

Extracurriculum

extracurriculum

Student activities outside the regular classroom designed to facilitate student growth and learning.

Educators also recognize a fourth type of curriculum—the **extracurriculum.** This consists of all the "extras" or outside activities sponsored by schools, such as chess clubs, debate teams, volleyball teams (and other sports), and Spanish clubs. Many high school students find the extracurriculum the most powerful aspect of their school experience. The public also values extracurricular activities, with 63% judging them to be "very important" to a young person's education (Rose, Gallup, & Elam, 1997, p. 53).

Some scholars make a distinction between extracurriculum and co-curriculum. The "extra" curriculum is that which is in addition to the academic curriculum; the "co" curriculum consists of those activities directly linked to the school's formal curriculum. For example, if a school teaches drama and also has a drama club, then this activity would be co-curricular. On the other hand, a chess club at a school would be considered extracurricular because there is no corresponding chess class. However, the National Association of Secondary School Principals (NASSP, 1996) suggests that "the concept of extracurricular serves no useful purpose" (p. 18) and favors co- curricular instead. Their reasoning is based on the belief that such activities are integral to education and extend student learning (NASSP, 1996, p. 11). Which term do you think is more appropriate?

REFLECTION QUESTIONS

- **Write your own definition of curriculum.**

....

- **Recall and describe a learning experience from elementary, middle, or high school that resulted from the hidden curriculum.**

....

- **What did you learn from extracurricular activities at your high school?**

....

How Is Curriculum Developed?

"Curriculum development is basically a process of making choices from among alternatives" (Oliva, 1988, p. 45). In fourth-grade math should we teach computational skills, problem-solving skills, or both? The most effective way to make this decision is to process it in a deliberate fashion. Although we can talk about this in the abstract, in practice the process is messier—sometimes it is a matter of "hit or miss."

Purposes Drive the Curriculum

One systematic process that is quite popular comes from Ralph Tyler's (1949) classic book, *Basic Principles of Curriculum and Instruction*. This slim volume presents what has come to be known as the *Tyler Rationale*. It is based on the following four questions:

1. What educational purposes should the school seek to attain?

2. What educational experiences can be provided that are likely to attain these purposes?

3. How can these educational experiences be effectively organized?

4. How can we determine whether these purposes are being attained? (Tyler, 1949, p. 1).

Using these questions as a guide, teachers are more likely to achieve what Boyer (1995) calls a "curriculum with coherence." Based on Tyler's Rationale, it should be evident that the purposes drive the direction of curriculum. What are the goals of our educational efforts? Are students being taught for the purpose of becoming good citizens or independent thinkers or trained employees?

Discussions about the purposes of education have occupied the attention of those within and outside education for years. Nevertheless, determining educational purposes is a critical first step in developing curriculum. It is important to keep in mind that answering these questions is not a one-time occurrence. Curriculum is constantly changing and undergoing further refinement. Tyler (1949) emphasized the ongoing nature of curriculum development. Where do we begin to answer the questions posed by Tyler (1949)? His three sources for planning the curriculum are helpful beginning points.

Sources for Planning the Curriculum

Students

In planning the curriculum, we should consider the needs and interests of students. Content that is appropriate for third-grade students is not the same as content for tenth-grade students. Additionally, students may be particularly interested in a specific topic (e.g., dinosaurs). Knowledge of this special interest can be used to plan curricular experiences for these students. Asking students what they want to learn can offer insightful information as teachers determine what they will teach. Moreover, as students become more diverse in terms of their cultural backgrounds, it is vital that curricula be responsive to these changing demographics.

Contemporary Life

Curriculum is shaped by the times in which we live and will live. What issues are students currently facing? What will they be expected to handle once they leave school? As an example, the pervasiveness of computers in society today means that schools must give students the knowledge and skills to manage this technology. Thus we have seen an increase in computer labs and classes in schools. To illustrate further, students today must be able to interact effectively with individuals from many diverse cultures. A multicultural school curriculum can help students learn how to relate well with people of various backgrounds.

Subject Specialists and Standards

What do the "experts" say about the essentials of a particular subject area? Answers to this question are reflected in textbooks. Additionally, professional organizations today have a major role in shaping the curriculum. Most have developed voluntary curriculum standards that are influencing what and how teachers teach. For example, the National Council for Teachers of Mathematics (NCTM) has developed a set of standards that emphasize problem solving more than memorization, writing about mathematical processes, and using manipulatives to aid mathematical understanding. The National Council for the Social Studies (NCSS) and the National Council for Teachers of English (NCTE) have also created sets of standards for teachers' use. Standards in subject areas such as these are changing the ways teachers think about and plan for instruction.

Bloom's Taxonomy: A Tool for Curriculum Planning

A helpful tool in planning curriculum is Benjamin Bloom's (1956) *Taxonomy of Educational Objectives: Cognitive Domain*. This classification system offers a way of conceptualizing the thought processes involved in different learning tasks. There are six levels in Bloom's Taxonomy: *knowledge, comprehension, application, analysis, synthesis,* and *evaluation*. Each level requires a different and more complex thought process.

Teachers use Bloom's Taxonomy in making curricular decisions to ensure that they move students beyond the knowledge level and incorporate higher-order thinking. For example, let's say a teacher is planning a unit on the Civil War. She could expect her students to "list three causes of the Civil War," which would be a knowledge level objective. She could also ask students to "compare and contrast the Civil War with the War of 1812 in terms of military equipment, strategy, and leadership." This objective would be at

> ## NOTABLE QUOTE
>
> There are no rules or recipes that will guarantee successful curriculum development. *(Elliot W. Eisner)*

the analysis level. Bloom's Taxonomy helps teachers develop curriculum that challenges students to think.

How Is Curriculum Organized?

Subject-Centered

subject-centered curriculum

A way to organize curriculum that emphasizes the content of the disciplines or subject areas.

Curriculum development can be subject-centered, student-centered, or somewhere in between these two extremes. A **subject-centered curriculum** focuses on the content of various subject areas, whether that content primarily consists of knowledge (such as in history) or skills (such as in keyboarding or physical education). The teacher's job is to deliver instruction or to model skills in order to help students master the content. In a subject-centered curriculum, standardization exists whereby students are taught uniformly a body of knowledge. The curriculum of the typical high school is more subject-centered, with content mastery and course credits emphasized.

Core Curriculum

core curriculum

Common learning consisting of a set of required courses that all students are expected to acquire.

To help students see connections across disciplines, Boyer (1995) proposes a **core curriculum** that unifies several subjects into one topic or theme. Boyer offers the following eight core commonalities or themes for the basic (or elementary) school curriculum: *The Life Cycle, The Use of Symbols, Membership in Groups, A Sense of Time and Space, Response to the Aesthetic, Connections to Nature, Producing and Consuming, and Living with Purpose* (p. 85). These core commonalities are based on universal experiences shared by all people rather than artificial divisions between school subjects. At the high school level, Boyer recommends a core curriculum made up of more required courses and fewer electives. The notion of a core curriculum leans more toward a subject-centered curriculum.

Student-Centered Curriculum

student-centered curriculum

An approach to curriculum organization that stresses student attitudes and individual needs.

On the other hand, a **student-centered curriculum** focuses more on the process of learning and emphasizes affective goals (in contrast to cognitive and psychomotor outcomes). Constructivism, as discussed in Chapter 6, Philosophical Orientations, and Chapter 8, Make Decisions about Instruction, supports a student-centered curriculum whereby students "construct" their own meaning from knowledge. In a student-centered curriculum there is a greater focus on individual student growth and subjective perspectives. The teacher's role is that of facilitator in guiding students' development. The curriculum of elementary schools traditionally has been more student-centered, with a greater focus on designing activities that match students' needs and interests.

Integrated Curriculum

integrated curriculum

Blends together different subject areas whereby students can see how knowledge is interrelated.

You may have a mental picture of individual teachers working alone on curriculum development, yet from the perspective of teachers, groups working together control the content of the curriculum (Boyer, 1995, p. 36). Increasingly, an approach to curriculum development being used is called **integrated curriculum.** Boyer (1995, p. 84) found that 89% of teachers think that integrating the subjects is the most effective way to present the curriculum as opposed to teaching each subject separately. In addition, Germinario and Cram (1998) support an interdisciplinary approach to curriculum for the 21st century. Moreover, one recommendation of *Breaking Ranks: Changing an American Institution* (NASSP, 1996) stresses the integration of curriculum and values "depth over breadth of coverage" (p. 11). In the future, single-subject planning by individual teachers will become less the norm as connections between disciplines are stressed. Team planning is becoming more common in schools.

At the middle school level we often see an integrated curriculum that attempts to balance individual student needs with subject content by blending different disciplines in the curriculum so connections can be made. It can be seen in the organization of content into broader fields such as language arts and social studies. Integrated curriculum planning is often engaged in as teachers in different subject areas develop units of study that revolve around a common theme (Meinbach, Rothlein, & Fredericks, 1995). Themes can be found from many sources; local issues, special events, student interests, and literary themes are just a few examples. Once identified, themes provide a central focal point for teaching in two or more subjects.

For example, let's say "Getting Around in the World" was selected as a theme. In social studies, lessons could be designed to address the impact of different modes of transportation throughout history. In language arts, students could write descriptions of transportation in the future. In science, the mechanics and physics of movement could be studied. And in mathematics, distance problems could be solved and the use of vectors in air transportation could be discussed. An integrated approach to curriculum resembles more a student-centered curriculum.

What Forces Shape and Affect the Curriculum?

A school's curriculum is shaped by many forces. Tyler's (1949) sources for curriculum planning discussed earlier reveal several forces that shape a school's curriculum—namely, students, contemporary life, and subject specialists. There are, however, additional influential forces which this section discusses.

Tradition

One such influence on the curriculum is tradition, which plays a major role in determining what subject matter is taught. Teaching "the basics" is a primary expectation of the public, according to a report entitled *First Things First: What Americans Expect from the Public Schools* (Johnson & Immerwahr, 1994). Moreover, a recent Gallup Poll (Rose, Gallup, & Elam, 1997) confirmed the existence of public pressure for teaching the basics. Asked to define the meaning of the "basics," most of the public view it as math and English—similar to the traditional "three R's" of reading, writing, and arithmetic. However, at times the reasoning "We have always taught X so it must be important" can block curricular reform efforts.

Social Forces

What Tyler called contemporary life, Hass and Parkay (1993) labeled "social forces," which are another major influence. Changes in society often are reflected in the school's curriculum. When our economy was more agrarian based, the curriculum of the basic R's was sufficient. The curriculum must be responsive to the changing times and demands of society. For example, units on drug education were added to the school curriculum in the late 1960s as a result of the widespread use of illegal drugs in America. More recently, AIDS education has entered the curriculum because of the increasing number of individuals with this disease. Furthermore, technology is changing not only the content of curriculum but also the process of curriculum development. With the click of a mouse on the Internet, teachers and students have access to information that either was unavailable in the past or would have taken significant time and energy to locate.

Politics

National

Politics also play a part in determining what schools teach. In 1913 the National Education Association appointed the Commission on the Reorganization of Secondary Education, which issued its report, *The Cardinal Principles of Secondary Education* (1918). These seven goals continue to have an influence on the high school curriculum: *health, command of fundamental processes, worthy home membership, vocation, citizenship, worthy use of leisure time,* and *development of ethical character.* In fact, Germinario and Cram (1998) suggest that the curriculum of the 21st century will be a modernization and transformation of these very same principles: competency in the traditional core, social skills development, world citizenship, personal fulfillment, employability, and ethical behavior.

Other national events and reports have affected the school curriculum. After the launching of Sputnik in 1957, American schools placed more emphasis on math and science curricula. National legislation in the form of the National Defense Education Act (1958) made funds available for the development of curricular materials in these subject areas. More recently, the publication of *A Nation at Risk* (National Commission on Excellence in Education, 1983), which claimed that "mediocrity" characterized America's public schools, fueled numerous suggestions for curricular reform.

State

curriculum frameworks

State guidelines for developing curriculum in specific subject areas.

As a result of curricular reform in recent years, many states have what are called **curriculum frameworks.** These are intended to standardize curriculum in various subject areas throughout the state. School districts use these frameworks to develop their curriculum guides. Tests and textbooks are often aligned with these frameworks. However, Murray and Porter (1996) point out that "State frameworks and district curriculum guides vary dramatically in the degrees of discretion they leave to teachers" (p. 169). Nevertheless, the existence of curriculum frameworks provides a degree of structure and standardization to what students are expected to learn. State legislatures also mandate what schools must offer for graduation credit. State departments of education make policies that affect local schools.

Local

We can see local politics operating under the purview of the school board's actions. This is particularly evident in terms of how schools handle "hot topics" such as sex education. When local school boards vote on programs to implement in area schools, their decisions are heavily influenced by the values of the local community. For example, the school board may decide to offer Latin after several parents and other community members press for its inclusion. Likewise, in response to public demand, the school board may also vote to prohibit teachers' use of certain books. Thus local authorities have a major influence on the school curriculum. When teachers were asked who best controls the content of the school curriculum, fewer than half (27%) agreed that local authorities did (Boyer, 1995, p. 36). Regardless, teachers must abide by the policies approved by the local school board.

Business and Industry

Employer expectations within the business and industry sector have an influence on curriculum. We have already mentioned the now common trend of including computer courses in all levels of schooling. Another example results from the desire of employers to have workers who know how to learn. With the constant expansion of knowledge in today's age of information, what is learned quickly becomes obsolete. Thus schools have begun to emphasize the lifelong skills of learning how to learn. Additionally, places of business need workers who have collaborative skills and can participate in decision making. The school curriculum must find ways to respond to these expectations.

Textbooks

The textbook has a profound influence on what is taught (Eisner, 1979). There are both benefits and drawbacks to using textbooks. Textbooks help organize content for teachers and students. They make teaching more "manageable" (Murray & Porter, 1996, p. 169) and they offer what Eisner (1979) calls "security" (p. 27). However, Ben-Peretz (1990) cautions against teachers being too dependent on textbooks and advises that teachers see themselves as creators of curriculum not just as implementors.

Ben-Peretz (1990) encourages teachers to see their major role as "informed and creative interpreters who are prepared to reflect on their curriculum and to reconstruct it" (p. xv). When teaching becomes as technical as merely following the directions of a teacher's manual, it lacks the creative decision making that characterizes the art of teaching. Teachers need to go beyond the textbook to incorporate more meaningful and authentic curricular resources, including the expertise of family and community members. These "free" resources are often overlooked by teachers, but they can have a powerful effect on children's learning and motivation.

The influence of textbooks on the curriculum is especially strong in states that have statewide adoption. This means that schools are limited in their choice of textbooks and teachers must select textbooks from an approved list. Texas, Arkansas, and California are three states that have statewide adoption. Every five years or so a particular subject area (e.g., math) is up for adoption. Teacher committees in school districts examine texts and have input in the state's decision.

Reflections from the Field

A veteran teacher offered these words of advice: "I think that new teachers should appreciate resources for curriculum beyond the textbook. I think it is easy for teachers to become dependent on the textbook as 'the source' of the curriculum, which I believe not only stifles teacher creativity but also diminishes student interest."

- Obtain a textbook for the grade level and subject that you plan to teach. Read over the table of contents and skim the text.

- How would you rate the quality of the material?

- What suggestions for improvement would you offer?

Tests

Of even greater influence on the curriculum in recent years have been standardized tests. Increasingly, states are requiring students to pass mandated tests in order to pass to a higher grade and/or to graduate. The content of these "high stakes" tests is having an impact on the curriculum as well. It is often said that "what gets measured is what gets taught." Therefore, if proper punctuation is tested, then teachers will emphasize this skill. The impact of tests has been criticized by saying that teachers "teach to the test." When instructional time focuses on preparing students to pass standardized tests, other curricular areas are neglected. The difficulty lies in the inability of tests to measure all learning. However, the increasing use of performance-based tests is changing what and how schools teach.

New Theories

Another force operating on the curriculum is how we view the nature of knowledge and cognition (Hass & Parkay, 1993). As discussed in Chapter 5, a recent theory that is changing the way educators view teaching and learning is Howard Gardner's theory of multiple intelligences. In *Frames of Mind,* Gardner (1983) challenged the traditional view of intelligence as a single, fixed capacity and identified seven intellectual capacities. To illustrate, multiple intelligences theory (MI) defines intelligence as problem-solving ability and outlines seven types of mental ability: (1) verbal-linguistic, (2) logical-mathematical, (3) visual-spatial, (4) bodily-kinesthetic, (5) musical-rhythmic, (6) interpersonal, and (7) intrapersonal. Gardner has recently added an eighth intelligence: naturalist. Individuals tend to be stronger in certain intelligences than in others. Teachers, however, can design instructional activities to nurture different intelligences in students.

MI theory is used as the basis for curricula in many schools; it provides a "complex mental model from which to construct curriculum" (Campbell, 1997, p. 19). Teachers can use the MI theory to examine their existing curriculum, to determine where each intelligence is taught, and to find new ways of developing additional intelligences. As an organizing framework for delivering curriculum, MI has great promise.

Nelson (1995) tells how she "reinvented" her curriculum using Gardner's theory. As an example, a science lesson on earthquakes can have students at different learning stations where they engage in activities such as writing about why earthquakes occur, acting out the movement of colliding plates, drawing maps with fault lines, discovering how the level of force is measured, telling a partner what makes earthquakes occur, and composing music that portrays earthquake activity. The typical school curriculum emphasizes the verbal-linguistic and logical-mathematical intelligences. Through the lenses of MI theory, teachers can approach the teaching of topics in new ways and reshape the curriculum.

Teachers

The teacher plays a critical role in making curricular decisions. Although the teacher may not have selected the textbook, he or she decides in what order to present the content, what chapters to omit, what topics to emphasize, and how much time to spend on certain aspects (Murray & Porter, 1996). Teachers must use their judgment in selecting curriculum that best meets the needs of their learners. They must also be able to create curriculum, not merely implement it. In adapting available materials, teachers must be willing and able to pass curriculum through the filter of their own students' needs, interests, and abilities.

Curriculum is also shaped by a teacher's philosophy. A teacher who believes that the purpose of education is primarily to teach students to think critically will plan different activities than the teacher who thinks mastery of a body of knowledge is most critical. A teacher whose philosophical orientation is progressive would focus on educating the "whole child" and thus would include topics that reflect societal issues that affect students (e.g., environmental education). A teacher whose philosophical bent is essentialist would stress students' intellectual development and would emphasize teaching "facts."

The decisions that teachers make regarding content have implications not only for students but also for colleagues. What if a third-grade teacher decided not to teach cursive writing? What would her students do when they reached fourth grade? How would this teacher's decision affect the work of the fourth-grade teachers? Teachers' desire for autonomy in curriculum decision making must be balanced with the best interests of students, other teachers, parents, and additional public education stakeholders such as future employers.

Teachers overwhelmingly (70%) believe that they themselves should have the greatest influence in deciding what is taught in the public schools. Eleven percent said local school boards should have the greatest influence, 10% said state government, 3% said parents, and 2% indicated that the federal government should decide curricula (Langdon, 1997, p. 220). In *Teachers at Work*, Johnson (1990) described the increasing restraints being placed on teachers through prescriptive curricula. She also reported teachers' views on the importance of autonomy in curriculum decision making. A regimented curriculum stifles teacher creativity and devalues the teacher's knowledge of students' best interests.

A CASE STUDY

After reading the district's curriculum guide for tenth-grade biology, a newly hired science teacher, Carla, announces to a colleague next door, "I don't care what the school board tells me to teach, I am going to decide what to teach my students in biology. I'm the one who specialized in this area; therefore I'm the one most qualified to determine what students need to know. Don't you agree with me on this?"

How would you respond if you were Carla's colleague? What would you say if this science teacher has said: "They can't make me teach evolution as part of the science curricula. Evolution is just a theory with no basis. I am a creationist; I believe God created man in his image." By the way, approximately 40 states have science standards that place some emphasis on evolution. Some of these standards are mandatory, whereas others are voluntary. What is your opinion about this? Is evolution an exact science? Is the biblical story of creation an exact science? In short, this controversy is far from being settled.

Reflections from the Field

A junior high teacher, Wendy Dodge, when asked what was essential for prospective teachers to know about curriculum planning, offered this advice: "Seeing the big picture is essential in curriculum planning. Being a person who cannot see the forest for the trees, I have come to see the need for planning. The last time we reviewed the curriculum, I noticed a major part of my subject area not being fully addressed. The change was easy to implement, but I would not have seen the omission had it not been for the listing and charting that was part of the curriculum mapping activity. With a little planning with other teachers, we avoid duplicating what other teachers have done or are doing. I believe that a willingness to invest time in curriculum planning is a necessity and involves working as a team not only with those teachers on your grade level or subject area but also from kindergarten through twelfth grade. There is no substitute for this effort, and lack of effort will be felt far and wide."

European-American or Multicultural Curriculum: Which Perspective?

Ethnocentrism, the belief that one culture is superior to another, was the view of the Spanish and English explorers who came to the Americas in the 1500s. This narrow perspective prevented these colonists from appreciating the rich heritage that was already part of the Native American culture (Spring, 1997). It is not surprising then that American schools were patterned after European models; subsequently, curriculum reflected the dominant Anglo-Saxon culture. Has this changed in the last couple of decades? If so, how?

Increasingly, today's curriculum is departing from the traditional practice of exclusion and is beginning to integrate the morals and traditions of other cultural groups in our society, such as African Americans, Native Americans, and Hispanic Americans (Spring, 1994). As we learned in previous chapters, a change in demographics in America is profoundly affecting what is being taught in modern schools. Many states are requiring that the curriculum and textbooks adopt a multicultural orientation. According to Banks (1997), the curriculum should describe how various cultural groups have influenced Western civilization.

It should be noted that not everyone agrees with this position. In fact, this issue has become rather contentious. One critic, Schlesinger (1995), fears that we lose our national heritage when we place too much emphasis on multicultural content. Adler (1982), in *The Paideia Proposal: An Educational Manifesto,* supports a core curriculum that promotes the great literary works and fine arts representing primarily Western civilization. As we learned in the chapter on philosophy, adherents to essentialism oppose a broad-based curriculum. Instead they favor a curriculum narrow in scope—one that emphasizes basic academic subjects.

Hirsch (1987), in his book, *Cultural Literacy: What Every American Needs to Know,* asserts that in recent decades schools have "shrunk the body of information that Americans share, and these policies have caused our national literacy to decline" (p. 19). **Cultural literacy** as defined by Hirsch is the knowledge that "lies above the everyday level that everyone possesses and below the expert level known only to specialists" (p. 19).

cultural literacy

A term that means there is a core (or fundamental) body of knowledge expected of all people in our society.

> ❝ **NOTABLE QUOTE**
>
> Literate culture is the most democratic culture in our land: it excludes nobody; it cuts across generations and social groups and classes; it is not usually one's first culture, but is should be everyone's second. . . .
> *(E. D. Hirsch, Jr.)* ❞

You may enjoy reading "The List," located in the appendix of Hirsch's (1987) book, to see how "culturally literate" you are. To illustrate, we cite one word from each alphabetical group: abstract expressionism, Sir Francis Bacon, catharsis, "Doctor Livingston, I presume?", Ellis Island, farm bloc, Ganges River, Holy Grail, iambic pentameter, jazz, kill two birds with one stone, left-handed compliment, Moslem, Navajo Indians, optic nerve, paradox, quid pro quo, run-on sentence, separate but equal, thermonuclear, Unitarian Church, vigilantes, watershed, xenophobia, Yom Kippur, and Zen (Hirsch, 1987, pp. 152–215). Hirsch concludes that many parents may be assuming their children are learning this fundamental knowledge, when in fact, they are not. He is concerned about this lack of knowledge that is prevalent in our society.

REFLECTION QUESTIONS

Do you agree or disagree with Hirsch's premise that far too many Americans lack "cultural literacy"?

Should the curriculum take a European-American focus, or should it encompass all cultures and ethnic groups in our society?

Do we lose our national heritage when too much time is devoted to contributions of diverse cultural groups found in our current society?

Do we run a risk of diluting standards of excellence when teachers spend too much time trying to cover all cultural perspectives and contributions? Or do you think that we should concentrate on making sure that all students have learned essential knowledge (i.e., a core curriculum)?

Should the Curriculum Be Gender-Neutral?

In *Failing at Fairness: How Our Schools Cheat Girls*, Sadker and Sadker (1994) note several studies in the 1950s and 1960s that found textbooks were either ignoring girls in the literature or portrayed females in an unfavorable light or other derogatory ways. By the mid-1970s national textbook companies responded by establishing guidelines for authors that would prohibit sexist portrayals of women.

REFLECTION QUESTIONS

Do you think current textbooks perpetuate negative stereotyping? What evidence do you have to support your position? As a teacher, how would you address these issues? Should the curriculum be sensitive to negative sex-typing and purge any hint of sexual bias? What if your school offered an elective on "Studies in Women's Literature" and excluded males from taking the course or offered a course in mechanics and excluded females—would that be gender bias?

Does every individual, regardless of gender, have the right to pursue those areas that are of interest and choose freely among electives?

Reflections from the Field

Clearly it helps to have community support for one's school curriculum. Patty recalls an incident when she was in the twelfth grade (in the early 1970s) that applies here. "My senior year I took a humanities course. The English teacher required student presentations. One student, as part of her presentation on homosexuality, invited a guest speaker who was gay. It seemed like a good idea at the time. By the end of the day, many parents had been to the school; the teacher was called to the principal's office, and the student was reprimanded. After that day, I remember parents attending future student presentations (including mine, which was on the Amish). There was a flurry of letters to the editor in the school and local newspapers. This is the only time as a student that I remember there being 'negative' community involvement in the curriculum. I learned that divergent values raise emotions and can certainly create an uproar at school."

Lynda recalls an incident in the late 1980s that inflamed community members regarding the curriculum. "Many primary school counselors used a curriculum guide called 'Developing an Understanding of Self and Others (DUSO).' The program's mascot, a puppet dolphin, was named after the acronym. As part of the self-esteem program, DUSO the Dolphin would teach responsibility and decision making to students. A vocal group of parents tried to ban local school districts from using this curriculum. They claimed that teaching children to handle problems on their own negated divine intervention and usurped parental authority. Further, they claimed that self-esteem is equated with pride (being full of self), and they objected to teaching this to their children. Parents seemed to object most strongly to those class activities that used meditation and guided imagery, which they associated with New Age religion. This controversy raged for months, and both sides became defensive. The editorial sections in local newspapers were saturated with this 'hot' issue."

NOTABLE QUOTE

Every day in America little girls lose independence, achievement, and self-esteem … Subtle and insidious, the gender-biased lessons result in quiet catastrophes and silent losses. *(Myra Sadker & David Sadker)*

Conclusion

Curriculum is never developed in a vacuum. Teachers must recognize that many groups and factors contribute either directly or indirectly to curricular decisions. To stimulate relevant student learning, the curriculum must undergo constant change. A static curriculum will not prepare students for the 21st century. The work of teachers is steeped in curriculum. It forms the foundation on which the art of teaching is built. Teachers must see curriculum as more than just course content. They must be prepared to take an active role in creating, modifying, and adjusting curriculum to meet the needs and characteristics of learners.

As you have seen, by virtue of specialized training, a teacher's input is invaluable in determining what students should be taught in a particular discipline or grade level. As a prospective teacher, you will have an important part to play in shaping curriculum of the future. You may want to keep in mind though, that becoming an expert on curriculum development and being comfortable with that role is learned over time. Beginning teachers usually rely on the collective wisdom of the prepared curriculum. Aside from that, new teachers should consult with other teachers who teach the same course or grade level. Also they should consult with those who teach the sequential course or grade to make sure that their students have prerequisite knowledge and skills. As new teachers acclimate to this new role, they will probably want to become more involved in curricular decisions.

Web Sites
To learn more about curriculum, check out these sites:
Association for Supervision and Curriculum Development
http://www.ascd.org
Coalition of Essential Schools:
http://www.essentialschools.org
Alliance for Currculum Reform:
http://www.alliance-reform.org

AssessYourself

As you reflect upon what you have learned about curriculum, consider the following questions:

Would you be willing to serve on committees that are charged with writing and updating curriculum?

Would you enjoy making decisions about what the curriculum should include? Do you think you could go along with a prescribed curriculum? Why or why not?

Are you prepared to exercise creative planning skills in developing curricula for your students?

Are you willing and able to adapt materials to students' needs and abilities?

REFLECTION QUESTIONS

What changes in school curricula have you seen since you started making field observations?

What is your opinion of "teaching to the test"? Have you ever experienced this teaching behavior in a classroom?

How should the present curriculum be changed to prepare students for living in an information age and a competitive global economy?

What would be the advantages and disadvantages of enlisting community and parental input in curricular matters?

© Michael Pole/CORBIS

At the end of the chapter, you will be able to

- Identify computer applications that benefit teachers and students.
- Cite limitations of computer technology and explain means for overcoming those limitations.
- Articulate ways you might integrate technology in the classroom.

Integrating Computer Technology

A bird's eye view of what to expect in this chapter

In this chapter we examine how technology can be used to enhance classroom learning. Becoming facile with computer technology teaches students how to reason. By integrating technology into the curriculum we are teaching valuable and transferable skills such as critical thinking and problem solving. Increasingly, teachers are beginning to realize the array of benefits derived from utilizing computers. Today's teachers understand the advantages of integrating digital content into the curriculum. Fortunately there are many quality software programs on the market that enhance instruction and facilitate student motivation and learning.

Aside from instructional purposes, computer technology has streamlined numerous menial tasks assigned to teachers. For example, there are many computer applications that expedite tedious grading and record-keeping responsibilities. Also, word processing has facilitated teachers' correspondence with both colleagues and students. And the Internet provides links to Web sites internationally, which fosters communication and learning.

Of course, computer technology is not a nostrum for everything that ails education. In fact, there are ethical and logistical problems associated with computer usage that must be addressed. One pressing issue is the need to make computer technology available to all students. High school graduates must be computer literate to be competitive in the global economy; yet poorer school districts have difficulty keeping current. How to level the playing field so that all students have computer access is certainly a worthwhile question to consider.

W e are living in a very exciting time. Every day technology expands our opportunities to acquire knowledge and information. Without a doubt, computer technology is a very useful tool for instruction and to expedite work-related tasks. In this chapter, we explore various computer applications that can be of value to teachers. In Chapter 8, we first mentioned computer-assisted instruction (CAI); this chapter continues that discussion.

When you become a teacher you may find that many of your students know more about computers than you do. Those of us already "mature" in age when computers came on the scene are less comfortable with computer technology than others who were introduced to computers quite early. In spite of your level of comfort, as a teacher, you must exude a constructive and positive attitude about computers. You should start improving your computer skills now in order to assist your students later.

The Need for Technology in the Classroom

Since the development of personal computers (PCs) in the late 1970s and early 1980s, educators have been interested in their application to teaching. From the start, it became apparent that computers had the potential to assist in the educational process. Leaders in government, business, and education advocated that computer instruction be part of the core curriculum. By the early 1980s, school districts that could afford to do so began installing computers in schools to provide "hands-on" experiences for their students.

Table 11.1 Percentage of Students Who Reported Using a Computer at School, by Grade and Frequency of Use: 1984–1996

Frequency of Use	Grade 4						
	1984	1988	1990	1992	1994	1996	1984
Never	61.2	29.8	18.9	16.5	14.0	11.4	66.7
Less than once a week	12.5	17.4	14.5	22.0	15.8	16.3	17.0
Once a week	15.5	34.2	41.1	37.0	39.6	36.0	8.1
Two or three times a week	7.6	15.0	17.7	18.6	22.8	26.5	4.6
Every day	3.2	3.6	7.8	5.9	7.7	9.9	3.6

NOTE: Details may not total 100.0 due to rounding.

SOURCE: U.S. Department of Education, National Center for Education Statistics. *NAEP 1996 Trends in Academic Progress (NCES 97–985).*

The need for computer technology in the classroom is obvious. Information is power, and information is abundantly available to anyone with access to the Internet. For example, the U.S. Government Printing Office (GPO) transmits a massive amount of information electronically (Turock, 1996), which can be accessed by Internet users. Individuals untrained in sending and receiving information electronically will naturally be at a disadvantage in the 21st century.

In a survey by Turock (1996), it was discovered that only 1 out of 10 Americans had access to Internet databases, which tends to separate those who are "computer literate" from those who are not. The good news is that with each new year the number of people with access to the Internet increases dramatically. This is also true in our nation's schools (see Table 11.1); by 1999 over half of all classrooms were connected to the Internet. In spite of this, access to the Web should continue to be a priority until we can boast that 100% of our classrooms are electronically linked to the Internet.

Computer access is complicated by many factors. Even individuals who have access to a computer and requisite skills find it takes money to keep up with the latest technological advances. Rapid changes can be problematic for anyone trying to stay current. If private citizens have difficulty staying abreast of updates in technology, how are schools that operate on tight budgets expected to keep up? Very few people would question the premise that technology is essential in schools. As you read this chapter, consider ways to make computer technology available to all children.

Grade 8					Grade 11					
1988	**1990**	**1992**	**1994**	**1996**	**1984**	**1988**	**1990**	**1992**	**1994**	**1996**
41.8	40.5	37.6	27.7	23.3	55.0	44.7	44.9	27.2	26.1	16.0
22.2	19.3	23.9	26.9	29.2	20.9	24.0	26.5	31.5	30.9	34.2
13.9	12.9	12.8	16.1	14.5	5.7	6.4	6.6	10.8	8.0	15.3
12.2	16.0	15.1	14.5	16.2	6.3	9.7	8.3	11.3	12.4	16.5
9.8	11.3	10.5	14.9	16.7	12.1	15.2	13.7	19.2	22.6	18.1

REFLECTION QUESTIONS

- Think about your own experiences with computer software. Did you learn computer skills in school or at home (or both)?

- What stands in the way of providing students with multimedia computers that are wired to the Internet?

- Is lack of money the problem, or is it teachers' lack of knowledge about how to integrate technology into the curriculum?

A CASE STUDY

This is Terry's first teaching assignment as a reading specialist. She is 25 years old. She has "grown up with computers"; consequently she is looking forward to applying her knowledge of technology in classroom instruction. She can hardly wait to start selecting software packages that will help her children master reading. However, the first week of school she was informed that there are scant resources available for instructional computer programs. The librarian showed her the computer lab, but advised her to reserve space weeks in advance because other classes also have access. It baffles her to imagine how one computer lab could possibly meet the needs of an entire school. Terry is very disappointed because she was envisioning a classroom like the one she had. Terry just assumed that all schools had a cluster of computers in each room. As she thinks about it, her disappointment turns into anger as she realizes the injustice of the situation.

If you were Terry, what would you do? Is there anything a new teacher could do about this situation? Should she talk to the principal about her feelings? Or should she think of alternative ways to teach reading to her children? Are there ways to raise money for computers? What about writing a grant? What community sources might she enlist? What about the private sector; could she tap into those sources?

Technological skills are critical for the 21st century. All students must be computer literate to be competitive in the global economy.

Computer Hardware

Let's begin by describing basic computer hardware equipment. To many of you this section will be redundant because you already possess this level of knowledge about computers. If so, feel free to skip this part.

Central Processing Unit

central processing unit (CPU)

Computer hardware that runs programs and processes data.

Computers generally consist of several interconnected parts. The **central processing unit (CPU)** contains the hardware, including the "chip" such as a Pentium, Celeron, or other microprocessor that runs programs and processes data fed into it. The CPU also houses the hard drive and the random access memory (RAM), expressed in megabytes (MB). In the 1980s PCs had memory capacity of only 32 to 64 kilobytes (KB) of memory, which was sufficient for early software programs. Many programs today require 10 to 100 times the memory capabilities of the early computers to run the complex word processing packages, multimedia, and Internet applications on the market. Computers today commonly have 64 to 256 megabytes (MB) of RAM.

Input Devices

input devices

Those parts of a computer system (such as the keyboard, mouse, and scanner) that facilitate the input of data.

A computer system uses **input devices;** the most common is the keyboard. If you are not proficient in typing, we highly recommend that you take a keyboarding course or buy a tutorial program and learn on your own. Other input devices include the mouse, scanner, digital camera, touch-sensitive screen, and speech recognition equipment. Most programs today use Microsoft Windows or Macintosh operating systems, both of which allow control of the programs by clicking the mouse button.

Often, younger students are more nimble than teachers at using the mouse. The mouse is particularly helpful for young children who do not know how to type on a standard "qwerty" keyboard. Another useful input device for younger children is a touch-sensitive screen. All the child has to do is touch a particular part of the screen for the desired response.

Scanners are becoming common input devices. Any printed material can be scanned into a computer using a program such as Paperport and stored there in graphic format. Most of these programs also have an optical character recognition (OCR) program that converts printed material into electronic form (i.e., plain text) that can be modified in an ordinary word processing program such as Microsoft Word or Corel's WordPerfect. This function saves time by converting a printed document into an electronic word processing document without retyping it. A caution is in order: Some characters do not convert accurately or may not convert at all (for example, an OCR program may "see" the number "1990" as "I99O"; therefore the document must be read carefully and checked for errors. A classroom use of a scanner would be to scan students' artwork and then display the pictures on a home page.

Another interesting input device is the digital camera, which takes pictures and loads them directly into the computer. Students may wish to use the camera to photograph class members or events and post these pictures on their home page.

Speech recognition software is now available for computers. This software enables students to speak directly into a microphone, which controls computer operations. Can you imagine the benefits of speech recognition packages to students with motor problems or paralysis? In addition, software is available that converts text to speech. This is a particularly useful function for students who may need to hear how their writing is construed. MacArthur and Haynes (1995) contend that features such as this have the capacity to improve the quality of students' writing.

Output Devices

output devices

Those parts of a computer system that produce meaningful products and tasks (e.g., printer, monitor, speakers).

To be productive, a computer system also needs **output devices.** The most common output device is the printer. Many types of printers are available. Laser printers are more expensive but are excellent for writing letters or papers. Bubble-jet printers can be purchased for $200 or less and produce print quality near that of laser printers. Many printers have color capability, which is useful for making charts, maps, and graphs. Children enjoy working with color graphics. The major drawback to color is cost; color ink cartridges can range from $30 to $50. Although older 24-pin dot matrix printers can produce relatively good results at a reasonable cost, they are typically unsuitable for formal papers or business use.

Another output device is the monitor. Most computers today have color monitors with good resolution (800 × 600 pixels). A useful instructional purpose for monitors is that the screen can enlarge print for children with visual problems. Color on a monitor screen highlights important material, which makes for easier viewing.

Disks and Memory Storage

RAM, used for running programs, is lost when the computer is turned off. This necessitates a way to store data currently in the computer. The most common type of storage is the hard drive of the computer. Most computers have an internal hard disk drive that stores up to several gigabytes (1,000,000,000 bytes = 1 gigabyte) of data. Although the 3.5-inch floppy disk is still the most commonly used type of portable storage medium, these disks hold only 1.44 MB of data each. Consequently, large files that must be saved to portable media must be saved to a Zip disk or CD. Also, as a preventive measure, it is wise to frequently back up data on the hard drive to portable storage. Portable storage for backing up data include tape drives, Zip disks, Jazzes, and CDs. One major drawback of tape drives, however, is that it can take several hours to back up a hard drive.

Computer Applications

Many valuable computer applications are available for teachers, such as spreadsheets, e-mail, and CAI. Let's begin by looking at the value of computers for record keeping and statistical analyses.

Spreadsheets: Record Keeping and Statistical Analyses

Various spreadsheet programs such as Lotus 1-2-3, Microsoft Excel, and Quattro Pro are useful to teachers for recording grades and storing data. Spreadsheets can make the calculation of grades and other statistics easier and more accurate. Some companies also provide computer grade books with their text materials. With these products, students' grades and averages can be quickly calculated. One change on your part can modify the entire graphic display so you can see the whole picture in relation to the alteration. Graphs, statistics, and other information can also be generated from these spreadsheets (Table 11.2).

Another example of computerized record keeping is the documentation of the progress of a student with an Individual Education Plan (I.E.P.), which is required for many regular classroom students, in addition to all students who qualify under Section 504 of the Individuals with Disabilities Education Act (IDEA). Data documenting the success of students can be recorded with

Table 11.2   Grade Book Spreadsheet

First name	Last name	Test 1	Quiz 1	Total
Joe	Abrams	70	10	80
Suzy	Washington	80	8	88
Art	Handel	90	4	94
Joe	Heard	100	10	110
Betty	Nan	75	5	80
Sue	Oster	60	0	60
Peter	Wong	77	8	85
Michelle	Goldstein	55	3	58
Garry	Tie	95	3	98

a program called the I.E.P. Tracker (developed by PeopleSystem Software).* Graphs can show progress made on the academic, behavioral, and speech objectives for each goal. The "Daily Result Averages for: Test Student" from I.E.P. Tracker is shown in Figure 11.1.

Another feature of the I.E.P. Tracker program allows you to examine results over a 30-day period. For example, in Figure 11.2 you can see results calculated over two-week and one-day periods for this particular student, describing the extent the objective was met on each day of that period. This would be particularly helpful in showing results to supervisors and parents.

E-mail for Professional Correspondence

electronic mail (e-mail)

Technology used to send messages over local or global (i.e., Internet) networks.

local area network (LAN)

A group of computers linked to a local server.

Electronic mail (e-mail) has become increasingly popular over the last few years as a way to correspond and communicate with others via the Internet. There is a variety of e-mail programs available, many with similar features. For example, Pegasus and Eudora are two popular e-mail programs. Teachers can use e-mail to communicate with other teachers in the **local area network (LAN)** or with anyone connected to the Internet. LAN is a network made up of computers linked to a local server that can serve of-

*This program is available from Sopris-West (call 1-800-547-6747, or visit www.sopriswest.com).

FIGURE 11.1 Daily result averages from I.E.P. Tracker

Source: IEP Tracker
Demonstration Software.
Reprinted by permission of
PeopleSystem Software.

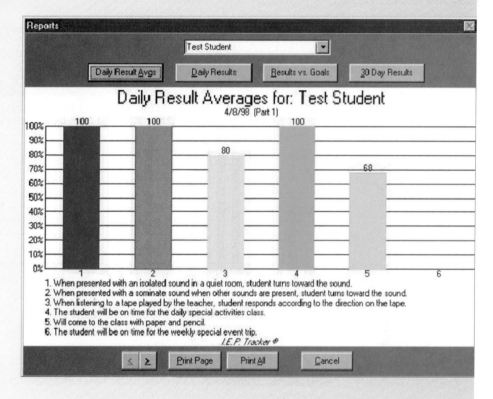

fices, schools, and businesses. Unlike phone communication, an e-mail message arrives inconspicuously and can be read at one's leisure. Assuming a person checks his or her e-mail regularly, information can be exchanged in a matter of minutes. Along with e-mail you can send "attachments." An attachment allows the recipient to extract an attached document and save it; in addition, it allows the sender to attach documents composed in other programs. This exchange of documents allows individuals to inexpensively share drafts with one another without the delay or inconvenience of regular mail (i.e., snail mail).

Another use of e-mail is listserves. A listserve is a computer-generated electronic mailing list. You must subscribe to a listserve in order to receive mail from its members. Members on a listserve can exchange valuable ideas and resources. If you are searching for a particular source, just ask. Someone on the listserve will probably have the information you seek. Be careful to subscribe to only a limited number of listserves or you will be inundated with mail. E-mail allows professional educators to communicate ideas and work on projects with colleagues all over the world. In other words, you can

FIGURE 11.2 Thirty-day test results from I.E.P. Tracker

Source: IEP Tracker Demonstration Software. Reprinted by permission of PeopleSystem Software.

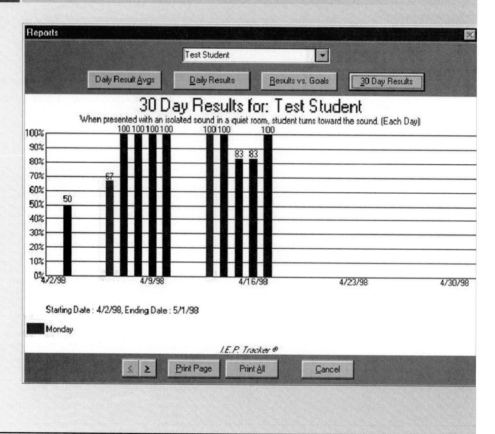

communicate with a person in Australia just as easily as with a person across the hall.

E-mail for Students' Use

Students' use of e-mail might begin with simple correspondence with their teachers. As students become more comfortable with e-mail, teachers can incorporate it into class projects. For example, if a student were studying the agricultural products of Denmark, he or she could communicate with a student from Denmark through epals to obtain first-hand information. Epals is a Web site initiated in 1996 that allows students to communicate with students from different cultures and countries. The epals classroom exchange page represents over 100 countries and 82 languages; it is used in over 13,600 classrooms. The purpose of this page is to encourage students from

Web Site

A notable education listserve is edresource. The e-mail address is: Edresource-subscribe@egroups.com.

Students not only like to use computers, but usage can improve reasoning skills.

© Julie Houck/CORBIS

Web Site

Visit epals classroom exchange page at http://epals.com.

all over the world to interact with each other. This page provides K-12 teachers and students with information about daily life in other countries. It allows for cultural and language exchanges between students from different countries. Epals can share classroom photographs, images, sounds, and video clips at minimal cost. Direct contact with international students is a good way to expand students' world view.

Aside from this, pen pal programs such as epals offer incentives for students. Students are motivated, for example, to improve their computer skills and thus become more computer literate. E-mail improves basic communication skills (mandatory for functioning in today's world). For children who are shy, e-mail might help build confidence, which could lead to enhanced class participation. Moreover, as students correspond with each other, writing skills improve. Clearly there are numerous benefits to electronic mail for students (as well as adults).

Computer-Assisted Instruction (CAI)

As mentioned in Chapter 8, there are many benefits to CAI. Let's look at word processing, for example. **Word processors** are very useful in helping students to fully develop ideas. CAI allows the tedious writing process to be broken down into manageable parts. Ideas can be quickly projected onto the computer screen and saved for later use.

Because word processors allow the user to move and manipulate text with ease, students are more likely to brainstorm, knowing they can rearrange

word processors

Computer programs for creating text documents.

Table 11.3 Selected List of Software Distributors

Broderbrund (Mattel Interactive), 17 Paul Drive, San Rafael, CA 94903;
Phone: 800-521-6263

Print Shop is an easy to use program to make signs, banners, and letters. It is a fine way to motivate students to write.

Compu-Teach, PMB 13716541 Redmond Way, Suite C, Redmond, WA 98035;
Phone: 800-448-3224

Kid Keys is an animated typing program that familiarizes children with keyboard functions.

Once Upon A Time Series lets students create and author their own books through a multisensory approach.

The Learning Company, 6493 Kaiser Drive, Freemont, CA 94555;
Phone: 800-852-2255

Reader/Writer/Math Rabbit Series works on different reading and writing skills, including letter recognition, word attack, number, and arithmetic concepts.

words, sentences, paragraphs, and pages later on. Unlike writing in longhand or on a typewriter, the flexibility of the word processor gives children the freedom to compose in an unrestrained, stream-of-consciousness fashion. Material can be easily cut and pasted, copied, edited, or deleted. In addition, word processors make it possible for students to write collaboratively on projects. Word processing can be used in cooperative learning projects, such as writing a short story as a group or publishing a class newsletter.

The tools available on many word processors can make writing even more efficient. For example, Microsoft Word allows you to choose among various templates for specific writing tasks. Suppose a student wants to learn how to write a cover letter for a job. A template for a letter style guides the student step-by-step through the actual writing of a business letter. Most word processors have spell checkers and grammar checkers. Other tools such as tables, spreadsheets, and graphics can enhance a student's manuscript. Table 11.3 lists some programs that have special tools.

drill and practice

Computer programs that provide repetitive, reinforced instruction in a particular subject area.

Another benefit of CAI, discussed in Chapter 9, is the **drill and practice** feature it provides. For an example, let's look at how "drill and practice" could improve students' reading skills. Jones, Torgesen, and Sexton (1987) found some students have trouble reading because of an inability to rapidly "decode" words. Inefficient decoding was found to be related to poor read-

FIGURE 11.3 | Illustration of Algebra II from a Senari screen

Source: The Algebra Class from Wm. K. Bradford Publishing. Reprinted by permission of Senari Programs.

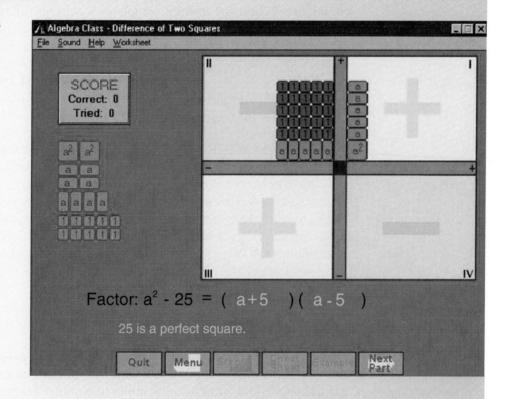

Web Site

Senari's e-mail address is senari@aol.com. The Algebra Class is available from Wm. K. Bradford Publishing Co. (800-421-2009), or visit the web site at: http://www.wkbradford.com.

ing; however, ample practice can greatly improve decoding skills (Jones, Torgesen, & Sexton, 1987).

Before computers entered the classroom, this type of rapid drill was difficult because it required one-on-one attention from a teacher or teacher's aide, as well as speed in the delivery. However, with CAI reading software, ample drill with immediate feedback has made this type of instruction possible. Along with time and speed, drill and practice activities require a patient instructor. Busy teachers and parents may not always have the time or patience for this type of tutoring. CAI can help with reading problems and other areas as well. There are many instructional programs available on the market. One that we have had experience with is Senari Programs. Senari Programs offers computerized instructional programs in many academic areas such as algebra, biology, and geography.

Let's look at one of Senari's programs. Figure 11-3 shows a screen from The Algebra Class. Feedback for correct answers and incorrect responses is immediate in this program. Some concepts are taught in a step-by-step mode and others in small chunks. Each time the student enters a concept, the previous score is erased. Students using this software typically repeat a concept until they achieve a high score. This feature boosts students' self-confidence. When the student completes a concept, he or she can go back to the main menu for more practice or a different concept. Students can, of course, work at their own pace and cover topics as needed.

Another advantage of this type of program is that at any time a teacher may choose to display the screen using an overhead projector for whole group work. Worksheets with randomly generated problems are also available for classroom use. A sample screen from Senari for factoring $a^2 - 25$ is shown in Figure 11-3.

Jones, Torgesen, and Sexton (1987) remind us that CAI does not replace the role of the teacher, it merely supplements teacher instruction. Specifically, the computer has the capacity to do endless repetition, which for some students is the key to academic success. In many schools, teachers are expected to teach 25 to 35 students in an algebra class; in such instances, there is no reasonable way to provide individualized instruction to ensure mastery of mathematical concepts. Finally, in addition to the obvious benefits, students tend to enjoy CAI. (And that fact alone justifies the use of CAI.)

Multimedia

multimedia

Computer programs employing a variety of media (i.e., sound, video, graphics) in their presentations.

Many software programs on the market today have **multimedia** capabilities that allow the user to interact with the subject matter. Multimedia programs include text, graphics, and audio to enhance learning. For example, a student studying Mozart could first view a video clip on Mozart's life and then listen to one of his musical compositions. Computer programs such as this permit students to zoom in on those things that are most intriguing about a subject. In fact, nonlinear instruction tends to sustain a student's interest for a longer period of time (Bender, 1998).

Clearly, multimedia programs are more intriguing intellectually and more stimulating to the senses, which in turn retains attention and facilitates learning. An example of a multimedia program that combines text, sounds, images, buttons, and video is Hypercard, developed by Claris Corporation. This type of interactive technology retains students' attention by presenting material in a fun way. Hypercard has simple, easy to learn commands. Yarrow (1994) used Hypercard in the schools in Carrollton, Texas. When programming, students used special effects, such as venetian blinds, to creatively simulate the movement (transition) from one topic to the next. Yarrow (1994) found programs like Hypercard have the propensity to motivate students who otherwise might find school boring.

Bender (1998) found that some students who were diagnosed with attention deficit hyperactivity disorder (ADHD) respond favorably to multimedia programs. A caution is in order here: Not all hyperactive children respond well to multimedia because it may provide too much stimulation. The array of features and the capability to move quickly from screen to screen may be too distracting for students who have trouble staying focused.

Internet Uses

There are many valuable uses for the Internet in education. As we discussed earlier in the chapter, e-mail can be used by students and teachers alike to access information and communicate with peers. The World Wide Web (Web) uses the same networks that compose the Internet, but the Web uses communication functions called browsers. Netscape Navigator and Internet Explorer are examples of browsers. Browsers allow the user to "surf the Web" using hypertext links.

Hypertext

hypertext

The system of information browsing and retrieval that contains associative links to other related documents.

Computer technology called **hypertext** allows the user to jump from one topic to another related topic with the "click" of the mouse. Hypertext facilitates learning by making connections between the text material and other related material. The student can move from one topic to another for clarification or explanation (MacArthur & Haynes, 1995). This capability allows the student to find further information about the given text by just clicking on an icon. In traditional instruction, the sequence of the material is determined by the text and/or teacher. Most classroom instruction tends to be linear in format. If by chance some topic happens to interest a particular student, he or she must wait until another time to pursue this.

In contrast, hypertext permits a student to pick and choose whatever links he or she wants for immediate clarification or explanation; furthermore, students can change quickly to slightly different material on the same topic or related topics (Bender, 1998). Research suggests that hypertext programs decrease student boredom and increase independent learning (Bender, 1998).

 **Web Sites**

Some single search engines are:

Infoseek
(http://www.infoseek.com)

Alta Vista
(http://www.altavista.com)

Excite (http://excite.com)

Search Engines

search engine

Computer software that helps locate Web sites based on key words.

An advantage of hypertext is that students can "surf" the Web at will. This method, however, is not efficient when looking for information on a particular subject (e.g., a topic for an oral presentation or a research project). A **search engine** is a more practical way to research a specific topic on the Internet; a search engine has access to massive databases relative to a given topic. By clicking on a screen icon, a student can call up a particular search engine, type in the desired topic, and receive an extensive list of relevant Web site addresses within seconds. This information is accessed using key words. A knowledge of Uniform Resource Locators (URL) or Web addresses can help you locate specific information about a topic on the Web. If you know the URL, you simply type it in; if you don't know the URL, you can go to a search engine to find this information.

When we went to the search engine Infoseek to locate "reading instruction in first grade," we found four references. (You try it; see what you find.) Other search engines such as Meta-search combine results from a single search engine to give a broader search. For example, we used Dogpile (http://www.dogpile.com) as a search engine for "reading instruction in the first grade" and found eight references from one engine. (See what you find.)

A directory search engine searches by subject matter. An example of this is Looksmart (http://www.looksmart.com). For example, Looksmart found these topics: Automotive, Reference, Education, Computer, and Internet. From these, you can extend your search further.

Yet another kind of search engine is a combined directory and search engine such as Yahoo! (http://www.yahoo.com). As you go through a directory search, Yahoo! allows you to enter a key word. When we chose "education" and initiated a key word search for "reading instruction in the first grade" (restricted to the category "Education"), the result was zero matches. In this case, we had better results with Dogpile.

Another strategy available for searching is Boolean operators. For example, in key word searching, you may end up with thousands of references if you key in "sex differences." You may wish to use the Boolean operators, which are *and, or, near,* and *not,* to define and narrow your search. If *and* is used, both key words must be in the document you are searching for; *or* requires that one of the key words be in the document; *near* requires that a specified key word be found within a certain number of words of another key word; and *not* will retrieve documents that do not contain the specified key word.

For example, on the search engine About.com (http://about.com), the word "differences" was used; consequently 27,582 references were found. Most of the search engines have hints about how to narrow your search to the most pertinent sources. A word of caution is in order: Even if students are searching for a legitimate topic, such as "sexual differences during development," X-rated sites could come up. (This happened to us when we were researching this chapter.)

Other uses of the Internet include locating references and teaching materials that can be used for whole-class instruction. There are many Web sites with information on specific lessons and units. There are lesson plans on the Internet available to teachers in mathematics, science, social studies, language arts, and so on.

Web Site
Visit the site for Classroom Connects Internet Lesson Plans at http://www.connectedteacher.com/home.asp, which offers grade-appropriate resources and lessons in many subject areas.

To illustrate, we downloaded a science lesson plan on the "Coriolis Effect" on the earth's rotation. The question was asked, "Which direction does water spin when it drains from the sink?" This lesson made suggestions to students such as: "Spin a globe and then turn it upside down to note the direction of the spin" or "Contact students in Australia (cyberpals) through a Web site at St. Olaf's College." By using cyberpals, students can collect data from the Southern Hemisphere so they can compare notes from the Northern Hemisphere.

Web Publishing

One final computer application we would like to include in this chapter is Web publishing. Williams (1997) has an excellent book showing teachers how to publish over the Web. Web publishing is similar to the hypercard program discussed earlier. These programs have cards linked to buttons that launch programs, play sounds, start videos, and so on. In the world of the Internet, buttons are hypertext links, cards are pages, and stacks are Web sites (Williams, 1997). Web pages have features that allow you to navigate the Internet. These pages can be read with browsers such as Netscape or Microsoft Internet Explorer. You can perform all the operations mentioned earlier, such as Web searches, using these browsers.

Web pages are written using a Web page writing program—Claris Home Page, Adobe PageMill, and Microsoft Front Page. Hypertext also can be written with the Netscape Editor. Web pages may be stored on a server on your Internet provider or on the local area network (LAN) for your school. Once this is arranged, you are ready to publish Web pages.

There are many reasons to publish on the Web, including the following:

- Enlarging one's world view
- Acquiring information from worldwide sources
- Learning new things from experts in the area
- Sharing what one has learned with others
- Improving writing skills, which results in better communication
- Writing collaboratively
- Modeling to students an interest in and enthusiasm about learning from the Web

There are concerns about the safety of students who publish over the Web. If, for example, a pedophile or sociopath sees a child's article or picture, is that student in danger? Williams (1997) contends that these risks are no greater than if the student's picture appeared in the newspaper or in the school yearbook; the chance of locating that student's phone number or address are about the same. However, Williams (1997) does offer safety guidelines. We have summarized some of the suggestions as follows:

- Keep personal information off the Internet. Don't publish full names and phone numbers of individuals.
- Obtain parental permission before publishing student information on the Web.
- Don't include students' e-mail addresses; instead use the school's e-mail address for responses.

And lastly, be aware that there are many sites accessible to students over the Internet that would be harmful for children to visit. Sometimes even a seemingly innocuous search can call up sites one would not want children to see (e.g., nudity, illicit graphics, and violence). Further, some of the text

Web Sites
Visit Cyber Patrol at http://www.cyberpatrol.com/fact.htm. Some other services are Surf Watch (http://www.surfwatch.com/) and Net Nanny (http://www.netnanny.com/).

information on the Web is unsuitable for impressionable and inquiring minds. The killing spree in Littleton, Colorado, in the spring of 1999 brought to public attention the fact that directions for building bombs and other explosives are easily accessible on the Internet. Fortunately there are software companies that provide "blocking" services for certain names and types of topics. At Cyber Patrol, for example, there are options for restricting access to certain times of the day, limiting total time spent online, and banning objectionable sites.

In addition, sites that contain appropriate material for children are also made known to parents or guardians. These sites are aptly called "yes sites." By the way, educational institutions wanting to block specific sites on their computers qualify for discounts. However, based on the First Amendment, recent court decisions have challenged the constitutionality of restricting Internet access. What the future holds regarding freedom of expression on the Internet is yet to be determined.

Distance Education

distance education

A trend in technology connecting specialists in another vicinity to students via two-way television equipment.

One way to correct for inequities among school districts is **distance education.** Small high schools, for example, may not be able to afford to offer all the advanced courses required by state standards. By using two-way television equipment that connects instructors with students, students living in remote areas have access to quality education. In schools in isolated areas, distance learning allows students to learn from specialists unable to visit the schools. All schools would benefit from this kind of access to experts who are unable to visit the schools. Distance education has great potential for education.

Critics of Educational Technology

With anything new, there are always nay-sayers; and computer usage in the classroom is no exception. Many critics question whether computers actually improve student learning. Skinner (1997) claims that much of the material gained from Internet sources has not been verified for accuracy and validity, and therefore the quality of the information is questionable. Himmelfarb (1997) warns that students may accept someone else's answer from a query over the Internet as more valid than knowledge gained by traditional sources; in essence, students may hastily accept any material gleaned from Web pages as authentic.

Skinner (1997) reminds educators that materials on the Internet may be limited in scope. Therefore teachers should not rely exclusively on the Internet for instruction; material from the Internet should be used as supplementary data to other sources of information. Aside from this, many are concerned that becoming proficient in technological skills might limit students to technical vocations because time was taken away from pursuing a strong liberal arts background.

Although we recognize the merit of the above arguments, we do not think they are strong enough to justify removing technology from education. There are ways that teachers can address the limitations inherent in telecommunications. As we mentioned earlier regarding Web publishing, anyone can put a page on the Internet, which means that teachers must teach students the value of checking all references for credibility and accuracy (just as you would anything in print). In sum, we believe that technology should be integrated into education, not replace education. There are ways to make technology work for us (not against us) if we are aware of these issues.

Selection and Evaluation of Software Programs

In closing, we would like to mention that today's teacher needs to know how to evaluate the usefulness and appropriateness of computer software programs. If you were asked, for example, to purchase a new software package for the foreign language department at your school, you must know what features are required. Some features to consider might be: (1) content (e.g., accuracy, appropriateness, and scope), (2) technical aspects (e.g., record-keeping features, presentation, and quality), and (3) documentation (e.g., technical information and instructor's guide). Additional information about software can be found on the Internet. The following are a few sites that may be helpful:

- The Software Publishers Association (http://www.siia.not) offers an extensive list of Web sites that review various educational software programs. Go to the search button at their site and search for "software reviews."

- The PEP (Parents-Educators-Publishers) Registry of Educational Publishers (http:// www.microweb.com/pepsite) provides information about various publishers of software. You can often purchase the program online at the publisher's Web site.

- North Carolina's Department of Public Instruction is a highly rated Web site that also provides evaluative information on educational Web sites (http://www.evalutech.sreb.org/criteria/index_frames.htm).

- Another useful site is the Association for Supervision and Curriculum Development (http://www.ascd.org). This site gives educational news, curriculum development information and information about educational meetings.

We understand you may not have the luxury to explore all the Web sites we have listed. Our aim is to let you know they exist and that there are many more than we have cited. If you become a teacher, it will help to know there are sites where you can chat with colleagues or consult with other educators worldwide about topics of interest to you. At your fingertips you can find assistance for practically any problem or question you may have. All you have to do is ask.

Clearly teachers today must be willing to integrate technology into the curriculum. If you become a teacher, would you be willing to stay abreast of new technologies?

Would you willingly attend workshops and inservice training to upgrade your computer skills?

Do you see yourself modeling a positive attitude to students about the need for becoming computer literate?

Conclusion

In this chapter we showed how computer technology can be very valuable to teachers in the classroom to enhance student learning. We began by demystifying computers by describing basic hardware and features. To demonstrate the benefits of technology, we presented classroom computer applications such as grading, record keeping, and CAI. Further, we illustrated how communication can be improved by using telecommunications media such as the Internet and the World Wide Web. Of course, there are limitations and problem areas involved with "surfing" the Web; teachers must provide proper instruction on usage. By understanding the disadvantages of technology, prospective teachers can plan in advance how to remedy some obvious shortcomings.

One glaring problem facing education today is the issue of inequity in computer technology. In a democratic society, all students must have the opportunity to become computer literate. It is negligent on our part to allow some students to lack the skills necessary to compete in a technologically advanced society such as ours. Without computer skills, students will be unprepared for the job market in the 21st century. After all, the goal of education is to set students up for success (not failure).

> ## NOTABLE QUOTE
>
> The key to successful implementation of technology into the curriculum is the teacher's attitude. *(Denise Johnson)*

Lastly, regardless of a teacher's level of comfort or competency with computers, he or she must recognize the grave responsibility of ensuring students are provided technological skills to excel. You must begin now to learn all you can about computers so you can help your students negotiate the demands of the 21st century and thus experience success. Our job as educators is to build thinkers; teachers can use technology to pique student interest and motivate students. We need students who are critical thinkers, not merely computer operators.

KEY TERMS

central processing unit (CPU)

distance education

drill and practice

electronic mail (e-mail)

hypertext

input devices

local area network (LAN)

multimedia

output devices

search engine

word processors

SUGGESTED READING

MacArthur, C. (1996). Using technology to enhance the writing processes of students with learning disabilities. *Journal of Learning Disabilities, 29,* 344–354.

National Council for Accreditation of Teacher Education. (1997). *Technology and the new professional teacher: Preparing for the 21st century classroom.* Washington, D.C.: Author.

Technology Counts '99. *Education Week: American Education's Newspaper of Record.* (September 23, 1999), Vol. XIX, Number 4, 4–110.

REFERENCES

Bender, W. N. (1998). *Learning disabilities, characteristics, identification, and teaching strategies.* Needham Heights, MA: Allyn & Bacon.

Himmelfarb, G. (1997). Revolution in the library. *American Scholar, 66*(2), 197–204.

Johnson, D. (1999). Nothing ventured, nothing gained: The story of a collaborative telecommunication project. *Childhood Education, 75*(3), 161–166.

Jones, K. M., Torgesen, J. K., & Sexton, M. A. (1987). Using computer guided practice to increase decoding fluency in learning disabled children: A study using the Hint and Hunt I Program. *Journal of Learning Disabilities, 20*(2), 122–128.

MacArthur, C. A., & Haynes, J. B. (1995). Student assistant for learning from text (SALT): A hyper-media reading aid. *Journal of Learning Disabilities, 28,* 150–159.

Skinner, D. (Summer, 1997). Computers: Good for education? *The Public Interest,* 98–109.

Turock, B. J. (1996). Libraries on the information superhighway: Connect or disconnect? In B. J. Turock (Ed.), *Envisioning a nation connected* (pp. 1–5). Chicago: American Library Association.

Williams, B. (1997). *Web publishing for teachers.* Foster City, CA: IDG Books Worldwide.

Yarrow, J. (March, 1994). Across the curriculum with Hypercard. *T.H.E. Journal,* 88–89.

UNIT 5

PROFESSIONAL ISSUES AND POLITICAL REALITIES

© CORBIS

At the end of this chapter, you will be able to

- Trace the history of teacher education.
- Identify criteria that distinguish professions from other occupations.
- Evaluate whether teaching is a profession.
- Cite ways that teachers can continue to grow as professionals.
- Summarize the roles and benefits of professional organizations.
- Describe recent changes in teacher education and the implications for teachers.

CHAPTER 12

Teaching as a Profession

A bird's eye view of what to expect in this chapter

This chapter begins with a brief history of milestones in teacher education that places teacher education in context. It also provides insight into the direction teaching is headed. As you examine the characteristics of a profession, you will be asked to decide whether teaching "fits the bill" of a profession. As you think about a career in teaching, you may not be concerned about whether you will be joining the ranks of a profession. However, becoming a member of a profession has important implications for your daily work as a teacher. Being affiliated with a profession will make a difference in how you perceive your work and in how others perceive you.

As a teacher you will be involved in activities that will make your school a better place for student learning. One way to do this is to see yourself as a learner along with your students. Teachers who are most successful make it a habit to engage in activities that enhance their learning and growth. We will show how professional development is a lifelong commitment to improvement.

One way teachers grow and develop is by becoming active members of professional organizations. There is much to gain from becoming involved in an organization for teachers. Membership in a professional organization not only builds excitement for what you have in common with other teachers, but it also facilitates your own growth and development as a teacher. Being affiliated with a professional association can be a helpful source of support. Sometimes just knowing that you are not alone can make a difference in your attitude and practice as a teacher. And lastly, you will learn about various reforms in teacher education and implications for you.

We begin this chapter with a case study. Consider the following dilemma.

Molly has looked forward to this year for a long time. Finally, she is in charge of her own classroom. Getting there was not easy. In preparation for this responsibility, Molly successfully navigated the route to becoming a teacher. She has taken courses, passed standardized tests, completed many hours of field experiences, served 16 weeks as a student teacher, and committed herself to continued learning. Molly knows her subject area (science) well. She knows about the learning process and various ways to enhance learning, she knows about adolescents and how to relate to them, she knows how to make informed instructional decisions, she recognizes the importance of her students' individuality and diversity, she possesses current technological skills, and she understands the cultural, historical, and philosophical foundations of education.

Now that she is a teacher, Molly has become aware of several new aspects of what it is like to be a teacher. Once her classes started, she noticed how little contact she has with other adults in the school. She has received various memoranda about meetings, deadlines, and mandates that affect her work; she has observed a veteran teacher whom she believes is detrimental to students' learning; and she has fallen behind with reading the two professional journals to which she subscribes. Moreover, she has responsibility for planning and delivering science instruction to five classes of 25 to 30 students who need both group and individual instruction. Based on her students' abilities, Molly would like to use a different textbook, but the committee has rejected her request.

In the midst of all these unexpected demands, Molly finds herself losing sight of the students' learning needs. In short, teaching does not seem to be the profession she imagined it would be. There is a gap between what she thought teaching would be like and what she is experiencing. Molly feels unprepared to deal with the unexpected challenges she now faces.

From what you have learned so far, what do you think Molly should do? What advice would you offer? Could you see yourself in this predicament? This chapter gives some hints as to how Molly could have avoided feeling frustrated and unprepared at this time in her career. Also, we will consider ways to more realistically prepare for one's future teaching career.

You can expect to learn a great deal about children and the act of teaching through field placements and student teaching experiences.

© David Young Wolff/PhotoEdit

History of Teacher Education

Before the spread of the common school, teachers received no formal training. Mostly males, with little more education than their students, held the position of teacher. Being a teacher was a temporary job. With the common school movement in public education came a need for more teachers who were better trained (Urban, 1990). Thus the first institution for the preparation of teachers emerged.

normal school

A 19th-century American teacher training institution.

This institution was called a **normal school,** so named for instructing prospective teachers in the "norms" (or accepted ways) of teaching. The first state-supported normal school was established in 1839 in Lexington, Massachusetts. For the most part, the founding of normal schools in the southern states did not occur until much later. Functioning as a "post-elementary, quasi-secondary school" (Urban, 1990, p. 61), a normal school consisted of a two-year program for the training of elementary teachers. Primarily unmarried females were attracted to these normal schools, which offered an avenue for viable employment until marriage. Generally, the curriculum of a normal school focused on pedagogy (i.e., how to teach), with some attention devoted to the subjects to be taught.

During the late 1800s and early 1900s, as high schools developed more widely, the need for training teachers in secondary education arose. Greater knowledge of subject areas was necessary. Thus most normal schools expanded into state teachers' colleges, which consisted of four-year programs. At the same time, the certification of teachers shifted from the local level to the control of state boards or departments of education. Previously, teachers with or without normal school completion could be hired at a local school board's discretion. When the states assumed more control of this process, they initially issued general teaching certificates, but by the 1920s specialized certificates for different areas and levels were commonplace (Urban, 1990).

Eventually, state teachers' colleges evolved into state colleges and later universities. These institutions of higher education offered expanded programs in more than just teacher preparation. Within universities, however, colleges of education were usually given lesser prestige and existed on the fringe (Clifford & Guthrie, 1988). This devalued position negatively affected many efforts to professionalize teaching.

With these changes in the education of teachers have come changes in the professional nature of teaching. Normal schools engaged in teacher training for a very narrow and specific purpose. Today we speak of *teacher education,* which, according to O'Neill (1988), has a broader, more encompassing connotation. Teacher education extends from the *preservice* (before practice) to the *inservice* (engaged in practice) levels of teaching. Teacher education recognizes the lifelong nature of learning to teach, whereas teacher training implies a one-shot approach.

The profession of teaching has an interesting history. Educators often have difficulty overcoming the past in the present. For example, a long-held belief that "anyone can teach" diminishes the view that teaching is a profession. Moreover, the "in loco parentis" doctrine suggests that the role of teachers was more associated with that of parents than that of other professions. Thus some of the early features of the teaching profession still linger and hold teaching back from becoming a full profession. Nevertheless, the trend is toward improving the quality of teachers by strengthening the ways in which they are selected and prepared.

Does Teaching Qualify as a Profession?

What is a profession? Does teaching qualify as one? When you hear the word "profession," what images come to mind? You might think of some of the following: advanced degrees, with diplomas on the wall; high standards for admission to a program of study; formally decorated offices; or titles of great respect, with nameplates on the office door. As you anticipate a career in teaching, it is important to examine the meaning you associate with the word "profession." How would you define the word profession?

Definition of a Profession

There are various definitions for a profession. Here are just a few to consider:

- "An occupation requiring considerable training and specialized study" (*American Heritage Dictionary of the English Language,* 1992).
- "A professional is an individual who performs a unique task that sets him or her apart from society" (Segall & Wilson, 1998, p. 29).

- "A profession is an occupation requiring expert knowledge that justifies a monopoly of services granted by government licensing" (Spring, 1998, p. 41).

Characteristics of a Profession

profession

An occupation that requires a body of knowledge and specialized preparation and renders a service to society.

Briefly, a **profession** is an occupation that rests on a solid body of knowledge, requires specialized preparation, and renders a service to society. The American Association of Colleges for Teacher Education (AACTE, 1976, pp. 6–12) in the report *Educating a Profession* identifies 12 characteristics of a profession as distinct from semiprofession, paraprofession, and skilled and unskilled trade.

As you read the list below, evaluate teaching according to these criteria. Where do you think teaching measures up? Where does teaching fall short?

1. Professions are occupationally related social institutions established and maintained as a means of providing essential services to the individual and society.

2. Each profession is concerned with an identified area of need or function (e.g., maintenance of physical and emotional health, preservation of rights and freedom, enhancing the opportunity to learn).

3. The profession collectively and the professional individually possess a body of knowledge and a repertoire of behaviors and skills (professional culture) needed in the practice of the profession; such knowledge, behavior, and skills normally are not possessed by the nonprofessional.

4. The members of the profession are involved in decision making in the service of the client, the decisions being made in accordance with the most valid knowledge available, against a background of principles and theories, and within the context of possible impact on other related conditions or decisions.

5. The profession is based on one or more undergirding disciplines, from which it draws basic insights and on which it builds its own applied knowledge and skills.

6. The profession is organized into one or more professional associations that, within broad limits of social accountability, are granted autonomy in control of the actual work of the profession and the conditions that surround it (admissions, educational standards, examination and licensing, career line, ethical and performance standards, professional discipline).

7. The profession has agreed-upon performance standards for admission to the profession and for continuance within it.

8. Preparation for and induction to the profession is provided through a protracted preparation program, usually in a professional school on a college or university campus.

9. There is a high level of public trust and confidence in the profession and in individual practitioners, based on the profession's demonstrated capacity to provide service markedly beyond that which would otherwise be available.

10. Individual practitioners are characterized by a strong service motivation and lifetime commitment to competence.

11. Authority to practice in any individual case derives from the client or the employing organization; accountability for the competence of professional practice within the particular case is to the profession itself.

12. There is relative freedom from direct on-the-job supervision and direct public evaluation of the individual practitioner. The professional accepts responsibility in the name of his or her profession and is accountable through his or her profession to the society.

Primary Aspects of a Profession

From these 12 characteristics of a profession, four primary aspects relative to teaching emerge. They are (1) knowledge base, (2) orientation, (3) autonomy, and (4) accountability.

Knowledge Base

knowledge base

The specialized knowledge acquired through a lengthy, intellectually rigorous period of education.

Do teachers have a knowledge base? The noun *profession* is built on the verb form *profess* meaning "to make a public declaration" or "to acknowledge." Thus at the foundation of a profession there must be a body of knowledge. In education, we refer to this as a **knowledge base.** Teachers, doctors, lawyers, and members of other professions have this specialized knowledge that members of the general public do not have. This possession of knowledge elevates members of a profession in the eyes of society to the level of "experts" (Hart & Marshall, 1992). Therefore what separates a profession from a non-profession is the multitude of judgments made based on knowledge. Such knowledge is acquired through a relatively lengthy period of education that is intellectually rigorous.

The importance of a knowledge base in teaching is stressed in a recent report by the National Commission on Teaching and America's Future (1996), *What Matters Most*: *Teaching for America's future:* "What teachers know and can do is the most important influence on what students learn" (p. vi). Consequently, more attention is being placed on strengthening the knowledge and skill base of future teachers.

Web Site
These standards, as well as other relevant information, can be found at the National Board for Professional Teaching Standards web site (www.nbpts.org).

Furthermore, the National Board for Professional Teaching Standards (1994) are based upon the following five core propositions, which help shape the knowledge base of teaching:

1. Teachers are committed to students and their learning.

2. Teachers know the subjects they teach and how to teach those subjects to students.

3. Teachers are responsible for managing and monitoring student learning.

4. Teachers think systematically about their practice and learn from experience.

5. Teachers are members of learning communities.

Because much of the practice of teaching has been based on personal experience and conventional wisdom, teachers have not always had a well-defined body of knowledge. As research continues to inform practice and these findings are disseminated through professional literature, the knowledge base of teaching continues to be developed and refined.

However, we do know that the key to teaching lies in the *application* of one's knowledge. Teaching is primarily a problem-solving venture that requires both knowledge and skill. The complexity of the work of teaching sets it apart from other occupations.

Orientation

What is the primary orientation of teachers? A profession has a strong service orientation—providing an essential service to society and to the individual. Although there may be some practicing physicians whose primary motive is financial gain, most doctors are committed to helping maintain or restore the health of their patients. This service ideal, according to Sockett (1993), is vital to teaching. A teacher's primary responsibility is to serve students. Implied in the service orientation is the sacrifice of self-interest (Hart & Marshall, 1992).

As we have noted many times in this textbook, some consider teaching a calling (Hansen, 1995). A commitment to others' betterment underlies any profession that seeks to serve. Ethical issues, as we also have seen, pervade teaching (Strike, 1988). In its relationships with others, a profession is guided by ethical standards. Even though the teaching profession does not have a unified code of ethics, as we will see in the next chapter on ethics, various education organizations, such as the National Education Association and American Federation of Teachers, do have such a statement.

Autonomy

How much autonomy do teachers have? For the most part, teachers have freedom within the classroom to teach as they best see fit. This independence influences teachers' level of satisfaction; overall, teachers carry out their daily duties with minimal supervision. However, as they make decisions, teachers must consider the expectations of parents and the values of the local community and school board. The freedom found in autonomy is tempered by accountability to others.

Being able to make important decisions about one's work is a large part of what it means to be affiliated with a profession (Sadker & Sadker, 1997). Hart and Marshall (1992) argue that public trust underlies self-governing professions. As a group, teachers have been relatively powerless—unable to affect decisions that have an impact on their work. For example, creating the class schedule is usually handled by the school principal and counselor. In addition, selecting textbooks is typically out of the hands of individual teachers because of the existence of state-adopted lists with lengthy time periods between adoption decisions.

Teachers experience more self-determination in some schools than in other schools. As mentioned in Chapter 7, the recent emergence of site-based (or school-based) management that permits teachers a greater voice in school matters has empowered teachers. Because teachers are becoming more involved in shaping decisions that affect their daily lives in the classroom, they are being given more autonomy than ever before. We discuss site-based management further in Chapter 14, Organization, Governance, and Financing of Schools.

Accountability

accountability

A trend in education that requires schools and teachers to be responsible for student performance.

The term for the practice of holding teachers and schools responsible for student learning is **accountability.** Do teachers have accountability? Thus far we have learned that teachers are responsible to many parties for their decisions and actions; they are accountable to their students, the parents and guardians of their students, other teachers, school administrators, and the public in general. The public has entrusted its young into teachers' hands for the purpose of education and has a right to expect results.

The question arises concerning how teachers can be *held* accountable. The ultimate measure of accountability rests in how well students learn. Yet, how should learning be measured? Are standardized tests the optimal way? Do teachers control all the factors that affect learning and achievement? What happens to teachers when their students do not learn? Although it is true that teachers demonstrate a level of accountability through the learning success of their students, the problem lies in finding equitable ways to assess these results.

One way schools have quality control over instruction is through their teacher evaluation system. Teachers undergo evaluation each year (beginning teachers have more frequent evaluations than veteran teachers). This evaluation is usually conducted by the principal; sometimes it is only a ritual encounter. Many school districts, however, are developing more meaningful ways to evaluate teachers involving the use of peer observation and portfolios. Assigning mentors to new teachers is another way to monitor teachers' performance.

We conclude this section by returning to the original question: Does teaching qualify as a profession? This particular question is often debated among educators. Hansen (1995) views teaching as a vocation. Others see it as a craft, based on skills such as those of artisans. Although teachers do belong to professional associations and exercise some control over their conditions, complete autonomy does not exist. Teachers perhaps could be more solidified if they identified as a group. Many teachers identify more with their individual disciplines (e.g., mathematics, language arts, reading, business education, etc.) than with their profession as a whole (American Association of Colleges for Teacher Education, 1976).

In spite of this limitation, current reforms (fortunately) are moving teaching forward in the direction of a profession on the continuum. To illustrate, the knowledge base is constantly changing and improving; the decision-making power of teachers is increasing; and the standards for admission to teacher education are being raised.

In sum, most authorities concur that teaching is an "emerging profession" or a so-called "semiprofession" (AACTE, 1967; Segall & Wilson, 1998). We suggest that if you become a teacher and you are dissatisfied with this status of "semiprofession," you get involved in ways that will change this image. Cooper (1988) reminds us that fulfillment in teaching comes more from the quality relationships we establish with students than with the idea of being in a profession. What do you think?

Value of Professional Development for Teachers

professional development

A teacher's commitment to engage in self-analysis and reflection to improve performance in the classroom.

A teacher's commitment to **professional development** is critical to success in the classroom. The public trusts teachers to hold themselves accountable as they engage in reflection and self-analysis. Teachers must seek to improve continually as they give their best to their students. Duke (1990) points out that "Professional development . . . is a dynamic process of learning that leads to a new level of understanding or mastery and a heightened awareness of the context in which educators work that may compel them to examine accepted policies and routines" (p. 71). Shortly we will elaborate on ways that teachers can enhance their professional development.

When you become a teacher, you will be a "work in progress" rather than a "finished product." One of the four teaching domains encompasses professional responsibilities—of which growth is a major focus (Danielson, 1996). Your commitment to professional development is critical. As Lieberman (1995) points out: an integral part of the daily life of any teacher should be his or her own development. The primary purpose of continuous personal and professional growth is to promote student learning (National Foundation for the Improvement of Education, 1996).

In the past teachers and schools perceived professional development in very narrow terms. Typically, an inservice workshop held after school or a staff development day was synonymous with the meaning of professional development. These one-shot attempts in which an outside expert came for a few hours or a day to "fix" teachers is now recognized as ineffective. Increasingly, professional development is conceptualized as being more teacher-directed, being individualized, and taking place within a school

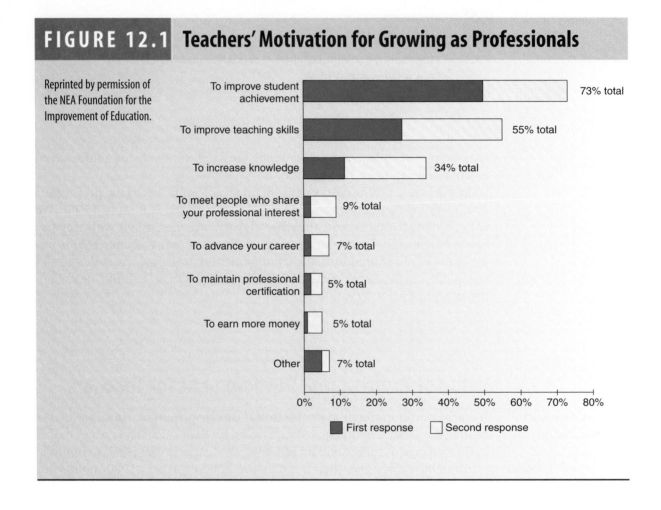

FIGURE 12.1 **Teachers' Motivation for Growing as Professionals**

Reprinted by permission of the NEA Foundation for the Improvement of Education.

among teachers. Rather than teachers being viewed as "passive recipients" of staff development, they are best seen as active participants in their own professional development (Lieberman, 1995).

New forms of orientation to professional development take into account teachers' perspectives and problems (Lieberman, 1995). These approaches recognize the importance of context, that is, the need to consider a particular teacher's school setting, learners' background, and subject matter. In addition, authors of recent views of professional development understand and value the long-term nature of professional growth.

The National Foundation for the Improvement of Education (NFIE, 1996) notes that teachers evaluate their own professional growth by its effects on students. In a survey of teachers, NFIE found that teachers' motivation for growing as professionals is "to improve student achievement" (73%), followed by "to improve teaching skills" (55%). In its report *Teachers Take Charge of Their Learning: Transforming Professional Development for Student Success* the National Foundation for the Improvement of Education (1996) urges teachers to do just that—to "take charge of their learning."

An important aspect of professional development is peer consultation and collaboration.

When it comes to professional development, teacher initiative is essential. Roland Barth (1990, p. 57) believes that professional development begins when a teacher says, "Here's what I want to try...." Thus taking professional risks by wanting to experiment and try different approaches facilitates professional growth.

Many school districts currently require teachers to develop a professional growth (or improvement) plan each year. This plan includes improvement goals the teacher has set for the year and ways (or strategies) to reach these goals. To complete such a plan entails taking stock of where one is as a teacher and where one wants to go. It requires that a teacher be aware of his or her strengths and weaknesses. *Breaking Ranks: Changing an American Institution*, the reform document of the National Association of Secondary School Principals (1996), recommends that educators create their own Personal Learning Plan. In formulating such a plan, a key question to pose is as follows: What knowledge and skills do I need to develop to improve student learning?

A teacher might decide that she needs to learn better ways to facilitate and assess critical thinking among students. Her plan to achieve this outcome might include watching a videotape on promoting higher-order thinking skills, reading a book or several articles on critical thinking, attending a professional conference session on that topic, observing a colleague who is noted for promoting students' critical thinking, or discussing with colleagues various strategies and ideas relative to the topic. Intended as a road map for lifelong learning, this Personal Learning Plan should be continually updated and modified as the needs of teachers and students change (NASSP, 1996).

Paramount to the growth process is interaction with peers (Danielson, 1996). To grow as professionals, teachers must seek ways to overcome the isolation that has pervaded schools and classrooms. A finding from the U.S. Department of Education (1986) is of particular note: "Students benefit academically when their teachers share ideas, cooperate in activities, and assist one another's intellectual growth" (p. 51).

Teachers can learn much about teaching from their colleagues. Through classroom observations and teaching conversations teachers can expand their views on how to promote learning. Teachers can interact with colleagues about such things as the design of assessment tools, the selection of textbooks and other curricular materials, and the creation of interdisciplinary units of study. These interaction opportunities provide teachers with means to grow, stretch, and improve their practice.

Additionally, teachers can form study groups to solve problems and discuss student motivation and learning. Elizabeth Hebert (1999) talks about using faculty meetings as more than announcement times and instead suggests using them as "rugtime" for teachers in which they can share experiences and solve problems collaboratively. She gives the example of a focused topic approach to meetings so that teachers come prepared to discuss concerns and viewpoints relative to a specified topic such as grief and loss or the organization of school space and time.

Activities That Promote Professional Growth

The types of activities that can enhance professional development are numerous and continue to expand as educators broaden their view of what constitutes professional development. Following is a list of possible activities that facilitate professional development:

❏ Conduct a demonstration lesson for peers

❏ Share knowledge gained from professional readings or conferences

❏ Lead a discussion group or book study group on a topic of interest or concern

❏ Assume the role of peer coach, student teacher supervisor, or team leader

❏ Write a journal article for publication or a grant for external funding

❏ Attend a conference of a professional organization

❏ Participate in a writing project

❏ Maintain a portfolio of teaching artifacts and reflections

❏ Undertake the task of national board certification

❏ Join a network of teachers around a common theme

❏ Engage in partnership activities with a college/university and/or business/community group

❏ Sign up for a listserv on a topic of interest or with a group of teachers with a similar background (e.g., foreign language teachers, middle school teachers, speech and drama teachers, reading teachers, etc.)

❏ Serve as a leader of an action research team to investigate an aspect of teaching/learning.

As Danielson (1996) outlines, contributing to the school and district is an important part of a teacher's professional responsibilities. As a teacher, you will need to seek opportunities to make contributions that make your school a better place for student learning. The activities listed here are ways to accomplish that. Underlying all professional activities is the process of reflection. Through reflection we are able to improve practice. Teachers who continue to grow constantly ask themselves "How can I contribute to students' growth and development?"

A Model for Professional Development

Our model for professional development (Table 12.1) is based on the ideas of Lieberman (1995) and Danielson (1996). The goal of the model is to improve teaching and learning. The foundation for these processes is reflection and collaboration.

Professional development became a national priority for teachers with the passage of the Educate America Act (1994) and its widely publicized Goals 2000. Perhaps you have seen or heard the statement: "The three best reasons to teach are June, July, and August." Such a statement damages the professional image of teaching. Quite the contrary, most teachers are involved in professional development activities that help them grow. For example, many teachers spend their summers reading professionally, developing curriculum, and attending graduate classes and workshops for teachers, and they rarely receive compensation for these activities. However, a recent report by the National Association of Secondary School Principals (NASSP, 1996) entitled *Breaking Ranks: Changing an American Institution* recommends that teachers have a 12-month contract to provide paid time for additional learning and development.

Within a school, students are not the only learners. It is important that teachers also view themselves as learners. Professional development should be an ongoing, personal responsibility (Gordy & Phelps, 1996) rather than merely the school's agenda through its staff development program. The National Commission on Teaching and America's Future (1996) views the lack of professional development as a barrier to improved teaching and

Table 12.1	Goal: Improved Teaching and Learning	
Content (what)		**Processes (how)**
Subject matter knowledge		Departmental faculty meetings
Pedagogy (instructional strategies)		School improvement council (self-study)
Assessment methods		
Curriculum standards and alignment		Mentoring relationships
Technology integration		Study Groups
Time and space learning		Electronic networks
		Professional organizations
		Workshops
		Peer review
		Student teacher supervision
		Leadership academy
		Informal networks

Adapted from Danielson, C. (1996). *Enhancing professional practice: A framework for teaching.* Alexandria, VA: Association for Supervision and Curriculum Development; and Lieberman, A. (1995). Practices that support teacher development. *Phi Delta Kappan,* 76(8), 591–596.

suggests a personalized approach that is also recommended by NASSP (1996) in the form of a personal learning plan for each educator. This plan would include knowledge and skills related to improved student learning. Keep in mind, however, that professional development involves not just knowledge but also an attitude toward change that includes the behaviors of listening, reading, reflecting, and asking others.

The critical importance of continued professional growth for teachers is embodied in the following statement:

> Probably nothing within a school has more impact on students in terms of skills development, self-confidence, or classroom behavior than the personal and professional growth of their teachers (Barth, 1990, p. 49).

When teachers remain learners they are better able to facilitate the learning process in their students. A true professional is committed to his or her own continued learning.

Your career as a teacher entails not only a commitment to students but to yourself and to others as well. As you contemplate joining the teaching profession, you may want to weigh your willingness to take the following pledge (Phelps, 1993, p. 154):

1. I will try, at least once, any approach that seems educationally sound.

2. I will seek the professional opinions of my colleagues on a regular basis.

3. I will share my experiences in the classroom with other educators in a positive manner.

4. I will aim to be a better teacher today than I was yesterday.

5. I will express my appreciation to students, administrators, parents, and peers for the success I have.

Taking such a vow will help you approach your teaching responsibilities in a more professional manner. Adhering to the pledge will enhance others' perspectives on teaching in a more professional direction.

A "To Do" List for Professional Development

There are some things you can do now to begin the path toward professional growth, such as the following:

- Continue to develop yourself as a person. Travel, read widely, explore special interests and hobbies, engage in sports, and so on. All these activities will not only make you a more well-rounded individual, but will also enrich your teaching.

- Find a professional mentor. This person might be a classroom teacher whom you admire, a former teacher, a college professor, or a leader in the educational community or in a field other than education. A rich source of potential mentors is retired teachers. Often these individuals can offer valuable insight.

- Stay up to date on current events and issues in education. Read in the field of education (not just in your subject field). One recommended resource is *Teacher Magazine*.

- Attend conferences of professional associations and organizations. Network with others preparing to become teachers and with current teachers.

- Develop your leadership skills by participating in clubs and organizations. Serving as an officer or committee chair will help hone your "people" skills.

- Maintain a portfolio to document your professional growth activities. Set goals for improvement areas and show evidence of your progress toward these goals. Share your portfolio with other teacher candidates for feedback.

- Acquire grant writing skills. Many continuing education departments at universities offer workshops. Teachers often need these skills to apply for grants to fund innovative teaching ideas. Keep a notebook in which to jot down ideas for which you might someday seek special funding.

Authors' Commentary

Being a member of a profession does not automatically make a person a professional. A professional is set apart on the basis of two dimensions: attitudes and behaviors. These manifestations are distinctly individual matters. For example, Mr. Johnson is a teacher, yet he constantly makes negative remarks about students. Other individuals (who may not be teachers) hear these remarks and comment that Mr. Johnson is not very professional. Or, for example, Ms. Blackburn is a teacher whose prevailing attitude is "Those lazy students just need to get it on their own." Her attitude would be characterized as "unprofessional."

Professionalism is earned. To act professionally is to translate one's attitudes, talents, abilities, and skills into actions that bring honor and respect. Worthy of reflection is the following statement by Cooper (1988): "Status (reward) and control are not the characteristics of professionalism; they are the byproducts" (p. 47).

REFLECTION QUESTIONS

Describe a teacher you have known whom you would characterize as "professional." Give reasons for your conclusion.

Contrast a "professional" teacher with one you have known whom you would consider "unprofessional."

Professional Organizations for Teachers

professional organization

A group or association of like-minded professionals that lobbies on behalf of members, publishes relevant materials, and offers other resources and support.

A **professional organization** is a group or association of like-minded members that provides support and other resources to members, publishes pertinent materials, and lobbies for the organization's cause. As a prospective teacher, there are numerous organizations for you to consider joining. These organizations fulfill many of the same needs as any organization: power, belonging, fun, and learning. Think about an organization to which you belong. Why did you join? What benefits do you receive by being a member? According to Segall and Wilson (1998), one of the distinguishing features of a profession is the existence of professional organizations. There are several types of organizations for teachers. We shall now look at two major types.

Study groups are invaluable to teachers as a means of generating new ideas and receiving support. This group of English teachers was participating in a writing seminar sponsored by the Bay Area Writing Project, Berkeley, California.

© Elizabeth Crews

General Professional Organizations

The first type of organizations fall into the general category. These appeal to a broad base of educators. The Association for Supervision and Curriculum Development (ASCD) is an example. This organization keeps teachers and administrators abreast of developments in the field of education. ASCD's publication is called *Educational Leadership,* and the Association holds an annual conference.

Specialty Professional Organizations

The second type of teacher organizations fall into the specialty category. Specialty organizations have in common a particular subject area or age-group. Their purpose is to unite members of the profession around this common concern. An example of an age-related specialty organization is the National Middle School Association (NMSA), which is for teachers and administrators who work at the middle school level. An example of a subject-related specialty organization is the National Council for Social Studies (NCSS), which is for social studies teachers. Even though these are national organizations, state-level organizations for the same areas also exist.

Professional organizations provide opportunities for teacher growth by means of their publications and other resources, as well as through their meetings. Networking is a primary advantage provided by the specialty organizations. For example, a foreign language teacher may be the only one in his or her school building. Through a professional organization such as the American Council for Teachers of Foreign Languages (ACTFL), one can

Table 12.2	Selected Professional Organizations for Educators
	Council for Exceptional Children (http://www.cec.sped.org)
	International Reading Association (http://www.reading.org)
	Music Teachers National Association (http://www.mtna.org)
	National Association for the Education of Young Children (http://www.naeyc.org)
	National Council for Social Studies (http://www.ncss.org)
	National Council of Teachers of English (http://www.ncte.org)
	National Council of Teachers of Mathematics (http://www.nctm.org)
	National Science Teachers Association (http://www.nsta.org)

interact with other foreign language teachers and stay informed about trends in the field through the publications offered.

When you take the time to examine the web sites of a few organizations, you will be amazed at the vast amount of information and support in the form of instructional materials that these organizations provide. You can also obtain information about their annual conferences and membership fees. Many organizations have reduced rates for preservice teachers (student memberships). For information on additional organizations, check the *Encyclopedia of Associations* or visit the web site of *Teacher Magazine* (http://www. teachermagazine.org).

National Organizations Influencing Educational Policy

National Education Association (NEA)

The oldest professional organization for teachers and administrators.

American Federation of Teachers (AFT)

A professional organization for teachers whose primary focus is to improve teachers' working conditions and salaries.

There are two very large education associations that have great influence over educational policies affecting teachers. They are the **National Education Association (NEA)** and the **American Federation of Teachers (AFT).** Lobbyists representing these organizations are very active in the national and state capitals. They seek support for educational legislation that positively affects teachers and schools. In addition, each organization has contributed a substantial amount of money to support the political campaigns of candidates for the offices of state governor and United States President. Benefits offered by both the NEA and the AFT include publications, annual conventions, insurance policies, and discounts for retirees. For several years these organizations have discussed merging. In 1998, members of the NEA rejected a proposal to join forces with the AFT. Let's briefly examine each of these powerful organizations.

National Education Association (NEA)

The NEA is the larger of the two organizations, with approximately 2.2 million members, consisting of both teachers and administrators. Teachers make up the majority of the membership. Originating in 1857 under the name of the National Teachers' Society, the NEA emerged in 1870, drawing teachers, normal school personnel, and administrators from mostly rural and later suburban areas. Bob Chase serves as national president of the NEA. There are state and local affiliates of the both the NEA and AFT. *Today's Education* is published by the NEA. Additionally, the NEA's Code of Ethics enhances the professional image of teaching and addresses professional behavior toward students and other teachers.

American Federation of Teachers (AFT)

The AFT has approximately 850,000 members; administrators may not join. When the Chicago Teachers Federation merged with other urban teacher associations, the American Federation of Teachers was formed in 1916. The primary focus of the AFT has been to improve teachers' working conditions and salaries. Affiliated with the American Federation of Labor and Congress of Industrial Organizations (AFL-CIO), the AFT has played a major role in bargaining for better conditions for teachers. Beginning in the 1960s the AFT has organized teacher strikes in several large urban districts. For this reason the efforts of the AFT have been labeled as more aggressive than those of the NEA. However, after the AFT supported strikes the NEA also endorsed the use of strikes to gain improved contracts for teachers.

Both organizations now use collective bargaining, thereby affecting the nature of teachers' relationships with local school boards. Led by Sandra Feldman, the AFT's membership consists of approximately one-half classroom teachers and one-half support personnel (e.g., school bus drivers, cafeteria workers, etc.).

Because of the association of unionism with the NEA and the AFT, some believe that these organizations contribute a nonprofessional flavor to the educational scene. Critics think that the use of union tactics has harmed society's view of teaching as a profession. Others say teachers would have remained "workers" without the advances made by these groups on behalf of teachers. The National Commission on Teaching and America's Future (1996) refutes the "myth" that unions block reform. Through the collective voices of the NEA and the AFT, which have challenged the status quo, conditions in schools have improved for teachers and students (NCTAF, 1996).

The NEA and the AFT are strong advocates for greater teacher autonomy. They are a large part of the political reality in the world of teaching. Understanding that opposing opinions on the value of the NEA and the AFT exist is important for you as a teacher candidate. As a condition of your teaching

> # NOTABLE QUOTE
>
> ...when teachers stop growing, so do their students. *(Roland Barth)*

AssessYourself

Are you presently a member of a professional organization? In what ways are these organizations of value? Which one(s) are you likely to join if you become a teacher? Why?

Select one professional organization for the age-group or subject area that you wish to teach. Find out more about this organization and investigate student membership. Locate its professional journal, examine the table of contents, and select an article to read and summarize.

contract, you may be required to join the AFT or the NEA. Whether their efforts diminish or increase the professionalization of teaching, only time and progress will tell.

Changes in Teacher Education

The preparation of teachers has undergone many changes in recent years. These changes continue today. Spring (1998) makes the point that changes in teacher education reflect changes taking place in the educational goals of schools. As society has become more complex and as conditions in schools have improved, so have the ways in which we prepare teachers.

The National Commission on Teaching and America's Future (1996) presents the teacher quality issue as a "three-legged stool" consisting of (1) accreditation, (2) licensure, and (3) certification. We next examine each of these dimensions of teacher quality, which are intended to raise standards and professionalize teaching.

Accreditation

Accreditation is earned when an external body positively reviews a program or an organization. The **National Council for Accreditation of Teacher Education (NCATE)** provides evaluation of teacher education programs on a voluntary basis. Approximately 500 of the 1,200 teacher ed-

accreditation

An external review process that organizations and programs undergo to ensure adherence to quality standards.

National Council for Accreditation of Teacher Education (NCATE)

An accrediting professional organization that evaluates teacher education programs on a voluntary basis.

ucation programs in the United States have earned NCATE approval. Some states, such as Arkansas, require that colleges and universities have NCATE endorsement in order to offer teacher preparation programs.

NCATE evaluates the quality of teacher preparation programs according to a set of rigorous standards. These standards are related to the quality of the teacher education faculty, the quality of library resources, the content and coherence of the curriculum, the governance process, and the incorporation of global perspectives and technology skills. NCATE determines whether programs of study for teacher candidates consist of comprehensive experiences grounded in general and professional studies.

NCATE is an umbrella organization that includes 30 other professional associations, such as the National Council for Teachers of Mathematics (NCTM) and the Council for Exceptional Children (CEC). To be NCATE accredited a teacher education program must use the standards of these member organizations to guide the content and outcomes of its specialty areas (e.g., the preparation of math teachers must follow NCTM standards). NCATE is a quality assurance measure endorsed by the National Commission on Teaching and America's Future (1996).

Standards-Based Reforms

Licensure

license

A document issued by an official body allowing practice of a specified trade or profession.

A **license** is a document that allows one to practice a specified trade or profession; it is issued by a board or other official body. Most recently, teachers have been licensed through their state departments of education by completing an approved teacher education program. (Most states use the term **certification** to describe the process of becoming recognized as one who can teach in the state's public schools.) In addition to course completion, most teacher candidates must also pass a written test—either a state test or the **National Teachers Exam (NTE).** The NTE is the standardized test developed by Educational Testing Service (ETS) that assesses communication skills, knowledge, and professional knowledge. Although requirements vary by state, there is a movement underway to standardize the initial licensure process.

certification

The process of meeting state requirements for teaching.

National Teachers Exam (NTE)

A national examination that measures general, professional, and common knowledge and subject areas.

Performance Assessment

PRAXIS Series: Professional Assessment for Beginning Teachers

A new licensing examination to test beginning teachers' knowledge and performance.

Increasingly, there is a recognition of the need to assess not only what teachers know but also what they can do. By focusing on the complexity of the teaching-learning process, as well as the need to apply knowledge, performance assessments move beyond conventional forms of testing by requiring the creation of evidence based upon performance (Eisner, 1999). Educational Testing Service (ETS) has recently constructed new teacher licensing tests known as the **PRAXIS Series: Professional Assessment for Beginning Teachers.** These tests are intended to replace the NTE.

PRAXIS III consists of "Classroom Performance Assessments" that involve classroom observations and semi-structured interviews (Danielson, 1996). Several states (e.g., California, Arkansas, and North Carolina) have adopted systems of performance assessment for teacher licensure. Successful completion of the *PRAXIS III* will lead to a permanent teaching license. A school-based mentoring component is typical, whereby experienced teachers assist beginning teachers in their development of teaching knowledge, skills, and dispositions.

National Standards Guidelines

Interstate New Teacher Assessment and Support Consortium (INTASC)

An association of state education agencies, higher education institutions, and national education organizations, established by the Council of Chief State School Officers.

Committed to standards-based reform in teacher education is the **Interstate New Teacher Assessment and Support Consortium (INTASC),** which is an association of state education agencies, higher education institutions, and national education organizations. Since 1987 INTASC, established by the Council of Chief State School Officers, has been developing licensure standards to provide a common ground among the states. These standards are intended to guide the initial licensing process to ensure teacher competence. INTASC is creating performance standards to assess beginning teachers in terms of their ability to plan effective learning environments for diverse learners, as well as other abilities vital to teaching/learning success. INTASC's core standards for licensing teachers are as follows*:

Principle 1: The teacher understands the central concepts, tools of inquiry, and structures of the discipline(s) he or she teaches.

Principle 2: The teacher understands how children learn and develop and can provide learning opportunities that support their intellectual, social, and personal development.

Principle 3: The teacher understands how students differ in their approaches to learning and creates instructional opportunities that are adapted to diverse learners.

Principle 4: The teacher understands and uses a variety of instructional strategies to encourage students' development of critical thinking, problem solving, and performance skills.

Web Sites
For more information about core standards for INTASC, visit http://www.ccsso.org/intascst.html. For information about PRAXIS, visit http://www.praxis.org.

Principle 5: The teacher uses an understanding of individual and group motivation and behavior to create a learning environment that encourages positive social interaction, active engagement in learning, and self-motivation.

Principle 6: The teacher uses knowledge of effective verbal, nonverbal, and media communication techniques to foster active inquiry, collaboration, and supportive interaction in the classroom.

*From Interstate New Teacher Assessment and Support Consortium. (1993). *Model standards for beginning teacher licensing and development: A resource for state dialogue* (pp. 1–29). A project of the Council of Chief State School Officers. Washington, D.C.: Author.

Principle 7: The teacher plans instruction based on knowledge of subject matter, students, the community, and curriculum goals.

Principle 8: The teacher understands and uses formal and informal assessment strategies to evaluate and ensure the continuous intellectual, social, and physical development of the learner.

Principle 9: The teacher is a reflective practitioner who continually evaluates the effects of his or her choices and actions on others (students, parents, and other professionals in the learning community) and who actively seeks out opportunities to grow professionally.

Principle 10: The teacher fosters relationships with school colleagues, parents, and agencies in the larger community to support students' learning and well-being.

REFLECTION QUESTIONS

- **Which of these changes in teacher education do you think is most important and why?**

- **What impact will such reforms have on your preparation as a teacher?**

- **What other changes do you think are critical? Why?**

National Certification: National Board for Professional Teaching Standards

National Board for Professional Teaching Standards (NBPTS)

A national board issuing a certificate signifying an advanced level of accomplishment.

Board certification is a new concept in teacher education. Accountants who wish to become CPAs or physicians who want to be board-certified family practitioners undergo the process of certification. In 1987 the **National Board for Professional Teaching Standards (NBPTS)** was established as recommended by the Carnegie Task Force on Teaching as a Profession in the report, *A Nation Prepared: Teachers for the 21st Century.* This Board issues a national certificate that signifies an advanced level of accomplishment. The National Board for Professional Teaching Standards (NBPTS) grants teachers who meet the rigorous criteria with the credential of NBCT (National Board Certified Teacher).

The fundamental purpose of NBPTS is to raise standards in teaching by recognizing those who excel in teaching. Membership on this 63-member national board consists primarily of K-12 teachers who develop standards and assessment processes leading to national certification. Each year additional standards for different subject areas (e.g., English) and developmental levels of students (e.g., early childhood and early adolescence) are developed, with 30 categories of certification planned.

Teachers who volunteer to apply for national certification undergo a rigorous assessment process by submitting an extensive portfolio including videotaped lessons and written reflections. Development of the portfolio takes an entire school year. In addition, a two-day assessment process takes place at the testing center, involving written tests of content knowledge and pedagogical skills. The National Board for Professional Teaching Standards (NBPTS) assessment process includes pedagogy and content knowledge of each discipline. Content knowledge and teaching skill application work in tandem and are essential pieces of both the portfolio and the test center experiences (as they are in actual teaching practice).

According to Cascio (1995), "the strength of the board is in its acknowledgment that outstanding teachers are the most important element in education" (p. 213). The dependence on teachers to assess teachers and to direct the national board's policies is a significant step toward increased professionalization in teaching. According to *What Matters Most: Teaching for America's Future,* the goal is to nationally certify at least one teacher in each school district by the year 2006; as of June 1996 a total of 374 teachers have met the criteria of the National Board for Professional Teaching Standards.

Whereas accreditation focuses on programs, certification concerns individuals. Of particular note, a major emphasis of the NBPTS is reflection upon practice. Teachers who qualify for national certification are those who engage in reflection and have documentation to that effect. Now is the time for you to seize opportunities to establish the habit of reflection.

In addition, the importance of collaboration with others—teaching colleagues and students' parents—is stressed by the NBPTS. As you pursue your teacher education program, seek ways to engage in collaboration. With more teachers opting to seek national certification, teaching will no doubt move to a new level of professionalism.

As a way to understand the process one goes through to be board certified, we asked Carol Shestok, who has received this honor, to tell us about her experience. Carol was a fourth grade teacher at Norman E. Day Elementary School in Westford, Massachusetts. In addition to her NBPTS credential, she has a Masters Degree in Education. She is also a PALMS Teacher Leader, Team Leader, and Co-Chair of the Science Curriculum Task Committee for the Westford School District. Currently Carol has been awarded a two-year sabbatical from the classroom to be K–8 Science Teacher Leader in the Westford Public Schools.

Reflections from the Field

"November 11, 1998, a very rainy Veterans' Day in Massachusetts, was an auspicious day for me. On that day I received notification that I had been awarded National Board Certification as a Middle Childhood Generalist. I had started the process more than a year ago. Although I teach fourth grade, this certification encompasses all subject areas in content knowledge and teaching skills for children ages 7 through 12. The process of National Board Certification provided a means through which

I grew professionally as a teacher of children and as a teacher of teachers. Through reflecting on my teaching and analyzing what I had done in relation to the national standards, I realized that some of our most loved lessons, although fun and educational in their own right, do not meet any national or state curriculum standard.

"Although the NBPTS process has changed me in some ways, I am still the same gal who loves teaching, has fun with teaching, loves children, uses much humor, and gets butterflies of anticipation, excitement, and wonder the first day of school, even after 21 years of teaching. Why? Because I want the youngsters' year with me to be a wonderful learning experience. I want their parents to be partners with me in their learning. I want to make a difference in their lives, even though I have them for only a brief school year. The moment the children enter the room, we begin to build a community of learners that continues to grow even as they become returning graduates.

"The portfolio I prepared for national board certification had to address the following six areas:

1. Writing: Thinking Through the Process

2. Thematic Exploration: Connections to Science

3. Building a Classroom Community

4. Building Mathematical Understandings

5. Documented Accomplishments I: Collaboration in the Professional Community

6. Documented Accomplishments II: Outreach to Families and Community

"I geared my portfolio work to my fourth graders' developmental levels, individual learning styles, and the various multiple intelligences in each of the six areas.

"Through the many hours of reading and planning for the work with the children, I became aware of the need to see the 'big picture.' Spelling out goal after goal in relation to standards; deciding which part of the entire interdisciplinary theme to use in my portfolio and which only to discuss; which children's work to analyze; and which original activities, assessments, and materials to use while remaining true to the district and state standards required many hours of thought and many choices. Analyzing and reflecting upon each theme area and selecting specific lessons and artifacts became the most rewarding professional development activity I had ever undertaken as I sought evidences of success (or lack of success) and specified changes.

"Describing, analyzing, and reflecting on the videotapes of my teaching was one of the most difficult tasks. It was very hard to watch myself on tape. Only 15 minutes of a specific discipline could be sent, and the video had to be unedited. The guidelines had to be strictly followed or the entire portfolio would not be read. Displaying my knowledge and teaching skill within the allotted pages was a challenge for me. Displaying the children's work, including pictures, required many choices.

"Most of us who have undertaken the NBPTS process are experienced teachers who have had student teachers, presented workshops, been involved in developing curricula, and had much interaction and communication with parents and are viewed as educational leaders by our districts. Portfolio entries should demonstrate, explain, reflect upon, and analyze these areas. A limited number of pieces of documented evidence had to be chosen and discussed in relation to the national standards.

"In addition to the portfolio documentation, I had to take an 8-hour test at a specified test site. The timed test consisted of questions, prompts, content, and case studies on children ages 7 through 12. Yes, that meant knowing what makes the third-grade child tick, as well as the 12-year-old child—quite a range. That meant knowing content of their curricula as well. Part of my study was to speak with teachers who work with these ages and read research in reading, math, science, health, and social studies. I think the most difficult phase of the whole process for me was taking the test. What made me more anxious was the timing component—90 minutes for each section. After submitting my portfolio and taking the test, then came the wait. Peers are the judges. Yet who is better qualified?

"I now realize that, regardless of the result, the entire process was the most diligent, rigorous, and beneficial professional development activity I had ever undertaken. I knew I was a fine teacher. Others had said I was a fine teacher. Why did I undergo this year-long rigorous process? At first I believe it was my ego and my natural inclination to meet a challenge. I did not know what the process entailed when I agreed to it. I had been approached by the Department of Education in Massachusetts. The state agreed to pay the entire fee of $2,000 if I undertook the process. I had been involved as a Teacher Leader in our state initiative, PALMS (Partners Advancing Learning in Math and Science). Thus I thought, 'Nothing ventured, nothing gained.' So I agreed. At that time no monetary reward was given by our state. Although some states do have such, Massachusetts did not. I went into this for me—to become a better teacher, to see if I was as good as I thought. (Now Massachusetts awards the 'Master Teacher' title to NBCTs; to those who become mentors of teachers in the state, a bonus is available. I have been awarded both title and bonus.) But what if I did not succeed? Was I less of a teacher? No, I was not less. I would have become even better no matter what."

AssessYourself

One thing is certain in this uncertain profession known as teaching: Change is inevitable. How do you handle and respond to change?

How do you feel about entering a career that is not unequivocally accepted as a profession? Does this bother you?

Would you stay and work to make it more uniformly seen as a profession? Or does it matter one way or the other to you?

Do you have an attitude of continued growth?

Do you see yourself as a "student" of teaching once you become a full-fledged teacher? How can you remain committed to this ideal?

Do you see yourself applying for National Board Certification, as Carol Shestok did, after you have become an experienced teacher?

Conclusion

Web Sites
For more information about the National Board for Professional Teaching Standards, visit their web site at www.nbpts.org.

In this chapter you were introduced to a brief history of teacher education. More importantly, we raised the question whether teaching fits the criteria of a profession. Like many other questions in this book, we left it unanswered. And for the same reason as before: because the future is unclear. It really depends on the next generation of teachers and the leadership that comes out of teaching.

Professional status is earned. Joining and becoming active in professional organizations at the national, regional, and state levels will greatly enhance your professional identity and growth as well as that of the "emerging" teaching profession. We concluded this chapter by describing recent changes in teacher education.

What is the future of teacher education? This is another of those questions we raised and left unresolved. As you consider teaching, Sarason (1993) suggests you ask yourself this question: "Am I the kind of person willing and able to enter a profession subject to all kinds of pressures, criticisms, and calls for change?" (p. 6). We, of course, believe it is exciting to think about the part you could play in changing teaching for the better. We would like you to think about becoming an agent of change.

KEY TERMS

accountability

accreditation

American Federation of Teachers (AFT)

certification

Interstate New Teacher Assessment and Support Consortium (INTASC)

knowledge base

license

National Board for Professional Teaching Standards (NBPTS)

National Council for Accreditation of Teacher Education (NCATE)

National Education Association (NEA)

National Teachers Exam (NTE)

normal school

PRAXIS Series: Professional Assessment for Beginning Teachers

profession

professional development

professional organization

SUGGESTED READING

Barth, R. (1990). *Improving schools from within.* San Francisco: Jossey Bass.

Connelly, F. M., & Clandinin, D. J. (Eds.) (1999). *Shaping a professional identity: Stories of educational practice.* New York: Teachers College Press.

REFERENCES

American Association of Colleges for Teacher Education: Bicentennial Commission on Education for the Profession of Teaching. (1976). *Educating a profession.* Washington, D.C.: Author.

American heritage dictionary of the English language (1992). (3rd ed.). Boston: Houghton Mifflin.

Barth, R. (1990). *Improving schools from within.* San Francisco: Jossey Bass.

Cascio, C. (1995). National Board for Professional Teaching Standards: Changing teaching through teachers. *The Clearing House, 68*(4), 211–213.

Clifford, G., & Guthrie, J. (1988). *Ed school: A brief for professional education.* Chicago: University of Chicago Press.

Cooper, M. (1988). Whose culture is it, anyway? In A. Lieberman (Ed.), *Building a professional culture in schools* (pp. 45–54). New York: Teachers College Press.

Danielson, C. (1996). *Enhancing professional practice: A framework for teaching.* Alexandria, VA: Association for Supervision and Curriculum Development.

Duke, D. L. (1990). Setting goals for professional development. *Educational Leadership, 47,* 71–75.

Eisner, E. W. (1999). The uses and limits of performance assessment. *Phi Delta Kappan,* 80(9), 658–660.

Gordy, S. H., & Phelps, P. H. (1996). Teacher educator as Ariadne. In J. Bowman & D. Fleniken (Eds.), *Modeling professional development: An Arkansas perspective* (pp. 155–161). Conway, AR: Arkansas Association of Colleges for Teacher Education.

Hansen, D. (1995). *The call to teach.* New York: Teachers College Press.

Hart, S., & Marshall, D. (1992). *The question of teacher professionalism* (ERIC Document Reproduction Services No. 349 291). Illinois: University of Chicago.

Hebert, E. A. (1999). Rugtime for teachers: Reinventing the faculty meeting. *Phi Delta Kappan, 81*(3), 219–222.

Lieberman, A. (1995). Practices that support teacher development. *Phi Delta Kappan, 76*(8), 591–596.

National Association of Secondary School Principals. (1996). *Breaking ranks: Changing an American institution.* Reston, VA: Author.

National Board for Professional Teaching Standards. (1994). *What teachers should know and be able to do.* Detroit, MI: Author.

National Commission on Teaching and America's Future. (1996). *What matters most: Teaching for America's future.* New York: Carnegie Corporation.

National Foundation for the Improvement of Education. (1996). *Teachers take charge of their learning: Transforming professional development for student success.* Washington D.C.: Author.

O'Neill, G. P. (1988). Teaching as a profession: Redefining our concepts. *Action in Teacher Education, 10*(2), 5–10.

Phelps, P. H. (1993). Bringing in the new: An induction ceremony for new teachers. *The Clearing House, 66*(3), 154.

Sadker, M. P., & Sadker, D. M. (1997). *Teachers, schools, and society* (4th ed.). New York: McGraw-Hill.

Sarason, S. (1993). *You are thinking of teaching? Opportunities, problems, realities.* San Francisco: Jossey Bass.

Segall, W., & Wilson, A. (1998). *Introduction to education.* New York: Prentice Hall.

Sockett, H. (1993). *The moral base for teacher professionalism.* New York: Teachers College Press.

Spring, J. (1998). *American education* (8th ed.). Boston: McGraw-Hill.

Strike, K. (1988). The ethics of teaching. *Phi Delta Kappan, 70*(2), 156–158.

United States Department of Education. (1986). *What works: Research about teaching and learning.* Washington, D.C.: Author.

Urban, W. J. (1990). Historical studies of teacher education. In W. R. Houston (Ed.), *Handbook of research on teacher education* (pp. 59–71). New York: Macmillan.

© Superstock

At the end of this chapter, you will be able to

- Articulate principles from the professional codes of ethics for teachers and apply those principles to specific teachers' attitudes and practices.

- Identify ways to protect yourself from being accused of wrongdoing.

- Clarify personal values, morals, and beliefs that could affect how you might respond to potential ethical and legal dilemmas that arise in school settings.

- Cite federal legislation and judicial decisions that affect teachers' legal responsibilities and civil rights.

CHAPTER 13

Ethical and Legal Issues

A bird's eye view of what to expect in this chapter

This chapter is an overview of ethical and legal issues affecting contemporary teachers. Our aim is to heighten your awareness of the risks associated with being a teacher in a litigious society such as ours. Throughout the chapter we accentuate teachers' ethical responsibilities toward students, in addition to discussing teachers' and students' legal rights. Moreover, we highlight some relevant statutes and judicial decisions. If you are considering teaching, you must be aware that litigation is on the rise and teachers are not exempt from civil or criminal lawsuits.

By becoming aware of ethical principles and legal standards, your chances of being a defendant in a lawsuit are lessened. Because ignorance of the law cannot be used as a defense, we have selected a few important legal precedents that directly relate to teachers' conduct (personal and professional). If you become a teacher, you should stay abreast of changes in national, state, and local school law in order to make prudent decisions. Your best protection from allegations of wrongdoing or from being named a defendant in a lawsuit is to recognize your vulnerability and stay informed about these critical issues.

n this chapter we will explore ethical and legal issues affecting teachers in today's changing and litigious society. It goes without saying that teachers should behave professionally, ethically, and lawfully in their everyday interactions with students, parents, administrators, colleagues, and support staff. In the majority of cases it is clear what kinds of behaviors satisfy acceptable conduct standards.

On occasion, however, teachers face situations in which doing what is ethical and legal is not so clear-cut. In this chapter we present dilemmas and then ask you to decide on an appropriate course of action if you were the teacher. The purpose of these scenarios is to demonstrate the ambiguous nature of some situations. You will be asked to consider possible actions, weigh respective consequences, and arrive at a decision you think is most appropriate for the present circumstances.

We wish we could provide you with a checklist that enumerates proper conduct, which would guarantee your freedom from public and legal scrutiny, but unfortunately no such list exists. As you read this chapter, be aware that charges can be brought against teachers for things they do as well as things they *fail to do* (omissions). Doubtless the peril is greatest for those oblivious to the "legal" minefields that surround them. Refusing to acknowledge the impending threat of lawsuits makes any teacher a "sitting duck" for allegations.

Thus it is imperative that prospective teachers are made aware of behaviors that could increase their vulnerability for litigation. In this chapter we are able only to scratch the surface of this topic; thus it is in your best interest to read further about this critical subject, particularly if you pursue teaching as a career.

Ethics

One obvious way to protect yourself from being a defendant in a lawsuit is to conduct yourself in an ethical and professional manner at all times. In theory this makes good sense; however, in actual practice it may not be so easy. Distinguishing what is ethical behavior in every situation raises interesting questions demanding reflection and speculation. Even a **code of ethics** written by a professional organization offers only guidelines (not absolutes) for proper conduct. Ethical codes embody ideals for members to strive for when deciding how to act as a professional. It would be virtually impossible to write ethical codes in definitive terms; there are just too many contingencies (extenuating circumstances) in human interactions.

It is reassuring to know that most ethical violations are committed innocently by teachers. However, regardless of whether the action was intentional or not, poor judgment can have dire consequences for a teacher. For example, did you know that a teacher who makes a derogatory comment about a student to a third party (another student or teacher for example) could be sued for defamation of character? The *National Education Association's Code of Ethics* (1975) states that "the educator shall not intentionally ex-

code of ethics

A professional organization's guidelines of appropriate behavior for its membership.

pose the student to embarrassment or disparagement." A naive teacher could inadvertently fall prey to "illegal" gossip just by socializing with colleagues in the teachers' lounge. Simply, teachers must be discreet about what they say regarding students and their families in the presence of others. Clearly, discretion is an imperative attribute for teachers to possess.

Professional Codes of Ethics

In an effort to avert being accused of wrongdoing, prospective teachers should begin by familiarizing themselves with the professional codes of ethics. Ethical codes represent a consensus of what the members in any given profession consider to be proper principles of conduct. As you examine the *National Education Association Code of Ethics* (1975) and the *American Federation of Teachers AFL-CIO Bill of Rights and Responsibilities for Learning: Standards of Conduct, Standards for Achievement* (1996), notice the abstract, vague wording. This merely underscores the need for professionals to use discretion and reasoning when interpreting and applying principles to actual behavior.

National Education Association Code of Ethics

Let's begin this discussion with the *National Education Association Code of Ethics* (Box 13.1). Take a few minutes to read the document in full. As you read, think of specific examples applicable to each principle.

American Federation of Teachers Bill of Rights and Responsibilities for Learning: Standards of Conduct, Standards for Achievement

Now read the *Bill of Rights and Responsibilities for Learning: Standards of Conduct, Standards for Achievement* (1996) by the American Federation of Teachers (Box 13.2). Again think of ways to apply these principles to actual teaching practices.

Teachers' Ethical Responsibilities

Web Sites
To learn more about NEA and AFT, visit their web sites: http://www.nea.org/info/code.html and http://civnet.org/civitas/partners/aft.htm.

Students have basic rights, and these rights should be respected and protected by school personnel. All teachers should behave ethically and responsibly in their interactions with students. To describe ethical attitudes and behaviors of responsible teachers, we have compiled a list of noteworthy ones for your review. We are sure there are other equally important behaviors we overlooked. Before reading our list, jot down your ideas regarding students' rights; then compare and contrast your list with ours.

BOX 13.1   **National Education Association Code of Ethics**

Preamble

The educator, believing in the worth and dignity of each human being, recognizes the supreme importance of the pursuit of truth, devotion to excellence, and the nurture of democratic principles. Essential to these goals is the protection of freedom to learn and to teach and the guarantee of equal educational opportunity for all. The educator accepts the responsibility to adhere to the highest ethical standards.

The educator recognizes the magnitude of the responsibility inherent in the teaching process. The desire for the respect and confidence of one's colleagues, of students, of parents, and the members of the community provides the incentive to attain and maintain the highest possible degree of ethical conduct. The Code of Ethics of the Education Profession indicates the aspiration of all educators and provides standards by which to judge conduct.

The remedies specified by the NEA and/or its affiliates for the violation of any provision of the Code shall be exclusive, and no such provision shall be enforceable in any form other than one specifically designated by the NEA or its affiliates.

Principle One: Commitment to the Student

The educator strives to help each student realize his or her potential as a worthy and effective member of society. The educator therefore works to stimulate the spirit of inquiry, the acquisition of knowledge and understanding, and the thoughtful formulation of worthy goals.

In fulfillment of the obligation to the student, the educator:

1. *Shall not unreasonably restrain the student from independent action in the pursuit of learning.*
2. *Shall not unreasonably deny the student access to varying points of view.*
3. *Shall not deliberately suppress or distort subject matter relevant to the student's progress.*
4. *Shall make reasonable effort to protect the students from conditions harmful to learning or health and safety.*
5. *Shall not intentionally expose the student to embarrassment or disparagement.*
6. *Shall not on the basis of race, color, creed, sex, national origin, marital status, political or religious beliefs, family, social or cultural background, or sexual orientation unfairly:*
   a. *Exclude any student from participation in any program.*

b. *Deny benefits to any students.*

c. *Grant any advantage to any student.*

7. *Shall not use professional relationships with students for private advantage.*

8. *Shall not disclose information about students obtained in the course of professional service, unless disclosure serves a compelling professional purpose or is required by law.*

Principle Two: Commitment to the Profession

The education profession is vested by the public with a trust and responsibility requiring the highest ideals of professional service.

In the belief that the quality of the services of the education profession directly influences the nation and its citizens, the educator shall exert every effort to raise professional standards, to promote a climate that encourages the exercise of professional judgment to achieve conditions which attract persons worthy of the trust to careers in education, and to assist in preventing the practice of the profession by unqualified persons.

In fulfillment of the obligation to the profession, the educator:

l. *Shall not in an application for a professional position deliberately make a false statement or fail to disclose a material fact related to competency and qualifications.*

2. *Shall not misrepresent his/her professional qualifications.*

3. *Shall not assist any entry into the profession of a person known to be unqualified in respect to character, education, or other relevant attribute.*

4. *Shall not knowingly make a false statement concerning the qualifications of a candidate for a professional position.*

5. *Shall not assist a non-educator in the unauthorized practice of teaching.*

6. *Shall not disclose information about colleagues obtained in the course of professional service unless disclosure serves a compelling professional purpose or is required by law.*

7. *Shall not knowingly make false or malicious statements about a colleague.*

8. *Shall not accept any gratuity, gift, or favor that might impair or appear to influence professional decisions or actions.*

Source: *National Education Association Code of Ethics* by the National Education Association. Copyright 1975 by the National Education Association. Reprinted by permission of the National Education Association, 1201 Sixteenth Street, N.W., Washington, D.C. 20036.

BOX 13.2

American Federation of Teachers AFL-CIO Bill of Rights and Responsibilities for Learning: Standards of Conduct, Standards for Achievement

The traditional mission of our public schools has been to prepare our nation's young people for equal and responsible citizenship and productive adulthood. Today, we reaffirm that mission by remembering that democratic citizenship and productive adulthood begin with standards of conduct and standards for achievement in our schools. Other education reforms **may** *work; high standards of conduct and achievement* **do** *work—and nothing else* **can** *work without them.*
   Recognizing that rights carry responsibilities, we declare that:

- *All students and school staff have a right to schools that are safe, orderly, and drug free.*
- *All students and school staff have a right to learn and work in school districts and schools that have clear discipline codes with fair and consistently enforced consequences for misbehavior.*
- *All students and school staff have a right to learn and work in school districts that have alternative educational placements for violent or chronically disruptive students.*
- *All students and school staff have a right to be treated with courtesy and respect.*
- *All students and school staff have a right to learn and work in school districts, schools, and classrooms that have clearly stated and rigorous academic standards.*
- *All students and school staff have a right to learn and work in well-equipped schools that have the instructional materials needed to carry out a rigorous academic program.*
- *All students and school staff have a right to learn and work in schools where teachers know the subject matter and how to teach it.*
- *All students and school staff have a right to learn and work in school districts, schools, and classrooms where high grades stand for high achievement and promotion is earned.*
- *All students and school staff have a right to learn and work in school districts and schools where getting a high school diploma means having the knowledge and skills essential for college or a good job.*
- *All students and school staff have a right to be supported by parents, the community, public officials, and business in their efforts to uphold high standards of conduct and achievement.*

Source: A Bill of Rights and Responsibilities for Learning: Standards of Conduct, Standards for Achievement *by the American Federation of Teachers. Copyright 1996. Reprinted by permission of the American Federation of Teachers, 555 New Jersey Avenue, N.W., Washington, D.C. 20001.*

Hold High Expectations for Students and for Self

Ethical teachers have high expectations for their students; they believe all children are capable of learning. They do not discriminate based on gender, race, ethnicity, socioeconomic status, sexual orientation or disability. In *Pygmalion in the Classroom*, Rosenthal and Jacobson (1968) found that teachers' expectations affected student achievement. At the onset of this study, teachers were told by researchers that certain students were academically "capable." Unbeknownst to the teachers, those students identified as "capable" had been randomly selected from the class rosters. At the end of the study, it was found that those students labeled as "capable" performed better than the others.

In spite of some limitations in research design, this study suggests that teacher expectations can affect students' learning and performance. In the literature the belief that students respond according to how they are treated is commonly referred to as **self-fulfilling prophecy.** If this is true, what could happen if a teacher expected less from students from certain minority groups based on negative stereotypes? Would students' performance reflect the teacher's bias?

Ability grouping, or tracking, is a practice used frequently in early grades whereby students are grouped according to some standardized test score. Lately this practice has been challenged because too often students placed in the lower groups become stigmatized unfairly. To explain, a teacher might expect less from students in the low reading group and generalize that poor readers are deficient in other areas as well. These students may also begin to perform consistently with what is expected from them. Of course there are some advantages to ability grouping, but we merely use it as an example to make a point about the importance of teachers expecting the best from their students. In sum, ethical teachers believe that all their students are capable of learning and achieving (albeit not in the same way or at the same pace). More will be said about the practice of tracking in Chapter 15.

Furthermore, ethical teachers hold high expectations for themselves. Students have a right to be taught by teachers who are confident in their ability to teach. In Chapter 3 we learned that efficacy is a belief held by effective teachers that they *can* make a difference in the lives of their students. Obviously efficacy is an attribute that ethical teachers possess. When teachers *believe* they can make a difference in students' learning, they *can* (Ashton & Webb, 1986; McIntyre & O'Hair, 1996). Students deserve to have teachers who are confident not only in their students' abilities to succeed but in their own abilities as well.

self-fulfilling prophecy

A belief that students behave according to how they are treated.

ability grouping

An instructional practice of grouping students by ability based on some type of assessment.

Handle Power Appropriately

As we discussed in Chapter 2, teachers as authority figures have power, and this power has the potential to be misused and abused. Students have a right to be taught by teachers who refrain from using power against them in malicious ways. Teachers who manipulate, goad, or mock students are exploiting their power and behaving irresponsibly. Belittling, embarrassing, and

Ethical teachers believe they can make a difference in the lives of their students. They hold high expectations for students and themselves.

© Robert Maass/CORBIS

intimidating students can be psychologically damaging to students; therefore such actions should be avoided by teachers. Being able to handle power responsibly and morally is a prerequisite for teaching; any misuse of power can be detrimental to students' self-esteem.

Teachers should accept and revere the power that comes by virtue of their position, and they should be very careful not to abuse or misuse this power. We want our students to behave, not out of fear, but because it is the right thing to do. If you delight in the idea of being an authority figure with immense power to hold over children, we suggest you rethink teaching as a career choice.

A CASE STUDY

A student in an introductory course to teacher education commented that he wanted to teach elementary school kids "because you can intimidate them more easily." The faculty member teaching this course was caught off guard by this inappropriate comment and did not respond. The class continued to discuss reasons why they believe they would work better with certain age-groups.

If you had been the instructor, how would you have handled the situation described in the case study? Would you have ignored the comment?

What message is sent when one lets such comments slide? What would you have said to that student in this situation?

REFLECTION QUESTIONS

- Do you remember teachers who were "power hungry" and seemed to enjoy manipulating students to do their bidding? Describe the experience.

- What is your position regarding whether teacher preparation programs have an ethical duty to screen applicants based on personal traits?

- Should an applicant with exemplary grades and high scores on standardized tests be denied admittance to a teacher education program based on questionable personality traits?

- If so, what defense should the screening committee offer to justify their rejection of a candidate on the basis of perceived "power" issues?

Set Healthy Boundaries

An ethical teacher recognizes professional boundaries between teacher and student and sets appropriate limits. Power issues come into play when teachers enter into unhealthy relationships with students. As discussed previously, the teacher-student relationship implies a power differential that makes the teacher more powerful than the student; this imbalance of power leaves students vulnerable. In the language of psychology, when a person in power plays one or more "conflicting" roles with a person of less power, the relationship is referred to as a **dual or multiple relationship** (Corey, Corey, & Callanan, 1998). Teachers must recognize that these types of relationships, because of the power discrepancy, have the potential to be problematic.

dual or multiple relationship
A relationship in which a person in authority plays two or more conflicting roles.

To illustrate, a teacher who becomes a friend to a student is entering into a dual relationship. On first glance, befriending a student (especially one who lacks nurturing at home) seems like a caring and appropriate behavior. But could there be unfavorable repercussions resulting from this relationship? The student could become overly dependent on the teacher. This type of relationship could jeopardize class morale because other students in the class may not understand or appreciate the unique circumstances that precipitated this special relationship. A dual relationship also creates problems when grading or assessing that student's work. Can a teacher be objective when evaluating an individual that he or she has known on a more personal basis? From a legal perspective, the teacher (as the person in authority) is the one who is responsible for any negative outcomes resulting from dual

Ethical teachers realize the importance of setting healthy boundaries with their students. They accept responsibility for drawing and maintaining those lines.

relationships. As you can surmise, there are many factors to consider before entering into a dual relationship with a student.

Please note that taking a special interest in a child who needs assistance is typically not considered "unethical" behavior. Teachers, especially those working with younger children in low-income areas, will find many students in need of extra attention and support. Fortunately, there are many discreet ways teachers can help children without appearing condescending or partial. For example, teachers who want to help economically disadvantaged children could donate food, clothes, toys, and school supplies to the school counselor or social worker, who, in turn, will distribute these items to the student or family. As you can imagine, it gives a teacher great satisfaction to know he or she has helped a student in some small way. Unaware of the source, the student benefits from the assistance without having to feel uncomfortable or indebted to that teacher. This allows the student to save face and allows the teacher a chance to make a visible difference in the life of a student.

Assess Performance Fairly

An ethical teacher is fair and just in grading practices; evaluations are based on objective criteria known in advance to all students (Strike, 1990). If a teacher cultivates a friendship with a student, that teacher's objectivity could be impaired when he or she attempts to assign a grade or evaluate the student's performance. Becoming too familiar with students could cloud one's judgment—even those teachers who take special care to avoid the possibility of subjectivity. In short, students have a right to be graded in an impartial manner.

This raises the question: Does being fair imply that students in a class are treated the same in every situation? Or does being fair mean that teachers must consider each student as an individual with varying needs and abilities? For example, should test conditions be uniform for all students or should teachers make adjustments based on students' needs? And if accommodations are made for some students, would that seem unfair to other students in the class? For example, should students whose native language is not English be expected to take the same written test under the same conditions as other students in the class? These are the types of dilemmas that teachers face daily.

Protect Confidentiality

Students also have a right to have test scores and other assessment results held in strict confidence; ethical teachers make every effort to protect students' confidentiality. A student can, of course, disclose test scores to other students—but teachers do not share that privilege. To release test scores without permission is not only unethical it is illegal. Do you remember teachers passing out test papers in such a way that other students could see your grade? Or posting the grade by your name, or calling the grade out in class? This practice is clearly not ethical. But is it legal? More will be said about the legality of privacy shortly.

It is interesting to note that neither NEA's or AFT's ethical codes specifically refer to confidentiality nor mention privacy rights. However, the *NEA Code of Ethics* (1975) indirectly alludes to confidentiality when it states that educators "shall not disclose information about students obtained in the course of professional service unless disclosure serves a compelling professional purpose or is required by law." Therefore ethical teachers respect students' privacy and do not divulge private information unless instructed to do otherwise.

Behave Consistently

An ethical teacher believes in what he or she teaches and reflects that commitment in actions. According to Strike (1990), ethical teachers' behaviors demonstrate respect for the subjects they teach. To do this, teachers must model behaviors consistent with what they teach; otherwise they could appear hypocritical. As we have mentioned numerous times in this text, responsible teachers are mindful of how their actions can be construed by their students. To be credible, teachers must try (within reason) to practice what they teach.

A few examples of incongruent behaviors are: A fourth-grade teacher teaches a unit on the importance of nutrition, yet is seen eating junk food

Ethical teachers avoid making value judgments and imposing their values on students. They can, however, model socially appropriate values.

out of the vending machine for her lunch. A ninth-grade civics teacher neglects to register to vote in the community in which he now resides. A physical education teacher is a chain smoker. An overweight coach scoffs at the idea of exercising. These are classic examples of teachers who are unfaithful to their chosen disciplines. From your experiences, identify examples of teachers' behaviors that were incongruent with what they taught and then identify examples of congruent behaviors.

Refrain from Judging or Imposing Personal Values

An ethical teacher must be careful not to judge students' personal values or impose his or her own values on students. Strike (1990) asserts that students have the right to determine for themselves what they believe. Let's say a teacher is a staunch vegetarian—should she preach ("teach") a lesson chastising those who eat red meat? What if a teacher were a recent convert to a religious sect, should he share his conversion experience with his students? Would this be ethical? Would it be legal?

If you are employed by a public school, you must remain neutral with regard to your faith or your religion. Although the courts have ruled prayers and Bible readings as unconstitutional in public schools, this does not preclude teachers from talking *about* religion (Fisher & Sorenson, 1996). Teachers cross the line, however, when they use their positions of influence to promote or impose a particular religious faith or doctrine. Furthermore, teachers cannot publicly depreciate someone else's personal beliefs or religion in general. Indoctrination is forbidden. In sum, teachers have a duty to protect the rights of all students, regardless of their faith—or lack of faith. Every student has the right to believe or not to believe in a higher being (Noddings, 1993).

This raises the question: Can a teacher ever voice a personal opinion about religion in the classroom? For example, if a student asks a teacher outright if he believes in God or what religion he belongs to, can the teacher respond truthfully without violating the law? Legally, because the student initiated the discussion, a teacher can respond, but the explanation must be brief. The teacher cannot, however, use this opportunity to promote and/or convert students to his religion or faith. To repeat, teachers whose salaries are paid by state funds cannot impose religious doctrine or personal faith on students.

Although teachers cannot impose their religious or spiritual views on students, this does not mean they cannot display their faith or values to students via actions. There is a big difference between imposing and displaying; imposing means pushing your beliefs on others (being dogmatic in your convictions), whereas displaying is demonstrating what you value by being a good example. Modeling appropriate morals and values to students is quite acceptable behavior for teachers. For example, a gentle, forgiving spirit can speak louder than words, especially when teachers are trying to teach their students to be understanding and forgiving of other students' shortcomings.

Ethical Dilemmas: Shades of Gray

In some situations, teachers are compelled to reevaluate their principles and convictions about what is right and what is wrong. Ethical dilemmas can create uncertainty (and sometimes anxiety) for teachers because solutions are not black or white. By definition ethical dilemmas are fraught with multiple shades of gray. Gray areas force teachers to stop and think before they act. For an example of this, let's look at the practice of giving gifts to teachers.

If you recall, the *NEA Code of Ethics* (1975) declares that educators "shall not accept any gratuity, gift, or favor that might impair or appear to influence professional decisions or actions." Based on this, one might infer that teachers who accept gifts from students are behaving unethically. But is this behavior unequivocally unethical? Do you see any shades of gray that preclude this being a "black and white" issue? Under what circumstances would it be "appropriate" for a teacher to accept a gift or a favor from a student or parent? What are some exceptions to this rule?

Let's say you are a third-grade teacher and one of your students gives you an ashtray made in art class; would you accept the gift? What if your car does not start and a student's parent offers to jumpstart your battery or tow your car, would you accept the favor? Does one automatically lose objectivity when he or she gets to know a student's family better? We pose these questions to underscore the ambiguous nature of many ethical dilemmas teachers face in a school setting.

REFLECTION QUESTIONS

- Why do you think the NEA's code of ethics includes the admonition about accepting gratuities, gifts, and favors?

- How might the practice of gift-giving put some students—who are unable to afford gifts—at a disadvantage?

- Are students who are able to give expensive gifts to teachers treated differently from those students who cannot give gifts? What have your experiences been regarding this practice?

- How would a student know whether a gift (or lack of one) was the reason behind how the teacher treated him or her?

AssessYourself

Did you ever give teachers gifts when you were in school, or was gift-giving against school policy? What do you think?

Is gift-giving an ethical issue? Why or why not?

What would be your policy regarding this practice?

If you are considering becoming a teacher, you may need to think about issues like this in advance. Sensitive and responsible teachers search for solutions to ethical dilemmas, they take into account how their actions will be interpreted by students. Students are impressionable. They are looking to the teacher for guidance, and they notice behavior and take cues from it. Teachers then must actively question their motives and actions to assess the impact of decisions on students. Teachers who downplay these kinds of concerns may regret later having taken such a nonchalant attitude. Losing your credibility or damaging that of the profession would be a high price to pay for thoughtless reactions to ethical predicaments. Simply put, it is very important to have the respect of your students and their families.

School Law

The significance of school law to educators cannot be overemphasized. Standard 1.D.1 of the *National Council for Accreditation of Teacher Education* (NCATE) (1995) states that "Candidates shall complete a well-planned sequence of courses and/or experiences in professional studies in which they acquire and learn to apply knowledge about...school law and educational policy" (p. 17). Of interest, very few teacher education programs require a course in school law (Gullatt & Tollett, 1997). Patterson and Rossow (1996) surveyed more than 700 teacher education programs and found 18 programs that offer a course in school law. If you pursue teaching, we recommend you learn as much as you can about educational law.

One place to begin is by reading a column written by Dr. Perry Zirkel, a professor of law and education at Lehigh University, called "Courtside," which periodically appears in the *Phi Delta Kappan. Phi Delta Kappan* is an educational journal published by Phi Delta Kappa International, Inc., a prominent educational fraternity. Because school law (and law in general) is in a state of flux, both experienced and novice teachers must stay abreast of changes that will affect them.

Sources of Educational Law

In the next section we address teachers' legal responsibilities toward students. As you may recall from your American government class, there are two main sources of laws. Laws can be made by the U.S. Congress and by state legislatures. These legislative laws are called *statutes* or *statutory laws*. Sometimes laws are declared "unconstitutional" by the courts. As you remember, the checks and balances system grants the judicial branch of government the power to determine the "constitutionality" of Congressional statutes. The U.S. Constitution and state constitutions provide the basis for these types of judgments.

These kinds of court decisions provide the second source of laws: *judicial law* (i.e., court law). The U.S. Supreme Court, for example, has played an instrumental role in education. The landmark case was *Brown* v. *Board of Education of Topeka* (1954), in which the court ruled that the "separate but equal" doctrine was inherently unequal. This decision reversed a historical pattern of segregated schools, subsequently leading to desegregation. More recent court decisions have addressed issues related to special education, school prayer, bilingual education, due process, tenure, search and seizure, sexual harassment, suspension, and expulsion, to name a few.

REFLECTION QUESTIONS

In the spring of 1999, Congress passed a law that permits public schools to post the *Ten Commandments.* Do you think this particular statute would be upheld by a court of law if it were ever challenged in the future?

Does this law violate separation of church and state and compromise First Amendment rights?

Teachers' Legal Responsibilities Toward Students

Teachers have certain legal responsibilities and can be sued if they are negligent in those duties. To be found negligent the plaintiff must prove (1) the teacher (the defendant) had a duty to protect the student from harm, (2) the duty was breached, and (3) the student was injured mentally or physically (or both) as a result of the breach. The client (plaintiff) must prove all three conditions to succeed in a negligence suit against an educator.

Basically, a judge tries to determine whether the defendant's behavior departed significantly from actions taken by any other "reasonable person" in that position in similar circumstances. If the judge concludes that a teacher did fail to provide a certain "standard of care," the teacher may have to pay compensatory damages to the client. Compensatory damages are usually awarded in civil (tort) suits; a **tort** is defined as a legal injury or wrong against a person or property. It is important to realize that criminal, as well as civil, charges can be brought against teachers. Penalties imposed on teachers found guilty of criminal acts include fines and imprisonment (or both) depending on the seriousness of the offense.

As you can see, being accused of wrongdoing is a grave matter; it could destroy a teacher's career. To illustrate, if a student charges a teacher with abuse, the accused teacher can face a criminal suit or a civil suit (or both). And because this is an alleged child abuse case, the state's child protective agency will likely get involved (Villaume & Foley, 1993). After a legal investigation is conducted, the state board of education and/or licensing board will probably conduct its own inquiry. A teacher's license or certification status could be suspended or revoked depending on the final outcome.

Because of the gravity of this topic, we have decided to list some behaviors that could put teachers at legal risk. Our list is far from encompassing,

tort

A legal injury or wrong against another person or property.

so we would like you to think of other behaviors that might indicate legal trouble for teachers.

Protect Students from Harm

Teachers and school personnel assume the place (role) of parents and guardians while students are under their care; this is called "in loco parentis" and was defined in earlier chapters as "in the place of parents." The *NEA Code of Ethics* (1975) states that teachers "shall make reasonable effort to protect the students from conditions harmful to learning or health and safety." The *AFT Bill of Rights and Responsibilities* (1996) states that: "All students and staff have a right to schools that are safe, orderly, and drug free." Thus teachers are duty-bound to ensure a safe environment for students while students are on school property or participating in school-sponsored events such as field trips, athletic contests, or other school-related activities. Responsible teachers take necessary precautions to lessen the risk of students' injuries.

Think about this example: A teacher is late for hall duty one morning; in her absence a fight erupts and a student bystander is hurt. Is the teacher liable? (Most likely yes.) On the other hand, if the teacher had been on duty and was paying attention and the fight still occurred, is the teacher liable now? (More than likely not.)

A related question is: What is a teacher's duty to protect students from impending danger? Obviously, teachers are not fortune-tellers. They cannot accurately predict dangerous situations. It is unrealistic to think a teacher could prevent mishaps or tragedies from occurring. Nevertheless, in the case above, if the teacher had been on duty as assigned, the injury might not have happened.

If a teacher is given advance warning of imminent danger and fails to act on this information, is the teacher liable? (In this case, probably yes). If, for example, a student reveals to a teacher that she intends to hurt another student, the teacher should notify the building principal at once. A student's threat against others or against self (a suicidal threat) must be taken seriously; teachers are obligated to report such threats to the proper authorities. Most schools today have comprehensive crisis management plans in place, which can be very helpful to a new teacher who may not know what to do in the event of an emergency.

At first glance, many recent court decisions relating to school safety appear to infringe on students' civil rights; however, on further analysis, that is not necessarily the case. To explain, most courts have upheld the right of school officials to conduct a random **search and seizure** on school property. Judges grant administrators latitude to conduct searches (even strip searches) when there is a "reasonable suspicion" to believe a student is concealing weapons, drugs, or other illegal items. Metal detectors have also been upheld by the courts as constitutional (Alexander & Alexander, 1998). These rulings support strong measures taken in schools today as a

search and seizure

The legal right to search an individual and property if there is "reasonable suspicion" that person has committed a crime or is concealing illegal items.

way to protect the common good. In other words, the means justifies the end (i.e., safety).

Safeguard Students' Privacy

School personnel are not at liberty to discuss or release students' test scores or academic records unless explicit approval has been granted. In 1974 the United States Congress passed the **Buckley Amendment** (*Family Educational Rights and Privacy Act*, P.L. 93-380), referred to as FERPA, which protects students' privacy rights. In essence, FERPA prohibits the release of students' test scores to anyone other than courts and school personnel (who have "a right to know") without written permission from the parents or guardians. Persons designated as having "a right to know" are those who have a "legitimate educational interest" in the student, such as classroom teachers. Obviously teachers should have access to academic files because the information therein can be extremely useful for individualizing instruction for students.

Although a teacher cannot be held liable for failing to comply with FERPA, the school district can be, which translates to losing federal funding. To prevent school personnel from inadvertently violating the Buckley Amendment, school districts have developed strict guidelines and procedures for accessing files, releasing information, and storing files. Beginning teachers should be informed at the outset of these procedures and must be willing to comply with FERPA's regulations. For example, a teacher who allows a student to distribute or call out grades is violating privacy rights under the Buckley Amendment.

Adhere to Copyright Laws

Educators must abide by copyright regulations. However, because teachers need quick access to printed materials for the delivery of instruction, those legal guidelines are less binding. To clarify teachers' rights to photocopy published works, the U.S. Congress in 1976 revised the original Copyright Act of 1909 to include a **fair use** provision. This clause provides specific guidelines for teachers to adhere to when copying printed materials.

A teacher, for example, can make a single copy of a published piece for instruction or research without prior permission from the author if the piece is less than 250 words (e.g., a poem). Lengthier pieces of more than 1,000 words or 10% of the printed material (whichever comes first) cannot be copied without the copyholder's permission. Nevertheless, if a teacher needs something right away for a particular class (making it impossible to obtain the author's permission in time), the teacher can make the copy—as long as it is from a single work and is used only once per semester in a given course.

In 1980 Congress amended the Copyright Act to include a "fair use" provision relative to computer software programs. In most situations, teachers

Buckley Amendment

An abbreviated name for the Family Educational Rights and Privacy Act (FERPA), passed in 1974 by Congress to protect students' privacy.

fair use

A revision to the original Copyright Act of 1909 passed by Congress in 1976 that allows teachers more latitude in photocopying published works.

can now make one backup copy of a software program. Keep in mind that as a rule it is illegal to copy software packages, as well as material off the Internet, unless otherwise stated. The following year, Congress passed legislation regarding the taping of live television broadcasts. Teachers can legally tape a television show as long as the video is (1) shown only once to any class within the first 10 days of taping, and (2) erased after 45 days. As you can see, teachers cannot collect tapes and create an educational library for future reference.

Even though copyright laws are less stringent on teachers, we must still exercise due care. Teachers need to pay close attention to the guidelines, not only because it is the "legal" thing to do, but also because we are demonstrating to our students how important it is to respect someone else's work. Giving credit where credit is due is one way of showing respect for an author's endeavors.

Teach Responsibly

educational malpractice

A claim made in court that a certain teacher or school district failed to adequately teach academic skills.

An **educational malpractice** suit is a claim made by a student that a certain teacher or school district failed to adequately prepare him or her to function effectively in a competitive society. As you can imagine, this type of malpractice suit is very difficult for students to win. Primarily because it is virtually impossible to prove that a student's academic deficiencies were caused by a teacher's breach of duty (or negligence). Obviously, there are too many "nonschool" factors that may have interfered with that student's progress in school. It is unrealistic to think that any teacher could promise that every student in class will meet certain levels of proficiency (Hartmeister, 1995).

Those few educational malpractice suits that have succeeded were claims made by special-education students who had been inaccurately labeled or diagnosed (Hartmeister, 1995). To date, courts steer clear of educational accountability cases. This may not continue to be the case, however, especially with the increased use of high-stakes tests that determine whether a student passes or graduates. Considering the rise in the number of claims made against other professionals such as doctors and lawyers, it is important to be aware of educational malpractice. (Laws can change, as can public opinion, so beware).

Defend Students' Freedom of Expression

freedom of expression

A fundamental right to express your beliefs that is protected by the First Amendment to the Bill of Rights.

Freedom of expression is a fundamental right protected by the First Amendment to the U.S. Constitution. *Tinker* v. *Des Moines Independent Community School District* (1969) was a landmark case establishing students' rights to free expression. In response to a group of students wearing black armbands to protest U.S. involvement in Vietnam, the Des Moines School Board instituted a policy forbidding the wearing of armbands. Students who refused to comply were suspended. The U.S. Supreme Court decided that as

Freedom of expression is a First Amendment right. Have we gone too far? Should there be dress codes and/or limits on students' civil rights?

long as the students' behavior (i.e., wearing armbands) did not disrupt the educational process, the student had the right to do so. This decision ultimately struck down the school's rule as an abridgement of students' rights to free expression.

Acknowledge Students' Right to an Education

due process

Specific procedures that protect the rights of individuals from arbitrary actions.

The U.S. Supreme Court in the *Tinker* decision also established students' rights to free education; hence schools cannot arbitrarily remove a student from school without **due process.** The right of due process is protected under the Fourteenth Amendment to the U.S. Constitution. To be deprived of an education curtails a student's "property" rights; to be suspended or expelled compromises a student's "liberty" rights.

In *Goss* v. *Lopez* (1975) the U.S. Supreme Court ruled that students suspended less than 10 days are entitled to oral or written notice of the charges that gives them time to respond to the charges. School expulsions and suspensions of more than 10 days require schools to follow even more rigorous due process procedures. School districts must inform students in advance of specific behaviors that warrant being removed from school. And when a student faces disciplinary actions, the school must adhere to proper procedures (i.e., due process) for a fair dismissal.

Report Suspected Cases of Student Abuse and/or Neglect

Most state laws designate teachers as mandated reporters, which means they are legally required to report suspected child abuse. If a teacher has reasonable cause to suspect child abuse and fails to report it, he or she could be held liable. Beginning teachers are often afraid to make reports; they fear the report could come back "unfounded" or "unsubstantiated." You should know that teachers are not liable if that were to happen; legislators cannot mandate a person to do something and then fail to protect the person for compliance. Mandated reporters are typically immune from prosecution because it is assumed they reported in "good faith and without malice" based on the information at hand. On the other hand, if a teacher fails to report a suspected abuse case and later the child is seriously hurt, the teacher *could* be held liable. Penalties for failing to report abuse include fines and jail sentences (or both). A caveat: It is better to report than not to report if you have reasonable cause to suspect abuse.

It is important to follow through on any report made, because sometimes cases get lost in the bureaucratic system. The reality is that most state agencies operate on shoestring budgets; consequently investigators are overworked, underpaid, overstressed, and underappreciated. It is wise to keep in touch with the school counselor, because most state agencies are legally required to report back to the counselor on the status of abuse cases. In the meantime, you can offer support and kindness to a student in an abusive situation (because abused children need and deserve all the help they can get).

Refrain from Engaging in Any Form of Child Abuse

In their book, *Teachers at Risk: Crisis in the Classroom*, Villaume and Foley (1993) warn that abuse of students by teachers is equivalent to child abuse and teachers can be held liable for it. Prospective teachers need to have a clear understanding of the different forms of student abuse as their best line of defense against being charged. Teachers must be very careful that their actions do not in any way constitute child abuse. Let's begin with emotional (verbal) abuse.

Teachers can be held liable for verbal or emotional abuse. According to Philip Villaume, a legal attorney who defends teachers and other professionals charged with white collar crimes, emotional abuse is defined as "any conduct, action, or words for that matter, that would cause mental injury to a child" (Villaume & Foley, 1993, p. 17). Teacher abuse includes things such as "badgering or overworking students . . . and using corporal punishment . . ." (Villaume & Foley, 1993, p. 18).

Teachers who call students "stupid," "dumb," or "slow" are verbally abusing their students. Do you remember former teachers who would belittle or

What will be your policy on touching students if you become a teacher?

demean students in public? Were you a victim of teacher abuse? As we learned in the chapter on classroom management, it is better to discipline students by taking privileges away rather than doing something that has the potential to embarrass students among their peers (Purkey & Novak, 1996). Threatening students (idle or not) is emotional blackmail and should be avoided.

Teachers can be held liable for physical abuse. According to Villaume and Foley (1993), 75% of teacher abuse cases involve corporal punishment (p. 21). Students who are hit, spanked, or restrained excessively by teachers can file charges against teachers for causing bodily harm or emotional abuse. A teacher could be found liable even in cases in which pain was inflicted accidentally or there are no visible signs of abuse.

As mentioned earlier, there is a fine line between abuse and punishment and it is up to the teacher to know when the line is crossed. Some teachers have problems recognizing abuse because of their own unresolved abuse issues. Admittedly, being a victim of severe punishment as a child can evoke intense emotions as an adult. If not dealt with honestly, however, this unfinished business could significantly impair a teacher's ability to manage students' misbehavior. Unresolved anger from your past can adversely affect your present relationships with students and others as discussed in Chapter 2.

Teachers can be held liable for sexual abuse. Any teacher who engages in sexual intimacies with students has blatantly crossed the line and thus faces serious charges. The media has publicized many cases of teachers charged with having illicit relationships with students. Judges tend, understandably, to be very hard on teachers found guilty of sexual misconduct with their students.

Title IX

A provision of the 1972 Education Amendment Act that prohibits gender discrimination in any educational setting receiving federal monies.

sexual harassment

Any unwanted sexual advance in the context of an unequal relationship of power.

Title IX of the Education Amendment Act, passed by Congress in 1972, prohibits gender discrimination in educational settings receiving federal monies. Since the decision in *Cannon* v. *University of Chicago* (1979), students have been granted leeway in filing civil suits against schools for **sexual harassment.** In *Franklin* v. *Gwinnett County Public Schools* (1992) the U.S. Supreme Court made it possible for students to collect monetary damages from school districts who violate Title IX. Since that ruling, the number of sexual harassment suits filed against school personnel has increased (McCarthy, 1998).

In *Mary M.* v. *North Lawrence Community Sch. Corp.* (7th Cir., 1997), on appeal a judge ruled that sexual conduct between a school employee and a student is never "welcomed" (McCarthy, 1998). Simply put, sexual contact with a student (consensual or not) is illegal and the school employee is the guilty party. A school district can also be held liable when one of its employees is found guilty of sexual harassment. In such cases, the Office for Civil Rights (OCR) in the U.S. Department of Education can discipline schools by withdrawing federal monies.

The safest policy is to avoid putting yourself in any precarious position that could be misconstrued as a sexual advance. Avoid any hint of impropriety that could be misinterpreted by a vulnerable child. Even innocent teasing and flirting could be legally lethal to a teacher. A simple hug could be perceived by a needy or vengeful student as a caress, which could lead to sexual allegations being made against that teacher.

What are the differences between "good touch" and "bad touch?" To minimize risks, some teachers decide on a "no touch" policy to avoid misunderstandings. Do you think a "no touch" policy is too extreme? After all, there are "good touches," such as hugs and pats on the back. Do you think these teachers are overreacting to a few isolated cases? Does the age of the child or grade level make a difference? If so, in what way? As a teacher, describe what your policy might be regarding touching students. What variables would you consider when deciding whether to touch students or not?

Dilemmas Between Ethics and Law

The moral dilemmas presented thus far have essentially represented ethical conflicts. The situation presented in the following case exemplifies a teacher's struggle between ethics and the law. When doing what is morally right conflicts with legal requirements, what should a teacher do? Apparently, dilemmas of this nature have even higher stakes, because a teacher who breaks the law can be prosecuted. How would you handle situations in which your convictions are at odds with your legal responsibilities? Would you compromise your values to protect yourself from legal ramifications, or would you adhere to what you believe is right in spite of possible consequences? As you read the case study, think about what you would do if you were this teacher.

A CASE STUDY

Ms. Gould has been teaching home economics in middle school for many years. Ms. Gould encourages her students to turn to her for support and guidance; her students see her as a mother figure. Late one afternoon one of her students, Josie, lingers after school ostensibly to help her clean up. Ms. Gould notices that Josie appears unusually nervous and distracted, so she asks what is wrong. Josie asks, "Will you keep a secret?" Ms. Gould nods her head affirmatively. Josie then reveals that her Mom's behavior has been unpredictable and aggressive lately. The previous night her Mom slapped her several times across the face just for failing to do the dishes on time. (Ms. Gould does not notice any apparent signs of swelling or bruising on Josie's face.) Josie discloses that she is afraid of what her Mom will do next. Ms. Gould looks at the clock and realizes that by now the school counselor and the principal have left for the day. If you were Ms. Gould, what would you do?

From what Josie has revealed so far, would you consider this child abuse? If you do, would you immediately report this to the Child Protective Services or would you wait until the next day and discuss it with the counselor? What questions would you ask at this point to better understand the situation? Would you ever consider taking students home with you in order to protect them from imminent danger?

A related ethical issue that must be weighed is that Josie asked her teacher not to tell anyone what she was about to divulge. Should a teacher make such a promise to a child? If you report an incident to Child Protective Services, when a student has asked you not to tell, would your action be seen as a betrayal? Would this breach compromise your existing relationship with this student? Under what circumstances is it appropriate to break confidentiality? To avoid a sticky situation like this in the future, what should a teacher do?

AssessYourself

Do you think there could be circumstances in which a teacher (who suspects abuse) decides not to report because it is in the student's best interest? For example, suppose one of your students told you his mother's live-in boyfriend beats his mom, and when the student steps in, the man turns his wrath on him. The student begs you not to report this (at least not now). He argues that he has the situation under control, and if things get more dangerous at home, he promises to notify you immediately.

Would you report this or remain quiet?

If this student were 17 and a star athlete, would that make a difference in how you would respond?

We raise these questions to point out the nebulous nature of many abuse cases. Beginning teachers are advised to consult with colleagues who are more experienced at handling abuse cases, such as the school counselor, social worker, or school nurse. You may be surprised that even those with experience in these matters may not always know for sure what is the "right" thing to do in every situation.

Nevertheless, teachers, as front-line helpers, must be knowledgeable about legal statutes and school policies pertaining to child abuse and maltreatment. When Ms. Gould weighed her options in the above scenario, hopefully she did so with full knowledge of her responsibilities under the law. If you are unfamiliar with your state's child abuse law, we recommend contacting your Attorney General's Office to obtain a personal copy. Examine this legal document in class, and discuss its implications for teachers. In most cases, teachers are mandated reporters, which means they are legally required to report cases of child abuse.

Let's look at one more case of a dilemma between ethics and the law. This situation has to do with a teacher's convictions regarding the inflicting of physical punishment on students. This issue is quite controversial, and many are opposed to the use of such punishment. In fact, there is evidence to suggest that some punishments (such as corporal punishment) tend to have effects opposite to those desired (Lefrançois, 1997). McFadden, Marsh, Price, and Hwang (1992) have found that using violence to punish violence tends to promote aggression rather than eliminating it.

Before we present the next case study, let's examine the legality of paddling children in schools. Is it against the law to use corporal punishment in the schools? In *Ingraham* v. *Wright* (1977), the U.S. Supreme Court ruled that schools can use corporal punishment at the discretion of the state. However, those states that choose to use corporal punishment should ensure that the punishment is "reasonable and not excessive."

In at least 27 states and the District of Columbia (D.C.), corporal punishment has been banned. Japan and most European nations have abolished the practice. National professional organizations, such as the American Medical Association, National Education Association, American Psychological Association, American Counseling Association, National Association for the Advancement of Colored People, and National Parent Teachers Association have taken a stand against corporal punishment in the schools. Furthermore, corporal punishment is prohibited in prisons. It is illegal to hit a prisoner, yet it is legal to hit a child. Think about it. What is your opinion?

As we learned Chapter 2, it is very important that teachers examine their past to recall specific ways they were disciplined and punished as children. You might say: "The past is history; why go there?" We disagree and so do others in the field. For example, it has been found that teachers tend to use disciplinary measures similar to those that were used on them as children (Kaplan, 1992). Were you reared in a democratic home, a family in which children were asked for input, and their feelings and opinions were considered? Or are you the product of a punitive home, where one or both parents dominated and controlled your every move? Did you feel you were punished fairly or unfairly as a child?

Which teachers use corporal punishment? The research suggests that teachers most likely to use corporal punishment were those who were spanked as a consequence for misbehavior as children (Kaplan, 1992). Note the word "likely," because there are certainly exceptions to this; many adults who were spanked when they were children are opposed to physical punishment and have consciously decided not to use corporal punishment. Did your parents or guardians spank you for misbehavior when you were a child?

Assess Yourself

What is your opinion regarding the use of physical force as punishment for misbehavior?

What stance do various religions take regarding the use of corporal punishment?

What are your views regarding the use of corporal punishment?

What is the origin of the adage, "Spare the rod and spoil the child"? Does "rod" literally mean stick or paddle, or could it be figuratively used to mean discipline?

A CASE STUDY

After the first nine weeks, a new teacher was called to the office by her principal to witness a paddling. Because it was the teacher's preparation period, the principal knew she was available. She was adamantly opposed to corporal punishment for any reason as a form of discipline, but was caught off guard by the principal's request. While he was administering the licks to the young man, she heard him say, "Now this will teach you not to hit another classmate again!" She was thinking: "How does striking this child help him learn not to hit others?" But she kept her thoughts to herself. Later that evening she reflected back on what she had done and wondered whether or not she had been true to her convictions.

What do you think she should do? Was the teacher acting cowardly in not standing up for her beliefs? Should she have said something to the principal or to the student? What should the teacher have done differently, if anything? What did this punishment teach the child? Does it teach that when you become an adult, with power, you can hit others with less power if you are trying to teach a lesson to a child about consequences for unacceptable behavior? Or do you think this is a mixed message for the child? Did he learn anything from this punishment? Some students may actually prefer this type of punishment because it is over quickly and nothing is lost from the misdeed. Some people argue that corporal punishment is the only way to get some students to obey. What do you think?

Tips for Avoiding Lawsuits

Our aim for discussing behaviors that leave teachers legally vulnerable is not to unduly frighten you, but rather to make you "duly" cautious. A reassuring caveat (stated earlier in the chapter) might be worth repeating now: Courts typically do not hold teachers liable as long as they exercised "reasonable care." Reasonable care, or "due care," is established by comparing an accused teacher's conduct with what other professional teachers would have done under similar circumstances. To stay informed, it behooves a teacher to join and become active in professional organizations. Further, members of the National Education Association or the American Federation of Teachers can purchase professional liability insurance at a group discount.

As you can see, it is extremely important that teachers stay abreast of ethical and legal requirements to avoid being a party in a lawsuit. Although there are no ironclad guarantees to prevent you from ever being charged with a crime, there are ways to lessen your chances of litigation. The following list recaps what we have learned so far in this chapter.

❑ Know your professional codes of ethics and be able to apply them to specific situations you may encounter as a teacher.

❑ Document in writing the procedures you followed when you have reason to suspect your actions could be questioned at a later time or subject to a lawsuit.

❑ Admit when you are uncertain about what to do in a particular situation that has legal and/or ethical undertones and be willing to ask for help from colleagues and administrators.

❑ Consult your attorney at the first sign of a legal snare to avert a pending lawsuit.

❑ Stay abreast of changes in school law by attending inservice and professional meetings that address legal and ethical issues, reading educational journals, and becoming informed about local and state politics.

❑ Establish firm professional boundaries with students and be sensitive to the ramifications of your actions, especially with regard to touching students and disciplining students. Determine personal policies in advance that meet ethical and legal criteria.

❑ Recognize any issues of past abuse that may negatively affect how you will relate to and interact with your students.

Teachers' Legal Rights

At this juncture, you may feel that teachers have no rights, which is not true. Teachers actually do have rights, and you should know what they are in order to protect yourself. It may relieve you to know that teachers can bring legal action against an administration whenever they feel their constitutional rights have been violated. In an increasing number of cases, courts are ruling in teachers' favor.

As a beginning teacher it is important that you understand your own professional employment rights so that you can protect yourself against unfair dismissal practices in addition to false allegations. As mentioned, professional organizations offer free advice to teachers who are unsure whether their civil rights have been abridged.

Freedom of Expression

A teacher's right to freedom of expression (just like that of any other citizen) is protected under the First Amendment of the U.S. Constitution. However, teachers do not have unlimited free speech, primarily because of the uniqueness of their audience (i.e,. impressionable and vulnerable children). This limits what teachers can say and do in a classroom. Spring (1998) enumerates three criteria judges use in cases involving free speech: whether the material or statements made by the teacher were "appropriate for the age of the students, related to the curriculum for that course, and approved by other members of the profession" (p. 273). Newman (1990) contends that courts tend to support teachers' methods and techniques if the teachers can produce reasonable evidence that other members of the profession consider the techniques valid (p. 114).

This raises an interesting question: Do teachers have the right to publicly criticize school policies or challenge administrators' decisions? Generally, courts have upheld a teacher's right to criticize a school policy, as long as this action does not interfere with the normal operations of the school. For example, in 1968 in *Pickering* v. *Board of Education of Township High School,* the U.S. Supreme Court overturned an appellate court's decision and found that Pickering (a teacher fired for writing a letter to the local newspaper criticizing the way the school board and superintendent had handled tax increases) had not spoken "falsely" or "recklessly." Therefore the school board had no right to dismiss him for exercising his right to free speech (Alexander & Alexander, 1998).

Tenure and Employment Rights

tenure

A status granted to a teacher after a successful probationary period that legally protects from unfair or arbitrary dismissal.

The Fourteenth Amendment, which protects citizens' rights to life, liberty, and property, applies to teachers as well. Courts have ruled that school boards cannot deprive a teacher of "property" without due process. As already mentioned, due process procedures basically protect individuals from arbitrary actions. Tenured teachers, for example, have the right to due process before they can be dismissed. **Tenure** is awarded to a teacher after a specified period of time and implies a contract of secure employment. Tenure has been interpreted as a "property" right under the law (Fischer & Sorenson, 1996). Therefore before a tenured teacher can be dismissed, he or she must receive proper notification in order to respond and defend his or her actions. During a hearing, both sides are given an opportunity to present their case before a final decision is rendered. Grounds for dismissal vary by state law; however, immorality, insubordination, and incompetence could be causes for dismissal.

Private Life

You may be wondering the extent to which a teacher's private life can be held up to public scrutiny. In other words, when are teachers officially off duty? Is it anyone's business what they do in their own time? As a rule, recent court decisions tend to uphold a teacher's right to a private life unless the conduct creates a "substantial disruption" to the educational process. For example, in *Morrison* v. *State Board of Education* (1969), the California Supreme Court ruled that a teacher's sexual orientation cannot be grounds for losing certification status unless that conduct becomes a matter of public controversy and thus impairs a teacher's effectiveness.

Today's courts generally distinguish between private and professional lives, and judges tend to support a teacher's right to privacy unless the behavior is seen as "immoral" or incites an unfavorable reaction within the community (Fischer & Sorenson, 1996). Of course, spelling out what is "immoral" is difficult to do. Morality is contingent on many factors, including the national climate, geographic region, and particular locale. And let's not forget that federal judges are appointed by the President of the United States, with Senate approval; thus politics enters into the equation. Nonetheless, the greatest influence comes from the values of the citizens in a local community. School boards are particularly sensitive to the sentiments of the people they serve.

AssessYourself

If you were a judge or an administrator, how would you rule on these cases?

A teacher smokes marijuana at home; a teacher lives with a lover without being legally married; a teacher is arrested for driving under the influence (first offense); a teacher frequents a local bar (even on school nights) and stays out rather late; a teacher poses nude for a magazine.

Would the gender of the teacher make any difference in your decisions?

Actions that Are Ethical and Legal but Unprofessional

In this chapter we have discussed ethical and legal limitations placed on teachers' private and professional conduct. Prospective teachers should realize that although some behaviors meet minimum ethical and legal standards and community "moral" standards, this does not necessarily indicate that the behavior is acceptable for a person in that position. Many teachers' behaviors could be viewed as unbecoming to a professional person. Conduct that satisfies the letter of the law could still miss the spirit of the law.

To explain, some teachers adhere to double standards—they expect students to do things they do not intend to do. Have you known teachers who established one set of rules for students and another set for themselves? Consider, for example, a teacher prohibits food or drinks in the classroom, yet she drinks coffee in class, or a teacher penalizes students for tardiness, yet he is habitually late to class (and offers no excuses or apologies). A teacher who adheres to a double standard runs the risk of alienating students.

Do you think it is appropriate for a teacher to groom in class (e.g., apply lipstick, file nails, or comb hair)? What if your teacher wore the same pants every day, failed to bathe, or wore unironed clothes—is this unbefitting behavior? What kind of examples do these teachers set for students to follow? We suggest that beginning teachers seek advice from senior faculty regarding personal behaviors such as dress and grooming. Experienced teachers are usually flattered when a new teacher defers to them by asking their opinion on such matters. Examples of relevant questions are: Do you think these pants are too casual? Do you think it is necessary to wear a tie to school? Is this skirt too short?

Is It Appropriate to Date a Former Student?

To conclude this section we pose one last question: Do you think it is appropriate for a teacher to date a former student who is of legal age, that is, after he or she has graduated from high school? Because the teacher is no longer in an evaluative position, what would be the harm? The *NEA Code of Ethics* (1975) states that the educator "Shall not use professional relationships with students for private advantage." Would this principle apply here? Take a minute to formulate your response to this question before reading our opinion.

A relationship with a former student originally began as a teacher-student relationship with a power disparity. It would be difficult to equalize that power imbalance in the new relationship. A relationship with a former student hints of impropriety. How could a teacher prove that the relationship did not start while that person was a student? If this relationship becomes known, administrators, colleagues, and parents may lose confidence in the teacher's abilities. They may begin to question the teacher's judgment on other matters as well. And most important, how will current students react when they learn that the teacher is dating a former student?

Is it really worth taking a chance like this? A caveat: A teacher is entering into dangerous territory if he or she enters into a relationship with a former student. A teacher's integrity is at stake. Adopting a policy of "Once a student, always a student," is doubtless the safest bet for any teacher. People in positions of authority (especially authority over minors) have to be exceedingly wary of how their actions will be perceived by others. In the final analysis, a teacher's behavior is not only governed by what is ethically and legally acceptable, but by public opinion as well. To gain credibility for our profession, teachers must aspire to high standards of conduct and morality.

Conclusion

Throughout this chapter we underscored the necessity for teachers to conduct themselves in a professional, ethical, and legal manner. Dilemmas were posed in this chapter to illustrate the fine line that can exist between doing what is right and doing what is required by law and/or school policy. Finding solutions that do not compromise one's integrity or the welfare of the student is not always easy. Teachers must question their values, beliefs, and actions to make sure they are behaving appropriately in every situation.

We also learned in this chapter that any professional educator could be sued; those teachers who minimize or deny the seriousness of this threat are most susceptible. If a teacher's actions cause psychological and/or physical harm to student(s) under the teacher's care, that person could be sued. If you decide to pursue teaching, you should learn everything you can about ethical and legal issues affecting teachers as a way to protect yourself, your students, the profession, and our democratic way of life.

AssessYourself

In this chapter you learned that teachers have rights, but rights carry immense responsibilities. Would you be willing to continually question your values, morals, and actions to discern if you are behaving in a manner consistent with public expectations?

Do you see the threat of litigation as necessary for ensuring that students' civil rights are protected? Or do you view it as a "burden" or an exaggerated response?

Can you live under a microscope and know that your judgments might someday be challenged in a court of law?

After thinking about this, do you still want to be a teacher?

REFLECTION QUESTIONS

What would you do if you discovered one of your colleagues was behaving unethically? For example, suppose you overheard a teacher giving her students hints when they were taking a standardized achievement test. What steps would you take? Or would you just ignore what you had heard? Would this be a legal issue as well as an ethical one?

Write your own professional code of ethics. Begin with: "As a teacher, I will strive to . . ." or "I believe . . ." or "I am committed to . . ."

Reflections from the Field

When Patty was asked to recall an ethical dilemma from her years of teaching, she remembered this incident: "During my second year of teaching (right before Christmas break), my Latin II students gave me a beautiful jewelry box with an engraved plaque on the lid. The students had collectively pooled their resources to purchase what seemed to me to be a very expensive gift. I remember being taken aback by their generous gift and feeling that it was not appropriate. The engraving was in Latin (some of which was incorrect form), and my first name was on it. I was uncomfortable with this, because I did not allow my students to call me 'Patty' to my face. This informality also caused me to feel the gift was 'too personal.' I did accept the gift and never mentioned that the Latin was wrong and my displeasure at the use of my first name. To this day, I fondly remember those Latin students. In retrospect, I do not think I granted them any special favors, and they continued to have difficulty with Latin translation! My only consolation was that it was a 'group' gift and not an individual one."

Lynda recalled several situations of an ambiguous nature that would qualify. Of those, this one stood out the most: "The week before high school graduation I caught a student cheating on the final exam. After class I confronted him, and he admitted he had done so under pressure (he needed to pass my course to graduate). My policy states that students found cheating on an exam earn a zero for that test. A zero in his case would prevent him from graduating with his peers. If he had cheated during the semester, he would have had a chance to raise his semester average through extra study that accrues bonus points (e.g., written assignments, oral reports, and papers). Because it was not possible to make amends (i.e., raise his grade), I was uncertain about what to do; the stakes seemed so high. Academic dishonesty creates such turmoil for me. In an ideal situation, students would never cheat, but we do not live in an ideal world. On occasion a student will cheat, and prospective teachers need to start thinking about how they would handle this kind of behavior. I'm not going to say what I did in this case, because I'd rather let you decide what you would do in a similar situation."

KEY TERMS

ability grouping (tracking)

Buckley Amendment

code of ethics

dual or multiple relationship

due process

educational malpractice

fair use

freedom of expression

search and seizure

self-fulfilling prophecy

sexual harassment

tenure

Title IX

tort

SUGGESTED READING

Goodlad, J., Soder, R., & Sirotnik, K. A. (Eds.). (1990). *The moral dimensions of teaching.* San Francisco: Jossey Bass.

Hartmeister, F. (1995). *Surviving as a teacher: The legal dimension.* Chicago: Precept Press.

Strike, K. A., & Soltis, J. F. (1998). *The ethics of teaching.* New York: Teachers College Press.

Villaume, P. G., & Foley, R. M. (1993). *Teachers at risk: Crisis in the classroom.* Bloomington, MN: Legal Resource Center for Educators.

REFERENCES

Alexander, K., & Alexander, M. D. (1998). *American public school law* (4th ed.). Belmont, CA: Wadsworth Publishing.

Ashton, P., & Webb, R. (1986). *Making a difference: Teachers' sense of efficacy and student achievement.* New York: Longman.

Brown v. *Board of Education of Topeka, Kansas,* 347, U.S. 483, 74 S. Ct. 686 (1954).

Corey, G., Corey, M. S., & Callanan, P. (1998). *Issues and ethics in the helping professions.* Pacific Grove, CA: Brooks/Cole Publishing.

Fischer, L., & Sorenson, G. P., (1996). *School law for counselors, psychologists, and social workers* (3rd ed.). White Plains, NY: Longman.

Franklin v. *Gwuinnett Country Public Schools*, 112 S. Ct. 1028 (1992).

Goss v. *Lopez,* 419 U.S. 565 (1975).

Gullatt, D. E., & Tollett, J. R. (1997). Educational law: A requisite course for preservice and inservice teacher education programs. *Journal of Teacher Education, 48*(2), 129–135.

Hartmeister, F. (1995). *Surviving as a teacher: The legal dimension.* Chicago: Precept Press.

Ingraham v. *Wright*, 430 U.S. 651 (1977).

Kaplan, C. (1992). Teachers' punishment histories and their selection of disciplinary strategies. *Contemporary Educational Psychology, 17,* 258–265.

Lefrançois, G. R. (1997). *Psychology for teaching* (9th ed.). Belmont, CA: Wadsworth.

Mary M. v. *North Lawrence Community Sch. Corp.* 7th Cir. (1997).

McCarthy, M. M. (1998). The law governing sexual harassment in public schools. *Research Bulletin No. 2.* Phi Delta Kappan Center for Evaluation, Development, and Research. May, pp. 15–18.

McFadden, A. C., March, G. E., II, Price, B. J., & Hwang, Y. (1992). A study of race and gender bias in the punishment of school children. *Education and Treatment of Children, 15,* 140–146.

McIntyre, D. J., & O'Hair, M. J. (1996). *The reflective roles of the classroom teacher.* Belmont, CA: Wadsworth.

Morrision v. *State Board of Education,* 82 Cal. Rptr. 175, 461 P.2d 375 (1969).

National Council for Accreditation of Teacher Education. (1995). *Standards, procedures, and policies for the accreditation of professional education units.* Washington, D.C.: Author.

Newman, J. W. (1990). *America's teachers: An introduction to education.* New York: Longman.

Noddings, N. (1993). *Educating for intelligent belief or unbelief.* New York: Teachers College Press.

Patterson, F., & Rossow, L. (1996). Preventive law by the ounce or by the pound: Education law courses in undergraduate teacher education programs. *National Forum of Applied Educational Research Journal, 9*(2), 38–43.

Pickering v. *Board of Education of Township High School*, 391 U.S. 563 (1968).

Purkey, W. W., & Novak, J. M. (1996). *Inviting school success: A self-concept approach.* Belmont, CA: Wadsworth.

Rosenthal, R., & Jacobson, L. (1968). *Pygmalion in the classroom.* New York: Holt, Rinehart and Winston.

Spring, J. (1998). *American education* (8th ed.). New York: McGraw-Hill.

Strike, K. (1990). The legal and moral responsibility of teachers. In J. Goodlad, R. Soder, & K. A. Sirotnik (Eds.), *The moral dimensions of teaching* (pp. 188–223). San Francisco, CA: Jossey Bass.

Tinker v. *Des Moines Independent Community School District,* 393 U.S. 503 (1969).

Villaume, P. G., & Foley, R. M. (1993). *Teachers at risk: Crisis in the classroom.* Bloomington, MN: Legal Resource Center for Educators.

© Michael Newman/PhotoEdit

At the end of this chapter, you will be able to

- Identify local and state school personnel and their respective roles.

- Describe how public schools are governed.

- Enumerate various school choice alternatives.

- Explain site-based management and its implications for teachers.

- Identify sources of educational funding, and describe how traditional state fund-ing formulas can result in school inequities.

- Describe ways to lessen the impact of school inequities.

CHAPTER 14

Organization, Governance, and Financing of Schools

A bird's eye view of what to expect in this chapter

In this chapter, you will be introduced to the vast infrastructure supporting schools. As you read this chapter, you will see how your educational experiences from the elementary, junior high (middle school), and high school years evolved from careful planning by countless people (many of whom you never knew existed). If you were to return to your former schools, you would be amazed at the number of people, along with teachers and administrators, who played interrelated roles in the educational process. This chapter begins by introducing the valuable individuals and groups who make education a reality for you and others.

You will also see how many schools today are undergoing organizational and governance changes. In some communities, parents are being given more choice about where their children attend school; in addition, parents are being given a greater voice in how these schools are run. Likewise, teachers are being given more authority in school management issues than ever before. We will conclude by examining funding sources that produce inequities among schools and look at ways to address these funding problems.

For better or worse, American education is in a state of transition, and what the future holds is yet to be determined. Hopefully, structural changes will be for the best, and these new reforms will remedy many of the flaws found in the existing system. As you read, try to picture yourself in the midst of these reform efforts. What role will you play in the reconstruction (or restructuring) of schools?

On a daily basis there is a multitude of people who make schooling happen for our youngsters. Running a school is a huge undertaking. You would be astonished at the meticulous planning that goes on "behind the scenes" to ensure that school operations run smoothly. Realizing the magnitude and intricacy of this enterprise may make you less critical and more forgiving of your local schools when things don't go your way.

Key School Personnel at the Local Level

Teachers

When you think back on your 12 years or more of schooling, the first image that probably comes to mind is that of *teachers*. By far, teachers make up the largest category of people who influence our educational experiences. Without classroom teachers, education and schooling would not exist; teachers, then, are essential players to the operation of schools.

Staff Members

A second group of key individuals is *staff members*. This group includes librarians, media specialists, guidance counselors, school psychologists, speech pathologists, and special-education teachers, to name a few. Also, instructional aides, called *para-professionals,* assist teachers and students in the classroom. The number of additional staff members employed by a school district generally depends on enrollment size and available resources.

Support Staff

A third group, likewise indispensable to day-to-day operations, is *support staff*. Often we fail to realize just how critical these staff members are to the daily routine of schools. Without their presence, there would surely be mass confusion. For example, remember the bus driver who brought you to school? What about the school nurse who bandaged your knee when you fell on the playground? Or the cook who made those wonderful rolls? Or the kind secretary who let you call home when you had a problem?

Building Principals

And how many of us could forget our *building principals*? You may still remember the names of your principals. (For some of us, our behavior meant getting to know these people too well!) A building principal is often considered the instructional leader of the school, as well as the manager of human resources (i.e., students, teachers, and support staff). In small schools, for example, two or more schools might share a principal or perhaps a senior faculty member might serve as both teacher and principal.

As chief administrators of their schools, principals are responsible for interviewing and recommending prospective faculty members, preparing budgets, scheduling classes, supervising and evaluating teachers and staff, supervising maintenance, administering school policy, and responding to student and parental needs. Principals also must ensure that local, state, and federal guidelines are met. Accountability has made a principal's job very demanding. Some administrators estimate they spend about half a day on paperwork, chiefly providing documentation that governmental regulations are being followed (Guthrie & Reed, 1991).

Some schools, depending on the organizational structure and size, have *assistant principals*. Assistant principals typically oversee student discipline and parental complaints, which puts them in direct contact with the student body on a daily basis. In the chain of command, assistant principals are accountable to their immediate superior, the building principal, and the building principal is accountable to the local school board and superintendent.

Superintendent of Schools

superintendent of schools

The chief executive officer (CEO) of the local school district, who is responsible to the local school board.

The administrative staff that works in the central office is another essential but maybe less familiar group of people. The **superintendent of schools** and the various directors of programs in the district are housed in the central office. The number of administrators in the central office varies with the size of the school district and the organizational structure. Usually, very large districts will have several assistant superintendents and perhaps a few administrative assistants. Some districts call these assistant superintendents *directors*. A district may have a director of elementary education, a director of secondary education, a director of special services, a director of adult education, a director of technology, and a director of curriculum, depending on the size of the school district. In smaller districts, there may be only one assistant superintendent of schools (Campbell, Cunningham, Nystrand & Usdan, 1980). All of the administrative staff members in the central office report directly to the superintendent.

The average profile of a superintendent is a white, middle-class male over 40 years of age who serves a term of five years. Only 6% to 7% of the superintendents in the United States are women (Konnert & Augenstein, 1998; Peterson, 1996). Many of us did not meet the school superintendent until commencement. Or if you did, the person you met originally was probably not the same person who awarded you your diploma at graduation. There is a great deal of turnover in the position, largely because superintendents are not eligible for tenure and the demands are inordinate.

There is usually a striking discrepancy between the superintendent's salary and the salaries of teachers because of the professional and personal demands of the superintendent's position (Guthrie & Reed, 1991). To illustrate, a superintendent supervises administrative staff; oversees the operation of the district; assists the board's president in preparing an agenda for meetings; attends school board meetings (as well as executive sessions, when his or her performance is evaluated); prepares school budgets; makes staffing recommendations; stays abreast of federal, state, and local policies and laws; attends state legislative meetings; oversees building construction and maintenance; sets goals for the district; serves as a liaison between the district and the community; and communicates with the media.

In addition, a superintendent must maintain a positive and active role in the community. This individual must be seen participating regularly in school and civic events. For all practical purposes, a superintendent is on call 24 hours a day, 7 days a week (Konnert & Augenstein, 1998). Therefore maintaining a conciliatory relationship with the community is critical to the position. Because of high visibility, a superintendent must be very careful about any display of emotion that could offend the community.

Local School Boards

In the chain of command, the superintendent as chief executive officer (CEO) of the local school district is responsible to the board of directors—the local school board. If he or she loses favor with the community or the board, a contract is not renewed. Thus a superintendent's job can be a highly political position.

Reflections from the Field

An urban elementary school teacher recalled a time when a superintendent exchanged sharp words with a popular local newscaster over an incident in the district. Although the superintendent felt justified in his curt reply, the public was not so forgiving. This sharp retort, along with several other grievances, convinced the school board the next year not to renew the superintendent's contract.

school board

The policy making body of a local school district.

The local board of education, commonly called the **school board,** is the policymaking body of the district. Although a school administrator may interview you for a teaching position, technically it is the school board that hires you. Even though you may never formally meet these members, they actually influence your job more than any other group because they determine teachers' salaries, class size, duties, and other responsibilities. The majority of school boards are composed of elected men and women who are citizens of the district in which they reside.

When a person becomes a member of a school board, he or she is deemed an official of the state. (There are a few boards to which citizens are appointed, but typically school board members are elected.) Constituents in smaller communities tend to elect school board members who are actively involved in civic organizations such as PTO, Little League, Scouts, Lions Club, Junior League, and other non-profit community organizations. Thus people who give freely of their time and expertise to community projects are likely candidates for school board positions. By contrast, in larger communities and urban cities, members who are public figures are more likely to be selected. You may know someone who is serving or has served on a school board. Former President Jimmy Carter and former U.S. Supreme Court Justice Lewis Powell were once school board members. Or perhaps you are or have been a school board member. If so, that experience will be invaluable if you do become a teacher.

School boards vary in size from 5 to 17 members; the average is 5 to 7 members on a board. These individuals are generally white males between the ages of 41 and 50; married, with one or more children in school; college graduates with professional occupations and substantial incomes; and entrenched in their community (Freeman, Underwood, & Fortune, 1991; Peterson, 1996). As is true of most state boards, there is little, if any, monetary compensation for members who serve in this capacity. The average term for a school board member is one to three years (Freeman, Underwood, & Fortune, 1991).

The local school board's first responsibility is to formulate policy for the district's schools. The board's duties include hiring the superintendent, administrators, teachers, and support staff; developing curriculum; approving textbooks; establishing attendance policies; drawing school boundaries; overseeing the administration of school facilities; supervising building construction; enforcing laws passed by the state legislatures; and implementing policies mandated by the state board of education. Last but not least, local school boards secure revenue for the operation of the district's schools. Raising funds often requires that the local school board levy taxes and issue bonds.

Interestingly, school board elections are nonpartisan—those running for office and those voting are not required to state political party affiliation. This is the only public election in which candidates are independent of political ties. Although school board members do not have to adhere to a party line, they do (as elected representatives of the local school district) have to please their constituents. Local citizens feel entitled to lodge complaints or offer advice on school-related issues whenever they choose, which means that school board members may be approached by dissatisfied parents or taxpayers or community members who wish to discuss school issues.

School board members are also under scrutiny by the local media, especially in small districts. As a result, boards take the brunt of criticism when problems arise. In one rural community, the local newspaper published a column called "Speak Out" to provide a forum for individuals to anonymously express opinions. When the school board convened, many residents took advantage of the opportunity to address issues, especially when controversial topics were being considered by the board. Due to anonymity, school board members could receive a stinging reprimand if a decision struck a negative chord with constituents.

School board members may find themselves at odds with the very people who elected them to office, which adds additional pressure to an already stressful job. The movie *Mr. Holland's Opus* demonstrates the far-reaching effects of one school board's decision to cut the music and drama programs from the high school and the public outcry regarding such actions. School finance depends mainly on bonds and tax increases, and dissatisfied communities often show their disapproval by voting against tax increases for local schools. The bottom line is that school board members have enormous power to implement change, but this power does not come without responsibility to the community and the possibility of criticism (Shannon, 1994).

One final comment on boards: A local school board reflects the values of its members and the ideology of its community. If the community is conservative and has strong religious and family values, board decisions typically mirror those sentiments. For example, in one community the school board prohibited the scheduling of extracurricular activities on Sunday—a day reserved for church attendance and family events. In a nearby community, school board members took a completely different stand and allowed extracurricular activities on Sundays. Ironically, two boards—a few miles apart—took opposite views on an identical issue.

For all the reasons cited above, it behooves the public to elect competent and dedicated people to board positions. The successful operation of any school depends on the members who serve on that board. A school board must simultaneously be responsive to the needs of its constituents while maintaining the overarching goal of providing quality education for students in that district.

AssessYourself

Does reading this information inspire you to want to run in the next school board election? Or does it dissuade you from taking on such a demanding role?

We desperately need insightful, committed people who will assume leadership roles on school boards. Think about it.

Maybe you could see yourself as an administrator or even a superintendent. Do you have the temperament to withstand public criticism and scrutiny?

Superintendents and school boards can become adversaries rather than partners when roles are confused (Konnert & Augenstein, 1998). To explain, if board members become overly involved in administrative duties, or a superintendent becomes heavily involved in policymaking, there could be a role clash. A superintendent could resent the fact, for example, that he or she has to defer to board members who lack appropriate credentials to run a school district. Admittedly, it is a rather peculiar situation—schools being run by people who are not trained or experienced in that field. On the other hand, board members may become indignant when a superintendent (hired by the board) questions their authority or fails to carry out their dictates.

A superintendent's job then depends on the consensus and goodwill of the school board's membership. With each election, a superintendent could be at odds with the majority opinion. If incumbents choose not to remain in office or are defeated, and new members do not share mutual goals, a superintendent may not be retained (McCloud & McKenzie, 1994). For example, in one community the school board hired a superintendent who favored a middle school, which the board also wanted. However, over the course of the next two elections the composition of the board altered dramatically, and the newly elected board members opposed, instead of supported, the middle school concept. Battle lines were drawn, and before long the superintendent was replaced.

Superintendents are extremely vulnerable to public opinion. Special interest groups, teachers, parents, community leaders, and the media are all free to express disapproval of the actions of the superintendent. However, when things go smoothly in a school district, a superintendent can enjoy many productive (and secure) years of employment. The selection of the superintendent is a critical decision for any school district. This person must be able to work cooperatively with a board who may not share the same credentials or vision.

A CASE STUDY

After the results of a local study on the sexual activity of teens was made known, a high school's student council submitted a proposal to the school board asking that condoms be made available in the restrooms of all junior and senior highs. When the local community heard this story, it became an overnight topic of controversy. Because a school board meeting is scheduled for the following evening, representatives from the student council, the teachers' association, the Parent-Teacher Organization (PTO), the administration, and other "concerned" taxpayers have requested time slots to voice their opinions. The local news media will definitely send a reporter to the meeting, because they anticipate that a "hot" story like this will attract viewers and readers.

What is your opinion on the so-called hot topic described in the case study? Do you take the position that students who engage in premarital sex should have easy access to condoms as a way to protect them from disease and unwanted pregnancies? Or do you think making condoms available encourages and condones premarital sex? If you were a parent, would this change your perspective? If you were on the student council, what arguments might you make to justify the proposal's request? As a teacher, what stance would you take? Or would you prefer to remain neutral on such a heated topic? As an administrator, what would be your position? And lastly, if you were a school board member, how would you vote? Let's complicate this inquiry by adding that you are up for reelection next fall, and a school bond proposal is scheduled for a vote next month. Does this change your opinion in any way? Would this issue be controversial in your community?

School Governance at the State Level

Individual states have been historically responsible for the education of their residents. It is amazing to think that the U.S. Constitution (1789) does not explicitly make provision for education. When the U.S. Constitution was amended in 1791 by the Bill of Rights, it was the Tenth Amendment that indirectly gave states the power to govern schools. "The powers not delegated to the United States by the Constitution, nor prohibited by it to the States, are reserved to the States respectively, or to the people." Consequently, the Tenth Amendment gives your state the authority to run its schools. Furthermore, because of the Constitution we do not have a national system of education.

Nationally, there are approximately 16,000 independent school districts overseeing the operation of 88,000 schools, of which approximately 66,000 are elementary schools and 22,000 are high schools (Tanner, 1993). As you might surmise from these demographics, individual states vary tremendously from one another in size, which ultimately creates a governing pattern that is unique to each state (Leinwand, 1992). In essence, there is no uniform organizational pattern appropriate for every school district in the nation (Guthrie & Reed, 1991).

Role of the Legislature

As a governing body, state legislatures have become increasingly involved with policies affecting school districts within the state. In the past, local districts had greater control over their schools. Because local school districts bore the major expense of education, they were entitled to a greater voice in how schools should be operated. As legislators became cognizant of inequities in schools, state legislatures have begun to take a more active role in educational funding and other school-related issues, which expands their scope and influence. Some related issues of interest to state legislators include the length of the school year and school day, mandated testing, and standards for teachers (Guthrie & Reed, 1991).

Role of the Governor

Governors today are becoming more active in issues affecting education. In many states, for example, candidates for governor might campaign for specific educational reforms. Moreover, it is not unusual to find staff positions created for the explicit purpose of keeping governors informed on critical educational issues (Tanner, 1993). Goals 2000, which was established under George Bush's administration and later extended under Bill Clinton's administration, was actually initiated by the **National Governors' Association.** This set a precedent for greater participation of governors in matters relevant to education.

National Governors' Association

Association of state governors involved in school reform and other school-related issues.

Role of the State Courts

Certainly one of the greatest influences on schools is found in that state's judicial system. Although governors influence and legislators enact educational laws, it is the state's courts that interpret the constitutionality of statutes governing schools. Teachers' rights, students' rights, school finance, and religious rights are various areas in which courts can and do exercise enormous power. In effect, court decisions influence and shape many educational policies.

Role of the State Board of Education

state board of education

The board that establishes policies affecting the supervision and structure of schools in a state.

The main function of the **state board of education** is to establish state school policies regarding the general supervision and structure of elementary, secondary, and vocational schools within the state. A state board can consist of 3 to 23 members; the average time served may be from seven to nine years (Guthrie & Reed, 1991). The majority of states authorize the governor to appoint members to the state board of education. Only 10 states elect their state board members. Because of the honor of being chosen by the governor and the influence granted to a state board, members usually consent to serve in spite of the lack of monetary compensation.

Policies implemented by state boards range from new testing requirements for high school students to setting curriculum standards for third graders. The state board of education also sets standards that regulate accreditation of schools within the state. As a prospective teacher, you will be affected by the state board's recommendation concerning the courses you must take to be qualified to teach.

Role of the Chief State School Officer

The **chief state school officer,** sometimes called the *director of the state department of education* or the *state superintendent* or the *state commissioner of education,* is the chief executive officer (CEO) for the state. It is the responsibility of the chief state school officer to implement the policies of the state board of education and to provide guidance and supervision to school districts (Guthrie & Reed, 1991).

The chief state school officer is often appointed by the state board of education with the approval of the governor. Although this person sits in on board meetings, he or she has no voting rights (like a superintendent who sits in on local school board meetings). As head of the state department of education, this individual serves as the liaison to the state board of education by relaying the state board's policies and mandates to the local school districts and to the department of education (Peterson & Kelley, 1998).

Role of the State Department of Education

The **state department of education** is not just one agency, but rather is a collection of agencies with diverse components ranging from departments of early childhood education to drug education. Every state except Hawaii has a department of education (Condoli, 1995). In the organizational chain, the state department of education operates under the state board of education and the state legislature. It is their responsibility to ensure that the state board's policies are met, as well as the educational laws mandated by the state. The state organizational structure operates much like a local school board, with a superintendent, administrative staff, and secretarial staff (Condoli, 1995; Guthrie & Reed, 1991).

The administrative duties of a state department of education include deciding how funds will be appropriated and distributed, certifying teacher applicants, accrediting schools in the various districts, setting and supervising instructional standards, administering federally funded programs, overseeing safety standards for school buildings and transportation, monitoring statewide testing programs, evaluating local school programs, and regulating nonpublic schools. When you apply to teach, you will contact the state department of education for guidelines regarding certification and/or licensure.

School Choice for Parents

It's hard to pinpoint the place or time that **school choice** became a rallying point for parents. One national report published in the early 1980s, *A Nation at Risk: The Imperative for Reform* (National Commission on Excellence in Education, 1983), generated considerable public concern about the status of American education. This report claimed that American students were performing below other countries on measures in math, science, reading, and other academic areas. Although the report was originally intended to bring people together in an effort to improve community schools, it seemingly had the opposite effect. Many interpreted the findings as proof to indict teachers and schools.

Admittedly, some of the wording of the report was rather strong and could have been misconstrued as stating the American educational system was on the brink of disaster. However, reading of the entire document (about 36 pages) shows that the message is more uplifting. The media and news commentaries selected excerpts from the report that painted education in the worst possible light. Consider, for example, the following section, which taken out of context does make it sound like education was in a state of emergency:

> ". . . the educational foundation of our society is presently being eroded by a rising tide of mediocrity that threatens our very future as a nation and a people. What was unimaginable a generation ago has begun to occur— others are matching and surpassing our educational attainments. If an un-friendly foreign power had attempted to impose on America the mediocre educational performance that exists today, we might well have viewed it as an act of war. As it stands we have allowed this to happen to ourselves" (National Commission on Excellence in Education, 1983, p. 5.)

When this report and others became known, parents began to vocally complain that the public schools today are not the same ones they knew as children. The public began to point to the lack of discipline, outbreaks of violence, and prevalence of drugs as evidence that public schools are preoccupied by problems clearly unrelated to academics. But what could parents do? At this time, parents had little discretion as to what schools their children attended or how those schools were run. The exception to this was "cross-district programs" that allowed parents to change schools—provided that the chosen school was racially balanced and had space (which was rarely the case). And of course, if a child was assigned to a school that fell short of parental expectations, families could either move to another district or enroll their child in a private school. Both options are hardly practical, because private schools are costly and moving one's residence is not only inconvenient but also expensive.

alternative school

A public or private school offering a more individualized or specialized approach to instruction than is available in a regular public school.

Alternative schools offer a range of options for parents who decide, for whatever the reason, their children would benefit from another type of school other than what the regular district school has to offer. Alternative schools can either be public or private. As we already know, no single program or formula works best for all students. Therefore it behooves us to creatively search for effective modes of delivery.

Public Alternative Schools

Alternative schools within the public school system have existed for the past 20 years or more. These schools were conceived to provide a choice for children who have special needs that mainstream public education was apparently not able to provide. Many alternative schools were originally started to help students having trouble in mainstream schools. Students who were disruptive or could not fit in traditional schools could be placed in an alternative school, where the routine was highly structured and the instruction was individualized. Many programs provide individual and group counseling to the students. This specialized attention has enabled many children to experience success. The goal, of course, is to bring the child back to the public school when he or she is capable and ready.

Alternative public schools today are attempting to be more responsive to the unique needs of individual students (Adelman & Pringle, 1995). One example, the **magnet school,** has become a selective alternative school within the public schools that offers a special curriculum to attract gifted and talented students from the community. Typically, students apply for a limited number of slots and may have to take a specialized test for admission. Initially these schools were created to encourage a voluntary desegregation that would ensure a racially and ethnically diverse student body. By offering specialization in the sciences, mathematics, or performing arts, these schools attempted to attract suburban students to the inner city; hence the name "magnet" was given to these urban schools (Unger, 1993).

Another type of alternative school, discussed in Chapter 7, is *charter schools*. These schools tend to promote positive, cooperative relationships between community and schools. Basically, charter schools delegate authority for the school into the hands of teachers and parents. Teachers, along with administrators, parents, and community representatives contract with the local school board or some other recognized regulating body, which in turn grants them the right to design and structure their school independent of the many rules and regulations that constrict traditional public schools. The rationale is that those people who join forces to contract are the ones who know their students' needs better than officials in the central office (Wallis, 1994).

Because local boards might reject a request for a charter school, the state government (in some states) has assumed this responsibility. Therefore, which governing body has the authority to grant a charter, and the number of charter schools that can exist, largely depends on the individual state. At any rate, the contract becomes the legal bond between that governing body and the organizers of the charter school. The contract lists goals, objectives, and responsibilities for both parties. Funding is also specified in the contract. However, the actual dispersal of funds is left up to the discretion of the specific school.

The charter also allows the school to set up its own governing body. Unlike a traditional school, in which the principal is in charge and the teachers and staff adhere to the principal's directives, the governing decisions emanate from teachers and parents. In the organizational structure of a charter school, the principal may assume the role of the director, but the decisions come from the bottom up. This bottom-up reform enables new leadership to emerge in schools. Although there is a high degree of autonomy, charter schools are held at an even higher level of accountability in student performance than traditional public schools (Wohlstetter & Anderson, 1994).

magnet school

An alternative school offering curriculum to attract gifted and talented students from segregated neighborhoods to urban schools.

Los Angeles Science Magnet School.

From their inception, charter schools overall have received bipartisan support. Many local, state, and federal leaders jumped on the bandwagon to endorse school choice. In his 1999 State of the Union Address, President Clinton asked states to increase the present number of charter schools. States began to examine this idea in hopes of restructuring and improving public schools. In 1991, Minnesota became the first state to take this bold initiative. Three years later, about 140 schools nationwide were granted charters (Wallis, 1994). The number continues to grow.

The charter school concept is clearly a deviation from the norm. Most of us attended schools where students, parents, and teachers were rarely consulted on school-related matters. We just accepted the dictates of administrators and local school boards. Even experienced and highly respected teachers were rarely consulted on administrative decisions. As you might surmise, top-down decisions can stifle creative and progressive ideas on the part of teachers.

In all fairness, we should point out that charter schools do not escape criticism. Some of the arguments against charter schools are as follows. Some opponents believe that the money allotted to charter schools is a misuse of funds. When money is reserved for students who attend charter schools, they claim that the local school district loses revenue. Thus, if the majority of students choose to attend charter schools, a sizable aggregate of money would be subtracted from the district's budget. Second, teacher unions tend to oppose charter schools because teachers in these schools are prohibited from collective bargaining. Third, some argue that charter schools recruit the more talented individuals away from traditional school settings. Last, some are concerned that the financing of charter schools can be susceptible to

Phillips Exeter Academy, Exeter, New Hampshire.

© Superstock

profiteering. In Michigan, a couple who owned a private school turned it into a public charter school and charged the district three times more per square foot for rental space on buildings than a public school would have cost (Toch, 1998). However, even in the midst of some of these concerns, the charter school concept continues to flourish, especially among those who believe in the free enterprise system for schools. In recent years, several millionaires and successful entrepreneurs have pledged huge sums of money to help finance these schools.

Private Alternative Schools

private school

A school run by an agency, private enterprise, or religious denomination and financed mainly by private funds.

Historically, parents who could afford it have always had the option of sending their children to **private schools.** There are, of course, advantages and disadvantages to private schooling. One obvious advantage is that because of the small enrollments, private schools can offer a close-knit family atmosphere. Most private schools are relatively small; a comprehensive K-12 private school may have an enrollment of under 1,000 students. Because of their size, private schools can provide more opportunities for teacher and student involvement. It is easier for students to establish personal relationships with teachers (which is truly an asset).

Supportive school environments have been found to correlate with better student discipline (Conway, 1992). Private schools, unlike public schools, are free to accept and retain only those students who comply with their mission. Thus disruptive students can be expelled more easily when their behavior creates a problem for school officials. In recent years the minority populations in private schools have steadily grown because many minority parents desire for their children the safer and more academically challenging environment that private schools can provide (Conway, 1992).

Some parents choose private religious schools for the education of their children. Generally there are two types of religious schools: (1) parochial schools, which are generally owned and operated by a church or religious sect, and (2) independent private religious schools that have no legal ties to a church. An elected board of trustees operates the latter. As court rulings over the past decades confirm a secular curriculum, many parents opt for religious schooling for their children.

Some conservative groups have argued that ignoring religion in schools has contributed to many of the social problems plaguing public schools today. These parents want to know that their children are receiving religious and moral instruction compatible with their values. They see private religious schools as safe and orderly environments where their children can receive moral education in addition to scholastic instruction (Unger, 1993).

Reflections from the Field

A teacher who now teaches in a private parochial school in St. Louis said he left public education because of administrators' lack of understanding about how things had changed in the classroom. The stress of teaching students who were disrespectful, coupled with indifferent parents, prompted this teacher to take a sizable pay cut just to get out. Although he admits the private school where he now teaches is far from perfect, he still believes he made the right move. He finds he is more effective teaching in an environment that values academic scholarship and promotes respect for authority.

REFLECTION QUESTIONS

- Apparently there are benefits that come from teaching in private and parochial schools as opposed to public schools. But there are limitations as well.

....

- From your vantage point, what are the benefits of teaching in a private school? What are the disadvantages?

....

- Would you take a cut in pay to teach at a private school? Where would you draw the line with regard to a salary reduction?

....

voucher

Coupons that can be used as cash for tuition to private schools.

Clearly one of the biggest disadvantages for parents who choose private schooling is the cost factor. Parents pay tuition while simultaneously paying taxes for public school education. And parents without the financial means to send their children to private schools have had no other recourse but to send their children to district public schools (Unger, 1993). However, in recent years school **vouchers** permit some low-income families to send their children to private schools.

For those of you unfamiliar with school vouchers, here is an example. Suppose you have a child who attends a school you consider unsafe. Aside from that, there are scant resources available for computer equipment and training. Because you cannot afford a computer in your home, you are afraid your child lacks computer skills. Realizing you qualify for a voucher, you begin shopping around for a school that better serves your child's needs. After making a selection, you apply for and receive a voucher, which you give to the new school. The school turns the voucher over to the local or state government for reimbursement. The voucher has helped to level the financial playing field. Your concerns about your child's education have been addressed.

Some states have their own programs that specify which parents qualify for vouchers and the types of schools they can choose (Guthrie & Reed, 1991). In the spring of 1999, Florida approved a state voucher program that allows those parents whose children attend "deficient" public schools a choice in schools. Some say that although vouchers appear to level the playing ground, in many ways socioeconomic class is still a limiting factor. For example, there are hidden costs that continue to create disparities for low-income families, such as transportation, clothing, extracurricular fees, and educational supplies. Proponents of vouchers insist that low-income families are willing to make whatever financial sacrifices are required to ensure quality education for their children.

Additionally, advocates of vouchers contend that their existence will make schools more accountable as they compete with others for parental endorsement (Martinez, Thomas, & Kemerer, 1994). Critics counter by claiming there has not been enough time to adequately assess the extent to which competition for vouchers actually produces better schools. Opponents of vouchers also argue it is too costly.

private enterprise school

Alternative schools financed by the private sector to improve public schools.

In recent years, the private sector has started getting involved in school restructuring. The number of these schools, called **private enterprise schools,** is on the rise. One such enterprise, the *Edison Project,* created a national network of private schools that could be emulated in both traditional and charter public schools. The Project's goal is to enroll two million students by the year 2010. Unlike public schools, Edison Project schools operate for profit. An interesting aspect of these schools is that day-care facilities are available to young mothers.

The multimillion-dollar reformer, Chris Whittle, is also committed to building new and better American schools that will emphasize technology in the marketplace. Whittle was the entrepreneur who introduced Channel One in the schools in 1990s. You may be familiar with Channel One—a

10-minute news broadcast with a 2-minute commercial carried in more than 10,000 public and private classrooms throughout the United States. To accomplish this, 6,000 miles of cable,10,000 satellite dishes, and 300,000 televisions sets were installed in American schools, quadrupling the number of sets in the schools. To raise the money for this project, Mr. Whittle sold two minutes of commercials to sponsors. This created quite a stir among the major education professional organizations such as the National Education Association and the National Parent-Teacher Association. Many claimed that commercials have no legitimate place in classrooms with captive young audiences. What do you think? Why?

In spite of criticism, private enterprises such as the Edison Project are being seriously discussed as a viable way to reform schools. In San Francisco, the billionaire founders of The Gap company pledged $25 million to hire the Edison Project to reform its schools (Toch, 1998). This departure from traditional public schools is yet another example of school reform generated by private concerns (Shannon, 1994).

Home Schooling

Home schooling is an alternative to public and private education. Parents who choose to teach their children at home want control over what and how their children are taught. Many of the same concerns driving parents to choose private schools are cited by parents who home school (e.g., school violence, poor discipline, declining morality, and low test scores). These parents think that home schooling is the best means to ensure that their children are taught the parent's values and morals (Koetzsch, 1997).

There has been tremendous growth in the number of families participating in home schooling. It has been estimated that currently one million children are being schooled at home. Home schooling is now legal in every state. Parents who home school their children confer with one another through group support teams, conventions, and Internet chat sessions. Standardized testing is required in many states to ensure that students are measuring up to their public school counterparts.

Critics of home schooling argue that these children miss out on learning that takes place through peer interaction. Also, they contend that home-schooled children may receive inadequate instruction because not all parents would be able to assist in the more advanced subject areas. Who monitors the academic qualifications of the parents? Will these children be able to compete nationally?

To respond to these concerns, home school advocates contend that their children, because of individualized instruction and attention, are competitive nationally. Also, they claim that their children do not waste valuable instructional time changing classes or sitting in study halls. Lastly, they believe that the family unit is strengthened by the parent's daily involvement with the children.

One thing is certain—the monopoly of mainstream public education no longer exists. Today, viable and successful schools, both public and private, represent a wide range of alternative approaches to education (Koetzsch, 1997). The *Almanac of Education Choice* lists 6,000 alternative schools in the United States (Koetzsch, 1997, p. 235).

Teacher Empowerment: Site-Based Management

In the organizational structure of the school system, teachers are usually placed at the bottom rung of the ladder. Decisions that directly affect what goes on in their classrooms tend to be made by others further up the ladder. For good reasons, teachers have been frustrated by the lack of shared decision making. Many are tired of decisions being handed down by others.

A reform effort gaining momentum today is the increase of shared involvement by teachers and parents in the operation of schools. This is called site-based decision making; it is sometimes referred to as school-based management, school-based decision making, or school-based leadership. In spite of terminology, teachers (and parents) in some places are being given a greater role in decisions affecting school governance.

By forging this new kind of relationship, individual schools may reap benefits from administrators and teachers collaborating as team players, rather than working as adversaries. In some schools, decisions affecting curriculum, program offerings, time allocations, and instructional decisions are made from the efforts of all of these individuals who are involved in the local school and community. In other communities, decision making is limited to some restrictions imposed by the central office.

Reflections from the Field

One former elementary school teacher recalled an incident in which she and a group of other teachers petitioned administrators and school board members to rethink the large class sizes based on current research. They recommended that class size be reduced, particularly in grades K-3. Because the director of elementary instruction in the central office recalled a time from his past when he taught large numbers of children without apparent repercussions, the teacher's proposal was stymied. She recalled that this type of thing happens more than it should—good ideas from teachers being rejected because of one person's agenda.

School Finance

Financing schools is much like operating a household budget: individuals do not always agree on how the money should be spent. And just as with a family budget, overspending has consequences. However, when a school district overspends, it is a legal offense. As you might suspect, there can be heated debates during the drafting of a district's budget.

Tax Structure

Because federal spending on education constitutes only about 5% to 6% of the total expenditures, local and state revenue are extremely important for school finance. Basically, taxes are generated through (1) *personal income tax* placed on individual earnings; (2) *state sales tax* placed on items of purchase; (3) *personal property tax* on homes, personal items, and businesses; and (4) *privilege tax* placed on licenses such as a driver's licenses, hunting licenses, and so on. In some states, revenue is generated from legalized gambling and/or a state lottery.

personal property tax

Tax on assessed value of a home or property.

Because almost half of school revenues come from local sources, we will focus on **personal property tax.** Historically, an individual's wealth was measured by land and taxes were levied accordingly. This situation remains true today regarding public schooling—the mainstay of financial support for schools comes from revenue generated from personal property taxes. The computation of local school taxes can be quite confusing. In the next section, we present two examples of how local school taxes are computed.

Let's say you owned a home with a fair market value of $100,000.00 (market value is the price you would ask for your home if you put it up for sale). Your home is assessed yearly by the county assessor or another designated official to determine its value. (Note that the assessed value is always lower than the market value). In this particular community, let's suppose the official assigns an assessed valuation of 20% of the fair market price, which gives your home an assessed value of $20,000.00. Assume that the school board has been authorized by the voters to take $3.48 from every $100.00 of assessed valuation. If this were the case, your school taxes for the year would be $796.00. The formula below shows how this figure was computed.

$$\frac{\$20,000.00}{100} = 200 \times \$3.48 = \$796.00$$

Some states operate on millage taxes; a mil generates $1.00 per every $1,000 of revenue. Using the same hypothetical case, with the assessed value at $20,000.00 and a millage rate of 30, for example, your school taxes for the year would be $600.00 based on the following formula.

$$\frac{\$20,000.00 \times 30}{1,000} = \$600.00$$

The school board determines how much revenue is needed to operate the schools; they cannot arbitrarily set millage amounts. Some states require a yearly vote by the public to determine the millage rate. Under these conditions, voters may elect to increase the millage rate or keep it the same. Fortunately, voters cannot lower the present millage rate for their schools unless a school board decides to give voters that option (Peterson & Kelley, 1998).

Opposition to Taxes

A high percentage of tax money for education comes from property owners; therefore a vote to increase school taxes often faces opposition. For retired homeowners who no longer have children in school, or those persons on fixed incomes, paying school taxes can be seen as an unwanted and unfair burden. (One board member contended that he could almost without exception predict the outcome of a millage rate increase, based on the percentage of senior citizens who voted in that election.) Furthermore, some property owners complain it is unjust that they must pay for schools, yet families who rent apartments or homes are exempt.

Additionally, some parents whose children go to private schools feel they are unfairly saddled by school taxes; after all, they are already burdened by costly tuition fees. Aside from these arguments, others have pointed out that schools are not producing sufficient outcomes, and thus they are undeserving of revenue increases. In those school districts where there is the most dissatisfaction with local schools, attempts to increase taxes are usually unsuccessful.

Issues that affect people's pocketbooks tend to create the greatest dissension. What do you think about property taxes being the main source of revenue for schools? Does this type of tax unfairly penalize those who own property? Or does this system seem fair? What alternatives would you propose?

Inequities in School Finance

The most obvious limitation of school districts' heavy reliance on local property taxes is, of course, the disparity found in local schools. In communities where property valuations are higher, the tax bases will inevitably be larger, which means that the district's schools will mirror that affluence. Thus one school district has an ample operating budget while another district barely can make ends meet. As mentioned already, this dilemma of unequal funding remains a bone of contention and a vexing source of concern for poorer school districts across the nation (Kowalski, 1994). Simply put, some of our nation's schools excel, some are mediocre, and others are in crisis financially.

To better understand this problem, we suggest reading: *Savage Inequalities: Children in America's Schools* by Jonathan Kozol (1991). After touring schools from East St. Louis, Illinois, to San Antonio, Texas, Kozol reported his find-

GREAT TEACHERS

Jonathan Kozol

© Bettman/CORBIS

Born in 1936, in Boston, Jonathan Kozol graduated with a B.A. from Harvard University in 1958. From 1958 to 1959, he pursued graduate studies at Magdalen College, Oxford, as a Rhodes Scholar. Kozol soon began working in the schools as an elementary teacher in Boston and Newton, Massachusetts. Then his career focus shifted to alternative schools, where he directed the Storefront Learning Center in Boston. At the Center for Intercultural Documentation Institute in Cuernavaca, Mexico, Kozol was an instructor in alternative education. He also was a teacher in remedial writing and reading programs in South Boston High School and became a director of the National Literacy Coalition in Boston. He has won numerous awards and honors for his works and writings on poverty, race, and education.

Kozol has contributed much to the field of education through his accounts of his experiences in public schools. For example, he documented the plight of black children in Boston's ghetto schools in *Death at an Early Age: The Destruction of the Hearts and Minds of Negro Children in the Boston Public Schools* (1967). Kozol describes the school he started in Roxbury, a black district of Boston, in his book *Free Schools* (1972). After extensive research, Kozol published an exploratory work on literacy called *Illiterate America* (1985), in which he outlined his plan for dealing with this enormous problem. In 1991, he shocked America again with *Savage Inequalities: Children in America's Schools.* In this book he compares the horrible conditions of inner-city schools in East St. Louis, Illinois, to affluent schools in Winnetka, Illinois, and Rye, New York. He has remained an important activist in education by speaking out against inequities in schools.

ings. In poorer schools, he observed clogged toilets; bathrooms without hot water, soap, or paper products; playgrounds without swing sets or jungle gyms; and outdated textbooks. The presence of support staff was negligible. At the opposite end of the spectrum, Kozol toured schools with carpeted hallways, music suites, and lounges for students. Study halls were fully

What do we want for our future leaders? Does the appearance of the school building and facilities affect student achievement? What about its effect on student pride and morale? What message are we sending our youth?

equipped with the latest technology, and libraries were stocked with state-of-the-art equipment. There were opportunities for students to perform or study abroad. He noted modern school buildings surrounded by trees and landscaped gardens, with spacious playing fields for sports. More support for staff and faculty was present in these schools. Kozol (1991) found ratios between counselors and students, for example, to be as low as 1 counselor to 24 students in some districts.

Kozol compared expenditures per student per year in 1987 and found that a fourth grader in East Aurora, Illinois, received $2,900.00 toward education, whereas a youngster in a nearby town (in the same grade) received $7,800.00. In New York, disparities in funding ranged from $5,500.00 to $11,000.00 per student. Although Kozol (1991) primarily described inequities found in inner-city schools, he noted the situation is no different in poor rural districts.

Reflections from the Field

A high school teacher, from a small school in a rural community with no industry or jobs other than farm labor, had this comment to make about her school: "I am very concerned about disparities in income levels, which translates to disparities among schools. In economically depressed school districts, such as the one my school is in, it is next to impossible to pass tax increases for schools. Even though I understand why taxpayers who are barely making ends meet would refuse to vote for a millage rate increase, I still find it deplorable that we allow this in an affluent nation such as ours. It is a travesty of justice for some students to have so little and others so much. It is unpardonable that students have to attend schools such as these. It is a disgrace to subject my students to conditions such as this. My students are shortchanged in every possible way (e.g., outdated materials, non-existent media and/or technology, and inadequate support staff, not to mention substandard facilities). And where is the toilet paper for the bathrooms? And forget about washing your hands with soap. Unequal opportunities for children in schools is a grave concern, and most people are unaware of what it is like in schools such as this."

Attempts to Correct for Inequities Among Schools

Inequities such as those described by Kozol (1991) have provided an impetus for school finance reform—federal, state, and judicial.

Federal Government's Response

categorical aid

Federal funding providing educational services and programs for special-needs children.

The federal government's role is and has been somewhat limited regarding school finance. However, the Department of Education, a Cabinet-level office created in 1979 by President Jimmy Carter, distributes grant money to schools. Most federal assistance has been in the form of **categorical aid,** which is earmarked for a specific school need such as a library, computers, reading programs, or free lunches for economically disadvantaged students. A large portion of categorical grants are reserved for schools with a high proportion of children from low-income families or other children whose special educational needs put them at a disadvantage. The drawback to categorical aid is that there are strings attached; the schools must use the monies for the designated purposes. There are strict federal guidelines that accompany these dollars. Stringent documentation is required from those schools accepting categorical aid.

block grant

Federal funding given to states with fewer federal restrictions than is the case with categorical aid.

During the 1980s, restrictions on local school administrators eased under the Reagan administration when another type of federal assistance known as a **block grant** was made available. Simply put, block grants came with fewer federal restrictions, which meant that schools were given more latitude as to how the money could be spent to best serve students' needs.

At the end of the 1990s, it was projected that public schools would spend $200 billion in federal, state, and local funds for K-12 (Leinwand, 1992). Regardless of the federal government's role in financing schools, the major financial burden of schools is and continues to rest on states and the local school districts (Guthrie & Reed, 1991).

States' Response

flat grant

State equalization of funding by distributing money based on student attendance.

equalization grant

State equalization of funding by redistributing surplus revenue to poor districts.

foundation grant

State grants made available to poor districts to supplement insufficient local funding.

In an effort to correct inequities, states are being asked to equalize funding among districts by flat grants, equalization grants, and foundation grants. A **flat grant** is based on the district's average daily attendance from the previous year. Then money is evenly distributed for each child within that district, with minor adjustments. This funding source explains why it is crucial for districts to keep meticulous records on attendance. An **equalization grant** requires that wealthier districts give back surplus revenue to the state, which will in turn distribute excess funds to poorer districts. A **foundation grant** is designed to provide poorer districts with state aid to compensate for insufficient local funding. Hence, local school districts that have trouble raising revenue because of low property values can receive assistance from the state to make up for these deficiencies. Most states require a minimum property tax for local communities to qualify for this grant (Guthrie & Reed, 1991).

Judicial Response

In some states the department of education is in conflict with state courts regarding the outcome of inequities in the funding of school systems. One of several landmark court cases affecting school funding was *Serrano* v. *Priest* (1971), which charged that the current system for financing schooling in California was unconstitutional. The plaintiffs argued that using property taxes to finance schools violated the Fourteenth Amendment to the U.S. Constitution. The Supreme Court of California upheld the parents' claim that the wealth of the state—not the wealth of property owners from local school districts—should be the determining factor for financing schools because it was clear that property taxes in poorer communities could not compete with property taxes in the wealthier communities. The court instructed the California State Legislature to revise the system to separate school funding from local property taxes.

After this ruling, cases were filed in several states, including the *San Antonio Independent School District* v. *Rodriguez* case. A federal circuit court ruled the same as in the *Serrano* case. However, in 1973 the U.S. Supreme Court reversed that decision and ruled that this funding practice was not unconstitutional because the right to an education is not guaranteed in the U.S. Constitution, although it might conflict with state constitutions. Nonetheless, the U.S. Supreme Court (1973) did recognize that there were inherent disparities in educational expenditures because of a flawed system of property tax funding. The court noted, however, that these kinds of issues should be addressed by state legislatures or state courts.

Let's look at two examples in which this problem of funding inequities was addressed on a state level. In 1989 the Texas State Supreme Court found the system of relying on property taxes for school revenue had led to inequities in pupil expenditures. In response the Texas State Legislature passed legislation in 1991 to redistribute funds from wealthier districts to poorer districts (i.e., districts that had lower property values). Likewise, Kentucky's method of school funding was found to be unconstitutional, which led to a complete overhaul of the system. Other states, along with Texas and Kentucky, are in the process of examining this problem more fully (Bell, 1993). What the future holds remains to be seen.

REFLECTION QUESTIONS

What is your opinion about how to remedy the impact of school funding inequities?

....

How would you address these kinds of issues?

....

Is it the role of the federal government to intervene in issues of school funding? Or is this the responsibility of the states? Defend your position.

....

Conclusion

In this chapter you are introduced to key personnel in the governance and operation of schools. Major changes are underway for schools; the traditional system of the past is under scrutiny by courts, legislators, taxpayers, and parents. Becoming impatient and disillusioned by what public schools can offer, the public is demanding greater accountability on the part of schools. School boards are feeling the pressure to make schools more efficient and effective.

To respond to constituents, school boards and administrators are becoming more receptive to outside input. Businesses and industries are being seen as allies in the quest to improve schools. Parents are being given more of a voice in matters pertaining to the education of their children. Furthermore, teachers are being given a greater voice in policymaking than ever before.

Finally, we have seen that school finance is a challenge with grave implications. Obviously, there are no easy solutions with regard to how to improve the financing of schools or how to correct for the inequities found in schools. This is a highly complicated matter. The good news is that the nation is aware of the problem, and policymakers are investigating solutions to this issue.

You will be affected by these reform outcomes, both as a professional (should you become a teacher) and as a parent. And if neither is your calling, you will still be affected. As concerned citizens, we must be interested in the schooling of our young people. We must work to ensure that all children (regardless of where they live) have equal access to quality education that will prepare them to work in a technical, global society. There is probably no such thing as a "perfect" school, but there may be such thing as a "good match" for a particular child. Perhaps current reforms will take us to that point.

KEY TERMS

alternative school	personal property tax
block grant	private enterprise school
categorical aid	private school
chief state school officer	school board
equalization grant	school choice
flat grant	state board of education
foundation grant	state department of education
magnet school	superintendent of schools
National Governors' Association	voucher

SUGGESTED READING

Kozol, J. (1991). *Savage inequalities: Children in America's schools.* New York: Crown Publishers.

Manno, B. V., Chester, E. F., Bierlein, L. A., & Vanourek, G. (1998). How charter schools are different: Lessons and implications from a national study. *Phi Delta Kappan, 79*(7), 489–498.

Sernak, K. (1998). *School leadership: Balancing power with caring.* New York: Teachers College Press.

REFERENCES

Adelman, N., & Pringle. (1995). Education reform and the uses of time. *Phi Beta Kappa, 77*(1), 27–29.

Bell, T. H. (1993). Reflections one decade after a nation at risk. *Phi Delta Kappan, 74*(8), 592– 605.

Campbell, R. F., Cunningham, L. L., Nystrand, R. O. & Usdan, M. (1980). *The organization and control of American schools* (4th ed.). Columbus, OH: Charles E. Merrill.

Condoli, C. (1995). *Site based management in education: How to make it work in your school.* Lancaster, PA: Technomic Publishing.

Conway, G. E. (1992). School choice: A private school perspective. *Phi Delta Kappan, 73*(7) 561–564.

Freeman, J. L., Underwood, K. E., & Fortune, J. C. (1991). What boards value. *The American School Board Journal, 178*(1) 32–36, 39.

Guthrie, J., & Reed, R. J. (1991). *Educational administration and policy: Effective leadership for American education* (2nd ed.). Needham Heights, MA: Allyn & Bacon.

Koetzsch, R. E. (1997). *The parents' guide to alternatives in education.* Boston: Shambhala Publications.

Konnert, M. W., & Augenstein, J. J. (1998). *The school superintendency: Leading education into the 21st century.* Lancaster, PA: Technomic Publishing.

Kowalski, T. (1994). Chasing the wolves from the schoolhouse door. *Phi Delta Kappan, 76*(6), 486–489.

Kozol, J. (1967). *Death at an early age: The destruction of the hearts and minds of Negro children in the Boston public schools.* Boston: Houghton Mifflin. (Revised edition, 1985). New York: A Plume Book/Penguin.

Kozol, J. (1972). *Free schools.* Boston: Houghton Mifflin.

Kozol, J. (1985). *Illiterate America.* New York: Anchor Press/Doubleday.

Kozol, J. (1991). *Savage inequalities: Children in America's schools.* New York: Crown Publishers.

Leinwand, G. (1992). *Public education (American issues).* New York: Facts on File.

Martinez, T., Thomas, K., & Kemerer, F. R. (1994). Who chooses and why: A look at five school choice plans. *Phi Delta Kappan, 75*(9), 678–681.

McCloud, B., & McKenzie, F. D. (1994). School boards and superintendents in urban districts. *Phi Delta Kappan, 75*(5), 384–386.

National Commission on Excellence in Education. (1983). *A nation at risk: The imperative for educational reform.* Washington, D.C.: Author.

Peterson, P., & Kelley, C. (1998). *School boards by design: A manual for structure.* Conway, AR: University of Central Arkansas, Center for Academic Excellence Publishers.

Peterson, P. (1996). The "typical" Arkansas board member. *The School Board Reporter, 14*(9), 1, 4–5.

San Antonio Independent School District v. *Rodriguez,* 411 U.S. 1, 93 5.Ct. 1278 (1973).

Serrano v. *Priest,* 5 Cal.3d 584, 9b Cal. Rptr 601, 487 P.2d 1241 (1971).

Shannon, T. A. (1994). The changing community school board/America's best hope for the future of our public schools. *Phi Delta Kappan, 75*(5), 394–397.

Tanner, D. (1993). A nation 'truly' at risk. *Phi Delta Kappan, 75*(4), 288–297.

Toch, T. (1998). The new education bazaar. *U.S. News & World Report, 124*(16), 35–42.

Unger, H. G. (1993). *How to pick a private school.* New York: Facts on File.

Wallis, C. (1994). A class of their own. *Time, 144*(18), 53–63.

Wohlstetter, P., & Anderson L. (1994). What can U.S. charter schools learn from England's grant-maintained schools? *Phi Delta Kappan, 75*(6), 486–491.

© Superstock

At the end of this chapter, you will be able to

- Discuss the purpose of schools.
- Describe what makes a school "a school."
- Identify what makes a school effective.
- Describe how schools are organized.
- Discuss the various school settings.
- Recognize the reforms that are affecting schools.

CHAPTER 15

Schools in the New Century

A bird's eye view of what to expect in this chapter

As a new century begins, several old questions about schooling have emerged in the education literature. Questions such as: Why do we have schools? What makes a school "a school"? What makes schools effective? How are schools organized? What forms of schooling exist? What reforms are affecting schools?

At first glance, these questions appear simple; the answers, however, are not as simple. Each answer is complex and depends on the individual's interpretation of what it means to be educated. Your interpretation of key educational words often provides a framework for answering these kinds of questions. For example, the words *education* and *schooling* are often thought to be synonymous. However, on close inspection, arguments can be raised to demonstrate their differences. A student can spend 12 years in the school system and yet not be educated. In contrast a person can be well educated and never enter a school building. Schooling can best be defined as a social or group process, whereas education is concerned with a process of learning that occurs over a lifetime.

T he following true story describes one of the many reasons that we have schools.

T he setting is inner-city Los Angeles. The school is Vaughn Next Century Learning Center and is one of many public charter schools in the Los Angeles Unified School District. Vaughan serves 1,640 K–5 students and 1,000 community members. Of these students, 99% are eligible for free or reduced-cost lunches and 88% of its students have limited English proficiency. Based on these facts, many would surmise that this school and its students have less prospect for success. But here is where the story begins.

Ten years ago Dr. Yvonne Chan, filled with a passion for teaching and learning, was hired as the school principal. Many community members believed that she would last only a few months. Ten years later, she is still filled with the same passion. President and First-Lady Hillary Clinton recently visited the school and declared it a "Blue Ribbon School." Why has Dr. Chan been so successful? The word "passion" describes it all. She believed that she could make a difference for children, youth, and families.

Today, this school has changed the lives of its students and their families. Accomplishments include standards-based instruction, rigorous multiple assessments, K–5 class size reductions, technology access and integration, community library services, longer school day and year, intensive teacher training and performance pay, proactive programs to end social promotion, expanded off-hour learning opportunities, child care, family center and Healthy Start program, special education inclusion, accelerated English language development, site-based governance, facilities modernization and expansion, on-site University Professional Development Center, joint ventures with local businesses, career ladder for parents, and community economic development. Furthermore, within the next two years, Vaughn Next Century Learning Center will add a secondary division (grades 6–12) to establish a Career Academy for Future Teachers. The students are the real winners in this story. Today, their eyes are bright with hope in a world that once offered them nothing.

Why Do We Have Schools?

Through the last century, the purpose of schools has been defined by most scholars as providing free public (or private) education to enlighten the citizenry, with the goal being equal opportunity available for all, to cultivate an investment in the human capital of a country. This perspective, for the most part, has been based on the idea that society should be able to demonstrate a return for its investment. Many feel that the first purpose of schools is to transfer academic knowledge.

As a new century begins, other theories of schooling are emerging that claim a basic education includes more than core curriculum. Many feel that schools should be a place where children can experience love and affection, foster ecological thoughts, encourage future studies, increase their understanding of global issues, and foster the technologies. These views point out the importance of preparing students for life, which is considered by many to be the real purpose of all learning.

The following scholars and reports provide a spectrum of thought as you consider the purpose of schools:

- Burrup, Brimley, and Garfield (1999, pp. 15–16) claim that "education [through schools] is now popularly referred to as an investment in human capital."

- *The Economist* (1997, p. 15) editorializes that "educational achievement and economic success are clearly linked—the struggle to raise the nation's standards is fought first and foremost in the classroom."

- Goodlad and McMannon (1997, p. 6) are much more specific in their deliberation of schooling, as follows: "Recent studies of schools and school districts suggest that parents have difficulty choosing among academic, social, vocational, and personal educational goals for their children. They want them all."

- Ted Sizer (1997, p. 40) writes the following: "Public education is an idea, not a mechanism. It promises every young citizen a fair grounding in the intellectual and civic tools necessary to have a decent life in this culture and economy. It promises the rest of us that the rising generations have tools to keep America a place worthy of residence. It signals that we are all one."

The last two statements imply the importance of the child becoming an active citizen in society and that schools reflect the values of their communities. However, in all the above citations the significance of learning or growing in knowledge is the one common characteristic of the purpose of schools.

Socialization of the Student

Socialization of the student is one of the purposes of schools. Those who strongly believe this argue that if teachers do not help children become adjusted to society, then academics are meaningless. They believe that if a child is worried about a life skill, such as friendship, abusive home relations, or drugs and alcohol abuse, then learning mathematics will merely become secondary.

Socialization of the child often includes some of the following life skills: drug education, human sexuality, parenting, child abuse, peer relationships, money management, extracurricular activities, and transmitting the culture.

To compound the issue, teachers, often without any specific education in life skills curriculum, have the responsibility of teaching these classes.

The answer to these arguments from the teaching profession is often, "We will do what is best for each student." What are your thoughts? Do you think teachers should be responsible for how a student adjusts to society? Or should the role of schooling be purely that of academics?

Another relevant question is the impact of the Internet on teaching and learning. Acquiring knowledge is becoming more than a social process. The information explosion through the World Wide Web is making it insufficient to merely memorize facts. Rather, it is far more important that students learn how to process information through a critical eye. Learners must construct their own education, which requires much more of schools than merely what is outlined in the curriculum.

The idea of teachers and students coming together to learn is known as "teaming." In other words, learning is not an isolated task. Rather, learning is viewed today as requiring social interaction with others to find personal meaning. This was referred to in the orientation of this textbook as "social constructivism."

As we have seen, schools and homes are partners in the educational enterprise. This partnership over the years has not always been easy. Parents often view their child's education differently than do teachers and administrators. For example, how schools track student progress has been a point of contention for many years in most American schools.

Tracking

tracking

The official and unofficial records of students' progress in academic and nonacademic curricula.

The official and unofficial records of student progress in academic and nonacademic curricula is known as the **tracking** system. Schools have a responsibility to screen students for various tracks that prepare them for different careers and lifestyles. Some of these tracks are remedial, college, honors, and vocational. As you may recall, tracking was discussed in Chapter 13 under the heading "ability grouping."

There is much research today related to the negative aspects and injustices of tracking. Many school districts are opting for the elimination of tracking procedures, claiming they are unfair. They ask: What right has any school system to determine a student's career options? In 1985 Jeannie Oakes authored a benchmark research publication entitled *Keeping Track* to show that tracking is harmful. Despite this research and the research of many others, tracking remains a feature of most junior and senior high schools. Some of the problems with tracking are as follows:

- The most competent teachers often teach the higher-track students.

- Students in lower tracks often are provided a less demanding curriculum.

- Learning activities featuring critical and reflective thinking are usually presented only to higher-track students.

- Less is expected of lower-track students.
- Students in lower tracks often have poor self-esteem.
- Students in lower tracks do not have career choices that are offered to higher-track students.
- Students who do not do well on tests might be assigned lower tracks when their abilities may be similar to those of higher-track students.

Historical Perspective

In the Great Depression of the 1930s and later in the 1940s, a "life-adjustment" curriculum evolved. The idea of schools as social organizations began to surface. Social dance, debate, clubs, drama, art, and music began to be part of the school routine. But this focus on helping the child to be a well-adjusted individual and lifelong learner was short-lived. In the early 1980s, President Reagan was concerned that schools were no longer teaching academic standards and that schooling had taken over responsibilities of the home with a curriculum that included drivers' education, sex education, social dance, parenting, and so on.

The President Commissions an Educational Study. For the first time in American history, a president appointed a commission to study the status of public education. The commission's report, entitled *A Nation at Risk: The Imperative for Educational Reform,* by the National Commission on Excellence in Education (1983), forced Americans to realize that students suffered as a result of low academic standards. The report outlined some of the problems with schools, as follows (pp. 8–9):

1. Average achievement of high-school students on most standardized tests is now lower than when Sputnik was launched.

2. The College Board's Scholastic Aptitude Tests (SAT) demonstrated a virtually unbroken decline from 1963 to 1980. Average verbal scores fell over fifty points and average mathematics scores dropped nearly forty points.

3. Many seventeen-year-olds do not possess the "higher order" intellectual skills we should expect of them. Nearly forty percent cannot draw inferences from written materials: only one-fifth can write a persuasive essay; and only one-third can solve a mathematics problem requiring several steps.

Over the following years, this reform report stimulated important improvements, but it lacked a comprehensive, specific vision of what students actually needed to know and be able to do at specific grades/levels of their education. Many states, such as California, have attempted to define what students need to acquire at each grade/level from K–12. The country has undertaken a "back to the basics" journey since 1983, but the correct road has yet to be discovered.

REFLECTION QUESTIONS

- Recall tracking experiences you have had in schools and their relation to your present education.

....

- What is your opinion about some of the problems outlined in *A Nation at Risk*?

....

- Did Americans overreact or underreact to its message?

....

AssessYourself

What success stories do you know of people who changed the lives of others?

What caused these people to do what they did?

What do you think is missing in schools today?

What could you do to implement change?

What Makes a School "a School"?

Think of your school experiences and what made your school "a school." The following are most often given by students when asked this question: friends, extracurricular activities, teachers, learning, stories, field trips, tests, homework, report cards, and thinking. Their perspectives of what makes a school a school developed through their experiences in the traditional public schools (this concept will be covered in more detail in the section How are Schools Organized?) or through one or more of the following notions of "school": *school within a school, school as community, factory model, shopping mall school*, and *alternative arrangements for schooling*.

School Within a School

The reorganization of schools into smaller, self-contained learning communities is fast becoming standard practice in the restructuring efforts of large comprehensive schools. Restructuring not only combats student alienation, but it can reduce teacher isolation, hopefully increasing collegiality and col-

When you think about your schooling experiences, what memories are most vivid? From your perspective, how important were extracurricular activities?

© Bachmann/PhotoEdit

school within a school

The reorganization of schools into smaller, self-contained learning communities.

laboration among faculty. Many believe that the idea of the little red schoolhouse is emblematic of the concept known as **school within a school.**

There are positive and negative perspectives to the one-room, little red schoolhouse that existed in the early 1900s. The positive features included the following: teachers knew their students academically and socially, the entire community was involved in the educational process, and a moral perspective was evident in the curriculum and the teaching process. In contrast, some problems with this thinking were: special education students were rarely accommodated, one teacher attempted to teach all grades, and rote memory was the method commonly used in the learning process.

Over the years, schooling has become big business, with a single school serving thousands of students. Many educators and some teachers know little about each student's personal and academic life. Many believe this lack of connectedness is the main cause for the increase in school violence. Thus the return to the ideas of community, safety, and personalization has begun to surface in the education literature.

For example, Ken Smith Middle School, with a population of approximately 1,200 students, demonstrated that schools with large student populations can serve the needs of individual students. The school restructured its organization to divide the student and teaching populations into smaller units. The school was organized into three equal school communities, called "pods," with approximately 405 students in each pod, including sixth, seventh, and eighth graders. About 27 educators were assigned to each of the pods, one of them an assistant principal. In such schools the entire student body comes together for assemblies and sporting and drama events. For most daily operations, the school's communities are conducted as three separate pods, each caring about how approximately 405 students live and learn.

Schools as Community

Thomas Sergiovanni, a leading author in school-as-community literature, makes the following claims in his book *Leadership for the Schoolhouse* (1996):

> Schools are responsible for more than developing basic competence in students and passing on the culture of their community. They are also responsible for teaching habits of the mind and habits of the heart. Everything that happens in the schoolhouse has moral overtones that are virtually unmatched by other institutions in our society. (p. xii)

school as community

The philosophy that education is the responsibility of all citizens.

The idea of **school as community** is central to the life of the community. What this means is that education becomes the responsibility of all citizens. Parents, teachers, school administrators, social agencies, grandparents, and others all work together to ensure that the children receive a quality education.

It Takes a Community to Educate a Child

The Department of Education in the State of California has made enormous strides to help students achieve at high levels. This has largely been accomplished through partnerships with local school officials, teachers, families, businesses, and community agencies to make a difference in how students learn (California Department of Education, 1999).

Framed within this thinking is how schools are organized. Schools are not organized to prepare "things" for life; rather they are organized to prepare "children" for life. Further, nothing is more prized by a parent than his or her child, and parents view educators as having the "awesome" responsibility of enhancing their child's opportunities in life. Thus Sergiovanni's statement of schools having a moral responsibility rings true.

teacher leader

A teacher empowered to lead and to initiate change.

Sergiovanni and others (1996) believe that school leadership within the concept of schools as community rests with the teacher rather than the principal. When teachers become empowered to lead and initiate change, the term **teacher leader** or *leadership from the middle* is used. Teacher leaders make all the difference in the change process in that they most often initiate restructuring processes based on the needs of their students. Change comes from the level closest to the students, and teachers have more ownership for the daily operation of the school.

Orem Junior High School in Utah investigated leadership from the middle. This school was successfully restructured to increase student academic performance and social success. At the beginning of the process, most teachers in the school referred to any reform movements as being the ideas of the new principal. However, when the principal began to shift responsibility for what was happening in the school to others—mainly chosen teacher leaders—the language of the school also changed. Instead of discussing "her" idea, the teachers began to talk about "our" programs. The principal had moved the apex of decision making to the center rather than the top of the pyramid.

This principal took time to involve others, talk to others, and, more importantly, listen to what others thought were important for teaching and learning in the school. Ultimately, all that really mattered was what changes would benefit students most. When this goal was adopted, things began to happen.

Current researchers Lynn Beck and Joseph Murray, in their book *The Four Imperatives of Successful Schools* (1996), assert that everything that happens in the school should be directed toward improving student academic performances and that teachers should play a direct role in this mission. Decisions about facilities, capital expenditures, curriculum, selection of resources, partnerships, and other issues should be based on determining what is best for the student in the classroom. One might ask if all decisions presently made in schooling are based on what is best for the student. Unfortunately, so many daily decisions must be made in schools today that it is often hard to discern the motives of those making the decisions. For example, the time of day children eat lunch at school is often based on what time best suits others rather than on when is the best time for students to have lunch in order to be academically successful. Timetables, staff schedules, busing hours, budgets, and so on are often designed for convenience to the system rather than on children's academic interests.

Consider the following situation. A school is about to purchase a series of textbooks for a particular discipline. Often, students are not consulted as to the textbook that appears most appealing for their learning—the administration and sometimes teachers make those decisions. Such decision processes are not the fault of anyone; they result from the nature of the system and the expectations placed on schools today.

Some of the following activities occurred in one school only because teacher leaders took the initiative to make the educational process serve students better.

- Setting up a web page for a class or for a school to keep parents and students informed
- Organizing a parent council to handle telephone messages: one or two parents to coordinate organizational activities throughout the year
- Sending home monthly newsletters
- Encouraging parents to sign up for classroom involvement
- Visiting the homes of their students throughout the school year
- Inviting parents and grandparents to speak to the class about their professions, life experiences, heritage, and so on

Student-Centered Schools

student-centered school

A school that puts students first in all matters pertaining to how teaching and learning are conducted.

teacher-centered school

A school that emphasizes teacher-directed instruction and traditional testing measures.

Schools as community are most often described as student-centered schools. A **student-centered school** places students first in all matters pertaining to how teaching and learning are conducted. The opposite of a student-centered school is a **teacher-centered school**. A walk through a student-centered school can usually reveal the following characteristics: supportive

school mission statement, student work displayed in classrooms and hallways, parental involvement, a sense of "*we*-ness" within the building, and evident student leadership. Such schools have student involvement at the apex of teaching and learning. This usually occurs when teachers allow students to be part of the decision-making processes. The following experience provides a conceptual framework for the idea.

Reflections from the Field

When a new teacher was interviewed about her most meaningful experiences during her first year of teaching, she said, "During my first year of teaching, I had the opportunity to meet with the superintendent of schools, who was about to retire after 35 years in the profession. I wanted to hear what his thoughts were to a question I often think about: *How would you describe a great teacher?* His response was simple and to the point. 'A great teacher is one who has less sage on the stage and more guide on the side.' "

Another interview—with a school principal—provided an important perspective related to how students learn in a student-centered environment: "Through my years of teaching children and adults, I have learned one secret about how learning best occurs. This one idea has carried me through my years of teaching and learning and has never failed to reach students. The idea comes from an old Latin saying, *docemur docendo*, 'He or she who teaches learns.' "

In teacher-centered schools *(left)*, test scores and grades are used to measure student learning. In contrast, student-centered schools *(right)* deemphasize traditional testing measures and encourage authentic assessments, which accentuate students' ideas and creativity.

Educators throughout history have recognized that teaching is a powerful strategy for learning. John Comenius, a 17th-century Moravian educator, advocated learning by teaching. He believed that he who teaches others learns himself. "This is true, not only because constant repetition impresses a fact deliberately on the mind, but because the process of teaching in itself gives a deeper insight into the subject taught . . . if a student wished to make progress, he should arrange to give lessons daily in the subjects he was studying, even if he had to hire his pupils" (Gartner, Kohler, & Riessman, 1972, pp. 14–15).

Table 15.1 illustrates some of the differences between student-centered and teacher-centered teaching and learning.

The Factory Model

factory model

A model of schooling based on the business-based concepts of efficiency and accountability.

The **factory model** of schooling was developed from concepts found in the business community, namely factories, during the early 1900s. Efficient production was all that was important in factories during this time. Human beings were secondary in the process of producing "things."

The metaphor of a bottle factory comes to mind with respect to how students learn. Students instead of bottles move through the school's assembly lines. Into open bottles (student's minds), teachers pour ingredients of knowledge. The process is mechanical, and each step can be accounted for. During each step in the process, a supervisor knows exactly what is happening to the

Table 15.1	Differences Between Student- and Teacher-Centered Learning

Student-Centered	Teacher-Centered
Students actively involved	Teacher-directed
Student-to-student interaction	Teacher-to-student interaction
Student ideas welcomed	Teacher less interested in student ideas
Students working with peers to learn	Teacher-directed learning process
Personal life/content–related discussion encouraged	Discussion is mostly focused on teacher-directed topics
Tests and grades do not direct teaching and learning	Tests and grades are the measures of what is taught and learned
Students help direct the class rules and goals	Class rules and goals are decided by the school and teacher

bottle and exactly how many bottles per hour should come off the assembly line. Thus efficiency can be measured.

Another mechanical metaphor, that of the cookbook, often surfaces with respect to how teaching is conducted in the factory model. Teachers are prescribed a step-by-step recipe of exactly how a concept should be taught. The lesson plan dictates exactly what to say and what questions to ask, expected responses, test questions, and so on.

Within these schools, the factory model is a mechanical method for how teaching and leaning occur. Does this model exist in schools today?

The Shopping Mall School

shopping mall school

The idea that schools are shopping centers of knowledge where students choose among courses and personalize the curriculum.

The **shopping mall school** is one that offers students choices to meet their individual learning tastes. The shopping mall school was derived from the idea of shopping centers, where consumers have a choice of stores in which to shop and a choice of products to buy. In other words, schools adopting this model would become shopping centers of knowledge. Students choose the school and personalize their curriculum. The movie *Fast Times at Ridgemont High* is about a high school and its resemblance to a shopping mall. The book The *Shopping Mall High School* (Powell, Farrar, and Cohen, 1985) provides an in-depth study of such high schools.

A factory-model mentality can be the unfortunate by-product of high teacher–student ratios and overcrowded school facilities.

© Tony Freeman/PhotoEdit

Web Site
For more information on home schooling, visit the National Home Education Research Institute's web site at http://www.nheri.org.

Web Site
The Home School Legal Defense Association's web site can be found at http://www.hslda.org.

Alternative Arrangements for Schooling

Alternative arrangements to public education, more commonly labeled as school choice, include private and home schooling, charter schools, school choice/voucher programs, and state takeovers. Many of these alternative arrangements are the result of parents becoming more involved in school choice. The school-choice movement began in the 1980s, about the time that the greatest increases in home/private schooling situations were recorded. School choice allows parents to decide the school they would like their child to attend, and tax dollars then are moved to that school. School choice seeks to improve student achievement by broadening the menu of available school options.

Although the motives for the school choice movement appear to be worthy, many educators and parents have expressed concern. "It centers on the introduction of capitalistic competition into public school education by allowing consumer-parents to select the best schools for their children" (Unger, 1999, p. 5). There are many implications to this approach. Education might seem to be moving more toward elitism in that those who can afford it are able to transport their children to schools out of their neighborhood district. Another interpretation is that many schools would be judged on unestablished criteria or popular school myths. Many fear that education will have to be run as a business and that the human side of educating may become less important than efforts to obtain consumer dollars for some of the alternatives to public education.

The following examples provide insight into various arrangements for school organization:

- Mrs. Hirsche takes her six-year-old son to work with her. The company she works for has an on-site elementary school. Mrs. Hirsche not only participates in her son's education by being available to volunteer at the school during her lunch hour, but she can also observe her son in his classroom through her computer via a webcam.

- C. J., who is seven years old, lives with his grandmother, who has no formal education. Each day they go to school together. Many adults, like C. J.'s grandmother, are part of the second-grade class. These adults learn together with their children. Often you can see cooperative education in action. For example, when C. J. reads with his grandmother, helping her to sound out words, his grandmother takes time to explain certain words, such as "gramophone," to C. J.

- Teague and Nicholas are being home schooled by their mother. Their home is connected to the World Wide Web, and Teague and Nicholas are able to conduct educational research with the help of their mother. To enhance their extracurricular education, they join other students their own age for recreational experiences at the local community recreation center. They also are active in many Internet chat rooms in order to have social and academic interaction with other students their age.

- Mercedes attends a charter school organized by parents, teachers, and business leaders that is exempt from state and local regulations. Mercedes's parents were instrumental in helping form the school's mission statement, which supports learning through a moral perspective. Seven years ago charter schools did not exist. Today there are just under 1,700 in the United States.

Two School-Choice Movements: Home/Private Schools and Charter Schools

Home and private schools provide the greatest variety of choices to families. As this book goes to press, the National Private School registry lists just over 130,000 members. This number does not take into account the many private schools that exist and yet are not registered. The number of home schools throughout the United States is approximately 750,000 (Lyman, 1998). Both of these movements antedate the current wave of discontentment with public education. Parents often choose home schooling over private and public schooling for their children for the following reasons:

- To customize their children's education
- To provide a learning environment that offers opportunities for social, emotional, spiritual, and academic growth
- To instill certain religious values
- To protect their children from violence and allow them to learn in a safe environment
- To strengthen the family by bringing education back to where it originated

Many decisions are involved in the choice of a private school: the cost, the school's specialization, and the location. In the 1990s, charter schools were

Web Site

For more information on family education, you may want to visit http://www.familyeducation.com.

introduced in the United States and Canada. They are public schools because they are funded through tax dollars, but they resemble private schools in that they do not have an assigned population and students must apply for admission. Their operation is usually independent of the school district and the state. At this time, Arizona leads the nation in the number of charter schools; however, even in Arizona only 3% of children attend charter schools.

A charter, in its most basic application, is a grant of permission to engage in an activity. According to the Department of Education of New Jersey, charter schools hold the promise of creating a new kind of publicly funded school—one that breaks the traditional mold in an effort to help children achieve at higher levels. The charter school program enables teachers, parents, community leaders, private entities, and institutions of higher learning to take the lead in designing public schools that will provide unique and innovative approaches toward achievement of high academic standards.

AssessYourself

Should schools be known for their academic rigor? Or should schools be known for their expanded learning opportunities—that which goes beyond the academics?

Describe what was rigorous in your K–12 experiences. Describe other learning experiences that were less rigorous but socially enhancing. Which experiences are more memorable? Which ones would you want to include to ensure your students experience success?

REFLECTION QUESTIONS

- Considering schooling since the time of the little red schoolhouse, is education better or worse today?

- How should schools of the future be organized?

What Makes a School Effective?

effective school

A school that has achieved success for its students both academically and socially.

An **effective school** is a school that meets the academic and social needs of its students. This might sound simple, but most students, teachers, and parents are somewhat disgruntled with the process of schooling, which indicates that more research is required in determining what is effective.

The effective-school movement began in the 1980s with the intention of improving the quality of education within the United States. "Effective" was defined as including those attributes of the school that would increase success for students academically (meeting higher standards) and socially (experiencing less truancy and fewer school drop-outs). These emphases grew out of concern for possible educational discrimination against minorities and students of low socioeconomic status. Thus students in an effective school would demonstrate as much growth socially and academically as affluent students. This movement was based on the assumption that characteristics of successful schools could be identified, replicated, and be the basis for improving other schools.

The research on effective schools has identified characteristics that distinguish the most successful schools from the least successful. The differences in most cases are in the attitudes and actions of the administrators and teachers, not in the district's wealth or the students' family backgrounds.

The Coleman Report of 1966 designated family background as the predominant determiner of student achievement and is often considered to have provided the impetus for the Effective Schools Research. Researchers such as Edmonds (1979) and Brookover (1979) disagreed with the findings of the Coleman Report and examined other factors that affect student achievement.

Generally, research found that most effective schools exhibited the following characteristics; this list has become known as the Correlates of the Effective Schools Movement (Edmonds, 1979):

1. Strong instructional leadership

2. High expectation that all students will learn

3. An orderly and positive climate that supports learning

4. A carefully developed instructional focus

5. Regular measurement of student learning

Correlates 2 and 5 are worthy of further discussion.

Correlate Two: High expectation that all students will learn. Effective schools pride themselves on serving the needs of all students. Thus the movement toward inclusion of students with disabilities in the general public education system gained momentum through the effective schools movement. Although the intent to serve all students within the framework of public schools is a worthy ambition, not everyone has been supportive of this idea. Proponents of inclusion have suggested that placement of students with disabilities in general education settings will improve every facet of the students' experience, including grades, academic skills, social acceptance, and social skills.

The opponents of inclusion see inherent flaws in this system, stating that it is not based on empirical evidence. They contend that the argument for inclusion is a moral one and is not based on sound scientific investigation or data.

These opposing factions do agree that most of the inclusion research has centered on children with disabilities as a broad category, not on specific populations of disabled children, especially those with unique needs.

One of the neglected groups is students with emotional and behavioral disorders (McMillan, Gresham, & Forness, 1996). Educators need to look more specifically at this population to identify the particular effects of inclusion on students with this form of disability. Commonly, students with emotional and behavioral disorders are served in the most restrictive of settings, more so than most other categories of special-needs children. Figures from the 1994 U.S. Department of Education's key report to Congress indicate that the students identified as having behavior disorders are commonly served in separate classrooms (37%); private, separate facilities (6%); or residential hospital facilities (5%). However, only 16% are served in general classroom settings.

Educators are asking whether students with emotional and behavioral disorders are best served in a more restrictive, structured environment or in a regular classroom. Some authorities recommend providing a full range of continuous services, extending from most restrictive to full inclusion. They claim that full inclusion programs or inclusion programs with support services for students with emotional and behavioral disorders are necessary, important, and functional.

One of the unresolved issues involved with inclusion is how assessment occurs. Although the idea of authentic assessment is often debated in the literature, this concept is gaining more acceptance as a valid measure of learning.

Correlate Five: Regular measurement of student learning. We have long known that children who learn only to pass examinations do not retain much of the information learned. For the most part these students could be called passive learners. The teacher teaches, and the student listens. Active learning allows a student to retain and remember what was learned because the student has been involved in the process. In active learning the student becomes in part his or her own teacher. Authentic assessment is concerned with representing the world the way it is. It requires students to use knowledge in deriving solutions to real-life issues based on their knowledge base. The tasks do not call for recipes or "canned" answers such as one would expect on a multiple-choice examination. Instead the student is expected to solve problems based on his or her interpretation of the knowledge base and life experiences.

Table 15.2 illustrates that how much we remember is directly related to the method of instruction. The same idea holds true for assessment. Meaningful authentic assessment allows the student to be actively involved in the process of evaluation and thus learning from the experience is student centered rather than teacher centered.

A form of authentic assessment is a project in which students in an English class create a weekly school newspaper. They use all their skills of writing, researching, reading, and listening to create something new rather than merely answer routine questions. Another example is for students to design

Table 15.2	How We Learn Best	
Amount We Remember	**Ways We Learn**	**Level of Involvement**
10%	Reading	Passive
20%	Hearing words	Passive
30%	Looking at pictures	Passive
50%	Watching a movie Looking at an exhibit Watching a demonstration	Passive Passive Passive
70%	Participating in a discussion Giving a talk	Active Active
90%	Teaching	Active

a city after studying and learning about the role and expectations of the community. These students might ask themselves questions such as: To best serve the people, where in the community should the bank be placed? The school? The senior citizen center? The market?

Twenty years later, the American Association of School Administrators affirms the essentials of the Correlates of the Effective Schools Movement of 1979. Effective schools are those that exhibit the following characteristics (American Association of School Administrators, 1999, pp. iii–iv):

- Contemporary technology
- Integrated, dynamic, competency-based curriculum
- Focus on student performance
- Student-centered systems
- Broad academic and social context
- Effective standards and assessment
- Environmentally responsive infrastructure and facilities
- School-community linkages
- Information/knowledge age teaching
- Responsive governance
- Targeted funding
- Research-based improvement

Meaningful learning and authentic assessments tend to encourage students to take ownership for their work.

© Cindy Charles/PhotoEdit

REFLECTION QUESTIONS

How effective would you describe the K–12 schools you attended?

What are your experiences with the "inclusion" process?

What are some of your experiences with authentic testing?

If you were planning a new school, what characteristics of school effectiveness would you include?

How Are Schools Organized?

Elementary School

American schools have traditionally been organized into two categories: elementary schools and secondary schools. The elementary schools evolved in the early 1800s from the thinking and efforts of Horace Mann, who implemented the first state-supported "common school" in Lexington, Massachusetts. The common school was the beginning of his dream to ensure that all students would receive an education. Education for the most part was free, open to all students (socially and intellectually), and situated in the center of community life.

Middle School

Today we have another tier of schooling called junior high schools, and more recently, middle schools. These schools were introduced to reach a population of youth who were an academic and social challenge to the elementary and high schools. The junior high school most often serves students in grades seven to nine, and the middle school serves students in grades six to eight. The purpose of these divisions is to enhance academic growth while ensuring that the students' social and emotional development will be taken into account.

High School

At the secondary level, Latin grammar schools evolved in the early 1600s, followed by English grammar schools in the 1700s. The idea of academies began in the late 1700s and early 1880s as a combination of the Latin and English grammar schools, with an emphasis on college preparation. The idea of high schools began in the late 1800s and exists today.

In What Settings Are Schools Found?

Schools are further organized according to their locations: rural, suburban, and urban.

Rural

The rural school, often classified as a one-room school, began the schooling movement throughout most of North America. Today, however, few one-room schools exist in the United States.

Reflections from the Field

Ms. Patterson is a teacher in a rural school who believes that the best education is delivered and received in small settings. In other words, she claims that less is better. She further states: "Students learn best when they are few in number, when their teacher knows them and their families, and when they help each other to learn." Presently, Ms. Patterson is the only teacher of 35 K–8 students in a one-room school in Nevada.

Suburban

On the increase is the suburban school. Families are choosing to move from rural and urban centers in hopes of finding a better education for their children. Suburban centers often offer newer school facilities, younger teachers, and more innovation with respect to curriculum and delivery.

Urban

Urban schools are under close review today largely because of their oversize populations and increasingly diverse school population. Much research and funding is focused on better understanding how to ensure a quality education for students attending these schools.

Garfield High School in East Los Angeles is one of many urban schools that has been restructured for student success. In the late 1970s this school was on the brink of losing its accreditation. The movie "Stand and Deliver" was made about Garfield High School and the success of its committed teachers, students, and parents. In this school, one teacher, Jaime Escalante, assisted colleagues, students, and parents to realize that all students can succeed. His students surprised the nation with their standardized test scores. In fact, his students were required to retake the test because some thought the students' scores were impossibly high and that perhaps some form of cheating had occurred. However, in the second test, these same students received even higher test scores, proving that all students can succeed if their teachers and parents believe in them.

The idea of building fewer facilities and allocating money toward those items that would enhance student learning has been popularized. Thus year-round schools were conceived and extended-day schedules were implemented. In the year-round school, students and teachers are placed on tracks with a given number of days in school, usually 45, and then a vacation, generally 15 days. All students usually receive the same Christmas, spring, and two-week summer breaks. Other than these common breaks in their schedules, classes are placed on different tracks of on-and-off-school. The extended-day schedule also allows schools to maximize facility use (see Figure 15.1).

REFLECTION QUESTIONS

- What were the best years of your K–12 education? Why?

- Are students in rural and suburban schools better educated than students in urban schools?

- What success stories do you know about schooling?

FIGURE 15.1 Extended-Day Schedule

	Track I	Track II	
Teacher Arrival 7:30 AM			
Student Arrival	8:00 AM	8:00 AM	Provide Prep
		8:40 AM	Chorus, Study Hall, etc. 9:30 Students
		9:20 AM	
Core		9:30 AM	Student Arrival
			1st Rotation Specialty
		10:20 AM	
			2nd Rotation Specialty
3rd Rotation	12:15 PM	12:15 PM	
Specialty			
4th Rotation	1:05 PM		
			Core
Specialty Student Dismissal	2:00 PM		
Chorus, etc.	2:10 PM		
8:00 Students Teacher Prep	2:50 PM		
		3:30 PM	Student Departure
Teacher Departure	4:00 PM		

Reflections from the Field

Dr. Tuttle is a university professor in a teacher education program in New York. He believes that the present idea of student teaching in schools will soon be replaced with online teaching experiences. He further claims that unless schools and students become electronically wired, they will become obsolete.

What Reforms Are Affecting Schools?

Undoubtedly attempts at school reform and restructuring will continue. The report *A Nation at Risk: The Imperative for Educational Reform—A Report to the Nation and the Secretary of Education* (NCEE, 1983) declared that our educational system, if left as is, would soon cripple the United States of America. Because this was the first document of its kind to be issued through the president's office, nations such as Canada also read and listened to its conclusions with great interest. The document generated extensive research and thought about what was and was *not* happening to education in the United States.

Since the NCEE report was published, the world has experienced a deluge of reports, some commissioned by the federal and state governments and others financed by various interest groups. Most of these reports have asserted that schools are in trouble. Some of the reports provided suggestions for changes to schooling, and others merely reported on what was observed. One suggestion was to look for the "good" in schooling and build upon it.

The desire of parents to become more involved in the educational process was seen as a movement that was beneficial to students. The idea of site-based management evolved. Parents were encouraged to be part of the school decision-making process, forming parent councils with teachers, community representatives, and school administrators so as to work together in governing the school.

Successful School Restructuring (Newmann & Wehlage, 1995) was initiated some 10 years after the NCEE report through the Center on Organization and Restructuring Schools. Newmann and Wehlage researched 1,500 schools throughout the United States to learn what educators consider quality education and what is successful in schools.

They determined that the quality and success of education did not depend on techniques, practices, or facilities. Rather it depended on basic human and social resources. The commitment and competence of the educators are the most important aspects of working with students who want to learn. In keeping with this finding, Newmann and Wehlage developed a circle model as a representation of support to students. It begins with the focus on student learning, which was determined to be the focus of all that matters in schooling.

From this core of learning, the next circle is authentic pedagogy. Authentic pedagogy encircles student learning and encourages teachers to teach toward a vision that enhances successful student learning practices. The word *authentic* is used because it refers to the importance of ensuring that the student is active in the learning process. He or she is thinking, acting, and doing, rather than passively soaking up knowledge.

In the third ring of the circle is school organizational capacity. This ring supports the professional community. It was found to be important that educators work in an environment that supports continuous improvement and that everything that happens within this community is focused toward supporting student learning. This can be accomplished as teachers work in teams in an environment that supports collective and cooperative ventures. The professional community should allow for risk taking and for the germination of ideas so that teachers and parents work toward new perceptions that might assist the teaching and learning processes.

In the outer ring of the circle is external support. For the schools of today to meet the needs of the students and the society they will live in tomorrow, they must receive the financial, technical, and political support that they need from their communities. Thus teachers and administrators need to look beyond the school for partnership and entrepreneurial involvement to ensure that teaching and learning are competitive with other community activities.

The Good High School

Sara Lawrence Lightfoot wrote an entire book about the "goodness" within high schools. She discovered that "goodness" within schools was supported by an external school community. In her award-winning book *The Good High School: Portraits of Character and Culture* (1983), Lightfoot describes six different high schools, seeking to capture the culture of these schools and thus their individual styles and rituals. The appealing idea about this book (winner of the American Educational Research Award) is that it is concerned about the "goodness" in the school—the success stories. Lightfoot believes that enough had been written about the things that are wrong with education. She found much "goodness" within the walls of the six schools she studied (permeable boundaries that reflect shifts in societal trends; leadership style that reflects qualities of being feminine and masculine; teachers having authority; consistent, unswerving attitudes toward students; and safe and regulated environments for building student-teacher relationships).

The purpose and design of her study have been a template for many other educational studies seeking to know "what works best in schools." The following is an excerpt:

First, we searched for goodness—exemplary schools that might tell us something about the myriad definitions of educational success and how it is achieved. Second, we wanted diversity among the secondary schools—diversity of philosophies, resources, populations, and type. And third, we were eager to have geographic representation. Our selection was not scientific. No random sample was taken, no large-scale opinion surveys were sent out in order to identify good schools. They were chosen because of their reputation among school people, the high opinion of them shared by their inhabitants and surrounding communities, and because they offered easy and generous entry. (Lightfoot, 1983, p. 11)

Tradionally the school uniform was the standard attire of parochial and private school students. Today, however, some public schools have adopted school uniforms.

© Philip Gould/CORBIS

Why Education?

Another scholar who has studied schools in order to help others understand what works best is John I. Goodlad. What Lightfoot discovered in 1985, Goodlad confirms in 1997. In his book *In Praise of Education* (1997) Goodlad further expands our thinking about success in schools by elaborating on the "why" of education.

Goodlad does not view education in economic terms, nor does he believe that schools should be thought of in a market-driven context. For Goodlad, schools should not be focused on the utilitarian idea of preparing young people for jobs. Rather, schools should undertake helping the youth to think, survive, and make good decisions based on thought and reflection. Many educators believe that students taught to think will be students who will acquire positions in life that are self-satisfying first to the individual and then to society.

The following quote from *Preparing Schools and School Systems for the 21st Century* (AASA, 1999) is supportive of the direction of Goodlad, Lightfoot,

Newmann, Wehlage, Sergiovanni, Beck, Murphy, and other scholars cited in this chapter:

> As we move into the 21st century, what we expect of our schools is commutative. Schools are still expected to produce ethical, moral, civilized people who can help us sustain our democracy. They are expected to prepare students for employability. They are expected to prepare a new wave of immigrants for life in America. And as demands increase, expectations grow, and life accelerates, our schools are expected to produce people who can effectively lead us into a global knowledge/information age. (AASA, 1999, p. 94)

Conclusion

As the new century begins, the topic of what it means to be educated has never received more discussion or more criticism. Part of the reason for placing education in this reflective light has been our inability to understand and agree on what constitutes an education. Because the majority of North American children receive their K–12 education within the boundaries of public schooling, schools are often linked synonymously with education.

However, what makes a school a school today is rapidly changing. Thus the idea of what it means to be educated is also changing. With the onset of the electronic classroom and the explosion of knowledge, questions abound regarding the purposes of schools and how they should be organized to ensure students are educated.

The idea of nontraditional settings for teaching and learning has never been more inviting. However, being on the frontiers of these new horizons brings the skills and the tools to evaluate the effectiveness within the educational setting. Further, the increasing numbers of these reform reports indicate that the idea of accountability has yet to be determined. Who *is* accountable for how children learn?

As you make meaning of education and schooling in this most exciting time in history, you will want to ensure that you equip yourself with the tools to evaluate change so that the needs of learners are best served.

KEY TERMS

effective school

factory model

school as community

school within a school

shopping mall school

student-centered school

teacher-centered school

teacher leader

tracking

SUGGESTED READINGS

American Association of School Administrators. (1999). *Preparing schools and school systems for the 21st century* (pp. 4–5). Council of 21, John Glenn, Honorary Chair. Recommendations from the Mount Vernon Conference. Author.

Goodlad, J. I., & McMannon T. J. (Eds.) (1997). *The public purpose of education and schooling.* San Francisco: Jossey-Bass.

Lightfoot, S. L. (1983). *The good high school: Portraits of character and culture.* New York: Basic-Books.

REFERENCES

American Association of School Administrators. (1999). *Preparing schools and school systems for the 21st century* (pp. 4–5). Council of 21, John Glenn, Honorary Chair. Recommendations from the Mount Vernon Conference. Author.

Beck, L., & Murphy, J. (1996). *The four imperatives of a successful school.* Thousand Oaks, CA: Corwin Press.

Brookover, W. B. (1979). *School social systems and student achievement: Schools can make a difference.* New York: Praeger.

Burrup, P., Brimley, V., & Garfield, R. (1999). *Financing education in a climate of change.* Boston: Allyn & Bacon.

Coleman, J. S. (Ed.). (1965). *Education and political development.* Princeton, NJ: Princeton University Press.

DePree, M. (1989). *Leadership as an art.* New York: Dell Publishing.

The Economist. (1997). Education and the wealth of nations. March 29–April 4, p. 15.

Edmonds, R. E. (1979). Programs of school improvement: An overview. *Educational Leadership 40*(3), 4–7.

Gartner, A., Kohler, M. D., & Riessman, F. (1972). *Children teach children: Learning by teaching.* New York: Harper & Row.

Gibb, S. A., Allred, K., Ingram, C. F., Young, J. R., & Egan, W. M. (1998). Lessons learned from the inclusion of students with emotional and behavioral disorders in one junior high school: Behavioral disorders. *Journal of the Council for Children with Behavioral Disorder, 24*(2), 122–137.

Goodlad, J. I., & McMannon T. J. (Eds.) (1997). *The public purpose of education and schooling.* San Francisco: Jossey-Bass.

Lightfoot, S. L. (1983). *The good high school: Portraits of character and culture.* New York: BasicBooks.

Lyman, I. (1998). *Homeschooling: Back to the future? Policy analysis* (p. 294). Washington, D.C.: The Cato Institute.

McMillan, D. L., Gersham, F. M., & Forness, S. R. (1996). Full inclusion: An empirical perspective. *Behavioral Disorders, 21,* 145–159.

National Commission on Excellence in Education. (1983). *A nation at risk: The imperative for educational reform* (pp. 8–9). Washington, D.C.: U.S. Government Printing Office.

Newmann, F. M., & Wehlage, G. G. (1995). *Successful school restructuring.* Washington, D.C.: American Federation of Teachers.

Oakes, J. (1985). *Keeping track: How schools structure inequality.* New Haven: Yale University Press.

Powell, A. G., Farrar, E., & Cohen, D. (1985). *The shopping mall high school.* Boston: Houghton Mifflin.

Sergiovanni, T. I. (1996). *Leadership for the schoolhouse.* San Francisco: Jossey-Bass.

Sizer, T.R. (1997). *Horace's school: Redesigning the American high school.* New York: Houghton Mifflin Co.

Unger, H. G. (1999). *School choice.* New York: Checkmark Books.

© Michael Newman/PhotoEdit

At the end of this chapter, you will be able to

- Describe the developmental phases of the career teacher's life cycle.

- Identify trends in the job market for teachers.

- List steps to undertake in order to secure a teaching position.

- Plan "next steps" if you decide not to pursue a teaching career.

- Summarize challenges that teachers face in the 21st century.

- Identify rewards that come to those who teach.

CHAPTER 16

Is Teaching for You? Expectations for the Future

A bird's eye view of what to expect in this chapter

At this time you may have mixed feelings about becoming a teacher. In this final chapter we attempt to answer any lingering questions or address any doubts you may still have. To do this, we highlight future trends and issues that may affect you if you choose to become a teacher. Admittedly, we have covered many of these points already, but by repeating ourselves we bring closure to this topic. Also as promised, we offer suggestions to those of you who decide that teaching is not a good match.

As you weighed the pros and cons of a career in teaching, you were asked to keep your personal values and background in sight. As we have learned, self-knowledge is critical to making a wise decision. We ask you again: What do you seek in a career? What kind of career would make you happy? What experiences have you already had that lead you to believe that you may be suited for teaching? What experiences in your background "fight against" your choosing a teaching career? The decision to teach, as you know, is one that no one else can make for you (although you can certainly be influenced by others).

Deciding to teach is like deciding to get on a thrilling new ride at the amusement park. The ride is unpredictable yet exhilarating. Those who choose teaching must commit to a lifelong pursuit of excellence in both living and in learning. As models of the human experience, teachers accompany students on this breathtaking ride as they prepare together for the future. In this chapter, we ask if you are willing and able to get on board.

A s we begin this chapter, consider the following case study.

....

D avid, a fourth-grade teacher, is in the middle of his second year of teaching. Having survived the first year of teaching, David thought the next year would be smooth sailing. Now he is very discouraged and constantly questions his effectiveness. Sometimes he wonders why he ever entered the teaching field.

Several of David's colleagues talk about enrolling in a master's degree program at the local university. The thought of returning to school does not excite David. He is already keeping long hours at Central Elementary School. The needs of his students are greater and more diverse than anticipated. The demands of parents and administrators press upon him constantly. Reading about educational issues is the last thing he wants to do!

David has lost touch with his mentor from last year. He also rarely interacts with other teachers except during faculty meetings. Mary Beth, another fourth-grade teacher, recently attended a workshop on the new math curriculum initiative. David has many questions but is hesitant to ask Mary Beth for help because he is afraid of appearing incompetent. Finding himself preoccupied with his upcoming evaluation, David stays in his own classroom even more than usual. David wonders what his life will be like over the next 35 years.

Should David leave teaching before it is too late to start over in another career? Or should he wait a few years to see if his attitude changes? What could David do to revive his enthusiasm for teaching? What advice would you offer him?

Adopting a Career Perspective

Now that you have extended your knowledge and understanding of the teaching field by reading this text, perhaps you are ready to commit to a career in education. Undertaking a teaching career requires a strong personal commitment. When teachers lack commitment to their work, they are more likely to leave the profession (or never enter it) and they are less likely to be effective in the classroom. As described in the case study, David seems to lack commitment to his work as a teacher. We believe that having a career perspective will aid you in developing a sense of commitment.

Life Cycle of the Career Teacher

It may be difficult at this point in your exploration of teaching to focus on the big picture—that is, to have a career perspective. One useful model is Steffy and Wolfe's (1997) life cycle of the career teacher. This model can help you see where you fall at this point and where you are headed. Specifically, Steffy and Wolfe propose six phases over the lifetime of a teacher: *novice, apprentice, professional, expert, distinguished,* and *retiree/emeritus.*

Novice

Most likely, you are at the novice phase (or will be shortly). This phase begins when you engage in field experiences (or school-based practica) that are intended to shape your development as a teacher. As you become aware of the realities of today's classrooms, it is only natural that you might feel unsure of your ability to handle all the demands placed on teachers. As a novice, you are just beginning to learn what it means to teach. And if you become a teacher, this learning does not stop; you will continually be learning about what it means to be a teacher.

Apprentice

The second phase of the career life cycle is that of apprentice. Most preservice teachers become apprentices during their student teaching experience. Self-confidence increases as newly acquired skills are put into practice. Apprentice teachers are noted for their enthusiasm and energy. The apprentice phase often will extend into your second or third year of classroom teaching.

Because about one third of all newly hired teachers leave the field within the first few years (National Commission on Teaching and America's Future, 1996), it is important to be prepared to avoid such a fate during your apprenticeship phase. Many schools have a **mentorship program,** in which beginning teachers are guided by mentor teachers. Should you secure a teaching position at a school that does not have a formal mentor program, be sure to seek out an experienced teacher whose positive attitude and classroom success you would like to emulate. This teacher can become your "unofficial" mentor. Having a mentor during the first few years of teaching can help you through the "rough" spots as you learn to stand on your own feet. David, as described in the case study, is still an apprentice, or a teacher-in-training; however, he has cut himself off from sources of support (which is not prudent).

mentorship program

A program in which a novice is assigned to an experienced teacher who serves as a model and counselor.

Professional

The professional phase of the teacher's life cycle comes with even more increased self-confidence as focusing on student learning becomes paramount. Interactions with students and other teachers bring the greatest joy to professional teachers. They value professional growth and use a variety of professional development opportunities to help them grow. Having met state licensure requirements, teachers in the professional phase are competent and dependable; they form the "backbone" of the teaching profession (Steffy & Wolfe, 1997).

Expert

The expert teacher has met the expectations set forth by the National Board for Professional Teaching Standards (even though he or she may not have officially sought such certification). The expert teacher has a reputation as a master teacher. Holding leadership positions in professional associations, expert teachers seek the newest ideas in the profession and model continuous learning for their students. Described as competent, caring, and qualified, this level of teacher is what every student deserves, as declared in the report *What Matters Most: Teaching for America's Future* (National Commission on Teaching and America's Future, 1996).

Distinguished

Distinguished teachers are few in number. They exceed current expectations for what excellent teachers should exhibit. The *National State Teachers of the*

The professional phase of the teacher's life cycle is characterized by increased self-confidence and commitment to student learning. Teachers in the professional phase are competent and dependable.

© Peter Turnley/CORBIS

Year (NSTOY) are considered distinguished teachers. Such teachers serve as spokespersons for the profession and often are able to influence policy decisions that affect classrooms.

Retiree/Emeritus

Teachers who are retirees have made important contributions to education and can continue to be a resource to their communities. Some may even earn the status of *emeritus teachers* by continuing to remain active in the field. These teachers serve as mentors, as volunteers, and sometimes as lobbyists. Finding ways to connect with schools and students characterizes the work of emeritus teachers.

Learning to Teach Is a Developmental Process

Understanding the existence of these six phases may help you feel less overwhelmed as you look at teaching from your current vantage point. Learning to teach is a developmental process. Thus you are not expected at this time to be an expert or even a professional teacher. Having a career perspective should help you realize that becoming a teacher is a journey—not a destination. You can and should pack your suitcase and make travel plans, but remember that the process of "getting there" is just as meaningful as "having arrived." Along the way the pursuit of excellence (through reflection and renewal) should guide your efforts. When you devote time to thinking about your teaching and you engage in activities that help you to renew yourself, you will find that greater energy and enthusiasm result.

Retired teachers often derive great satisfaction from remaining active in the field.

© Layne Kennedy/CORBIS

Demographics and Knowledge About the Job Market

Selecting teaching as a career requires sound knowledge of the field. This section contains important information to consider before deciding whether a teaching career is for you. As you contemplate a future in teaching, you should be aware of several demographic characteristics of the teaching force and examine the implications of each.

Age

How old will you be when you start teaching? The average age of teachers is 43 years old (National Center for Education Statistics, 1997). This average age has risen in recent years, an indication that the teaching force is aging. Therefore many retirements are anticipated within the next decade. U.S. Department of Education Secretary, Richard Riley, predicts that 2.2 million new teachers will be needed in the next 10 years (Henry, 1999).

Gender

Approximately 75% of teachers are female. Certain fields have a greater proportion of female teachers than others (e.g., kindergarten vs. secondary level). According to your gender, will you be in the majority or minority in the teaching field? If you are male, will this proportion present a problem for you? Would you mind being the only male teacher in an elementary school? (Note: Children need male role models in the early years, as well as the later years.)

Racial and Ethnic Composition

The racial and ethnic composition of the teaching force during the 1993 to 1994 school term was predominantly white, non-Hispanic (National Center for Education Statistics, 1997). Of concern to many educators is the disparity between the proportion of minority students compared with minority teachers. Whereas approximately 12% of students are Hispanic, only 4% of teachers are Hispanic; whereas 16% of students are African American, only 9% of teachers are African American (National Center for Education Statistics, 1997, p. 10).

Salary

How much can you expect to earn as a teacher? According to the National Center for Education Statistics (1998), the average annual salary of all public school teachers is $38,921.00. Beginning teachers receive an average salary of $25,462.00. With more years of experience and higher levels of education, teachers move up the salary schedule. In some schools, teachers can receive additional pay for extracurricular activities and coaching. This is particularly true at the secondary level.

Furthermore, teacher salaries vary according to different areas of the nation. For example, teachers in rural areas and small towns are paid an average annual salary of $33,829.00 and teachers in central cities average $37,837.00. The highest average salaries are paid to teachers in urban fringe areas or large cities ($42,060.00). In which geographic region are you interested in seeking work?

Job Market

The job market for teachers varies according to geographic area and subject area. Even though almost half of all public schools are located in rural or small town communities (National Center for Education Statistics, 1997), those areas with growing population need more teachers than areas that are declining in population. In some parts of the country, rural areas are increasing in population as urban areas are decreasing. You will need to investigate trends in population shifts in the particular area of the country where you wish to teach.

The teaching fields of science, mathematics, foreign languages, special education, and bilingual education have the most favorable outlook (Darling-Hammond & Cobb, 1996). A school district's educational goals will often determine the subjects being emphasized and thus the teaching positions needing to be filled. For example, a rural school may stress vocational training more than a suburban school. Additionally, large urban schools often emphasize courses in the arts (i.e., dance, music, and art) and thus hire more teachers in these subject areas.

The supply of and demand for teachers are influenced by several factors. Darling-Hammond and Cobb (1996, pp. 21–22) identified the following three factors to explain recent increased demand for teachers: (1) increasing birth rates and immigration, (2) declining pupil to teacher ratios, and (3) increasing turnover of teachers, primarily because of retirement. As Darling-Hammond and Cobb (1996) note, teaching shortages are never absolute but rather are always tied to certain locales and subject areas. Supply and demand also depend on which level you intend to teach. According to the Bureau of Labor Statistics (1999), more secondary school teachers will be needed through the year 2006 than elementary teachers. Does this kind of information influence your decision about which level to teach?

Guidance for Novice Teachers

In view of the preceding information, we are offering some practical advice for those of you who decide to go forward with the idea of becoming a teacher.

Stay Abreast of Trends in the Marketplace

Web Site
You may want to visit the
Manpower, Inc. web site at
www.manpower.com.

There will always be a need for teachers. Predictions for the early part of the 21st century are optimistic. Each quarter Manpower, Inc. conducts an employment outlook survey. Recent survey results revealed that 17% of schools intend to add more staff and only 3% plan to decrease the number of workers. Attending a job fair is an excellent way to conduct your own research. Typically sponsored by the career planning office at a university, these events give you a feel for the area job market and experience in interacting with personnel directors.

Keep Options Open

Too many beginning teachers limit themselves geographically and are unable to locate a job opening. If at all possible, be careful not to lock yourself in geographically, because sometimes relocation is necessary to secure a teaching position. For example, urban areas in Texas recruit heavily for teachers from other states. Another way to keep your options open is to seek as many areas of licensure as you can reasonably manage. The more areas in which you are certified to teach, the greater your chances of landing a teaching position will be.

Expand Contacts with Young People

Seek as many opportunities as you can to interact with children of all ages. After you decide which age-group you feel more comfortable with, seek more opportunities to work with this age-group. Unquestionably, this will enrich your preparation for teaching success. Opportunities include the following: substitute teach whenever you have a break from school, work in a day care center, become a camp counselor, or take a summer job that involves working with kids. In non-school settings (e.g., malls, skating rinks, parks) observe closely the behavior of kids. Watch how they act, look at what they wear, and listen to what they say. These observations will extend your understanding of the students you will eventually teach. Such informal observations can also help you decide whether you really want to teach a particular level of students.

Develop as a Person

The more well-rounded you are as an individual, the greater the variety of resources you will bring to teaching. Develop hobbies, travel, read, play sports; there is no limit to activities that cause us to grow. These experiences will enrich your teaching by increasing your ability to make many connections with and for your students.

Become involved in campus organizations (or community-based groups). Such involvement helps to develop your leadership skills. Your communication and collaborative skills are built through such organizations. Teachers are not only leaders in their classrooms, but also are expected to provide school-level leadership in curriculum and instruction.

You should also become a student member of relevant professional associations. Usually there is a discount rate for student memberships in such organizations as the National Science Teachers Association, the National Council for Social Studies, and the Council for Exceptional Children. By joining your professional association, you will have opportunities to attend conferences and you will receive professional literature to help you stay current in your field.

Web Site
Visit teacher-related web sites such as Kappa Delta Pi's Teacher's Lounge at www.kdp.org.

Whether you join a professional organization or not, you should seek ways to become a "student" of teaching. Read educational journals regularly (e.g., *Phi Delta Kappan* and *Teacher Magazine*). Interact with teachers

> ❝ **NOTABLE QUOTE**
>
> One of the beauties of teaching is that there is no limit to one's growth as a teacher, just as there is no knowing beforehand how much your students can learn. *(Herbert Kohl)* ❞

and listen carefully to what they say. Ask questions to find out more about the teaching profession and stay abreast of educational issues.

Create a Portfolio

As the field of teacher education becomes more performance-based (i.e., it focuses on what teachers can do rather than just what they know), it is important to document teaching-related skills that you possess. A portfolio is a collection of work that reflects your abilities in a certain area. "Reflection Questions" can be used as potential entries for your teaching portfolio.

Most states require you to take a test in order to obtain a license. Keeping a portfolio should help you prepare for the new version of the National Teacher Examination, called *PRAXIS*, which was developed by Educational Testing Services (ETS). The PRAXIS Series is more performance-based than other earlier teacher assessments. It is a series of examinations constructed by ETS and administered at different times to measure beginning teachers' performance.

Web Site
For additional information on PRAXIS, visit the Educational Testing Services web site at www.ets.org.

The value of a portfolio rests in its capability to present a more complete picture of your strengths. As you continue in your teacher preparation program, you will want to include in your portfolio lesson plans you develop, photographs of group learning activities you direct, videotapes of lessons you teach, and samples of student work.

As part of your portfolio, maintain a journal in which you examine your beliefs about learning and teaching. Record your reflections on experiences you have. Ask yourself hard questions—those that require analytical and evaluative thinking. Be critical as you think about the meaning of each experience and how you might use a particular experience to enhance your own teaching.

Include in your portfolio a copy of your resume. Keep this updated as you undertake new part-time jobs and experiences. Separate from your portfolio but equally valuable are the files of materials you should begin to collect. Clipped articles, sample lesson plans, and lists of resources are all helpful materials that should be organized in files that you can easily access. These materials will prove invaluable during the apprentice phase of your career.

Anticipate Interview Questions and Prepare for Success

It may seem entirely too early to think about interviewing for a position as a teacher. However, anticipating interview questions can not only improve your present practice but also increase your confidence to handle a future interview well. As you take additional coursework and complete field experience assignments, ask yourself what a principal or fellow teachers might want to know in order to judge your suitability for their school.

Most interviews offer an opportunity for you to share your personal philosophy of education. You should begin developing a statement of your philosophy. At each step along the way toward becoming a teacher, you should be able to articulate your beliefs about teaching and learning. As you grow and develop as a teacher, your philosophy will continue to evolve.

Contemporary teachers need to hold positive attitudes about computer technology and model these attitudes to their students. They need to be comfortable with computers so they can integrate technology into the curriculum.

To help you formulate your thoughts about your future role as a teacher, you can jot ideas in your journal. It may also be useful to think about your answers to possible interview questions. You might try answering the following questions with a partner:

● How will you handle discipline problems in your classroom?

● How will you involve parents in your classroom?

● How will you teach to meet all students' needs?

● What strengths will you bring to the classroom and to our school?

● Why do you want to teach?

Affiliate with a Professional Development School

professional development schools (PDS)

Education programs that form partnerships with area public schools to better prepare teachers for the classroom.

As mentioned earlier in the text, many schools of education are forming partnerships with area public schools to better prepare teachers to link theory with practice. Similar to "teaching hospitals" in the medical field, these **professional development schools (PDS)** are designed to make teacher preparation more meaningful. Being involved with a PDS can help strengthen your teaching knowledge and skills, as well as help you network with other professionals. This network can keep you informed of upcoming openings and opportunities in teaching. As is true in many professions, teaching positions are often filled before they are formally posted or advertised.

Develop Technological Skills

Computers will continue to have a significant impact on how students learn and the ways teachers teach. Technology is a powerful teaching and learning tool. You should update your technological skills through hands-on workshops and self-directed learning. In your field experiences look for ways to integrate technology with your teaching. Collect a list of interesting web sites related to your field. Become familiar with educational software suitable for your teaching area.

Ask Questions

Throughout this text we have encouraged you to ask questions of a personal nature. Inquiry is a cognitive tool that leads to discovery. Additionally, you have seen how important it is to ask the right questions. In fact, the type of questions we ask of ourselves and our students is critical to arriving at the solution. In the same vein, Laurence Boldt suggests that sometimes individuals ask the "wrong questions" when selecting their life's work. According to Boldt (1996), in his book *How to Find the Work You Love*, the following are examples of the wrong questions to ask while making a career decision about teaching:

- What do my parents want me to do?
- What will be most in demand?
- How can I achieve power, status, and prestige?

In contrast, Boldt (1996) suggests the "right questions" to pose might be as follows:

- What was I "born to do"?
- What would be my greatest contribution to others?
- What would I really love to do?
- What is the best use of my life?

Reflections from the Field

Pamela Allen, a first-year teacher (four months into the new school year) gave this account. "I was very discouraged when I discovered upon graduation that finding a job in my hometown was going to take a while. I had to take a job in a related area, but it was not what I had been prepared to do, nor was it what I wanted. Of course, if I had been willing to move to an urban area, I easily could have found a teaching job (and with a better salary). My husband and I discussed moving to Texas, where there were many job openings for new teachers. In fact, I had been offered a job in an inner-city school in Memphis, but before accepting the position, I found out I was pregnant. This changed everything; the thought of moving away from family at a time when family support was needed took precedence over securing a teaching job. We decided to stay in the rural community where we were raised, and I would wait it out for a teaching position. Eventually a job did come up. It was hard to have to wait a couple of years for it, but the wait was worth it; I love my job! One really never knows how things will turn out. There are many factors to consider when deciding where to live and work."

Qualities to Develop

We have described many qualities and skills to develop that will enhance your effectiveness. Begin striving now to cultivate and refine some of those attributes.

For starters, we recommend that you read Martin Haberman's (1995) book, entitled *Star Teachers of Children in Poverty*. Based on over 1,000 interviews with teachers who succeed with "at-risk" urban students, Haberman describes attitudes and attributes of star teachers. As you anticipate entering the teaching profession, you can work on sharpening some specific qualities now that will serve your students well in the future. Let's examine three of those characteristics.

Persistence

Persistence characterizes "star teachers." Haberman (1995) found that teachers who are persistent never give up on a student and always ask themselves, "What do I do now?" To develop such persistence, it is vital that you see teaching as a problematic practice. Problems pervade a teacher's daily life but should be seen as challenges to be overcome. As you face problems now, you can develop greater persistence by searching for solutions and looking for better ways to do things. During your field observations you can think about alternative ways to reach students and you can ask teachers to talk about how they have solved classroom challenges. In teaching you will find that persistence pays.

Reflections from the Field

Robert Ash, a graduate student in the counseling psychology program at the University of Wisconsin, Madison, offered this touching story about his recollection of a teacher from his past that changed his academic career. "I'll never forget Ms. Peterson, my second-grade teacher. I was a real terror, but she never gave up on me. I'd push her to the limit. For example, I can still remember screaming at her in the coat closet; she would just deal with my temper outbursts. When I was initiated into the Honor Society in Senior High, I invited her as my guest. And she came! Who could forget this woman who never gave up on me."

Organizational Ability: Time Management Skills

"Star teachers" possess keen organizational ability. They manage time well. Their planning focuses more on what students will be doing and less on what the teacher does (Haberman, 1995). Teachers with good organizational

> ## " NOTABLE QUOTE
>
> You must have a love for teaching and a love for kids—someone has to love these kids. Your students may need basic skills such as math and reading, but they also need nurturing. If your goal is to make a difference in the lives of children, then education is the field to go into. But if you are only thinking about holidays, vacations, and summers off, these are not good enough reasons to become a teacher. *(Pamela Allen, a first-year teacher)* "

ability are able to coordinate several activities at the same time. You can begin now to seek and create situations that will hone your organizational skills. These opportunities can arise outside the school setting. For example, planning a successful party requires the use of organizational skills.

Emotional and Physical Stamina

Finally, emotional and physical stamina are necessities to respond to the demands of teaching. You should not underestimate how emotionally and physically draining an occupation teaching is. Because of their high energy level and enthusiasm, "star teachers" are able to rebound from the disappointments they experience and to handle the stress. Interacting with kids builds up these teachers instead of wearing them down (Haberman, 1995). You can build your stamina now by keeping fit emotionally and physically. You should find healthy outlets for stress, such as exercise or hobbies. One way you can augment your enthusiasm is to become involved in learning something new.

What if You Decide Teaching Is Not for You?

Perhaps you have decided that teaching is not the career choice for you. It is important to realize that this decision is perfectly acceptable. You would rather know now than later—after you have devoted a great deal of time, energy, and money in a vocation that does not match your needs, interests, and strengths. So, now what? We suggest you take the following three positive steps.

Seek Career Counseling

Your college or university campus has a career planning office (or at least a counseling center) that can offer helpful guidance on other possible careers. Most counseling centers have available career inventory tests that you can take. These inventories can give you direction on different careers to explore. There are also written materials you can examine to help gather ideas about other possibilities. Investigate careers that perhaps have always appealed to you. For example, you may have always wanted to be a lawyer, but you know very little about what they do and what preparation is necessary. Make a point of learning more about any careers that may interest you.

Reflect on Personal Strengths

Make a list of your strengths. Consider ways you could put these strengths to work. By focusing on your strengths, you are able to look at alternative avenues in which to use them. You might also think about fields that are closely related to teaching, such as sales, public relations, library work, or social work. Furthermore, if you were most attracted to teaching because of a love for a particular subject area, seek information on careers in that field. For example, if you have a passion for English, you should know that the field of publishing is one that is especially accessible to English majors.

Solicit Feedback and Input from Others

In addition to career counselors, you can also seek advice from those who know you best. For example, a college professor might be able to offer insight on areas for which you might best be suited. Likewise, a good friend or adult mentor might offer direction. Talking with someone may not give you the answers, but it usually results in greater self-insight, which is critical in career decision making. Being able to talk with someone who will listen to your concerns is helpful because sometimes talking aloud about an issue can help crystallize what you are actually thinking (it sharpens your lenses so you can see the whole picture better).

We assure you, there is no reason to be concerned if you decide a career in teaching is not for you. Knowing what career to pursue also includes knowing what careers *not* to pursue.

REFLECTION QUESTIONS

Some questions to ask yourself as you identify the direction you wish to take are as follows:

....

What aspect of teaching originally appealed to me?

....

What aspects of teaching continue to attract me?

....

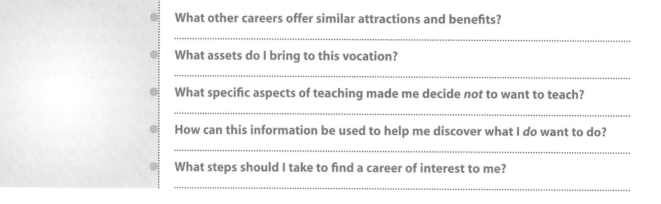

What other careers offer similar attractions and benefits?

....

What assets do I bring to this vocation?

....

What specific aspects of teaching made me decide *not* to want to teach?

....

How can this information be used to help me discover what I *do* want to do?

....

What steps should I take to find a career of interest to me?

....

Make a plan of action right now. To procrastinate in your search will only lead to frustration and disappointment.

Challenges Ahead

Teachers in the 21st century will face multiple and complex challenges. As you have seen, numerous unresolved questions remain regarding education. The following issues are stated in question form to highlight that the search for answers to these critical yet complicated issues is ongoing.

- How do we ensure that all children receive a quality education?
- How do we engage students in the process of learning?
- How do we correct for inequities in school funding?
- How do we ensure that students become technologically competent?
- How do we ensure that students see themselves in the faces of their teachers?
- How do we handle issues of a religious nature in public schools?
- How do we treat students individually yet fairly?
- How do we ensure that minority groups and others who historically have been denied full participation in education be granted that now?
- How do we best serve bilingual students?
- What services should we provide for children who are gifted and talented?
- How do we help children to overcome the problems they face in society, such as homelessness, poverty, racism, discrimination, crime, and other insidious conditions that rob them of success?
- How do we correct for unfavorable stereotypes that damage students' perceptions of themselves?
- How do we teach students to respect themselves and others?

- How do we develop the curriculum to teach values and reflect morals?
- How do we solidify ties with the community?
- How do we forge partnerships with parents and increase parental involvement in education?
- What role should the federal government play in education?
- How much choice should parents be given in the selection of schools for their children?
- How much voice should teachers be given regarding school-based management?
- Should the curriculum reflect a multicultural emphasis, or should it focus primarily on transmitting the dominant culture?
- Are local schools and teachers accountable to parents and the community for test scores and achievement levels of students?
- Should parents have a stronger voice and role in the governance of local schools?
- Will charter schools be a solution or a detriment to public education?
- Will students who are home schooled receive education comparable to that of their peers?
- What role should private enterprise have in education?
- To what extent should computer technology be integrated into the curriculum and instruction?
- How do students learn best?
- How do we tap into students' unique learning styles to enhance learning?
- How can we motivate students to accept the principle of lifelong learning?
- How do we get teachers to become reflective decision-makers and lifelong learners?
- What steps should we take to improve the image of teaching, and to solidify our image as a profession?

This list is far from complete; however, it is a reminder of how much material you have covered and also that we must continue to search for solutions.

Rewards Ahead

Many challenges await you if you become a teacher, but there are ample rewards as well. The title of this book, *Introduction to Teaching: Rewards and Realities,* was selected to portray that idea. Because teaching continues to nourish our souls and gratify our intellect, we were pleased and honored to tell you this story. Almost without exception the teachers we interviewed for this book were positive in what they had to say about this profession. We hope that you are not deterred by the challenges that you might face as a teacher, but instead are inspired to tackle these obstacles and overcome them.

Reflections from the Field

To end this story about what it's like to teach in today's schools and classrooms, we would like to share a few succinct yet powerful comments made by teachers in the field. We believe these comments aptly capture the heart and soul of why teachers choose teaching and stay.

Corey Oliver, eighth-grade English teacher: "The teaching profession has many meaningful rewards. Although many professions offer an abundance of extrinsic motivations (with few or no intrinsic motivations), teaching offers many intrinsic motivations and rewards."

Lisa Oates, sixth-grade special education teacher: "I love having a relationship with students. I like seeing the positive changes I can make when my students are experiencing academic and/or personal problems."

Dionne Latin, seventh-grade English teacher: "The reward in teaching is knowing that I have played some part in a student's life...teaching him or her what he or she will need to know in order to succeed and be a productive citizen."

Anita Cegers-Coleman, keyboarding and math teacher: "One reward in teaching is making a student aware that he or she is worthwhile that he or she can actually do something, like a math problem or achieve certain goals."

Frank Baker, Horace Mann Magnet Middle School, 19 years teaching experience: "The intangible rewards are probably more gratifying than the tangible benefits. It's extremely rewarding to make a conscious choice to give my best to my students each day. It's a tremendous opportunity for me to shape and sculpt the minds of the future without robbing them of their individuality."

Eric Jensen (1995), in his book *Super Teaching* states, "[Y]ou knew there was more to education than showing up and waiting for the last bell. Teaching is so much more than that. It is discovery, sharing, growing, excitement, and love. It's not a burden, it's a joy. And it's like a consuming, fulfilling bonfire that provides you with a glow of warmth and a blaze of passion. . ." (p. 342). After reading Jensen's heartfelt words, all we have to say is: "Well said" and "How true."

Leadership Is Needed

Clearly, schools in the new millennium are in the midst of reform, which means that changes could bring about positive transformations to our present educational system. A consensus among political factions and interest

> ## NOTABLE QUOTE
>
> The educator should be the *leading* learner. *(Thomas Groome)*

groups about the best way to proceed is not imminent; therefore education cries out for good leadership. To improve our schools and, in turn, the education of our youth, we need people with vision and insight, as well as concrete plans that work. We need individuals who will give more than lip service to the idea that children are important and that quality education is needed for all children. Will you join us to make that happen?

Hopefully, by now your interest in educational reform has been awakened (or reawakened) and you are eager to learn more about this field. If you are a person with good ideas about how to improve education, your services are required. If you are undeterred by criticism and discord and you possess a crusading spirit, education needs you.

AssessYourself

As you have seen by now, teaching as a career is certainly not for everyone. Teaching is for strategists who like to solve problems. Teaching is for those who are strong (mentally and physically) and who invite challenges.

Some individuals may want to be teachers but realize they do not have the temperament, qualities, or skills for effective teaching. Some have the disposition and attributes but lack the desire, which is a critical component to teaching.

Truly, teaching requires a unique person. Are you that special person?

REFLECTION QUESTIONS

- Make a prediction with regard to educational change for the next 30 years.

....

- In what ways do you see yourself playing a role in educational reform?

....

- What attributes do you believe will enhance your success as a teacher?

....

Is teaching for you? Do you see yourself as a teacher?

© David Young Wolff/PhotoEdit

Conclusion

In this textbook we underscore two basic themes: (1) teaching is fraught with challenge and (2) teaching is highly rewarding both professionally and personally. In this chapter we note the importance of keeping a "career perspective" in mind as you proceed along this path. By setting long-range goals and focusing on the future, you will be able to see the big picture and not get bogged down with day-to-day concerns. Simply put, to succeed in teaching, teachers combine knowledge of subject matter with passion for learning and compassion for students.

We believe that education can play a vital role in bringing justice to all Americans. Pessimism and apathy are enemies that should be resisted. Fortunately, negativism can be overcome by positive leadership and strong determination. It behooves us as parents and citizens to correctly identify those individuals who have the potential and willingness to take on leadership roles in our schools. We need teachers who will participate in any effort, that is, school-based or community-based efforts to improve the lives of students. We hope this inside glimpse of teaching in today's classrooms and schools inspires and motivates you to seriously consider the intriguing possibilities that await those who choose to teach.

What appears most encouraging is that America is abundantly rich in natural (and human) resources, which means our nation has the potential to achieve whatever it deems important. Borrowing from Abraham Maslow's theory, our nation has not reached its full potential; in the area of education, we are not yet self-actualized. The bottom line is that when our country realizes that our children are the most important asset we have, the educational system will reflect that commitment and the idea that all children deserve quality education will become a reality.

As we conclude this textbook, we hope that your interest and curiosity in American education has been piqued. And perhaps you might consider becoming part of our history by committing to teach the next generation of learners. Allow us to ask you one last question: Are *you* willing and able to join us in the collaborative effort to improve the education of our young people in the 21st century?

KEY TERMS

mentorship program

professional development schools (PDS)

SUGGESTED READING

Boldt, L. G. (1996). *How to find the work you love.* New York: Arkana.

Glennon, L., & Mohler, M. (1999). *Those who can—teach! Celebrating teachers who make a difference.* Berkeley, CA: Wildcat Canyon Press.

Jensen, E. (1995) *Super teaching.* Del Mar, CA: Turning Point Publishers.

REFERENCES

Boldt, L. G. (1996). *How to find the work you love.* New York: Arkana.

Bureau of Labor Statistics. (1999). *Occupational outlook handbook, 1998-99.* Washington, D.C.: U.S. Department of Labor.

Darling-Hammond, L., & Cobb, V. (1996). The changing context of teacher education. In Murray, F. B. (Ed.). *The teacher educator's handbook* (pp. 14–62). San Francisco: Jossey Bass.

Haberman, M. (1995). *Star teachers of children in poverty.* West Lafayette, IN: Kappa Delta Pi.

Henry, T. (February 16, 1999). "License all teachers," Riley says. *USA Today.*

Jensen, E. (1995). *Super teaching.* Del Mar, CA: Turning Point Publishers.

National Center for Education Statistics. (1998). *The condition of education 1998.* Washington, D.C.: U.S. Department of Education.

National Center for Education Statistics. (1997). *America's teachers: Profile of a profession, 1993-94.* Washington, D.C.: U.S. Department of Education.

National Commission on Teaching and America's Future. (1996). *What matters most: Teaching for America's future.* New York: Rockefeller Foundation.

Steffy, B. E., & Wolfe, M. P. (1997). *The life cycle of the career teacher: Maintaining excellence for a lifetime.* West Lafayette, IN: Kappa Delta Pi.

ability grouping An instructional practice of grouping students by ability based on some type of assessment. Separating students by ability can have adverse effects, particularly for students in the lower-achieving groups. Also known as *tracking*.

academic learning time (ALT) The amount of time students are engaged in learning and achieving a high rate of success.

academy A school that provides an education beyond elementary grades. The curriculum includes an academic track for students preparing for college and a vocational track for those preparing for work. The first academy was established by Benjamin Franklin in 1751 and is considered a forerunner of today's secondary schools.

accountability A growing trend in education that suggests schools and teachers should be held accountable for student performance.

accreditation An external review process that organizations and programs (e.g., schools and colleges) undergo to ensure adherence to certain standards.

active learning An approach to learning in which the individual is actively involved in finding personal meaning in the material being studied.

active listening The ability to separate emotional content from intellectual content by focusing on the core message another person is trying to convey.

aesthetics A branch of axiology concerned with developing an appreciation for beauty and art.

affective attributes Traits such as attitudes, feelings, values, and emotions, which cannot be measured quantitatively.

alternative school A public or private school that offers a range of options for parents wanting a more individualized or specialized approach to instruction for their children (compared to regular schools).

American Federation of Teachers (AFT) A professional organization for teachers founded in 1916; its primary focus is to improve teachers' working conditions and salaries. Affiliated with the American Federation of Labor and Congress of Industrial Organizations (AFL-CIO), the AFT plays a major role in bargaining for better working conditions for teachers.

Americans with Disabilities Act (ADA) Federal legislation passed by the U.S. Congress in 1990 to ensure that all citizens with disabilities are treated fairly. This act protects children with disabilities in both public and private schools.

applied behavior analysis (ABA) The application of behavioral concepts and techniques to shape and modify student behavior, such as positive and negative reinforcement. A more traditional term for ABA is *behavior modification*.

assertive discipline A structured, teacher-centered approach to classroom management developed by Lee Canter that applies basic principles of operant conditioning.

at-risk students Students who are at a greater likelihood for failure academically, vocationally, and personally due to adverse circumstances and backgrounds.

attending The ability to give one's full attention, physically and psychologically, to another person.

authentic assessment A recent trend in education, often referred to as *performance assessment*, that asks students to show evidence of learning by engaging in higher-order thinking such as analysis, integration, and self-reflection. Students solve problems that closely resemble real problems, with emphasis on what students can do.

authoritarian parents Parents who exercise absolute control over their children, have unreasonably high expectations, and may be unresponsive and lack warmth toward their children.

authoritative parents Parents who are confident and secure; they set challenging (albeit reasonable) goals for their children. They set limits and enforce rules in addition to providing explanations for the rules; they are warm and responsive to their children.

axiology   A field of study that presents philosophical questions on what is of value. There are two branches: ethics (morality and conduct) and aesthetics (beauty and art).

back-to-basics movement   An educational reform movement precipitated by the 1983 publication of a report by the National Commission on Excellence in Education called *A Nation at Risk: The Imperative for Educational Reform.*

behaviorism   A psychological theory and perspective that focuses on the behavior of a person rather than conscious experience. Behaviorism has directly influenced educational philosophy by providing a better understanding of human behavior and behavior management.

behavior modification   *See applied behavior analysis (ABA).*

bilingual education   An educational policy that allows non–English-speaking students the opportunity to receive instruction in their native language while they learn English.

Bilingual Education Act   The 1968 law passed by the U.S. Congress that allocates funds to schools to establish "English as a Second Language" (ESL) programs to assist students whose native language is not English.

block grant   A type of federal funding to schools that has fewer federal restrictions than categorical aid, allowing schools more latitude in determining the best way to use the assistance.

Brown* v. *Board of Education of Topeka   A 1954 landmark U.S. Supreme Court decision that ruled "separate but equal" was unconstitutional. Schools were instructed by the court to desegregate at "deliberate speed."

Buckley Amendment   An abbreviated name for the Family Educational Rights and Privacy Act (FERPA) passed in 1974 by Congress, which protects the privacy of students' test scores and academic records. School personnel are not at liberty to discuss or release private information on a student without written consent of the parent or guardian; exceptions to this rule include individuals with a "legitimate educational interest" in students' records, such as classroom teachers.

burnout   A condition caused by high levels of stress on the job, usually accompanied by a feeling of mental and/or physical exhaustion.

career anchor   An aspect of work that one is unwilling to give up. It consists of values that draw one to a particular occupation or job. Anchors explain why people choose and stay in certain careers.

Carnegie unit   A credit earned by a high school student for having successfully completed a course. Units are accrued for graduation and admission into college.

categorical aid A type of federal funding available to schools that provides educational services and programs for certain "categories" of students with special needs, such as children from low-income families. Sometimes funds are earmarked for specific projects such as libraries or computer equipment.

central processing unit (CPU)   Computer hardware that runs programs and processes data.

certification   The process of meeting requirements for teaching in each state. Many states are moving toward licensure that will be performance based rather than course driven.

character education   A movement that encourages schools to teach good character traits and values such as respect, cooperation, and responsibility.

charter school   Public schools that place the authority for governance with parents and teachers. A petition is filed by the organizers with a local governing body or state legislature and a contract is agreed upon. Even though charter schools are free from many state regulations, they are still accountable for student achievement.

chief state school officer   The executive administrator of a state board of education (sometimes called the director of the state department of education, state superintendent, or state commissioner of education), who is responsible for implementing the policies of the state board of education and providing guidance to school districts.

clarity   The quality of a message communicated to others in a clear manner.

classical conditioning   A theory of learning developed by Ivan Pavlov. It demonstrates that over time the repeated pairing of one stimulus, known to elicit a specific response, and a second stimulus, which does not normally generate this response, can eventually cause the second stimulus to produce the response in the absence of the first. In education, this theory can help to explain how some emotional responses to persons, things, or events may stem from past associations or experiences.

classroom management   Teacher decisions and actions intended to create an environment conducive to learning.

client-centered counseling   A nondirective therapeutic approach to counseling made popular by Carl Rogers that focuses on the needs of the client. In the 1990s client-centered therapy was renamed *person-centered therapy.*

code of ethics   A set of principles developed by a professional organization that represents guidelines for appropriate behavior of its members.

cognitivism   A theory of learning that attempts to explain human learning by studying internal processes of the mind. The goal is to find ways to help students process information efficiently and effectively to improve reasoning abilities.

common school movement   A network of elementary schools that exposed students to a "common" culture and curriculum. In the 1820s, Horace Mann fought for common schools in which every child would be entitled to a grade-school education at public expense.

community of learners   The concept of teachers and students working together to learn. All students' contributions are respectfully taken into account by the teacher, which facilitates a positive learning environment.

compensatory education   Federal programs that attempt to help schoolchildren overcome social and economic barriers such as poverty, neglect, and other forms of deprivation.. Project Head Start, Title I, and school-to-work programs are examples of compensatory education programs.

computer-assisted instruction (CAI)   A type of programmed instruction, also referred to as *computer-based instruction (CBI)*. CAI refers to those computer programs that take detailed information and reduce it to manageable frames. Students' responses to the stimuli can be immediately reinforced.

constructivism   A philosophical approach to learning that grew out of cognitive psychology. An individual connects new learning to familiar experiences to gain personal insight.

cooperative discipline   An approach to discipline that has been called "hands-joined" because teacher and student have joint responsibility for improved behavior. Behavior is goal-directed, and thus students choose their behavior. This approach was developed by Linda Albert (1989), and is based on the work of Dreikurs, Grunwald, and Pepper (1982).

cooperative learning   A teaching method that provides peer interaction and promotes cooperation rather than competition among students.

core curriculum   A set of required courses that all students are expected take in school.

core knowledge   *See cultural literacy.*

critical thinking   A higher-order type of thinking in which one carefully evaluates the reliability and validity of sources before making decisions. Reflective teachers develop and refine their critical thinking abilities in order to teach and model analytical thinking to students.

cultural literacy   A term coined by E. D. Hirsch for the core body of knowledge that every person must know to be considered culturally literate. These standards can be identified and should be made an essential part of the curriculum.

culture   Patterns of behavior and customs that include knowledge, beliefs, values, art, and morals. Culture has also been defined as a group's efforts to adapt to life's circumstances, resulting from competition for resources.

curriculum   Learning experiences provided under a school's direction; usually the term refers to a written plan of what students will be taught.

curriculum frameworks   State guidelines for developing curriculum in specific subject areas.

dame school   In colonial America, a co-educational school run by a woman in her home; a rudimentary education was provided for a small fee.

deductive reasoning   A type of reasoning that draws inferences from the general to the specific..

direct instruction   A systematic approach to learning basic skills and knowledge; the teacher organizes and presents the content or skill in a step-by-step (sequential) manner.

discovery learning   A term coined by Jerome Bruner, based on Piaget's work, for instruction delivered in such a way that students are able to make connections and find meaning for themselves. *Constructivism* is a current name used to describe this teaching approach.

disengaged students   A term taken from Lawrence Steinberg's research that describes students who are uninvolved in their schoolwork. These students perform minimally, exerting little effort or energy.

distance education   A new trend in technology that transcends distance by connecting specialists in one location to students in another location via two-way video equipment. Distance learning also includes the Internet and web-based instruction.

drill and practice   Computer software programs that provide repeated, reinforced instruction on a topic, such as practice in multiplication.

dual or multiple relationship   A relationship in which a person in authority plays two or more roles that conflict with one another. A teacher socializing with a student outside of school is an example of a dual relationship that could have adverse consequences.

due process A specified set of formal proceedings that protects the rights of individuals from arbitrary and unreasonable actions by individuals in positions of power. For example, before terminating a tenured teacher, a school board must give advance warning, allowing the teacher time to plan a proper defense for the hearing. Students also have due process rights in special education decisions and disciplinary actions.

eclecticism A method or system whereby an individual freely chooses from a variety of ideas or sources based on what he or she thinks is the best approach under the circumstances.

Education for All Handicapped Children Act A federal law (PL 94-142) passed in 1975, providing federal funding to schools to ensure all children receive a "free and appropriate education." It was amended in 1990 by the Individuals with Disabilities Act (IDEA), which extended access to public education to all children with disabilities between the ages of 3 and 21.

educational malpractice A claim made in a court of law that a certain teacher or school district has failed to adequately teach academic skills. These kinds of liability suits are harder to prove than medical malpractice; cases that have been successful have involved special education students.

effective school A name given to a school which has achieved success for its students both academically (by meeting higher standards) and socially (by reducing truancy and school dropouts).

efficacy In education, the ability of teachers to have an effect on the lives of students.

electronic mail (e-mail) Text messages sent electronically over the Internet. In addition to providing an efficient means of correspondence with students, e-mail makes it possible for teachers to consult quickly with colleagues anywhere in the world.

Elementary and Secondary Education Act (ESEA) Legislation passed in 1965 for federal funding of education that is considered to be the most comprehensive to date. A sizable portion of the ESEA's budget is reserved for schools in low-income areas that are willing to provide compensatory programs to disadvantaged students.

emotional intelligence A type of intelligence, proposed by Peter Salovey and John D. Mayer in 1990, that includes self-awareness, impulse control, persistence, zeal, self-motivation, empathy, and social skills.

empathy The ability "to put yourself in another person's shoes" to more fully understand that person's feelings and his or her situation without becoming emotionally involved. Empathy is an essential quality for teachers to possess.

engaged students A term coined by Lawrence Steinberg that describes students who are psychologically connected to what is going on in their classes. In contrast, disengaged students are uninvolved in their schoolwork and exert minimal effort or energy.

English as a Second Language (ESL) An instructional method of teaching English to those who are not native speakers.

English grammar school A historical school intended to prepare young men who were not planning to attend college for adult civic roles. The curriculum emphasized applied courses rather than classical courses.

epistemology A field of study that raises philosophical questions about the nature and origin of truth and knowledge. There are primarily five sources of knowledge: empirical, revealed, authoritative, rational, and intuitive.

equalization grant A way that some states equalize school funding by requiring that wealthier districts return surplus revenue, which is then distributed to poorer districts.

essentialism An educational philosophy similar to perennialism (and also influenced by idealism and realism) that focuses on scholastic subjects (core knowledge) that will develop students' intellectual abilities and subsequently produce good citizens.

ethics A branch of axiology that is concerned with personal and societal standards of morality.

ethnicity As defined by James Banks, a shared feeling of common identity derived chiefly from a common ancestral origin and a common set of values and experiences.

ethnocentrism A belief that one's culture or way of life is superior to other cultures. This type of narrow thinking prevents people from learning and benefiting from what others have to offer.

excellence in education A reform slogan, first heard in the mid-1980s, calling for higher academic standards and a more rigorous curriculum for students and teachers alike.

existentialism A philosophical attitude that perceives reality to be nothing more than what is perceived to be real from an individual's perspective. Existentialists believe that people are free to make choices and must assume responsibility for those choices.

explicit curriculum   The stated or adopted set of learning outcomes (knowledge, skills, and attitudes) students are expected to be taught, sometimes referred to as the *formal curriculum.*

extracurriculum   Student activities outside the regular classroom designed to facilitate student growth and learning.

extrinsic reward   A benefit that is derived from the tangible "positives" of a job, such as salary, security, and schedule.

factory model   A model of schooling developed from the business community, which holds teachers and schools accountable for student achievement. Efficiency is stressed and individuals are secondary to producing tangible outcomes.

fair use   A revision to the original Copyright Act of 1909, passed by the U.S. Congress in 1976, that allows teachers more latitude in photocopying published works. The provision sets forth guidelines for the use of copyrighted works without obtaining permission from the author.

field experiences   School-based placements made through teacher education programs designed to help prospective teachers learn more about the teaching profession.

flat grant   A way that the state equalizes funding by distributing money based on student attendance.

formal curriculum   *See explicit curriculum.*

foundation grant   Grant money from the state that is available to poorer districts to compensate for insufficient local funding.

freedom of expression   A fundamental right to express personal beliefs that is protected by the First Amendment to the Constitution.

full-service community school   An outgrowth of school-based health clinics that expands the scope and depth of the health services provided to children. Many states have or are in the process of initiating full-service community schools.

genuineness   A trait that expresses sincerity in thought and motivation. Being perceived as "genuine" is an essential quality for teachers to possess.

G. I. Bill of Rights   A federal law passed in 1944, also known as the Servicemen's Readjustment Act, that provided education stipends to veterans returning home from World War II. The G. I. Bill has had many incarnations since 1944, but has always offered education incentives in exchange for military service.

gifted and talented students   Students who have demonstrated high levels of performance in intellectual, creative, and/or artistic areas, shown exceptional leadership skills, or excelled in a specific academic area.

Goals 2000: Educate America Act   An act passed by the U.S. Congress in 1994 that outlined eight educational goals to be met by the year 2000. Although these goals were not completely achieved by the year 2000, they are still worthy of pursuing.

Head Start   A preschool educational program funded by federal legislation in the mid-1960s that provides enrichment opportunities to children who are from low-income families. The aim is to help children from disadvantaged backgrounds "catch up" with other children who come from middle- and upper-class homes.

hidden curriculum   *See implicit curriculum.*

hierarchy of needs   A pyramid of affective needs that must be gratified in sequence for a person to ascend to the next level. Abraham Maslow conceptualized this hierarchy of human growth needs as a way to explain human motivation.

holistic approach   A teaching approach that takes into account all developmental aspects of a student's life (e.g., physical, mental, social, cognitive, and spiritual) when planning instruction.

home schooling   An alternative to public education in which parents teach their children at home. The practice of educating children at home is as old as American education, but the increase in the number of parents choosing this type of schooling has risen dramatically in recent years.

hornbook   The first primary text used in colonial America. Hornbooks were made out of wood in the shape of a paddle, hung from a student's neck, and contained the alphabet, numbers, and the Lord's prayer.

humanism   An approach to teaching developed from existential philosophy that recognizes the worth and dignity of all human beings.

hypertext   Electronically stored information in a database format that contains associative links to other related documents.

idealism   A school of philosophy that considers truth to be a fixed set of ideas and reality to consist primarily of those ideas.

implicit curriculum   The unstated teachings of the school that derive from its practices, sometimes known as the *hidden curriculum* or the *informal curriculum.*

inclusion   The current practice of placing physically and/or mentally challenged students in regular classrooms as much as possible rather than isolating such students in resource rooms for separate instruction.

individualized education program (IEP)   A provision of the Individuals with Disabilities Act (IDEA) that requires an individualized plan for each child that receives special education, detailing short-term and long-term learning objectives, services, and evaluative methods.

Individuals with Disabilities Education Act (IDEA)   A federal law passed in 1990 that expanded the provisions of the Education for All Handicapped Children Act of 1975.

inductive reasoning   A type of reasoning that moves from the facts (specifics) to an understanding of general principles (generalizations).

information processing theory   A theory that explains how individuals take in, store, and retrieve information.

in loco parentis   A Latin term that translates as "in place of parents." Teachers must often serve as surrogate parents to their students during the school day.

input devices   Those parts of a computer system, such as keyboard, mouse, and scanner, used to facilitate the input of data and commands.

integrated curriculum   Designing lessons so that students can understand how knowledge in different fields overlaps (e.g., the study of a scientific concept such as electricity can be looked at from a social studies perspective at the same time). Also known as *interdisciplinary curriculum*.

interactive stage   The second cognitive stage of teaching in which the live action takes place. In this stage, teachers respond to the moment, which calls for spontaneity and flexibility.

Interstate New Teacher Assessment and Support Consortium (INTASC)   An association of state education agencies, higher-education institutions, and national education organizations established by the Council of Chief State School Officers. Since 1987 INTASC has been developing licensure standards to provide a common ground among states that can be used to guide the initial licensing process to ensure teacher competence.

intrinsic reward   A type of benefit internally derived from feelings of satisfaction.

Jim Crow laws   State statutes that segregated the races in public facilities, including schools. These laws were held constitutional until 1954, when the U.S. Supreme Court, in *Brown* v. *Board of Education of Topeka*, struck down the "separate but equal" clause as unconstitutional.

kaleidoscope metaphor   An interpretation of diversity that describes the "American" culture as dynamic, fluid, and evolving. The American culture continually shifts and splinters, producing splendid and interesting configurations, like those observed through the lens of a kaleidoscope.

kindergarten   Literally "a child's garden," the term refers to a preschool for children. Rooted in the ideas of the German educator Friedrich Froebel, the concept came to the United States with German immigrants in the mid-19th century. Susan Blow founded the first public kindergarten in St. Louis.

knowledge base   Specialized knowledge known to members in a particular profession that the general public does not have. Such knowledge is acquired through a relatively lengthy period of education that is intellectually rigorous.

Latin grammar school   A secondary school intended to prepare young men for advanced education in seminaries or universities by offering a curriculum steeped in the classics. The first Latin grammar school was founded in Boston in 1635. Today's prep schools are similar in philosophy to early Latin grammar schools.

learning   Any relatively permanent change in behavior or mental associations resulting from experiences.

learning theory   An attempt to systematically organize complicated human phenomena in an effort to better understand, explain, and predict behavior.

least restrictive environment (LRE)   Under federal law, students who qualify for special education are to receive instruction in the least-restrictive environment, which means they remain in the regular classroom with peers as much as possible (i.e., inclusion) rather than being segregated in resource rooms or separate schools.

license   A document issued by a board or other official body that allows one to practice a specified trade or profession.

local area network (LAN)   A group of computers linked to a local server. A LAN may serve an office, a school, or a business.

logic   A branch of philosophy that asks questions about how humans reason. Two types of reasoning are inductive (moves from specific facts to general principles) and deductive reasoning (moves from general principles to specific facts).

logical consequence   An action imposed by the teacher that is connected to the student's behavior.

magnet school   An alternative urban school that offers a special curriculum to attract gifted and talented students from segregated suburban neighborhoods. By offering specialties, such as mathematics, sciences, performing arts, and technology, magnet schools help achieve voluntary desegregation.

Massachusetts Act of 1642   A law passed by the Massachusetts Bay Colony that made parents responsible for educating their children. This piece of legislation is considered the first educational law in America's history.

Massachusetts Act of 1647   A law passed by the Puritan elders, referred to as the *Old Deluder Satan Act,* which deemed local communities responsible for the education of their youth. The following year the first property tax was levied to support local education.

melting pot metaphor   An interpretation of diversity that suggests cultures of various ethnic groups are gradually absorbed into a single "American" culture.

mentor   A wise and trusted counselor or friend who offers advice, insight, and encouragement to another person and is worthy of emulation. A mentor may be a college professor, a former teacher, an employer, a family member, or a close friend.

mentorship program   In education, a program that pairs an inexperienced teacher with an experienced teacher who serves as a role model and wise counselor.

metacognition   The knowledge people possess about how they learn best. As individuals grow, they learn cognitive strategies that enhance personal learning.

metaphysics   Philosophical system concerned with the nature of reality. Questions about the cosmos (the origin of the universe), theology (the nature of God), anthropology (the study of man), and ontology (the study of existence) are central to metaphysics.

multicultural education   A compilation of teaching and learning approaches that fosters an appreciation and respect for cultural pluralism and promotes democratic ideals of justice, equality, and democracy.

multimedia   Computer programs that employ a variety of media in their presentations, including text, graphics, and audio.

multiple intelligences   A theory advanced by Howard Gardner that contends intelligence is not a single entity but is multifaceted.

A Nation at Risk: The Imperative for Educational Reform   A national report published in 1983 by the National Commission on Excellence in Education that painted a bleak picture of student performance. This report alarmed policymakers and their constituents, who launched a "back-to-basics" movement and demanded massive educational reforms.

National Board for Professional Teaching Standards (NBPTS)   A national board established in 1987 at the urging of the Carnegie Task Force on Teaching as a Profession in its report *A Nation Prepared: Teachers for the 21st Century.* The NBPTS issues a national certificate (not intended to take the place of state licensure) that signifies an advanced level of accomplishment.

National Council for Accreditation of Teacher Education (NCATE)   An accrediting professional organization that evaluates teacher education programs on a voluntary basis. Approximately 500 of the 1,200 teacher education programs in the United States have earned NCATE approval.

National Defense Education Act (NDEA)   In response to the launching of the Soviet satellite Sputnik in 1957, the U.S. Congress passed the NDEA in 1958. This act poured massive amounts of money into education to enhance math and science programs and to identify and encourage gifted and talented students to pursue majors in the hard sciences.

National Education Association (NEA)   The oldest professional organization for teachers and administrators. There are state and local affiliates of the NEA.

National Education Goals   The eight goals set by The Goals 2000: Educate America Act to be realized by the year 2000.

National Governors' Association   The association of state governors, which is actively concerned about and involved in school reform and other school-related issues. The Goals 2000: Educate America Act, passed by the U.S. Congress in 1994, was initiated by this body.

National Teachers Exam (NTE)   A national examination developed by Educational Testing Services that measures general knowledge, professional knowledge, common knowledge, and subject areas. This examination is being phased out by the PRAXIS series.

normal school   A 19th-century American institution that trained teachers in the "norms" (or accepted ways) of teaching. The first state-supported normal school was founded in 1839 in Lexington, Massachusetts.

nuclear family   A family unit with both parents living in the home.

null curriculum   A name for the nonexistent or neglected curriculum, which is content that schools do not teach.

occupational fit   An intuitive calling among those who easily identify with the work of teachers and who see themselves fulfilling the demands of that role.

operant conditioning   A model of learning developed by B. F. Skinner postulating that reinforced responses are likely to increase in frequency and duration, whereas ignored or punished responses will likely decrease in frequency and strength.

output devices   Those parts of a computer system, such as monitors and printers, that use data from the computer to produce a useful or meaningful product.

parochial schools   Schools established and controlled by a church parish.

pedagogy   An educational term that means the systematic study of teaching and the scientific application of teaching methods and instruction.

peer facilitators   A practice in which students help other students to learn, benefiting both the helper and the one being helped. The notion of peer helpers or tutors is not new, but there has been a recent increase in programs using peer facilitators.

perennialism   An educational philosophy emanating from Idealism and Realism in which truth is absolute and that seeks to develop student intellect and appreciation for classical literature, humanities, and the fine arts.

performance assessment   *See authentic assessment.*

permeable families   Elkind's term to describe families in which parental boundaries have been diffused and children's needs have been overlooked.

permissive parents   Parents who are disorganized, inconsistent, and insecure. They fail to set limits or enforce rules and demand very little from their children.

PL 94-142   *See Education for All Handicapped Children Act.*

Plessy v. Ferguson   An 1896 U.S. Supreme Court decision that upheld "separate but equal" accommodations for blacks and whites. This fateful decision was a major setback for African-American students, who continued to be schooled in segregated schools until *Brown* v. *Board of Education of Topeka* (1954).

portfolio   An assessment tool used to display and evaluate an individual's achievements and personal growth.

pragmatism   A philosophy that considers truth to be relative and knowledge to be altered by one's unique experiences. Pragmatists believe that knowledge is in a state of flux, and therefore it is important to know how to learn. The process of learning is considered more important than the knowledge one learns.

PRAXIS Series: Professional Assessment for Beginning Teachers   A new licensing exam constructed by Educational Testing Service (ETS) designed to test beginning teachers' knowledge and performance. These assessments move beyond conventional forms of testing by requiring evidence of what the teacher can do. The PRAXIS series was developed to replace the National Teachers Exam (NTE).

preactive stage   The first cognitive stage of teaching. This stage involves planning that allows teachers to decide what, how, and whom to teach, in addition to how to measure learning.

private enterprise schools   Alternative schools that are financed by the private sector. These for-profit enterprises, such as the Edison Project, aim to reform (improve) the public schools.

private school   A school run by an agency, a private enterprise, or a religious denomination that is financed mainly by private funds. Because recent court decisions have affirmed a secular curriculum in the public schools, many parents who favor smaller schools with moral and/or religious instruction—and who can afford it—have opted for private schooling for their children.

procedures   Routines developed and taught by teachers to facilitate order and save instruction time.

profession   An occupation that requires a mastery of specialized knowledge and preparation and that renders a service to society.

professional development   A teacher's commitment to engage in self-analysis and reflection in order to improve performance in the classroom. Professional development is becoming more teacher-directed and individualized and is occurring within a school among peers.

professional development schools (PDS) Many schools of education are forming partnerships with area public schools to better prepare teachers for life in the classroom. The aim is to link theory with practice, which will make teacher preparation more meaningful.

professional organization   A group or association of like-minded professionals that lobbies for the organization's members, publishes noteworthy news and materials, and offers other relevant resources and support.

progressivism   An educational theory, based on pragmatism, contending that the optimal way to prepare children for a democratic society is to teach independent thinking. Progressivists take the whole student into account (holistic approach). The student-centered approach to curriculum and teaching is emphasized, and students are taught critical thinking and problem solving in addition to cooperative learning.

projective stage   The final cognitive stage of teaching, based on prediction and commitment. In this stage, the teacher tries to predict what would have happened if an alternative method had been used and then proceeds differently the next time.

property tax   A tax on the assessed value of a person's home (and in some states, personal items such as cars and furniture). Most school funding is derived from property taxes. Because of disparities in personal incomes, there are obvious inequities in funds among school districts. Such inequities have prompted national and state finance reform.

race   A group among humans that possesses inherited traits that are distinct enough to characterize its members as a unique people. Such divisions are often used by anthropologists to aid in classification. In a racially mixed society, any strict adherence to a classification scheme is limiting and problematic.

rapport   A feeling of connection that develops between two people based on mutual cooperation and respect.

realism   A school of philosophy that believes there is a natural order to the universe independent of the ideas we hold about it and that these laws of nature can be revealed through scientific inquiry. Realists believe knowledge is real and ideas should be tested. Modern sciences and mathematics grew out of realism.

reception learning   An instructional method for teachers, introduced by David Ausubel in the 1970s. Teachers begin a lesson by describing main ideas and concepts to be taught, called *advance organizers,* which help structure information so students can connect new information to familiar knowledge.

reflective stage   The third cognitive stage of teaching—analyzing and evaluating. In this stage the teacher processes what transpired during instruction and adjusts accordingly.

reflective thinking   A processing skill whereby one consistently questions and evaluates his or her attitudes, beliefs, values, and actions in an attempt to improve practice. Good teachers cultivate and refine reflective thinking abilities in order to model this skill to students.

resilient   The ability of certain individuals to overcome seemingly impossible odds and become well-adjusted, contributing members of society.

rules   Stated teacher expectations that guide student behavior.

salad bowl metaphor   An interpretation of diversity that suggests various ethnic groups, living side by side, complement each other without sacrificing their unique cultural differences.

school as community   A belief that education becomes the responsibility of all citizens. Specifically, parents, teachers, school personnel, social agencies, and even grandparents work together to ensure that young people receive a quality education.

school-based decision making   *See site-based management.*

school board   The local board of education is the policymaking body of the district. This group of (usually) elected members determines teachers' salaries, class size, and teachers' duties and responsibilities.

school choice   A movement that allows parents an opportunity to decide where, among several schools, they would like their children to attend. The rationale is to improve student achievement by expanding the range of available schools.

school health programs   A partnership between the school and community that provides comprehensive health services to schoolchildren. This coordinated health initiative emerged in recent years as a response to gaps in services to children. The aim is to improve the overall mental and physical health of students through an active alliance with the community.

school within a school   The reorganization of schools into smaller, self-contained learning communities.

search and seizure   The legal right to search an individual and his or her property if there is a "reasonable suspicion" to believe that person has committed an unlawful act or is concealing weapons, drugs, or other illegal items.

search engine   An Internet-based computer application that can search millions of databases in seconds and provide an extensive list of hyperlinks related to the requested topic.

self-actualized   The pinnacle of Abraham Maslow's hierarchy of needs in which all deficiency needs have been met and one has realized his or her full potential. Although human beings strive to fulfill their innate capacity, rarely will an individual achieve self-actualization.

self-fulfilling prophecy   A belief that suggests students behave according to how they are treated. Hence teachers should be careful to communicate high expectations for all their students.

sexual harassment   Any unwanted sexual advance in the context of an unequal relationship of power. School officials are prohibited under Title IX of the Education Amendment of 1972 from making unwelcomed verbal comments or physical contact with students of the same sex or opposite sex. If a teacher is found guilty of sexual harassment, a student can collect monetary damages under the law.

shaping   An operant learning technique that reinforces any response or effort that comes close to the desired behavior.

shopping mall school   The idea that schools (usually secondary schools) are like shopping centers of knowledge where students may choose among courses and personalize their curriculum.

site-based management   A reform effort in which teachers and parents are involved in the daily operation of schools. This is also referred to as school-based management, school-based decision making, or school-based leadership; all imply shared decision making at the level of the individual school rather than at the state or district level.

social cognitive learning theory   A theory of learning developed by Albert Bandura and other cognitive psychologists postulating that students form expectations about consequences, and those expectations (i.e., cognitions) motivate them to behave in certain ways.

social constructivism   An educational philosophy in which the learner actively constructs meaning from the acquisition of new material gleaned in a social context.

social distance   The amount of intimacy between groups or individuals, which defines the terms of the relationship.

social learning theory   Bandura's theory of learning (sometimes called *observational learning*), which postulates that students learn by observing and imitating others who serve as models of behavior.

social reconstructionism   An educational philosophy that grew out of progressivism. Social reconstructionists try to ameliorate societal ills. The teacher's role is to raise students' political and social consciousness and to find ways to tackle social problems that plague our country, such as crime, poverty, homelessness, inequality, and violence,

state board of education   The board that establishes school policies affecting the supervision and structure of elementary, secondary, and vocational schools. Additionally, the state board of education sets accreditation standards for district schools.

state department of education   A collection of related agencies that operate under the state board of education and the state legislature. Responsibilities include but are not limited to: accrediting schools, setting instructional standards, administrating federal programs, regulating local school programs, overseeing public and non-public schools, and certifying or licensing teachers.

student-centered approach   An approach to instruction in which the student is primarily responsible for his or her own learning.

student-centered curriculum   An approach to curriculum organization that stresses student attitudes and individual needs.

student-centered school   A school that places the student foremost in all matters pertaining to how teaching and learning are conducted. A few characteristics of the student-centered school include a supportive mission statement, parental involvement, student leadership, and a sense of "we-ness."

subject-centered curriculum   A way to organize curriculum that emphasizes the content of the disciplines or subject areas.

superintendent of schools   The chief executive officer (CEO) of the local school district, who is responsible to the local school board.

teacher-centered approach   A traditional approach to teaching in which the teacher is mainly responsible for dispensing knowledge and information to the student.

teacher-centered school   A school that emphasizes teacher-directed instruction and assesses students with traditional testing measures such as test scores and grades.

teacher efficacy   A teacher's belief that he or she can make a positive difference in the lives of students.

teacher leader   A teacher empowered to lead and to initiate school change.

tenure   A status granted to a teacher after a successful probationary period that protects the teacher from unfair or arbitrary dismissal. Due process procedures must be adhered to before a teacher's contract can be terminated.

theory   The study and analysis of complicated facts and how they relate to one another. Theory aids in an attempt to systematically organize complicated human phenomena in an effort to better understand, explain, and predict behavior. Theoretical constructs make it possible to systematically examine and seek solutions to human problems.

Title I Federal assistance made available to schools with a large number of children from low-income families. Title I (formerly Chapter I) is included in the Elementary and Secondary Education Act (ESEA).

Title IX A provision of the Education Amendment Act, passed by Congress in 1972, that prohibits gender discrimination in educational settings receiving federal monies. Students can file civil suits against schools for sexual harassment.

tort A legal injury or wrong against a person or property. Teachers can have charges brought against them in a civil (tort) case for failure to provide a reasonable standard of care to students.

town school A colonial school in New England built on land donated by the town as required for areas with 50 families or more. Townships were later divided into larger school districts.

tracking The method of screening students based on ability and placing them on tracks or educational pathways. Because a student may be unfairly placed due to race, ethnicity, or gender, tracking is a controversial practice. *See ability group.*

unconditional positive regard An attitude of total acceptance of another person's worth without judgment.

uninvolved parents A parenting style in which parents are permissive, unresponsive, and lack concern for their children. These parents neither try to control their children nor hold expectations for them.

values Those things that matter most to an individual. A career decision requires that one is aware of and willing to examine personal values.

Vocational Rehabilitation Act A federal law passed in 1973 to ensure that the civil rights of handicapped persons are not violated in the workplace. This includes students with disabilities attending public schools under Section 504. In recent years, the courts have ruled that children with AIDS cannot be discriminated against in public schools under the provision of Section 504.

voucher Coupons that can be used as cash for tuition to private schools. The voucher gives parents who cannot afford to send their children to another school the option for private or public education in another school.

withitness A term coined by Kounin and associates that describes adept teachers as those who appear to know what is going on in their classrooms at all times. It is as if these individuals have a second set of eyes (in the back of their heads).

word processors Computer software programs designed to produce text documents using automated text processing features. These software programs have built-in tools to check spelling, grammar, and punctuation. Editing tools allow the manipulation of font, point size, line spacing, text alignment, as well as the placement of pictures, graphs, and tables.

zone of proximal development The area or range between a student's current level of ability and his or her potential is the place most conducive for learning. Lev Vygotsky postulated that a child working within this range is capable of learning new material presented by an adult or an experienced peer. As the student becomes more self-reliant, outside assistance can be gradually decreased.

Adelman, N., & Pringle. (1995). Education reform and the uses of time. *Phi Beta Kappan, 77*(1), 27–29.

Adler, M. J. (1982). *The paideia proposal: An educational manifesto.* New York: Macmillan.

Albert, L. (1989). *A teacher's guide to cooperative discipline.* Circle Pines, MN: American Guidance Service.

Albert, L. (1995). Discipline: Is it a dirty word? *Learning, 24*(2), 43–46.

Alexander, K., & Alexander, M. D. (1998). *American public school law* (4th ed.). Belmont, CA: Wadsworth Publishing.

Alexander, L. (1993). School choice in the year 2000. *Phi Delta Kappan, 74*(10), 762–767.

Allen, J. D. (1995). Classroom management: Creating a positive learning climate. *Kappa Delta Pi Record, 31*(4), 178–181.

American Association of Colleges for Teacher Education: Bicentennial Commission on Education for the Profession of Teaching. (1976). *Educating a profession.* Washington, D.C.: Author.

American Association of School Administrators. (1999). *Preparing schools and school systems for the 21st century* (pp. 4–5). Council of 21, John Glenn, Honorary Chair. Recommendations from the Mount Vernon Conference: Author.

American Association of University Women (1992). *How schools shortchange girls.* Washington, D.C.: Author.

Arlin, M. (1979). Teacher transitions can disrupt time flow in classrooms. *American Educational Research Journal, 16*(1), 42–56.

Armstrong, T. (1994). *Multiple intelligences in the classroom.* Alexandria, VA: Association for Supervision and Curriculum Development.

Aronson, E., & Gonzalez, A. (1988). Desegregation, jigsaw, and the Mexican-American experience. In P. A. Katz & D. A. Taylor (Eds.), *Eliminating racism: Profiles in controversy.* New York: Plenum Press.

Ashton, P., & Webb, R. (1986). *Making a difference: Teachers' sense of efficacy and student achievement.* New York: Longman.

Aspy, D. N., & Roebuck, F. N. (1977). *Kids don't learn from people they don't like.* Amherst, MA: Human Resource Development Press.

Ausubel, D. P., Novak, J. D., & Hanesian, H. (1978). *Educational psychology: A cognitive view* (2nd ed.). New York: Holt, Rinehart & Winston.

Bagley, W. C. (1941). The case for essentialism in education. *NEA Journal, 30*(7), 201–202.

Bandura, A. (1977). *Social learning theory.* Upper Saddle River, NJ: Prentice Hall.

Banks, J. A. (1994). *An introduction to multicultural education.* Boston: Allyn & Bacon.

Banks, J. A. (1997). *Teaching strategies for ethnic studies* (6th ed.). Boston: Allyn & Bacon.

Banks, J. A., & Banks, C. M. (1997). *Multicultural education: A cultural perspective* (3rd ed.). Boston: Allyn & Bacon.

Banner, J. M., & Cannon, H. C. (1997). *The elements of teaching.* New Haven, CT: Yale University Press.

Barth, R. (1990). *Improving schools from within.* San Francisco: Jossey Bass.

Batey, C. S. (1996). *Parents are lifesavers: A handbook for parent involvement in schools.* Thousand Oaks, CA: Corwin Press.

Baumrind, D. (1967). Child care practices anteceding three patterns of preschool behavior. *Genetic Psychology Monographs, 75,* 43–88.

Baumrind, D. (1971). Current patterns of parental authority. *Developmental Psychology Monograph, 4,* 1–103.

Baumrind, D. (1991). The influence of parenting style on adolescent competence and substance use. *Journal of Early Adolescence, 11,* 56–95.

Beck, L., & Murphy, J. (1996). *The four imperatives of a successful school.* Thousand Oaks, CA: Corwin Press.

Bell, T. H. (1993). Reflections one decade after a nation at risk. *Phi Delta Kappan, 74*(8), 592–605.

Ben-Peretz, M. (1990). *The teacher-curriculum encounter: Freeing teachers from the tyranny of texts.* Albany, NY: State University of New York Press.

Bender, W. N. (1998). *Learning disabilities, characteristics, identification, and teaching strategies.* Needham Heights, MA: Allyn & Bacon.

Bennett, C. I. (1995). *Comprehensive multicultural education: Theory and practice* (3rd ed.).

Bennett, K. P., & LeCompte, M. D. (1990). *How schools work: A sociological analysis of education.* New York: Longman.

Benson, P. L. (1997). *All kids are our kids: What communities must do to raise caring and responsible children and adolescents.* San Francisco: Jossey-Bass.

Birch, S. H., & Ladd, G. W. (1996). Interpersonal relationships in the school environment and children's school adjustment: The role of teachers and peers. In J. Juvonen & K. Wentzel (Eds.), *Social motivation: Understanding children's school adjustment.* New York: Cambridge University Press.

Bloom, B. (Ed.) (1956). *Taxonomy of educational objectives: The cognitive domain.* New York: Longmans, Green & Company.

Boldt, L. G. (1996). *How to find the work you love.* New York: Arkana.

Boyer, E. L. (1995). *The basic school: A community for learning.* Princeton, NJ: The Carnegie Foundation for the Advancement of Teaching.

Brookover, W. B. (1979). *School social systems and student achievement: Schools can make a difference.* New York: Praeger.

Brooks, J. G., & Brooks, M. G. (1993). *The case for constructivist classrooms.* Alexandria, VA: Association for Supervision and Curriculum Development.

Brown v. *Board of Education of Topeka, Kansas,* 347, U.S. 483, 74 S. Ct. 686 (1954).

Bruner, J. (1966). *Toward a theory of instruction.* New York: Norton.

Bureau of Labor Statistics. (1999). *Occupational outlook handbook, 1998–99.* Washington, D.C.: U.S. Department of Labor.

Burrup, P., Brimley, V., & Garfield, R. (1999). *Financing education in a climate of change.* New York: Allyn & Bacon.

Calabrese, R. L. (1990). The public school: A source of alienation for minority parents. *Journal of Negro Education, 59*(2), 148–154.

Campbell, L. (1997). How teachers interpret MI Theory. *Educational Leadership, (55),* 14–19.

Campbell, R. F., Cunningham, L. L., Nystrand, R. O., & Usdan, M. (1980). *The organization and control of American schools* (4th ed.). Columbus, OH: Charles E. Merrill.

Canter, L. (1988). Assertive discipline and the search for the perfect classroom. *Young Children, 43*(2), 24.

Canter, L. (1989). Assertive discipline: More than names on the board and marbles in a jar. *Phi Delta Kappan, 71,* 57–61.

Canter, L. (1992). *Assertive discipline: Positive behavior management for today's classroom.* Santa Monica, CA: Lee Canter & Associates.

Canter, L. (1996). First the rapport—then, the rules. *Learning, 24*(5), 12, 14.

Cascio, C. (1995). National Board for Professional Teaching Standards: Changing teaching through teachers. *The Clearing House, 68*(4), 211–213.

Chapman, E. (1988). *Be true to your future.* Los Altos, CA: Crisp Publications.

Charles, C. M. (1996). *Building classroom discipline* (5th ed.). White Plains, NY: Longman.

Chavkin, N. F. (1989). Debunking the myth about minority parents. *Educational Horizons, 67*(4), 119–123.

Christensen, E. W. (1989). Counseling Puerto Ricans: Some cultural considerations. In D. R. Atkinson, G. Morten, & D. W. Sue (Eds.), *Counseling American minorities: A cross-cultural perspective* (3rd ed.) (pp. 205–212). Dubuque, IA: W. C. Brown.

Clifford, G., & Guthrie, J. (1988). *Ed school: A brief for professional education.* Chicago: University of Chicago Press.

Cole, M., John-Steiner, V., Scriber, S., Souberman, E., & Vygotsky, L. S. (1978). *Mind in* Coleman, J. S. (Ed.). (1965). *Education and political development.* Princeton, NJ: Princeton University Press.

Collins, M., & Tamarkin, C. (1982). *Marva Collins' way.* Los Angeles: J. P. Tarcher.

Combs, A. (1965). *The professional education of teachers.* Boston: Allyn & Bacon.

Comer, J. P. (1988). Is "parenting" essential to good teaching? *NEA Today, 6,* 34–40.

Comer, J. P., Haynes, N. M., Joyner, E. T., & Ben-Avie, M. (1996) *Rallying the whole village: The Comer process for reforming education.* New York: Teachers College Press.

Condoli, C. (1995). *Site based management in education: How to make it work in your school.* Lancaster, PA: Technomic Publishing.

Conway, G. E. (1992). School choice: A private school perspective. *Phi Delta Kappan, 73*(7), 561–564.

Cooley, J. J. (1998). Gay and lesbian adolescents: Presenting problems and the counselor's role. *Professional School Counseling, 1*(3), 30–34.

Cooper, M. (1988). Whose culture is it, anyway? In A. Lieberman (Ed.), *Building a professional culture in schools* (pp. 45–54). New York: Teachers College Press.

Corey, G., Corey, M. S., & Callanan, P. (1998). *Issues and ethics in the helping professions* (5th ed.). Pacific Grove, CA: Brooks/Cole.

Costa, A. L., & Garmston, R. (1985). Supervision for intelligent teaching. *Educational Leadership, 42,* 70–80.

Costa, A. L., & Garmston, R. J. (1994). *Cognitive coaching: A foundation for renaissance schools.* Norwood, MA: Christopher-Gordon Publishers.

Counts, G. S. (1934). *The social foundations of education.* New York: Charles Scribner's Sons.

Counts, G. S. (1945). *Education and the promise of America.* New York: Macmillan.

Cruickshank, D. R. (1987). *Reflective teaching: The preparation of students of teaching.* Reston, VA: Association of Teacher Educators.

Curwin, R. L., & Mendler, A. N. (1988). *Discipline with dignity.* Alexandria, VA: Association for Supervision and Curriculum Development.

Curwin, R. L., & Mendler, A. N. (1997). *As tough as necessary: Countering violence, aggression, and hostility in our schools.* Alexandria, VA: Association for Supervision and Curriculum Development.

Danielson, C. (1996). *Enhancing professional practice: A framework for teaching.* Alexandria, VA: Association for Supervision and Curriculum Development.

Darling-Hammond, L. (1997). *The right to learn: A blueprint for creating schools that work.* San Francisco: Jossey-Bass.

Darling-Hammond, L., & Cobb, V. (1996). The changing context of teacher education. In Murray, F. B. (Ed.). *The teacher educator's handbook* (pp. 14–62). San Francisco: Jossey Bass.

De La Rosa, D., & Maw C. E. (1990). *Hispanic education: A statistical portrait 1990.* Washington, D.C.: National Council of La Rosa.

Deane, F. P., & Chamberlain, K. (1994). Treatment fearfulness and distress as predictors of professional psychological help-seeking. *British Journal of Guidance and Counseling, 22*(2), 207–217.

Dejnozka, E., & Kapel, D. (1991). *American educators' encyclopedia.* New York: Greenwood Press.

DePree, M. (1989). *Leadership as an art.* New York: Dell Publishing.

Dewey, J. (1915). *Schools of tomorrow.* New York: E. P. Dutton.

Dewey, J. (1916) *Democracy and education: An introduction to the philosophy of education.* New York: Macmillan.

Dewey, J. (1933). *How we think.* Boston: Heath.

Dewey, J. (1958). *Philosophy of education (problems of men).* Totowa, NJ: Littlefield, Adams.

Dornbusch, S., Ritter, P., Leiderman, P., Roberts, D., & Fraleigh, M. (1987). The relation of parenting style to adolescent school performance. *Child Development, 58,* 1244–1257.

Doyle, W. (1986). Classroom organization and management. In Wittrock, M. C. (ed.), *Handbook of research on teaching* (pp. 392–431). New York: Macmillan Publishing.

Dreikurs, R., & Cassel, P. (1972). *Discipline without tears.* New York: Hawthorn.

Dreikurs, R., Grunwald, B. B., Pepper, F. C. (1982). *Maintaining sanity in the classroom* (2nd ed). New York: Harper & Row.

Dryfoos, J. G. (1994). *Full service schools: A revolution in health and social services for children, youth, and families.* San Francisco: Jossey-Bass.

Duke, D. L. (1990). Setting goals for professional development. *Educational Leadership, 47,* 71–75.

Edmonds, R. E. (1979). Programs of school improvement: An overview. *Educational Leadership 40*(3), 4–7.

Egan, G. (1975). *The skilled helper: A model for systematic helping and interpersonal relating.* Monterey, CA: Brooks/Cole Publishing.

Eisner, E. W. (1979). *The educational imagination: On the design and evaluation of school programs.* New York: Macmillan.

Eisner, E. W. (1994). *The educational imagination: On the design and evaluation of school programs* (3rd ed.). New York: Macmillan.

Eisner, E. W. (1999). The uses and limits of performance assessment. *Phi Delta Kappan, 80*(9), 658–660.

Elkind, D. (1995) *Ties that stress.* Cambridge, MA: Harvard University Press.

Ellis, T. I. (1984). Motivating teachers for excellence. ERIC Clearinghouse on Educational Management: ERIC Digest, 6, *ERIC Document Reproduction Service,* No ED259449.

Emmer, E. T., Evertson, C. M., & Worsham, M. E. (2000). *Classroom management for secondary teachers* (5th ed.). Boston: Allyn & Bacon.

Epstein, J. L. (1987). Parent involvement: What research says to administrators. *Education and Urban Society, 19,* 119–136.

Epstein, J. (1995). School/family/community partnerships: Caring for the children we share. *Phi Delta Kappan, 76*(9), 701–712.

Epstein, J., Salinas, K. C., & Jackson, V. E. (1995). *TIPS manual for teachers: Language arts, science/health, and math interactive homework in the middle grades.* Baltimore: Center on School, Family, and Community Partnerships, Johns Hopkins University.

Evans, T. D. (1996). Encouragement: The key to reforming classrooms. *Educational Leadership, 54*(1), 81–85.

Evertson, C. M., & Harris, A. H. (1992). What we know about managing classrooms. *Educational Leadership, 49*(7), 74–78.

Faber, A., & Mazlish, E. (1995). *How to talk so kids can learn at home and in school.* New York: Simon & Schuster.

Falk, P. J. (1989). Lesbian mothers: Psychosocial assumptions in family law. *American Psychologist, 44*(6), 941–947.

Fay, J., & Funk, D. (1995). *Teaching with love and logic: Taking control of the classroom.* Golden, CO: The Love and Logic Press.

Finders, M., & Lewis, C. (1994). Why some parents don't come to school. *Educational Leadership, 51*(8), 50–54.

Fischer, L., & Sorenson, G. P., (1996). *School law for counselors, psychologists, and social workers* (3rd ed.). White Plains, NY: Longman.

Fisher, C. W., Berliner, D. C., Filby, N. N., Marliave, R., Cahen, L. S., & Dishaw, M. M. (1980). Teaching behaviors, academic learning time, and student achievement: An overview (pp. 7–32). In D. Denham & A. Lieberman (Eds.), *Time to learn.* Washington, D.C.: U.S. Department of Education.

Fitzpatrick, J. P. (1987). *Puerto Rican Americans* (2nd ed.). Englewood Cliffs, NJ: Prentice-Hall.

Franklin v. *Gwuinnett Country Public Schools,* 112 S. Ct. 1028 (1992).

Freeman, J. L., Underwood, K. E., & Fortune, J. C. (1991). What boards value. *The American School Board Journal, 178*(1) 32–36, 39.

Freiberg, J. (1996). From tourists to citizens in the classroom. *Educational Leadership, 54*(1), 32–36.

Fried, R. (1995). *The passionate teacher.* Boston: Beacon Press.

Fuch, L. H. (1990). *The American kaleidoscope: Race, ethnicity, and civic culture.* Wesleyan: University Press.

Fuqua, D., Newman, J., Anderson, M., & Johnson, A. (1986). Preliminary study of internal dialogue in a training session. *Psychological Reports, 58,* 163–172.

Galassi, J. P., & Gulledge, S. A. (1997). The middle school counselor and teacher-advisor programs. *Professional School Counseling, 1*(2), 55–60.

Garcia, E. E. (1994). *Understanding and meeting the challenge of student cultural diversity.* Boston: Houghton Mifflin.

Gardner, H. (1983). *Frames of mind: The theory of multiple intelligences.* New York: Basic Books.

Gardner, H. (1993). *Multiple intelligences: The theory in practice.* New York: Basic Books.

Garrett, S., Sadker, M., & Sadker, D. (1994). Interpersonal classroom skills. In Cooper, J. (Ed.). *Classroom teaching skills* (pp. 189–231). Boston: Houghton Mifflin.

Gartner, A., Kohler, M. D., & Riessman, F. (1972). *Children teach children: Learning by teaching.* New York: Harper & Row.

Gehrke, N. J. (1987). *On being a teacher.* West Lafayette, IN: Kappa Delta Pi.

Germinario, V., & Cram, H. G. (1998). *Change for public education: Practical approaches for the 21st century.* Lancaster, PA: Technomic Publishing.

Gibb, S. A., Allred, K., Ingram, C. F., Young, J. R., & Egan, W. M. (1998). Lessons learned from the inclusion of students with emotional and behavioral disorders in one junior high school: Behavioral disorders. *Journal of the Council for Children with Behavioral Disorder, 24*(2), 122–137.

Ginott, H. G. (1976). *Teacher and child.* New York: Avon.

Glasser, W. (1965). *Reality therapy: A new approach to psychiatry.* New York: Harper & Row.

Glasser, W. (1969). *Schools without failure.* New York: Harper & Row.

Glasser, W. (1986). *Control theory in the classroom.* New York: Harper & Row.

Glasser, W. (1990). *The quality school: Managing students without coercion.* New York: HarperCollins.

Glasser, W. (1993). *The quality school teacher.* New York: HarperCollins.

Glasser, W. (1998). *Choice theory: A new psychology of personal freedom.* New York: HarperCollins.

Glasser W. (1998). *The quality school: Managing students without coercion.* Revised edition. New York: Harper Perennial.

Glazer, N., & Moynihan, D. P. (1970). Beyond the melting pot: The Negroes, Puerto Ricans, Jews, Italians, and Irish of New York City (2nd ed.). Cambridge: The M.I.T. Press.

Goleman, D. (1995). *Emotional intelligence: Why it can matter more than IQ.* New York: Bantam Books.

Gollnick, D. M., & Chinn, P. C. (1994). *Multicultural education in a pluralistic society* (4th ed.). New York: Merrill.

Good, T. L., & Brophy, J. E. (1994). *Looking in classrooms* (6th ed.). New York: HarperCollins.

Good, T. L., Grouws, D. A., & Ebmeier, H. (1983). *Active mathematics teaching.* New York: Longman.

Goodlad, J. I. (1984). *A place called school.* New York: McGraw-Hill.

Goodlad, J. I., & McMannon T. J. (Eds.) (1997). *The public purpose of education and schooling.* San Francisco: Jossey-Bass.

Gordon, R. (1998). Balancing real-world problems with real-world results. *Phi Delta Kappan, 79*(5), 390–393.

Gordon, T. (1989). *Discipline that works: Promoting self-discipline in children.* New York: Penguin Books.

Gordon, T., & Burch, N. (1974). *Teacher effectiveness training.* New York: Peter H. Wyden.

Gordy, S. H., & Phelps, P. H. (1996). Teacher educator as Ariadne. In J. Bowman & D. Fleniken (Eds.), *Modeling professional development: An Arkansas perspective* (pp. 155–161). Conway, AR: Arkansas Association of Colleges for Teacher Education.

Goss v. *Lopez,* 419 U.S. 565 (1975).

Gough, P.B. (1997). Editor's Page: A transfusion for democracy. *Phi Delta Kappan, 78*(8), 590.

Grant, C. A., & Gomez, M. L. (1996). *Making schools multicultural: Campus and classroom.* Englewood Cliffs, NJ: Merrill.

Greenwood, G., & Hickman, C. (1991). Research and practice in parental involvement: Implication for teacher education. *The Elementary School Journal, 91*(3), 279–288.

Gullatt, D. E., & Tollett, J. R. (1997). Educational law: A requisite course for preservice and inservice teacher education programs. *Journal of Teacher Education, 48*(2), 129–135.

Guthrie, J., & Reed, R. J. (1991). *Educational administration and policy: Effective leadership for American education* (2nd ed.). Needham Heights, MA: Allyn & Bacon.

Haberman, M. (1995). *Star teachers of children in poverty.* West Lafayette, IN: Kappa Delta Pi.

Hall, E., & Hall, M. (1987). Nonverbal communication for educators. *Theory into Practice, 26,* 364–367.

Hansen, D. (1995). *The call to teach.* New York: Teachers College Press.

Harris, L. (1995). *The Metropolitan life survey of the American teacher 1984–1995: Old problems, new challenges.* New York: MetLife.

Hart, S., & Marshall, D. (1992). *The question of teacher professionalism* (ERIC Document Reproduction Services No. 349 291). Illinois: University of Chicago.

Hartmeister, F. (1995). *Surviving as a teacher: The legal dimension.* Chicago: Precept Press.

Harvard Family Research Project. (1997). *New skills for new schools: Preparing teachers in family involvement.* Cambridge, MA: Author.

Hass, G., & Parkay, F. (1993). *Curriculum planning: A new approach* (6th ed.). Boston: Allyn & Bacon.

Hebert, E. A. (1999). Rugtime for teachers: Reinventing the faculty meeting. *Phi Delta Kappan, 81*(3), 219–222.

Henderson, A. T. (1988). Parents are a school's best friends. *Phi Delta Kappan, 70*(2), 148–153.

Hendren, R. L. (1994). *HealthWise: A Bulletin for School Health, 13*(2), 1–2.

Henry, T. (February 16, 1999). "License all teachers," Riley says. *USA Today.*

Hernandez, H. (1997). *Teaching in multilingual classrooms.* Upper Saddle River, NJ: Merrill.

Hervey, L. E., Calhoun, R. E., & Holmes, B. (1997). Am I *Everybody's* Teacher? Presentation to the 1997 Minority Student Today Conference. San Antonio, TX.

Himmelfarb, G. (1997). Revolution in the library. *American Scholar, 66*(2), 197–204.

Hirsch, E. D. Jr, (1987). *Cultural literacy: What every American needs to know.* Boston: Houghton Mifflin.

Hlebowitsh, P. S., & Tellez, K. (1997). *American education: Purpose and promise.* Belmont, CA: West/Wadsworth.

Holland, J. L. (1985). *Making vocational choices* (2nd ed.). Englewood Cliffs, NJ: Prentice Hall.

Hoover-Dempsey, K., Bassler, O., & Brissie, J. (1987). Parent involvement: Contributions of teacher efficacy, school socioeconomic status, and other school characteristics. *American Educational Research Journal, 24*(3), 417–435.

Horton-Parker, R. J. (1998). Teaching children to care: Engendering prosocial behavior through humanistic parenting. *Journal of Humanistic Education and Development, 37,* 66–77.

Huberman, M., Grounauer, M., & Marti, J. (1993). *The lives of teachers.* New York: Teachers College Press.

Hunter, M. C. (1982). *Mastery teaching.* El Segundo, CA: TIP Publishing.

Hutchins, R. M. (1954). *Great books: The foundation of liberal education.* New York: Simon & Schuster.

Hutchinson, G., & Johnson, B. (1994). Teaching as a career: Examining high school students' perspectives. *Action in Teacher Education, 15*(4), 61–67.

Ingraham v. *Wright*, 430 U.S. 651 (1977).

Irvine, J. J. (1990). *Black students and school failure: Policy, practices, prescriptions.* New York: Greenwood.

Jackson, P. (1968). *Life in classrooms.* New York: Holt, Rinehart & Winton.

Jensen, E. (1995). *Super teaching.* Del Mar, CA: Turning Point Publishers.

Johnson, D. (1999). Nothing ventured, nothing gained: The story of a collaborative telecommunication project. *Childhood Education, 75*(3), 161–166.

Johnson, J., & Immerwahr, J. (1994). *First things first: What Americans expect from the public schools.* New York: Public Agenda.

Johnson, S. M. (1990). *Teachers at work: Achieving success in our schools.* New York: Basic Books.

Jones, E. N., Ryan, K. & Bohlin, K. E. (April 1999). *Teachers as educators of character: Are the nation's schools of education coming up short?* Washington, D.C.: Character Education Partnership.

Jones, K. M., Torgesen, J. K., & Sexton, M. A. (1987). Using computer guided practice to increase decoding fluency in learning disabled children: A study using the Hint and Hunt I Program. *Journal of Learning Disabilities, 20*(2), 122–128.

Joyce, B., Weil, M., & Showers, B. (1992). *Models of teaching* (4th ed.). Needham Heights, MA: Simon & Schuster.

Kaplan, C. (1992). Teachers' punishment histories and their selection of disciplinary strategies. *Contemporary Educational Psychology, 17*, 258–265.

Kessler, R. C., McGonagle, K. A., Zhao, S., Nelson, C. B., Hughes, M., Eshelman, S., Wittchen, H. U., & Kendler, K. S. (1994). Lifetime and 12-month prevalence of DSM III-R, psychiatric disorder in the United States. *Archives of General Psychiatry, 51*, 8–19.

Koetzsch, R. E. (1997). *The parents' guide to alternatives in education.* Boston: Shambhala Publications.

Kohn, A. (1996). *Beyond discipline: From compliance to community.* Alexandria, VA: Association for Supervision and Curriculum Development.

Konnert, M. W., & Augenstein, J. J. (1998). *The school superintendency: Leading education into the 21st century.* Lancaster, PA: Technomic Publishing.

Kounin, J. S. (1970). *Discipline and group management in classrooms.* New York: Holt, Rinehart and Winston.

Kouzes, J. M., & Posner, B. Z. (1993). *Credibility: How leaders gain and lose it, why people demand it.* San Francisco: Jossey-Bass Publishers.

Kowalski, T. (1994). Chasing the wolves from the schoolhouse door. *Phi Delta Kappan, 76*(6), 486–489.

Kozol, J. (1967). *Death at an early age: The destruction of the hearts and minds of negro children in the Boston public schools.* Boston: Houghton Mifflin. (Revised edition, 1985). New York: A Plume Book/Penguin.

Kozol, J. (1972). *Free schools.* Boston: Houghton Mifflin. Revised edition published as *Alternative schools: A guide for educators and parents*, Continuum, 1982.

Kozol, J. (1985). *Illiterate America.* New York: Anchor Press/Doubleday.

Kozol, J. (1991). *Savage inequalities: Children in America's schools.* New York: Crown Publishers.

Lakein, A. (1973). *How to get control of your time and your life.* New York: Penguin Group.

Lamborn, S. D., Mounts, N. S., Steinberg, L., & Dornbusch, S. M. (1991). Patterns of competence and adjustment among adolescents from authoritative, authoritarian, indulgent, and neglectful families. *Child Development, 60*, 25–39.

Langdon, C. A. (1997). Poll of teachers' attitudes toward the public schools. *Phi Delta Kappan, 79*(3), 212–220.

Lasley, T. J., & Matczynski, T. J. (1997). *Strategies for teaching in a diverse society: Instructional models.* Belmont, CA: Wadsworth.

Lazear, D. (1991). *Seven ways of knowing.* Palatine, IL: IRI/Skylight Training and Publishing.

Lefrançois, G. R. (1997). *Psychology for teaching* (9th ed.). Belmont, CA: Wadsworth Publishing Company.

Leinwand, G. (1992). *Public education (American issues).* New York: Facts on File.

Levin, J., & Nolan, J. F. (1996). *Principles of classroom management: A professional decision-making model* (2nd ed.). Boston: Allyn & Bacon.

Lickona, T. (1991). *Educating for character: How our schools can teach respect and responsibility.* New York: Bantam Books.

Lieberman, A. (1995). Practices that support teacher development. *Phi Delta Kappan, 76*(8), 591–596.

Lightfoot, S. L. (1983). *The good high school: Portraits of character and culture.* New York: BasicBooks.

Locke, D. C., & Ciechalski, J. C. (1995). *Psychological techniques for teachers,* (2nd ed.). Washington, D.C.: Accelerated Development.

Lortie D. (1975). *School teacher: A sociological study.* Chicago: University of Chicago Press.

Lyman, I. (1998). *Homeschooling: Back to the future? Policy analysis* (p. 294). Washington, D.C.: The Cato Institute.

Lyons, O., & Mohawk, J. (Eds.). (1992). *Exiled in the land of the free: Democracy, Indian nations, and the U.S. Constitution.* Santa Fe: Clear Light Publishers.

MacArthur, C. A., & Haynes, J. B. (1995). Student assistant for learning from text (SALT): A hypermedia reading aid. *Journal of Learning Disabilities, 28,* 150–159.

Maccoby, E. E., & Martin, J. A. (1983). Socialization in the context of the family: Parent-child interaction. In P. H. Mussen (Series Ed.) & E. M. Hetherington (Vol. Ed.), *Handbook of child psychology: Vol. 4, Socialization, personality, and social development* (4th ed.) (pp. 1–101). New York: Wiley.

MacKenzie, R. (1996). *Setting limits in the classroom.* Rocklin, CA: Prima Publishing.

Mager, G. (1980). Parent relationships and home and community conditions. In D. R. Cruickshank & associates, *Teaching is tough* (pp. 153–197). Englewood Cliffs, NJ: Prentice-Hall.

Manning, M. L., & Baruth, L. G. (1996). *Multicultural education of children and adolescents.* Boston: Allyn & Bacon.

Martin, N. K. (1997) Connecting instruction and management in a student-centered classroom. *Middle School Journal, 28*(4) 3–9.

Martinez, T., Thomas, K., & Kemerer, F. R. (1994). Who chooses and why: A look at five school choice plans. *Phi Delta Kappan, 75*(9), 678–681.

Mary M. v. *North Lawrence Community Sch. Corp.* 7th Cir. (1997).

Maslow, A. H. (1954). *Motivation and personality.* New York: Harper & Row.

Maslow, A. H. (1968). *Toward a psychology of being* (2nd ed.). Princeton, NJ: Van Nostrand.

Mauk, G. W., & Taylor, M. J. (1993). Counselors in middle level schools: Issues of recognition, reclaiming, redefinition and rededication. *Middle School Journal, 24*(5), 3–9.

McCarthy, M. M. (1998). The law governing sexual harassment in public schools. *Research Bulletin No. 2.* Phi Delta Kappan Center for Evaluation, Development, and Research. May, pp. 15–18.

McCloud, B., & McKenzie, F. D. (1994). School boards and superintendents in urban districts. *Phi Delta Kappan, 75*(5), 384–386.

McCormick, T. (1984). Multiculturalism: Some principles and issues. *Theory into Practice, 23,* 93–97.

McFadden, A. C., March, G. E., II, Price, B. J., & Hwang, Y. (1992). A study of race and gender bias in the punishment of school children. *Education and Treatment of Children, 15,* 140–146.

McIntyre, D. J., & O'Hair, M. J. (1996). *The reflective roles of the classroom teacher.* Belmont, CA: Wadsworth.

McMillan, D. L., Gersham, F. M., & Forness, S. R. (1996). Full inclusion: An empirical perspective. *Behavioral Disorders, 21,* 145–159.

Meinbach, A. M., Rothlein, L., & Fredericks, A. D. (1995). *The complete guide to thematic units: Creating the integrated curriculum.* Norwood, MA: Christopher-Gordon.

Miller, D. (1998). *Enhancing adolescent competence: Strategies for classroom management.* Belmont, CA: West/Wadsworth Publishing Company.

Miller, N. E., & Dollard, J. C. (1941). *Social learning and imitation.* New Haven, CT: Yale University Press.

Mirande, A. (1986). Adolescence and Chicano Families. In G. K. Leigh, G. W. Peterson (Eds.), *Adolescents in families.* Cincinnati, OH: Southwestern.

Moore, K. D. (1998). *Classroom teaching skills* (4th ed.). Boston: McGraw Hill.

Morrision v. *State Board of Education,* 82 Cal. Rptr. 175, 461 P.2d 375 (1969).

Morrison, G. S. (1997). *Teaching in America.* Boston: Allyn & Bacon.

Murphy, J. J. (1997). *Solution-focused counseling in middle and high schools.* Alexandria, VA: American Counseling Association.

Murray, F. B., & Porter, A. (1996). Pathway from the liberal arts curriculum to lessons in the schools. In F. B. Murray (Ed.), *The teacher educator's handbook: Building a knowledge base for the preparation of teachers* (pp. 155–178). San Francisco: Jossey Bass.

Myrick, R. D. (1993). *Developmental guidance and counseling: A practical approach* (2nd ed.). Minneapolis, MN: Educational Media Corporation.

National Association of Secondary School Principals. (1996). *Breaking ranks: Changing an American institution.* Reston, VA: Author.

National Board for Professional Teaching Standards. (1994). *What teachers should know and be able to do.* Detroit, MI: Author.

National Center for Education Statistics. (1997). *America's teachers: Profile of a profession 1993–94.* Washington, D.C.: U.S. Department of Education.

National Center for Education Statistics. (1998). *The condition of education 1998.* Washington, D.C.: U.S. Department of Education.

National Commission on Excellence in Education. (1983). *A nation at risk: The imperative for educational reform* (pp. 8–9). Washington, D.C.: U.S. Government Printing Office.

National Commission on Teaching and America's Future. (1996). *What matters most: Teaching for America's future.* New York: Carnegie Corporation.

National Council for Accreditation of Teacher Education. (1995). *Standards, procedures, and policies for the accreditation of professional education units.* Washington, D.C.: Author.

National Education Association Handbook, NEA resolution C-29: 1999–2000, p. 301.

National Education Association, Commission on Reorganization of Secondary Education (1918). *Cardinal principles of secondary education.* Bulletin 35. Washington, D.C.: U.S. Bureau of Education.

National Education Goals Panel. (1995). *The National Education Goals Report.* Washington, D.C.: Author.

National Foundation for the Improvement of Education. (1996). *Teachers take charge of their learning: Transforming professional development for student success.* Washington D.C.: Author.

National School Boards Association. (January 1993). Report of the National School Boards Association on Violence in Schools. *The Los Angeles Times.*

Neill, A. S. (1960). *Summerhill: A radical approach to child rearing.* New York: Hart.

Nel, J. (1994). Preventing school failure: The Native American child. *The Clearing House, 67,* 169–174.

Nelsen, J., Lott, L. & Glenn, H. S. (1993). *Positive discipline in the classroom.* Rocklin, CA: Prima Publishing.

Nelson, K. (July/August 1995). Nurturing kids' seven ways of being smart. *Instructor, 104*(9) 26–34.

Newman, J. W. (1990). *America's teachers: An introduction to education.* New York: Longman.

Newmann, F. M., & Wehlage, G. G. (1995). *Successful school restructuring.* Washington, D.C.: American Federation of Teachers.

Noddings, N. (1988). An ethic of caring and its implications for instructional arrangements. *American Journal of Education, 96*(2), 215–230.

Noddings, N. (1992). *The challenge to care in schools: An alternative approach to education.* New York: Teachers College Press.

Noddings, N. (1993). *Educating for intelligent belief or unbelief.* New York: Teachers College Press.

O'Neill, G. P. (1988). Teaching as a profession: Redefining our concepts. *Action in Teacher Education, 10*(2), 5–10.

Oakes, J. (1985). *Keeping track: How schools structure inequality.* New Haven, CT: Yale University Press.

Oliva, P. (1988). *Developing the curriculum* (2nd ed.). Glenview, IL: Scott, Foresman, & Company.

Ormrod, J. E. (1998). *Educational psychology: Developing learners.* Upper Saddle River, NJ: Prentice Hall.

Ornstein, A. C. (1982). Curriculum contrasts: A historical overview. *Phi Delta Kappan, 63* (6) 404–408.

Palardy, J. M. (1992). Behavior modification: It does work, but. . . *Journal of Instructional Psychology, 22,* 127–132.

Palmer, P. J. (1998). *The courage to teach: Exploring the inner landscape of a teacher's life.* San Francisco: Jossey-Bass.

Patterson, F., & Rossow, L. (1996). Preventive law by the ounce or by the pound: Education law courses in undergraduate teacher education programs. *National Forum of Applied Educational Research Journal, 9*(2), 38–43.

Perrone, V. (1991). *A letter to teachers: reflections on schooling and the art of teaching.* San Francisco, CA: Jossey-Bass.

Persi, J. (1997). When emotionally troubled teachers refer emotionally troubled students. *The School Counselor, 44,* 344–352.

Peterson, P. (1996). The "typical" Arkansas board member. *The School Board Reporter, 14*(9), 4–5.

Peterson, P., & Kelley, C. (1998). *School boards by design: A manual for structure.* Conway, AR: University of Central Arkansas, Center for Academic Excellence Publishers.

Phelps, P. H. (1993). Bringing in the new: An induction ceremony for new teachers. *The Clearing House, 66*(3), 154.

Piaget, J. (1952). *The language and thought of the child.* London: Routledge and Kegal Paul.

Piaget, J. (1954). *The construction of reality in the child.* New York: Basic Books.

Pickering v. *Board of Education of Township High School,* 391 U.S. 563 (1968).

Place, A. W. (1997). Career choice of education: Holland type, diversity, and self-efficacy. *The Journal for a Just and Caring Education, 3*(2), 203–214.

Powell, A. G., Farrar, E., & Cohen, D. (1985). *The shopping mall high school.* Boston: Houghton Mifflin.

Prawat, R. S. (1992). From individual differences to learning communities: Our changing focus. *Educational Leadership, 49*(7), 9–13.

Punch, K. F., & Tuettemann, E. (1990). Correlates of psychological distress among secondary school teachers. *British Educational Research Journal, 16,* 369–382.

Purkey, W. W., & Novak, J. M. (1996). *Inviting school success: A self-concept approach to teaching, learning, and democratic practice.* Belmont, CA: Wadsworth.

Ralph, E. G. (1993). Beginning teachers and classroom management: Questions from practice, answers from research. *Middle School Journal, 25*(1), 60–64.

Renzulli, J. S. (1977). *The enrichment triad.* Wethersfield, CT: Creative Learning Press.

Riley, R. W. (1998). Our teachers should be excellent, and they should look like America. *Education and Urban Society, 31*(1), 18–29.

Rogers, C. R. (1961). *On becoming a person.* Boston: Houghton Mifflin.

Rogers, C. R. (1962). The interpersonal relationship: The core of guidance. *Harvard Educational Review, 32,* 416–429.

Rose, L. C., Gallup, A. M., & Elam, S. M. (1997). The 29th annual Phi Delta Kappa/Gallup Poll of the public's attitudes toward the public schools. *Phi Delta Kappan, 79*(1), 41–56.

Rosenshine, B., & Furst, N. (1973). The use of direct observation to study teaching. In R. M. Travers (ed.), *Second handbook of research on teaching.* Chicago: Rand McNally.

Rosenshine, B., & Stevens, R. (1986). Teaching functions. In M. C. Wittrock (Ed.), *Handbook of research on teaching* (3rd ed.). New York: Macmillan.

Rosenthal, R., & Jacobson, L. (1968). *Pygmalion in the classroom.* New York: Holt, Rinehart and Winston.

Rothstein, P. R. (1990). *Educational psychology.* New York: McGraw-Hill.

Ryan, K., & Cooper, J. M. (1998). *Those who can, teach* (8th ed.). Boston: Houghton Mifflin.

Sadker, M. P., & Sadker, D. M. (1997). *Teachers, schools, and society* (4th ed.). New York: McGraw-Hill.

Sadker, M., & Sadker, D. (1986). Sexism in the classroom: From grade school to graduate school. *Phi Delta Kappan, 67*(7), 512–515.

Sadker, M., & Sadker, D. (1994). *Failing at fairness: How our schools cheat girls.* New York: Simon & Schuster.

Salovey, P., & Mayer, J. D. (1990). Emotional intelligence. *Imagination, Cognition, and Personality, 9,* 185–211.

San Antonio Independent School District v. *Rodriguez,* 411 U.S. 1, 93 S.Ct. 1278 (1973).

Sarason, S. (1993). *You are thinking of teaching? Opportunities, problems, realities.* San Francisco: Jossey Bass.

Sartre, J. P. (1957). *Existentialism and human emotions.* New York: Philosophical Library.

Sizer, T. R. (1997). The meanings of "public education." In Goodlad, J. I. & McMannon, T. J. (eds.). *The public purpose of education and schooling.* (pp. 33–40). San Francisco: Jossey Bass.

Schein, E. H. (1993). *Career anchors: Discovering your real values.* San Francisco: Pfeiffer.

Schlesinger, A. (1995). The disuniting of America. In J. Noll (Ed.). *Taking sides: Clashing views on controversial issues* (8th ed.) (pp. 227–236). Guilford, CT: Dushkin.

Search Institute. (1997). *The asset approach: Giving kids what they need to succeed.* Minneapolis, MN: Author.

Segall, W. E., & Wilson, A. V. (1998). *Teaching in a diverse society.* Upper Saddle River, NJ: Merrill/Prentice Hall.

Segall, W., & Wilson, A. (1998). *Introduction to education: Teaching in a diverse society.* New York: Prentice Hall.

Sergiovanni, T. I. (1996). *Leadership for the schoolhouse.* San Francisco: Jossey-Bass.

Serrano v. *Priest,* 5 Casl.3d.584, 96 Cal. Rptr 601, 487 P.2d 1241 (1971).

Shafritz, J. M., Koeppe, R. P., & Soper, E. W. (Eds.) (1988). *The facts on file dictionary of education.* New York: Facts on File.

Shannon, T. A. (1994). The changing community school board/America's best hope for the future of our public schools. *Phi Delta Kappan, 75*(5), 394–397.

Skinner, B. F. (1953). *Science and human behavior.* New York: Macmillan.

Skinner, D. (1997). Computers: Good for education? *The Public Interest,* summer, 98–109.

Slavin, R. E. (1983). *An introduction to cooperative learning.* New York: Longman.

Slavin, R. E. (1987). *Cooperative learning* (2nd ed.). Washington, D.C.: National Education Association.

Sleeter, C. E., & Grant, C. A. (1999). *Making choices for multicultural education: Five approaches to race, class and gender* (3rd ed.). Upper Saddle River, NJ: Merrill. *society: The development of higher psychological processes.* Cambridge, MA: Harvard University Press.

Sockett, H. (1993). *The moral base for teacher professionalism.* New York: Teachers College Press.

Spring, J. (1994). *American education* (6th ed.) New York: McGraw-Hill.

Spring, J. (1997). *The American school* (4th ed.). New York: McGraw-Hill.

Spring, J. (1998). *American education.* Boston, MA: McGraw-Hill.

Stallings, J., & Kaskowitz, D. (1974). *Follow through classroom observation evaluation, 1972– 73.* Menlo Park, CA: Stanford Research Institute.

Steffy, B. E., & Wolfe, M. P. (1997). *The life cycle of the career teacher: Maintaining excellence for a lifetime.* West Lafayette, IN: Kappa Delta Pi.

Steinberg, L. (1990) Interdependence in the family: Autonomy, conflict, and harmony in the parent-adolescent relationship. In S. S. Feldman & G. R. Elliot (Eds.), *At the threshold: The developing adolescent* (pp. 255–276). Cambridge, MA: Harvard University Press.

Steinberg, L. (1996). *Beyond the classroom: Why school reform has failed and what parents need to do.* New York: Simon & Schuster.

Steinberg, L., Brown B. B, & Dornsbusch, S. M. (1996). *Beyond the classroom: Why school reform has failed and what parents need to do.* New York: Touchstone Book, Simon & Schuster.

Stoops, E., & King-Stoops, J. (1981). Discipline suggestions for classroom teachers. *Phi Delta Kappan, 63*(1), 58.

Strike, K. (1988). The ethics of teaching. *Phi Delta Kappan,* October, *70*(2), 156–158.

Strike, K. (1990). The legal and moral responsibility of teachers. In J. Goodlad, R. Soder, & K. A. Sirotnik (eds.), *The moral dimensions of teaching* (pp. 188–223). San Francisco, CA: Jossey Bass.

Sue, D. W., & Sue, D. (1990). *Counseling the culturally different: Theory and practice* (2nd ed.). New York: John Wiley.

Suzuki, B. H. (1984). Curriculum transformation for multicultural education. *Education and Urban Society, 16,* 294–322.

Tanner, D. (1993). A nation 'truly' at risk. *Phi Delta Kappan, 75*(4), 288–297.

Tavris, C. (1992). *Mismeasurement of women.* New York: Simon & Schuster.

The Economist. (1997). Education and the wealth of nations. March 29–April 4, p. 15.

Thorndike, E. L. (1913). Educational psychology. In *The psychology of learning,* Vol. 2. New York: Teachers' College Press.

Tinker v. Des Moines Independent Community School District, 393 U.S. 503 (1969).

Toch, T. (1998). The new education bazaar. *U.S. News & World Report, 124*(16), 35–42.

Turock, B. J. (1996). Libraries on the information superhighway: Connect or disconnect? In B. J. Turock (Ed.), *Envisioning a nation connected* (pp. 1–5). Chicago: American Library Association.

Tyler, R. W. (1949). *Basic principles of curriculum and instruction.* Chicago: The University of Chicago Press.

Tyler, R. W. (1989). Educating children from minority families. *Educational Horizons, 67*(4), 114–118.

Tyson, H. (1999). A load off the teachers' backs: Coordinated school health programs. *Phi Delta Kappan, 80*(5), 1–8.

U.S. Department of Commerce, Bureau of the Census. (1991). Characteristics of the Population Below the Poverty Level. Current Population Reports, Series P-20. no. 181.

U. S. Department of Education. (1994). *Strong families, strong schools: Building community partnerships for learning.* Washington, D.C.: Author.

U.S. Department of Education. *Meeting the Needs of Homeless Children and Youth: A resource for schools and communities.* (1997). U.S. Department of Education, Compensatory Education Programs Office of Elementary and Secondary Education. Waschington, D.C.

Unger, H. G. (1993). *How to pick a private school.* New York: Facts on File.

Unger, H. G. (1999). *School choice.* New York: Checkmark Books.

United States Bureau of the Census. (September 1993). Washington, D.C.: U.S. Government Printing Office.

United States Department of Education National Center for Statistics, U.S. Digest of Educational Statistics (1997) Table 52, p. 65.

United States Department of Education. (1986). *What works: Research about teaching and learning.* Washington, D.C.: Author.

Urban, W. J. (1990). Historical studies of teacher education. In W. R. Houston (Ed.), *Handbook of research on teacher education* (pp. 59–71). New York: Macmillan.

Villaume, P. G., & Foley, R. M. (1993). *Teachers at risk: Crisis in the classroom.* Bloomington, MN: Legal Resource Center for Educators.

Wagner, T. (1996). Bringing school reform back down to earth. *Phi Delta Kappan, 78*(2), 145– 149.

Walker, H. M., Colvin, G., & Ramsey, E. (1995). *Antisocial behavior in schools: Strategies and best practices.* Pacific Grove, CA: Brooks/Cole.

Wallis, C. (1994). A class of their own. *Time, 144*(18), 53–63.

Wallis, C. (1994). A class of their own. *Time, 144*(18), 53–63.

Watson, J. B. (1913). Psychology as the behaviorist views it. *Psychological Review, 20,* 158– 177.

Watson, J. B. (1925). *Behaviorism.* New York: W. W. Norton.

Watts, W. D., & Short, A. P. (1990). Teacher drug use: A response to occupational stress. *Journal of Drug Education, 20,* 47–65.

Weinstein, C. S. (1996). *Secondary classroom management: Lessons from research and practice.* New York: McGraw Hill.

Weiss, B., Dodge, K. A, Bates, J. E., & Pettit, G. S. (1992). Some consequences of early harsh discipline: Child aggression and a maladaptive social information processing style. *Child Development, 63,* 1321–1335.

Wentzel, K. R. (1997). Student motivation in middle school: The role of perceived pedagogical caring. *Journal of Educational Psychology, 89*(3), 411–419.

West, B. E. (1993). The new arrivals from Southeast Asia. *Childhood Education, 60,* 84–89.

Williams, B. (1997). *Web publishing for teachers.* Foster City, CA: IDG Books Worldwide.

Winzer, M. A., & Mazurek, C. (1998). *Special education in multicultural contexts.* Upper Saddle River, NJ: Merrill.

Wiseman, D. L., Cooner, D. D., & Knight, S.L. (1999). *Becoming a teacher in a field-based setting.* Belmont, CA: Wadsworth.

Wittmer, J., & Myrick, R. D. (1989). *The teacher as facilitator.* Minneapolis, MN: Educational Media Corporation.

Wohlstetter, P., & Anderson L. (1994). What can U.S. charter schools learn from England's grant-maintained schools? *Phi Delta Kappan, 75*(6), 486–491.

Wong, H., & Wong, R. (1998). *How to be an effective teacher: The first days of school.* Sunnyvale, CA: Harry R. Wong.

Yao, E. L. (1985). Adjustment needs of Asian immigrant children. *Elementary School Guidance and Counseling, 19,* 222–227.

Yarrow, J. (March, 1994). Across the curriculum with Hypercard. *T.H.E. Journal,* 88–89.

Zeichner, K. M., & Liston, D. P. (1996). *Reflective teaching: An introduction.* Mahwah, N.J.: Lawrence Erlbaum Associates.